DEADLY FORCE

DEADLY FORCE

A Police Shooting and My Family's
Search for the Truth

Lawrence O'Donnell, Jr.

WM

WILLIAM MORROW
An Imprint of HarperCollinsPublishers

HarperCollins books may be purchased for educational, business, or sales promotional use. For information, please email the Special Markets Department at SPsales@harpercollins.com.

A hardcover edition of this book was published in 1983 by William Morrow.

FIRST WILLIAM MORROW PAPERBACK EDITION PUBLISHED 2018.

Library of Congress Cataloging in Publication data has been applied for.

ISBN 978-0-06-287013-1

18 19 20 21 22   DIX/LSC   10 9 8 7 6 5 4 3 2 1

For Patricia, Eurina and Jamil

Preface to the Paperback Edition

Thirty years. I tried to get America to face the problems associated with police use of deadly force for thirty years. And I failed.

Then, all of a sudden, the country woke up. But Michael Brown had to die first. The people in his Ferguson, Missouri, neighborhood watched as his eighteen-year-old body was left lying face-down on the street riddled with police bullets for over four hours on a hot August afternoon in 2014, the year that changed everything.

While Michael Brown's body was still on the street, word spread that he was unarmed and that he was shot multiple times. The next day protest marchers began demanding to know what happened. They got no answers. Later that night two weeks of nighttime rioting began in Ferguson. And America woke up. Nothing snaps America to attention like a riot.

We have had riots after killings by police for over fifty years, but this was the first one in the era of twenty-four-hour cable TV news and social media. TV reporters held their positions on Ferguson sidewalks for hours on end. The governor declared a state of emergency, sent in the state police and the National Guard, and imposed a curfew. Every night America watched and waited to see if the curfew would hold. Michael Brown's three-hour funeral was carried live on national television. And Barack Obama became the first president of the United States to acknowledge that police abuse of deadly force is a serious problem.

Thirty years ago we didn't know how many people were killed

by police. We still don't. The federal government vacuums up millions upon millions of statistics about almost everything we do, but one thing that isn't counted is how many people the government kills in the United States. How many people get the death penalty on the street without ever getting their day in court? How many of them deserve it? How many don't? We don't know.

The *Washington Post* started keeping its own count in 2015 and recorded 991 killings by police that year. Thirty years ago our best estimates indicated there were at least six hundred killings by police in a typical year. Today's higher numbers reported by the *Post* are probably not because of an increase in killing by police but because the internet and social media allow the *Post* to collect much more accurate information than we were able to get decades ago by literally cutting stories out of newspapers around the country. We knew we were missing a lot of cases, especially in smaller towns, but we could only guess how many.

There are several reasons police are probably killing fewer people now than thirty years ago. The year after this book was first published, the U.S. Supreme Court ruled that it was no longer legal to shoot fleeing suspects simply because they were fleeing. Police rules on the use of deadly force were rewritten to comply with the Supreme Court ruling. Police training is still not adequate but it has improved. Police are no longer completely confident that they can cover up a bad shooting now that the news media is alert and ready to cover possible bad shootings by police. And police are now facing much less crime, which means they are facing fewer bullets fired at them. The Federal Bureau of Investigation has always kept an accurate count of the number of police killed in the line of duty and it has dropped from 129 in 1975 to 66 in 2016.

Black America has always known there is a problem. A friend, a neighbor, a cousin witnessed or heard about cases of unjustifiable police use of deadly force and passed the word. But it took a series of technological developments for white America to hear these stories: 24-hour cable news, the internet, social media, police dash cam and body cam video, and, most importantly, a camera-phone in everyone's pocket. This book is about what it was like before all that—before we all knew the names Michael Brown, Eric Garner, Tamir Rice, Laquan McDonald, Stephon Clark and many others who have inspired protestors to chant, "Black lives matter!" What is shocking is how little has changed except for the new public and political awareness that there is a problem.

When this book was published in 1983, it was the first of its kind—an exposé of how a badge could become a license to kill focusing on the Boston Police shooting of James Bowden. He was a young black husband and father who was shot and killed by two white police officers right after visiting his mother in a Roxbury housing project. That I was able to gather the facts to tell his story was something close to a miracle at the time. Cracking the blue wall of silence in a police department was virtually impossible. It helped that I was white with an Irish last name and a Boston accent. That made some Boston cops comfortable enough to do interviews with me—too comfortable. Some of the cops spoke to me the way they spoke to each other, including casual use of the N-word. In 1970s Boston, racist language was common and in the police department it was even more common. I wish the N-word was as shocking for me to hear from white Boston cops then as it would be now. Race relations in Boston have improved much more than I expected.

This book was the single biggest breakthrough in the then slim journalistic history of police use of deadly force. But this story would never have been told if it were not for the extraordinary commitment of one man who used to be a member of the police force that killed James Bowden. Without him James Bowden's death would have been known only to the Bowden family, and their friends and neighbors. The way he died would have been whispered at his funeral and then perhaps never spoken of again, just held as a private pain too hurtful to discuss.

My father was a Boston police officer who decided to work his way through college and law school. He was the lawyer James Bowden's widow found when she wanted to know the truth about what happened to her husband. As soon as my father heard her story, he knew what he had to do. He knew how hard it would be. He knew it would take years. He knew that his old police department would go to war with him. But he knew no other lawyer had the right experience to fight this kind of war—the ex-cop's inside knowledge of how bad cops try to cover their tracks. So he didn't think he had a choice. And now we know the truth.

DEADLY FORCE

Prologue

My father still asks me why I'm not a lawyer. Other people ask, too, as soon as they find out about my family. My father is a lawyer. My three brothers, all older, are lawyers. My only sister, four years younger, just finished law school. My mother is not a lawyer, but she is in the life. She is the financial manager of a small Boston law firm called—to the amusement of the legal community—O'Donnell, O'Donnell & O'Donnell. Senior Partner: Lawrence O'Donnell. Partners: Michael and Kevin O'Donnell. Associate: William O'Donnell. Law Clerk and soon-to-be Associate: Mary O'Donnell.

As I tell my father, it's not that I wouldn't like lawyering. In fact, trial work—his specialty—has always held great appeal for me. I've been a devoted fan of his since I could barely see over the bench in front of me. Before I was a teenager, I was tagging along as errand boy and briefcase carrier in the big trials. I found unparalleled anxiety and excitement in the three minutes it takes a jury to file into a courtroom and announce its verdict. The first one I heard was a "not-guilty" in a murder case. The second was a "guilty" in another murder case. The defendant's wife, whom I had come to know that summer in Suffolk Superior Court, burst into tears at the sound of the word. She writhed, minutes later, when the judge told her husband he was to die by electrocution. It has been nearly twenty years since I heard those verdicts announced, and in all the baseball, basketball, and football games I've played and watched since then, in all the books I've read, in all the movies and plays I've seen, in all the elections I've witnessed, I have known no more suspense and drama. No, there is nothing about the family trade that I dislike.

It isn't the family, either. My father is a hot-tempered, moody, unpredictable, difficult man, but I lived with him a long time, still see him almost every day, and we have left our communication problem far behind. We could work together with ease. My mother is a warm, selfless woman whose only flaw is excessive frugality. Her presence is ever a pleasure. Michael and I never agree on our views of the world. We're always laughing at each other. Kevin and I can go for long stretches without speaking, but the ice melts. William was my childhood best friend. And Mary, well, I hardly know.

That I write for a living seems to have happened by accident. In college I was an economics student who avoided courses that required term papers. By graduation I had decided that school no longer agreed with me. But I might have eventually succumbed to the inevitability of law school if, of a summer evening in 1977, my father had not left the office and taken a stroll through the grand oaks of the Boston Common with me in mind.

He emerged from the Common on the corner of Boylston and Charles. The Colonial Theatre was to his left. It was dark for the season. The Playboy Club was to his right. The Trailways bus station was straight ahead. Within a block were several bars featuring three-piece bands and naked dancing girls. Also nearby were about a dozen bookstores open only to adults. Women in loud colors walked the streets in groups. The neighborhood has long been known as "The Combat Zone." I started working in the Zone as a part-time parking attendant during my second year of college. It was now more than a year since I'd received my diploma, and I was still a parking attendant. My father walked past the bus station, across Eliot Street, and onto my hundred-car lot.

New York, New York was playing in the Sack Cinema across the street, but *Star Wars* and the Red Sox, who were on their way to finishing two games behind the Yankees, were playing far from the Zone and pulling in all the parking business that summer. I had time to talk.

"You should come up to the office and take a look at the Bowden case," my father said. "There's a good story in that file."

(He liked my writing. His collection of it amounted to four letters addressed to him from Williston Academy, a boarding school one hundred miles due west of Boston. He had sent Bill and me there after we achieved persona non grata status at Catholic Memorial High School. My letters were pleas for a pardon. After eighty-eight days served, they turned the trick, and to Williston's relief, we found another local parochial school willing to take a chance on us.)

I knew a little about the Bowden case already. I had been dragged into it in a small and funny way two years earlier, when I was arrested. My father didn't have to remind me of that.

"We've got the police reports and a bunch of depositions now," he said, plainly hoping I'd be tempted.

I had never read a police report, and, as a night-shift worker, I had plenty of free time during the day. I went to the office the next morning.

The Bowden file occupied its own four-drawer filing cabinet in Michael's office. In a few weeks, I had read all of it. What was supposed to be in the thirty-two Boston Police reports—the reason two patrolmen shot and killed James Henry Bowden, Jr.—was not there. The reports told a story, but it was obviously false. O'Donnell, O'Donnell & O'Donnell was on the side of truth in this one.

Michael and I fell into long discussions of the evidence. We talked about the cops a lot, too. The way they thought. Why they said this or that in a report or a deposition. I actually knew one of them; Michael didn't know any, but he didn't have to. They were guys like us. They had grown up in our kind of Irish neighborhood, gone to Catholic schools, probably been altar boys, hung on our kind of street corner.

On such street corners there is always talk about black people—or "niggers," as they are called. *Nigger* is still a widely accepted term in blue-collar Boston. (One of the unusual features of life in the O'Donnell home was that though we could get away with profanity, racial and ethnic slurs were forbidden.) There is idiomatic usage like "What are we? Niggers?" which someone might say to a friend when receiving bad service in a restaurant, or one workmate might say to another when assigned an undesirable task. Many of my lifelong friends try not to use the word *nigger* around me. But I don't think I will ever stop hearing "nigger" idioms—even from people who believe they have purged themselves of racism.

There is another usage, one that carries intense malice. It is the talk about how much someone "hates niggers" or wants to "kill niggers." Sometimes the "kill niggers" stuff is drunken bravado, sometimes it is a joke, sometimes it is serious, but always it is really talk about how much the speaker fears black people. The fear is largely of the unknown, since black life and white rarely intersect in Boston.

I imagine that squeezing the trigger of a gun is easier when you fear your target. And I imagine that the conscience of the Boston Police Department was at ease with the cover-up of the killing of James Bowden not just because the police instinct is to side with the officers involved in such a shooting, but also because James Bowden was black.

One day, as we were joking about the cop talk in one of the reports (the author says he yelled to Bowden: "Remove yourself from the vehicle!") my father walked in with a proposal. "Why don't you get in this thing with us? There's a lot you can do. You can be our . . . what do they call them now, Mike?"

"Paralegal assistant."

"Right. What do you say?"

"Okay."

That night was my last in a parking lot.

I stayed in the O'Donnell office for about a year. When the Bowden trial was over, I started working on this book, and soon found myself studying the national picture of what police rule books call "the use of deadly force." There was trouble everywhere. New York City, Los Angeles, Chicago, Philadelphia, Houston, Seattle, Baltimore, New Orleans, Nashville, Memphis, Indianapolis,

Milwaukee, Providence, and Fort Lupton, Colorado, along with many other cities and towns of all sizes, had recently experienced needless killing by police. Some of it was accidental, some of it reckless, some of it vicious, some of it insane. (On Thanksgiving Day 1976, New York City Patrolman Robert Torsney walked up to a fifteen-year-old black boy named Robert Evans and, after a short conversation, shot him point-blank in the head. Torsney originally claimed that the boy had pulled a gun on him. At his subsequent murder trial, however, Torsney, to the jury's satisfaction, pleaded not guilty by reason of temporary insanity. He spent a year in a mental hospital, was pronounced cured, and was released.)

In the fall of 1979 I wrote an article for the *New York Times* that outlined the problems involved in police use of deadly force. Those problems, and the national statistics behind them, have not changed. First among them is that many of the country's fifteen thousand or so police departments have no deadly force rules. That leaves state law as the only word on when an officer can shoot, and ignores the question of when he *should* shoot.

All states allow police to kill in self-defense or defense of others. Most states also allow police to kill fleeing felony suspects. The fleeing-felon law is grounded in centuries-old English common law, which classified only eight crimes—treason, murder, and rape among them—as felonies, all punishable by death. The American list of felonies has come to include many crimes, such as car theft (and, in one state, spitting on a policeman), that seldom draw a jail sentence in court if you are convicted but can, and all too often do, draw an instant death sentence on the street if a cop suspects you are guilty and you try to run away from him.

Killing by the police is investigated by the police, if investigated at all. Not surprisingly, less than 1 percent of the killings are ruled unjustifiable by police departments. A much tinier percentage lead to homicide charges against police. And usually zero percent of those lead to convictions.

Until recently, the general public was unaware of a problem. A 1970 Harris poll showed that 77 percent of the citizenry believed that when a police officer killed while on duty, the killing was automatically justified. In the *Times,* I said that police have an all but "unlimited license to use their deadly force."

A month later the Department of Justice invited me to Washington for a conference it was sponsoring on police use of deadly force. I was surprised to discover copies of my article being handed out to the five hundred or so attendees, who had come from every region of the country. Among them were police officers of every rank (none from Boston), federal and state prosecutors, congressmen, mayors, civil rights lawyers, community activists, and all the researchers whose work I had been studying. It was three days of speeches, seminars, and trading horror stories—amplified versions of Justice's current log of objectionable killings. A sample:

Brooklyn, New York. Five police officers fired 24 bullets at 26-year-old Hispanic male (an autopsy report revealed that he was struck 21 times and died instantly). Victim had a history of mental illness, allegedly threatened the police officers with a pair of scissors after his mother requested police assistance because he was tearing up the linoleum in the house.

New Rochelle, New York. Black male, 18, allegedly approached by police officer as a suspect in a stolen car incident. Youth allegedly fled from officer, who fired one shot, striking victim in the back and killing him.

Cincinnati, Ohio. Black male, 17, shot in back and killed while fleeing scene of a burglary.

Detroit, Michigan. Black youth, 18, observed by police in vicinity of stolen car. While officers were searching companions, victim attempted to run away. One of the officers gave chase and fired three shots, hitting victim— who died next day.

Seattle, Washington. Black male, 21, was shot in back and killed by uniformed Seattle police officer. Officer had received radio report of burglary suspect in area. After pursuit of victim (joined by several other police officers) on foot, one officer shot victim, first in foot and then in back. No contention that victim was armed or believed dangerous.

Anchorage, Alaska. Black male shot and killed by uniformed state police officer. Officer took notice of victim after victim entered and left service station in early morning. Officer followed in marked car, and victim reportedly incurred several traffic violations before abandoning car and fleeing on foot. Victim fell and allegedly reached for his ankle; officer contended he thought victim was going for a concealed weapon. Shot and killed victim. Victim later discovered to be unarmed.

Los Angeles, California. Black woman shot by police after reportedly threatening officers with butcher knife. Officers had been called to scene after complaint filed by gas company worker, whom victim had allegedly threatened earlier the same day.

East Los Angeles, California. Hispanic male shot and killed by sheriff's deputies investigating complaint about male with gun. Gun later determined to be a toy.

San Diego, California. Black male burglary suspect killed when he was struck on head by police officer using service revolver.

Las Vegas, Nevada. Black male, 20, shot to death by police. Victim was suspected of stealing a purse.

Waco, Texas. A Mexican illegal alien, 34, was shot and killed by a police officer who mistook the victim to be a fleeing burglar. The victim was shot at about 50 feet in the back of the head, as he fled his home in the dark following a domestic quarrel with his common-law wife.

Rosenberg, Texas. A 14-year-old Hispanic male was shot and killed by a Ft. Bend County sheriff's deputy responding to a burglary call. At the scene, two suspects were seen fleeing. One officer fired a shot at the victim, believing that he was pointing a weapon at the deputy. It was later determined that what appeared to be a weapon was a white sock.

Socorro, Texas. A 16-year-old high school football player was killed by an El Paso sheriff's deputy at a school party. The deputy was investigating a disturbance complaint at the party. Witnesses say the deputy pointed the shotgun at the boy who pushed the weapon aside, moved back, and was then shot.

Georgetown, Texas. A white soldier was shot and killed by sheriff's deputies following his arrest and attempted escape. The victim had been stopped for speeding and drunken driving. After being handcuffed, he stole a Department of Public Safety patrol car and evaded road blocks before running into a tree. Deputies allegedly mistook the gleam of handcuffs for a gun, prompting the shooting.

Laredo, Texas. A 32-year-old Mexican citizen (with naturalization papers and work permit) was stopped at the border by an off-duty policeman. The victim was riding in a van with two brothers when stopped. The officer held a shotgun to the victim's head while searching the others, and the gun went off.

Tampa, Florida. Black male allegedly involved in no felonious activity. Police officer, on routine patrol, reportedly spotted victim speeding on motorcycle. Officer allegedly gave pursuit and stopped victim some distance away. Officer emerged from his patrol car with his pistol drawn and shot victim in the face, according to witnesses. Victim died from the gunshot wound.

St. Petersburg, Florida. Black male, 20, shot dead in the act of running away from police officers. Officer on routine patrol saw a group of young men apparently drinking alcoholic beverages from a bag, and stopped to investigate same. An incident erupted when the legality of the officer's checking the contents of their bag was discussed.

When the officer attempted to arrest another individual, the victim interceded and the shooting occurred. The victim was not armed.

Pine Hill, North Carolina. Black male shot dead by police chief. Victim reportedly not involved in felonious activity. Police chief called to scene reportedly by white citizen complaining about blacks shooting dice in area of café. Allegedly the chief was attempting to place victim in pickup truck by poking him in the side and back with a gun. Victim is claimed to have grabbed for gun and was shot about five times. Victim was not armed.

Philadelphia, Pennsylvania. Male, 15, shot and killed while attempting to flee from police officers. When ordered to stop by uniformed police officers, victim continued his attempt to scale a fence. Was shot in back by one of the officers.

Philadelphia, Pennsylvania. Black male, 19, shot and killed by police officer after being arrested for traffic violation. Two officers were escorting victim to police headquarters; he fled from officers, with his hands cuffed behind his back. After pursuit, one officer apprehended victim, who struggled and was shot.

No one at the conference had heard of the Bowden case. I didn't mention it much. I was there to listen to the experts.

Lawrence Sherman, the research director of the Police Foundation, lamented "the paucity of official data." The Federal Bureau of Investigation's annual crime report tells us the number of police killed in the line of duty—about one hundred per year—but no one keeps an accurate count of how many people the police kill. It was Sherman's recent groundbreaking survey that provided us with a conservative estimate: about six hundred per year. An earlier study indicated that 25 percent of the victims are felony suspects—and even misdemeanor suspects—who flee from arrest; 25 percent of the victims are unarmed.

Sherman pointed out the irony of public debate raging on capital punishment while ignoring deadly force, although deadly force has always been "by far the most frequent method by which our government has intentionally taken the lives of its own citizens." He thought that ignorance was the explanation: "American society simply does not know how many of its citizens are killed each year under the authority of the state."

James Fyfe, a former New York City police lieutenant, whose doctoral dissertation was a study of his department's use of deadly force, led the conference to a consensus: Stricter deadly force rules were needed. Thinking that "the best solution to a potential confrontation is one that minimizes bloodshed," Fyfe said that the New York City Police Department tightened its rule in 1972 to something approximating a defense-of-life shooting policy. What followed was a sharp reduction in shooting and killing by police and, to everyone's surprise, shooting and killing *of* police. Fyfe told us that this was proof that restrictive deadly force rules do not, as police unions often contend, make a policeman's job more dangerous by giving an advantage to gun-wielding criminals who obey no rules.

All deadly force studies support one statistic: Half of the people killed by police are black.

A week after the conference, Arthur McDuffie, a young black insurance man and father of three, died in a Miami hospital. Cause of death: multiple skull fractures sustained when a group of Dade County police officers stopped McDuffie for speeding. The original police story was that McDuffie was injured in a traffic accident. Witnesses ruined that one in a matter of days, and soon four of the policemen involved were suspended, then fired. Five months later they went to trial on manslaughter charges. The prosecutor told the jury: "Five to seven officers were hitting him with nightsticks and flashlights, and there was a second row standing around reaching over the officers to hit Mr. McDuffie while he was lying on the ground." The defense maintained that McDuffie violently resisted arrest and the police did not use excessive force in subduing him. On May 17, 1980, the all-white jury quickly returned not-guilty verdicts, and within a few hours one of the worst riots in American history was sweeping through Miami. Centered in the black neighborhood of Liberty City, the rampage lasted three days. Some $80 million in property damage was done. Police arrested 855 people. Eighteen people were killed. Through it all, rioters chanted one word: McDuffie.

I thought of something that Chicago patrolman Howard Saffold, a middle-aged black man with the air of someone who has seen it all, had told me at the conference: "Cops can do things in a minute or a second that will sour a community for a generation."

That seems to be what happened in Miami. Rioting broke out again for two days in December of 1982, when a twenty-three-year-old patrolman shot twenty-year-old Nevell Johnson in the face. Johnson died the next day. His cousin and other witnesses said that Johnson had a gun in his pocket when two officers approached him, but admitted it to the police and did nothing to provoke them. The riot was confined to the neighborhood of Overtown. One killed. At least twenty-five seriously injured. Forty-five arrested. Property damage figure not yet calculated.

Because Nevell Johnson was armed, his death should not have been immediately regarded as a blatant case of police murder. (The officer was charged with manslaughter and was acquitted by an all-white jury.) I doubt that it would have provoked violent reaction were it not for still-smoldering anger over the killing of Arthur McDuffie. Howard Saffold is right about the souring of a generation.

The efforts of the Department of Justice, law-enforcement academicians, interested civic organizations such as the National Association for the Advancement of Colored People, mayors, city councillors, aldermen, progressive police administrators, and, I think most important, the public attention drawn to the McDuffie case and its aftermath have led to some isolated changes in the deadly force picture.

More police departments have instituted deadly force rules. Philadelphia finally has one, and police shooting there has declined. Police shooting has also declined in Chicago and Los Angeles, after highly controversial killings in each city made deadly force a public policy issue. Many departments that have had rules for a long time have nudged them toward—without in any case going all the way to—a self-defense-and-defense-of-others shooting policy.

Still, with American police killing about six hundred people a year, an October 1981 report by the U.S. Commission on Civil Rights concluded that "no effective protection from police misconduct seems to exist for the individual citizen." The commission called for nationwide restrictions on police shooting "to defense of life in those circumstances where it is reasonably believed to be the only available means for protecting the officer's life or the life of another person." In preparing the report, the commission held hearings in Philadelphia and Houston, the trouble spots of the 1970s, and reviewed the experiences of those and other cities and towns.

The commission paid no attention to Boston. Deadly force studies rarely do, because since 1974, the Boston Police Department's deadly force rule has included virtually everything the Department of Justice and the Commission on Civil Rights have suggested. The police commissioner and his predecessor have reputations in law enforcement as enlightened, honest police administrators. Boston police kill very few people. In the two years following the Bowden killing, they killed no one. Then, in 1978, they killed once; in 1979, once; in 1980, twice; in 1981, four times; and in 1982, six times. In each of the 1982 incidents the officers involved said they were either being attacked with a deadly weapon or being run down by a car. Boston police shooting seems to have been effectively limited to defense-of-life situations—if we take the department's word for it.

Once a police department has adopted a good rule, the deadly force issue becomes one of trust. When the police are the only witnesses to one of their killings, can we confidently accept their account of what happened? If we cannot accept the account, can we then expect that police investigators—Homicide and Internal

Affairs detectives—will reveal the truth? If the investigators miss or hide the truth, can we rest assured that police chiefs and commissioners—usually the final judges of police conduct—will see through any lie, remove any cover-up, punish any bad cops, and tell us the real story?

I found the answers to each of these questions in the Bowden case.

CHAPTER 1

She had been a widow for thirty minutes, but she didn't know it. When the telephone began ringing at seven o'clock that rainy evening, Patricia Bowden and her two children were in the bathroom. She was giving her six-month-old son, Jamil, a bath. Her four-year-old daughter, Eurina, was helping by handing Pat whatever she asked for—soap, washcloth, towel—and telling her baby brother not to cry. Pat was on her knees beside the tub. Eurina was standing. At the first ring, Pat told Eurina to hold Jamil, then pulled herself up with a groan. She had put on a lot of weight in her first pregnancy and never lost it. Now, at age twenty-five, she was a tall, heavy woman who couldn't spring to her feet the way she could six years earlier when she was still a nurse's aide at Boston City Hospital. She grabbed a small towel, dried her hands as she took four steps down the hall, turned left into the kitchen, and picked up the wall phone.

"Hello," she said in her effervescent manner which must leave some telephone callers thinking she's a teenager.

"Hello. Is this the home of James Bowden?" asked an anxious female voice.

"Yes," said Pat. "Who's this?"

"This is the Brigham Hospital. Are you related to Mr. Bowden?"

Pat closed her eyes, squeezed the phone, took a deep breath, and promised herself not to alarm the kids. "What's happened to him?" she asked softly.

"Well, are you related to Mr. Bowden?"

Remembering the routine on the caller's end from her days at City Hospital, Pat said calmly, "Yes, he's my husband."

"Well, Mrs. Bowden, I'm sorry to have to tell you this, but your husband is here in the emergency ward and I think you should come over here."

"What happened to him?"

There was a pause, and the hospital voice said, "He was shot."

With her eyes still closed, Pat hung up the phone and flattened her palms on the wall to steady herself against the pounding shock that blurred everything and left her working on instinct. She doesn't remember dialing the phone, but it was suddenly in her hand again and she was crying, "James got shot!"

"What?!" her mother shrieked.

"James got shot!"

"Oh, no!"

As she scrambled for her coat and her purse, Pat heard her mother's footsteps coming down the back stairs from her apartment in the free-standing wood-shingled house that Boston calls a three-decker. She came through the back door into the kitchen. The two women looked at each other. They said nothing. They were both crying.

"Mommy," Eurina called.

Pat turned and charged down the hall and out the front door. Her mother dried her eyes and walked to the bathroom, where she found Eurina still holding Jamil. Eurina didn't know what the commotion was about, but had heard her mother and grandmother crying, and was now crying herself.

Pat ran to Washington Street, the busiest street in Roxbury, Boston's black ghetto. She hailed a taxi. Though it couldn't have been more than ten minutes, the ride to the hospital seemed to take forever. Pat didn't talk to the driver after telling him where she wanted to go. "I don't know what I was thinking during that ride," she says. "I wasn't thinking James was dead, but I don't know what else I was thinking. . . . I was doing a lot of praying, I guess.

"When I got there I just went inside and a lot of nurses and doctors were standing right there. I told them I was Mrs. Bowden and a nurse said, 'Come in.' So, I went inside the emergency room—a typical emergency room, you know—and I saw James lying there. I think he was the only one there 'cause he was like in the middle. It was a big room and he was in the middle. He didn't have a T-shirt on or his shirt or his jacket or anything. He was bare-chested. The nurse was looking at me and I was looking at James. His eyes were closed. So, I looked at the nurse and she starts shaking her head no. I think I . . . I didn't pass out or anything. I just shook all over. Oh, it was terrible. And I asked her, 'Is he dead?' I didn't even get it out and she told me that he was.

"Then she took me away. Two other nurses helped me into a little room. It musta been someone's office. It seems like a lot of people were talking to me, but I couldn't hear anything. I was standing there. I could see mouths opening, but . . ."

Pat does not remember speaking to the police at the hospital. She says she came out of her "little daze" when a nurse asked her if there was anyone she wanted to call. "I called my mother," Pat recalls. "I told her that James was dead. Just like that. There was a silence and then she hung up. I didn't know what else to say. I guess she didn't either. Then I just left that place. I didn't even sign anything. I walked right out on the street. When I was leaving, I met James's brother, Walter Lee Bowden. I told Walter Lee that James was dead, but he already knew."

Walter Lee Bowden had been escorted into the emergency ward by a nurse who told him that his brother was dead on arrival. He grimaced when the nurse pulled back the sheet covering his brother's face. The eyes were closed. The mouth was hanging open. There wasn't a trace of blood. Walter Lee wouldn't let himself cry. "Doesn't look like he went through the windshield," he mumbled, just to say something.

"No, he didn't," said the nurse. "He was shot."

"No!" he said incredulously. "What do you mean?" Minutes

after the incident on Smith Street, he had heard through the neighborhood grapevine that James had been involved in a car accident and had been rushed to the Brigham. No one had said anything about a shooting.

"I'm sorry," said the nurse. "I thought you knew. . . . He was in a gunfight or something like that. He was shot by the police."

"No! No! You don't know . . . James'd never . . ." Walter Lee's voice trailed off. He shook his head and stared at his brother.

"I'm sorry, Mr. Bowden," said the nurse.

Then Walter Lee turned angry. He and his brother had grown up in the poverty and grime of the Mission Hill housing project, a place where kids were street-wise and tough before they reached their teens, and a far cry from Pat's middle-class surroundings half a mile away. Walter Lee, his mother, and two older married sisters still lived in the project. Standing over his brother's body, he was in no mood to trust anyone in the hospital.

"Then where'd he get shot?" he demanded as he reached out to the body. "I mean, where's the bullet hole?" He pulled the sheet down to the waist. "I don't see anything!" He ran a hand over the top of the head and down the back of the neck. He thought he felt some blood. He pulled the head forward. "Please don't do that," said the nurse. Walter Lee found a bullet hole in the back of the head.

"Jesus Christ," he said.

"He was also hit here in the left arm," said the nurse, pointing to a hole in the biceps, "and once in the back."

"The back!"

It took all his strength for the short, wiry Walter Lee to jerk his brother's heavy body up almost to a sitting position. Holding it up with his arms around the shoulders, he got a look at the hole in the back, an inch-wide crater in the skin. Again he murmured, "Jesus Christ."

Walter Lee and Pat took a cab back to her house. Pat's mother had put the kids to bed. "News started traveling fast," Pat remembers, "especially over there in the project where it happened, and before you know it this place was jammed. You know, his relatives, my relatives, and friends." Some were crying softly, others talking in low voices, all aware that the children were sleeping in the bedroom at the end of the hall. The dizzying swirl of people coming and going left Pat unsure of exactly how and when she learned her husband was killed by police.

A *Boston Globe* reporter arrived sometime after nine. Through streaming tears, Pat told him everything she knew about the last day of her husband's life. She thought it was like any other workday for him: up at six; out the door forty-five minutes later; at City Hospital from seven till three-thirty washing the floors; back home about quarter to four; play with the kids; watch TV; dinner at five; then over to Mission Hill to visit his mother and pick up the evening *Globe*. Pat said she had expected him home by seven-thirty. The reporter asked to borrow a picture of James to use in the newspaper. Pat gave him the only one she could find, her wedding picture.

When the reporter left, Pat called the Roxbury police station. "They acted like they didn't know what happened," she says. "I was put on hold, and transferred to someone else, and transferred to someone else. To me that was a dead giveaway. I mean, they knew they were in the wrong." Eventually, Captain William MacDonald came on the line. "I remember yelling at him," says Pat. "It was terrible. I started yelling and screaming. I was really carrying on. I was cussing like I never used cuss words before. I was calling him everything and he didn't even hang up on me. Then my brother came down the hall and grabbed the phone and said something to him and slammed the phone down."

It was 2:00 A.M. when the last visitor left. Pat went to the kids' room. Eurina was awake and wanted to know what was going on. Pat coaxed her back to sleep by promising to tell her about it the next day. Then she took Jamil out of his crib and went to the living room, where she spent the night sitting on her clear-plastic-covered couch, staring at her husband's bubbling aquarium, and holding her sleeping baby in her arms.

She wasn't in danger of losing her home. Her mother owned the three-decker. But she would have to go back to work to support the kids. Her marriage had ended six days after her fifth wedding anniversary.

CHAPTER 2

The next morning visitors filled the Bowden home again. It was an angry group. Everyone had read the police explanation of James Bowden's death in the *Globe*. No one believed it.

According to the newspaper, it had been a matter of self-defense. Two plainclothes patrolmen shot and killed James as he tried to kill them. They had approached him after he got into his parked car and pulled away from a curb in the Mission Hill project. They had been waiting for him ever since they spotted his empty Buick and identified it as the getaway car used only four hours earlier in an armed robbery of a variety store in the neighboring city of Cambridge. The *Globe*'s short article, tucked into a corner of page 4 under a one-inch photo of James Bowden's smiling face, said nothing that cast doubt on the police version of what happened. But true to journalistic form, the article did end with an outraged comment by the grieving widow: "'The police shot him through the head and killed him, and he'd only gone to the project to see his mother and pick up the evening newspaper.'"

Having had the last word in the *Globe* was no concession to Pat. She felt betrayed. The reporter, who had seemed so sympathetic the night before, had in print treated the killing of her husband as routine police work. She swore she would never talk to another reporter. So when Dave O'Brian arrived and identified himself as a reporter, he ran into trouble. Pat refused to talk to him. Nearly everyone else eyed him suspiciously. One man told him that the Bowdens' ten-year-old niece, Jessina Stokes, had seen the shooting from her bedroom window and could flatly contradict the police story. O'Brian asked if he could interview the girl. The man said no and, at the whispered urging of others, tore out of O'Brian's notebook the page where he had written her name. By now, everyone was guessing that O'Brian was a cop. It began with a few Mission Hill people who thought they had seen him in the group of cops surrounding James's car right after the shooting.

On looks alone, Walter Lee decided that the short, chubby, twenty-nine-year-old O'Brian was not a cop. Worried that the scene could turn violent, he took O'Brian aside before sending him on his way. He told him that his brother James was a hard-working family man who had been employed for the last seven years in the housekeeping department of Boston City Hospital and had never committed a crime in his life. "He has no criminal record," said Walter Lee. "You can check that. And he wasn't in Cambridge yesterday. You can check that too."

O'Brian set off to do just that. He cranked up the heater in his rattling but still reliable car and aimed for Cambridge. He dodged potholes and double-parked cars on Roxbury streets, and soon he was crossing the Charles River on the B.U. Bridge. Underneath him the Harvard crew slid across the water into a blinding afternoon sun. Joggers on the grassy Cambridge bank of the river wore gloves and ski hats and ran through puffy clouds of their own breath. The distinctly unathletic O'Brian envied them not at all. He loosened his scarf and left the river behind. At Central Square he took a right onto Massachusetts Avenue, then another right onto Pearl Street. A few blocks from the square he found the Pearl Food Market, a two-cash-register, seven-day-a-week variety store that serves a three-decker neighborhood situated midway between the Harvard and M.I.T. campuses.

Ethel Caragianes, a lifelong resident of the predominantly Greek neighborhood, owned the store. She had inherited it from her father. Her husband, Jim, a friendly middle-aged man, was minding the shop when O'Brian walked in. He told the reporter that he hadn't been in the store at two-thirty the previous afternoon when it was robbed. But his wife was. She was at one of the

registers and got a good look at the robbers. Caragianes said that
O'Brian had just missed her. A police sergeant had come by and
taken her to the morgue to identify one of the robbers, the one the
cops killed in Roxbury. Caragianes was sure she would have no
trouble identifying him. He said, "My wife saw the picture in the
Globe this morning and said, 'That's him!' She didn't even have to
read the story. As soon as she saw the picture, she said it was one
of them. He was wearing a stocking cap to hold down his Afro,
but she remembered him all right."

O'Brian scribbled all this in his notebook. He made a note to
himself to check with Headquarters later to see if Mrs. Caragianes
had identified Bowden. As O'Brian headed for the door, Jim Caragianes offered a parting thought. "You know," he said, "everyone
on this street has been fighting to get the death penalty back. They
were right to shoot him. They got rid of a shit bum."

O'Brian drove back onto Massachusetts Avenue and stayed on
it past the columns of M.I.T., across the Charles again, through
the red-brick and tree-lined Back Bay, past the neon POPS sign
on Symphony Hall, and into a black slum called the South End
that he and many other budget-minded young white city dwellers
had recently moved to. He drove past his basement apartment
in a renovated brownstone and at the end of Mass Ave was lucky
enough to find a parking space a block from the sprawling complex of Boston City Hospital.

At the housekeeping office O'Brian checked Bowden's time
card of the previous day. It had been punched in at 7:09 A.M. and
punched out at 3:17 P.M. A man who refused to identify himself,
and who claimed to be a co-worker of Bowden's, told O'Brian that
Bowden had worked a full day and couldn't have been involved in
a two-thirty robbery.

The final stop for O'Brian that afternoon was Boston Police
Headquarters, a square seven-story downtown building nestled
among the higher homes of insurance companies, such as the
newly constructed John Hancock Tower. O'Brian found an available parking meter beside the Tower.

The press spokesman in the police commissioner's office told

O'Brian that about an hour earlier at the morgue James Bowden had been positively identified as one of the Cambridge robbers. O'Brian asked about Bowden's criminal record, expecting to hear a string of other crimes. The press man gave him an official "No comment" and explained that, by law, criminal records are kept confidential. O'Brian asked to see the reports of the patrolmen involved in the shooting. He was told that they were confidential too. As a consolation, the press man offered O'Brian a copy of a report written by a sergeant who had arrived on the scene fifteen minutes after the shooting. He said that the commissioner, in anticipation of requests like O'Brian's, had arranged for the release of this one report, which was the department's official version of what happened.

Back in his car, O'Brian studied the five-page document. He was already unsure about what had really happened when the police approached Bowden's car. Now he was becoming suspicious. The official version didn't make sense. At the moment the triggers were pulled, Dave O'Brian had been present, his notebook in his hand, and nothing he already knew agreed with the police report.

It had been planned as just another ride-along story, the kind every major newspaper from the *Boston Globe* to the *Seattle Post-Intelligencer* seems to run every few months. A reporter and photographer spend a day in the back seat of a patrol car and bring back an article that shows, in real-life up-close terms, the exhausting, depressing, anxiety-ridden, dangerous, and thankless work our surprisingly good-natured, tough, smarter-than-the-rulebook, and always smarter-than-the-courts big-city cops are doing for the public. The typical ride-along story is more talk than action, because on a typical patrol shift a typical cop sees no crime, makes no arrests, and experiences nothing at all nerve-racking or even mildly stimulating. The time cops spend in cars and on Dunkin' Donuts stools with ride-along reporters is usually filled with funny, touching, scary, and who-knows-how-true accounts of arrests made the day, week, month, or year before. Without that talk, cleaned up for general consumption, most ride-along stories would be studies in tedium. But Dave O'Brian's ride-along story was going to have at least two advantages over those that had already appeared in the local dailies: It would be well written, and it would include accurate dialogue, no matter how profane.

On January 29, 1975, Dave O'Brian was going to ride in an unmarked car with the Boston Police Department's only controversial—in some quarters, notorious—unit, the Tactical Patrol Force. The TPF had been established in 1962 as a quickly mobile and versatile band of extra police strength to be deployed in what a department press release then called "unusual situations and sudden emergencies." When Boston was the scene of repeated anti-war marches and demonstrations during the late 1960s and early 1970s, the Tactical Patrol Force was essentially a riot squad. The unit was outfitted with combat boots, blue jump suits resembling paratrooper combat fatigues, and unusually long and thick wooden clubs. By the mid 1970s the Tactical Patrol Force numbered 125 men, all volunteers and all young, in their twenties and thirties. When court-ordered school busing came to Boston in September of 1974, after federal judge W. Arthur Garrity, Jr., found that the Boston School Committee had been deliberately and systematically segregating its students according to race, with the decision came protest, violence, and bloodshed. And the TPF was in the center of the storm.

As had been widely predicted, violent opposition to the desegregation order began in South Boston, an Irish neighborhood of three-deckers and an all-white public housing project, the best-maintained project in the city. South Boston natives praise their crowded, rather bleak-looking turf in a song, "Southie Is My Hometown," which is so fiercely proud that it must have been born of embarrassment. To outsiders, Southie's only amenity is its couple of miles of beach, sandy and narrow at high tide, muddy and strong-smelling at low tide. Occasionally lured out of their landlocked Roxbury neighborhood by the hope of using Southie's beach, black people have usually found themselves beaten back to Roxbury within minutes. Police on horseback had to gallop onto the beach one hot afternoon in the summer before busing began to save some black tourists who had been looking for a place to swim and thought South Boston's Pleasure Bay, as described in their guidebook, sounded like just the spot.

Judge Garrity's busing plan had many white students from Southie being bused to other neighborhoods, including Roxbury, while black students were being bused into Southie. For the first year, if a school bus carrying black students to South Boston High School was stoned, and if the black students saw the carefully lettered NIGGERS SUCK signs painted in three-foot letters on the street, and if upon entering the school under heavy police guard they heard the hate and obscenity in the screams of hundreds of white parents and boycotting white students who gathered outside every day, then the hordes of print, radio, and television reporters at the scene would call it a relatively uneventful—even peaceful—day at South Boston High School. (*Peaceful* meant no bloodshed.) When a black man was dragged from his car by a crowd of anti-busing demonstrators in Southie and was nearly beaten to death before a quick-thinking patrolman saved his life by dispersing the crowd with a gunshot fired into the air, a Wire-photo of the black man trying to flee his hundred-or-so attackers appeared on front pages of newspapers from *The Times* of London to the *Los Angeles Times* and conveyed to the world the newly overt racism rampant in Boston in the fall of 1974.

After school opened that year, Southie had been flooded with police, including all 125 men of the Tactical Patrol Force. But within a month the TPF had been pulled out of Southie amid charges of police brutality. There were several individual complaints of TPF brutality in the first three weeks, but a Saturday night melee at a bar called the Rabbit Inn was what ended the TPF's days in the neighborhood. Twenty-four TPF men in combat boots, jump suits, and helmets entered the Rabbit Inn a few minutes after eight o'clock that night. Later, they said they were there to investigate the recurring problem of bottles and bricks being thrown at passing TPF cars. There is no dispute that what followed was a few minutes of furious TPF club swinging. It was self-defense according to the TPF, and unprovoked police attack according to Rabbit Inn patrons and its owner, who claimed that the bar sustained $20,000 worth of damage. One young man was arrested for "assaulting a police officer." Nine others were treated at Boston City Hospital for cuts and broken bones. The TPF suffered no injuries at the Rabbit Inn. The next day a thousand Southie residents gathered outside police headquarters to demand the removal of the TPF from their neighborhood. Demonstrators carried signs saying things such as SEND HITLER'S TPF BACK TO HELL! and GESTAPO = TPF / IS THIS AMERICA? The injured described their beatings to television interviewers. The police commissioner told a press conference that he had ordered a thorough investigation of the matter by Internal Affairs. He would not comment further until that investigation was completed. To the question of transferring the TPF out of Southie, the commissioner's response was uncharacteristically brittle. "The TPF will not leave South Boston," he said. "The people cannot tell the police what to do about safety measures."

The conservative, police-supporting, law-and-order Irish politicians of South Boston, who had never before complained of police brutality, now did so in unison. One spoke of "the Gestapo-like tactics" of the TPF. A joint statement released by a state representative, a state senator, and a city councillor said, "The Tactical Patrol Force, a special unit of the Boston Police Department, is responsive only to the Commissioner. So massive was the assault Saturday night that our community must draw one of two frightening conclusions: either the Commissioner has lost control of the men in this unit, or that he retains control and these men are acting with his approval." A hastily convened City Council hearing, featuring the testimony of Rabbit Inn patrons who appeared in bandages and casts, amplified the case against the TPF. Five days after the Rabbit Inn incident, the TPF was pulled out of Southie and scattered throughout the city's less troublesome schools and neighborhoods. Replacing the 125 men of the TPF in Southie, where sporadic violence had intensified since the Rabbit Inn incident, were 300 state police officers.

The day after the shift, the *Boston Globe* ran a front-page story under the headline THE TPF—CAUGHT IN THE MIDDLE. It portrayed the TPF as a hardworking, dedicated group of young men who had been unfairly expected to do the impossible job of keeping the peace in Southie. Captain Joseph Rowan, "the skipper and veteran of the elite force," complained about the long overtime hours his men had to work because of the busing troubles. The extra money was not compensation enough, Rowan said, without mentioning that nearly every one of his men was actually collecting about $500 per week in overtime alone. The *Globe* story contained not a word about the Rabbit Inn. It was the kind of cheerleading article the TPF would have welcomed from Dave O'Brian.*

The TPF office was in a handsome three-story Federalist-style brick building at the mouth of the Callahan Tunnel, an underwater route across the harbor to East Boston, the airport, and the northern suburbs. From the feet of its facade's columns to the small gold-leaf dome that caps its clock tower, the building looks like the slightly younger brother of nearby Faneuil Hall, but it carries none of its look-alike's centuries of historical significance. It was built in 1932 as a police station. Because of its downtown location, with immediate access to the city's principal highways, it became the ideal base for a police unit not bound by precinct or, in Boston terms, *district* boundaries. The TPF shared the building with the Boston Police Academy—the instructional center for new recruits—and a rent-paying tenant, the patrolmen's union. The TPF used one of the side doors, over which was the stone inscription SEMPER FIDELIS. It was through that door that Dave O'Brian and his photographer, Ken Kobre, walked shortly before two o'clock on that Wednesday afternoon.

Neither O'Brian nor Kobre could have been mistaken for rough

---

* The Internal Affairs investigation of the Rabbit Inn incident ultimately found a few of the involved officers guilty of misconduct and recommended suspensions from duty for each of them, but not before a full year had passed. The commissioner then ordered the suspensions, but the officers immediately mounted a successful Civil Service appeal and never missed a day of work.

and ready TPF men reporting for after-school patrol assignments. They looked like a couple of graduate students entering a library. They were both twenty-nine. O'Brian was a short, chubby guy with a receding crop of brown hair, a thin moustache on an owlish face, and permanently attached eyeglasses. He wore his winter work clothes that day: a ski parka, sweater, permanent-press pants, and waterproof shoes. In one pocket was his notebook and in another a couple of pencils. Pencils don't run out of ink and can write in the rain, something he thought he might have to do that day. Ken Kobre, a tall, lean Floridian with light wavy hair and a bushy moustache, carried a heavy camera bag over his shoulder. He was wearing a denim jacket, a thick sweater, faded jeans, and cowboy boots, which were then still a rare sight in Boston.

Waiting for O'Brian and Kobre at the front desk was Sergeant Harry Byrne, the TPF patrol supervisor of the afternoon. The pudgy, middle-aged sergeant introduced them to six plainclothes patrolmen who were standing around him: Eddie Holland, Dennis McKenna, Billy Dwyer, Mark Molloy, Frank MacDonald, and Loman McClinton. Byrne explained that the six would be working as a team split into three unmarked cars. Eddie Holland and Dennis McKenna would ride in one car, Billy Dwyer and Mark Molloy in another, and Frank MacDonald and Loman McClinton (the only black or even non-Irish member of the team) in the third. Sergeant Byrne told O'Brian and Kobre that they would first ride with Dwyer and Molloy and later switch to Holland and McKenna's car. McKenna politely asked O'Brian and Kobre to excuse them for a moment and led the cops across the room for a huddle.

Dennis McKenna did not want O'Brian and Kobre riding with the team. None of the other cops objected. McKenna reminded them that O'Brian was with the *Phoenix*. He warned them that they couldn't trust someone from a radical paper like that.* Though McKenna's teammates shared his suspicion of the *Phoe-*

---

* Founded in the 1960s, *The Boston Phoenix* had begun as an "underground" newspaper, but by 1975 the weekly had earned prominent newsstand displays

nix, they still liked the idea of appearing in a newspaper story. McKenna, a patrolmen's union representative, then made everyone wait while he rushed next door to union headquarters. Minutes later, he returned with the union's president and the union's lawyer, Frank McGee, who agreed with McKenna that *Phoenix* reporters shouldn't be granted ride-alongs. The three men went directly to the commander of the TPF, Joe Rowan.

Rowan was also wary of the *Phoenix*. Like most cops, he was only comfortable when dealing with regular police reporters from the dailies, mostly Irish guys like himself whom he had come to know well in his thirty years on the force. Guys he could trust. But Joe Rowan's orders on this matter had come directly from the commissioner, who had recently promoted him to the lofty rank of deputy superintendent. The commissioner would surely be unmoved by Rowan's or the union's or McKenna's concerns about the *Phoenix*.

Police Commissioner Robert J. di Grazia came to Boston in 1972 when Mayor Kevin White, surprising most people and shocking the rest, appointed him to the post. White had first offered the job to his friend Clarence Kelley, who was then the chief of police in Kansas City. But Kelley had turned down the offer, possibly knowing even then that he was going to become the next director of the FBI. When Mayor White asked Kelley whether there was anyone he would recommend for the job, Kelley suggested only one man: Robert di Grazia.

Like everyone else in Boston, Kevin White had never heard of Robert di Grazia, whose law-enforcement career had begun only twelve years earlier in a small California town called Novato, about thirty miles north of his hometown of San Francisco. It was not until 1960 that peaceful Novato decided to form a police department, and when it did, Bob di Grazia quit managing the

---

across the state and strong circulation in Boston's universities with its in-depth reporting on politics, sports, and the arts. The *Phoenix* has been consistently liberal, never radical.

local department store and joined the force. He spent the next nine years with the Novato P.D. During his last six years there, he was chief of the twenty-seven-man force. Di Grazia left California in 1969, moving halfway across the country to accept an offer to run the St. Louis County Police Department. Not to be confused with the police department of the city of St. Louis, Di Grazia's department was a three-hundred-man force that patrolled only the affluent western suburbs of the city. It was not a major urban police department, but it was a long way from Novato. It was there, in his three years as chief of police in St. Louis County, that Di Grazia developed a mutual professional respect and friendship with Kansas City's Chief Kelley, his colleague at the other end of the state.

The Boston press was caught by surprise when the new police commissioner's appointment was announced. Initially, both the liberal *Globe* and the conservative *Herald* had to rely exclusively on the mayor's press release for information on Di Grazia. Not surprisingly then, the first Di Grazia stories to appear in the local press were cluttered with adjectives like *progressive, hardworking, capable, honest, intelligent, innovative, witty,* and *handsome*.

The day after his appointment became public, Di Grazia flew to Boston. The *Herald* welcomed him with a front-page article describing him as, among other things, "a staunch Catholic," "a moderate drinker," and "an extremely honest man." The article also noted what to many of its ethnicity-conscious readers was a most important point: Di Grazia was the first non-Irish Boston police commissioner in thirty-eight years. The next sentence was quick to point out that Di Grazia's wife "is of Irish extraction." Mrs. di Grazia's heritage was no consolation to the most extremely parochial of the local Irish, for whom the appointment by an Irish mayor of an Italian police commissioner was an unpardonable betrayal of the trusted tradition of insular ethnic patronage. Of course, to the Italians, Boston's second-largest ethnic group, the appointment of the first Italian police commissioner was welcomed as a major victory in their continuing struggle for political parity with the Irish.

Bob di Grazia met the local news media on his first day in Boston. The new commissioner had a striking stage presence, standing before the television lights and cameras confidently fielding reporters' questions. The athletically trim and attractive man, six feet four inches tall, towered over everyone in the room. To virtually every questioner, he flashed a quick, natural smile before answering. On the lapel of his fashionable three-piece suit was pinned a small gold pig. When asked about it, he explained: "The pig has come to symbolize the police officer in a derogative sense. I am privileged and proud to be a police officer. This pig symbolizes Pride, Integrity, Guts, and Service. You'll find that symbol on the lapel of all my suits no matter where I am. It stands as a symbol of my pride in law enforcement." The next day's *Herald* ran a front-page headline: DI GRAZIA PROUDLY WEARS PIG SYMBOL.

In that first press conference Di Grazia instantly became a darling of the news media simply by being more talkative and amiable than any Boston police commissioner in recent memory. The only meaningful exchange he had with a reporter was with Dave O'Brian, who asked how he would maintain the integrity of the department, particularly in light of some recently discovered evidence of corruption throughout its ranks.

The corruption charges centered on a list, found in a raid on a bookie's home, which contained the names and telephone numbers of eighty-two high- and low-ranking Boston cops. A grand jury had begun studying the bookie's list and was hearing testimony on the same day Di Grazia was meeting the press. (In the end, the grand jury returned no indictments, but all the men on the list retired or resigned not long after Di Grazia took office.)

To O'Brian's question Di Grazia firmly replied, "I don't like bad cops. I will do everything possible to get rid of bad cops."

"How do you intend to root out the bad cops?" O'Brian asked.

"I certainly believe it can be done," said Di Grazia, "if you work from within."

By 1975, Bob di Grazia had solidified his popularity with the press and the public. My friends in Dorchester, the neighborhood where I grew up (and still live, long after the rest of my family has pulled out to the southern suburbs), thought him too liberal but respected him for his apparent honesty. But in his own department, he was disliked. He had hired a band of young civilian advisers whom he consulted more than the brass. Most cops thought Di Grazia and his gang swaggered around headquarters without any deference to experienced commanders and patrolmen and were trying to change too many of the old ways. One Di Grazia innovation that was extremely unpopular in the field, but which endeared him to the press, was his policy of allowing any reporter to ride in a patrol car at almost any time. The patrolmen's union had gone to court to try to end the wide-open ride-along system. Since the court had not yet acted on the union's case, Attorney McGee told Joe Rowan that Wednesday afternoon that he should call Di Grazia and suggest waiting for the court's opinion before granting any more ride-alongs. But Rowan knew that Di Grazia would view such a suggestion as just another union attempt to block his every move. Thus, Rowan turned a sympathetic ear to McGee's plea but didn't bother to call the commissioner. He finally closed the meeting by ordering Dennis McKenna to take O'Brian and Kobre out with the team.

McKenna returned to the front desk, where his teammates were waiting. He nodded to O'Brian and Kobre—who were off by themselves in a corner and had no idea what McKenna had been up to—and said, "Let's go." O'Brian and Kobre followed Billy Dwyer and Mark Molloy to their car. Eddie Holland and Dennis McKenna got into another car. Frank MacDonald and Loman McClinton got into a station wagon. It was 2:30 P.M. when they hit the street.

Three years later, McKenna told a jury that he and the other five cops were working as an Anti-Crime Unit that afternoon. "The Anti-Crime Unit work," he explained, "was generally to go into areas where people were being ripped off, mugged, assaulted, and try to saturate the area with a number of plainclothes police officers to take the muggers off the street." I remember watching these ACU teams at work from my stool in the parking lot. The sidewalk in front of the Hillbilly Ranch, a seedy bar across the street from my lot, was a favorite spot for ACU decoy operations. One TPF guy would pose as a stumbling drunk with some big bills sticking out of his pocket. Others would be scattered around the area in the guise of passersby, or hidden in dark doorways or in parked newspaper-delivery trucks. I used to try to pick out their hiding places before they came charging out at someone who allegedly reached for the money. They never took chances in those arrests. All six or seven guys going at the would-be thief would have their guns out every time. Even though I never saw the ACU teams meet any resistance or disarm anyone, I often saw them sticking guns to the heads of the black teenagers they had hooked. After the TPF's first night in front of the Hillbilly Ranch, all the pimps, prostitutes, pickpockets, and parking attendants in the area knew about the decoy setup and could spot it instantly. The TPF always claimed it was pulling in major-league criminals, but I found it hard to believe that any real bad guys could actually fall for it. It seemed more like a trap for Vermont farmers who had just dropped the harvest money at neighboring strip joints, where between shows the performers hustled a cruelly expensive imitation of champagne in exchange for seemingly fantasy-fulfilling, but ultimately frustrating, hugs. These were guys who, despite their booze-blurred vision, spotted the gas money they needed to get home sticking miraculously out of another drunk's pocket, and for the first time in their lives committed a crime.

In other locations, such as Roxbury, where purse snatching is an epidemic, some of the short and thin TPF patrolmen like McKenna would on occasion dress in women's clothing and walk the streets with invitingly loose grips on their purses—and teammates trailing them in unmarked cars. The Anti-Crime Unit was one of Di Grazia's innovations. In the first year of busing it was the TPF's regular after-school assignment.

Unmarked ACU cars were equipped with two types of radios. The one connecting them to Headquarters and the TPF office was the standard multi-channel set installed in all Boston police cars.

The other was a hand-held walkie-talkie used for calls among teammates. As the ACU team headed across town to Roxbury that day, the first thing to come over the air from Headquarters was a report, relayed from the Cambridge police, of an armed robbery of a variety store in Cambridge. The robbers were reported to be two colored males, in a blue Ford or Buick, Massachusetts number 4S•6368, last seen headed for Boston. Soon, a correction of the plate number was relayed from Cambridge. The "S" might be an "F". The messages on the radio about an armed robbery, only minutes into his ride-along, readied O'Brian for action. But there wouldn't be any for the next four hours.

Using the simple, old-fashioned stakeout method, the team went after purse snatchers. Each car went to a different spot favored by Roxbury muggers, and the cops just sat, waiting for something to happen. They stayed in touch with each other via walkie-talkie. Billy Dwyer pulled his Buick into a parking space a few hundred yards from an intersection near the Mission Hill housing project. Dwyer told O'Brian and Kobre that female drivers who had to stop for the traffic light there were being attacked by gangs who thought nothing of smashing their way through car windows with bricks and pipes so they could reach in and grab a pocketbook. Mark Molloy sat beside Dwyer, peering through binoculars at the intersection.

I had come to know Billy Dwyer about ten years earlier. He was the coach of a Dorchester baseball team for teenagers, and I was one of his outfielders one summer. He was in his early twenties then, not yet a member of the force. I think he was a clerk in a hardware store. Billy was chummy with the players he had known for a while, but was cool and distant with new guys like me. He always called me by my last name. Coaching was serious business for Billy. He was a former Dorchester High School pitching star and he liked showing us his stuff in batting practice. He'd whiz fast balls and curves by me effortlessly. Occasionally he'd let up so I could get the feel of hitting the ball. His pitching was better than anything we faced in games. It was great practice. I liked him and tried to impress him with every move. Billy once asked me if my father was "the lawyer." I said he was. At a game we played in Plymouth that summer, the only one my father saw, I introduced him to Billy Dwyer (an event my father was not going to remember ten years later when he read the name in Dave O'Brian's story).

Dwyer had hardly aged since that summer. O'Brian thought he was in his mid-twenties. Actually he was thirty-two. But then, little in Dwyer's life had changed. He'd put in six years on the force. He was still unmarried, and still lived with his parents in Dorchester. Softball had replaced baseball as his summer exercise. He was still trim, fit, and handsome. His blond hair had ripened to something browner and, like everyone else's, was longer and covered most of his ears. It came as no surprise to me to read in O'Brian's article that Dwyer was "acknowledged by his colleagues as the 'brains'" of the ACU team. While the other five looked tough and maybe smart, Dwyer looked smart and maybe tough. I remember sitting on the bench with him, thinking that his penetrating eyes were picking up more than mine ever could.

Dwyer and Mark Molloy had been partners since they joined the Tactical Patrol Force seven months earlier. Molloy was a year younger than Dwyer and had one less year on the force. He's from Charlestown, and looks it.

Charlestown produces Boston's toughest people. Most of my father's clients who have been accused of bank robbery grew up in Charlestown's Decatur Street housing project. It is not a dangerous place, if you live there. No black people do. Black sailors who used to make the mistake of wandering out of the old Charlestown Navy Yard were often beaten back into it. When delegates to the 1982 NAACP convention, held in Boston, visited Charlestown's Bunker Hill monument, they did so in the early morning under a heavy police guard of approximately one cop per black person.

I was fourteen the first time I set foot in Charlestown. I was with my brother Bill, who is a year and a half older than I, and our friend Bobby Gilbody, who had somehow acquired the nickname "Gooba" and was unquestionably Dorchester's toughest teenager of that era. We went to Charlestown's municipal ice-skating rink to see a friend of Bill's who worked there. We had just stepped in the door when Gooba, who had a gift for looking at people the wrong way, did just that. In Dorchester that was usually enough provocation for a fight. In Charlestown it was enough for murder. We turned to see Gooba being invited outside by a kid half his size. We tried to tell Gooba to ignore him, knowing that if he did it would be the first time in his life that he passed up a fight. As soon as Gooba squared off outside, the kid pulled a knife. No one but Bill and I in the crowd of about a hundred onlookers of adults, teenagers, and children seemed to consider this a violation of the honor code of street fighting. Gooba, who never carried a weapon, welcomed the knife as a way of evening the odds. Before he could make a move, though, a bigger kid jumped out of the crowd with a bigger knife, lunged at Gooba, and expertly slipped the blade into his belly. For a minute Gooba didn't falter. He continued to step carefully around the ring formed by the crowd, looking for the moment to go against the knives with feet and fists flying. Then Bill jumped in and grabbed Gooba from behind and started dragging him to our car. I was already on my way there. Gooba had been weakened enough so that he couldn't resist Bill's lead. Bill pushed Gooba into the car. I was in the front seat waiting for Bill to get behind the wheel. As he opened the driver's door someone grabbed him and slammed him against the side of the car. I leaned across the front seat and looked up to see a knife point actually touching my brother's throat.

"Don't ever come back here," the blade man said.

"Yes, sir," replied Bill.

Years later, the Charlestown story was one of many told at Gooba's wake. After serving with distinction, and possibly even pleasure, as an Army tank commander in Vietnam, where he was wounded more than once, Gooba went out in a flaming car crash on his way home from a softball game.

Anyway, Mark Molloy had moved out of Charlestown and settled with his wife and three young children in a neighboring suburb, but he was still a genuine Charlestown heavyweight, the toughest-looking guy on the ACU team. He was only an inch or two over six feet but his bulk made him seem truly massive. He had short, curly red hair and, because his ACU undercover role allowed it, a matching red beard. He was wearing a floppy denim hat that could take the day's on-again-off-again rain, a velour zipper-front shirt, a nylon windbreaker, and Hush Puppies.

Dwyer and Molloy had no luck on the intersection stakeout. It was a strangely quiet afternoon for Roxbury, Dwyer told O'Brian. Nothing came over the walkie-talkie from the other ACU cars either.

Ken Kobre had intended to save his film for the action he expected, but when it began to look like there wouldn't be any, he decided to take some pictures of Dwyer and Molloy. They were happy to oblige and posed according to Kobre's suggestions. From outside the car Kobre took some shots of Molloy sitting in the front seat looking through binoculars. Inside the car, he coaxed Dwyer into a series of more dramatic poses with loaded gun in hand and finger on the trigger.

As the afternoon dragged on, Dwyer and Molloy tried to fill the hours with you-should-have-been-with-us-yesterday stories. They told O'Brian and Kobre that the day before they had collared a whole gang of purse snatchers. They shared the credit for the arrest with Dennis McKenna and Eddie Holland. Molloy finished the story with the complaint that the arrest was meaningless because, "They'll just be sent to the Youth Service Board, which is nothing." Dwyer offered an explanation, without any fancy economic, sociological, or psychological trimmings, of what motivates purse snatchers and muggers. "All this talk that they do it for drugs is bullshit," Dwyer casually opined. "They're maggots, that's all."

After about two hours with Dwyer and Molloy, O'Brian and Kobre transferred to the car carrying Holland and McKenna. After a Dunkin' Donuts coffee break, Holland and McKenna began to cruise the Mission Hill housing project. McKenna was driving a beat-up Oldsmobile. O'Brian sat behind him. Kobre had to sit in the middle of the back seat because there was a milk crate on the right side holding up the front seat. As he later reported, O'Brian thought the car was "designed to look so much unlike a police cruiser that one would think your average, street-wise mugger would single it out instantly." Holland was covering the radios.

Ken Kobre, who has a better memory for feelings than facts, noticed something different about Holland and McKenna. "The first two cops we were with seemed pretty sensible," Kobre told me, "but these last two were, I don't know, just kind of different, almost weird." But the only differences Kobre remembers were that they were older than the others, wore shabbier clothes, were on the short side, and looked gaunt compared to Mark Molloy.

To Dave O'Brian, they weren't so different or at all weird. O'Brian liked McKenna despite his stated dislike of reporters and news photographers. "Reporters will write anything to sell a story," he told O'Brian. And to Kobre he said, "I've seen nosy photographers take a thousand pictures during this busing thing and only use the one of the cop with his stick raised."

"Denny McKenna," O'Brian wrote in the next week's *Phoenix*, "was the most open, honest and direct cop with whom I spoke that day."

I've never spoken to Denny McKenna or Eddie Holland. They have refused to talk to me, so I don't have much detail on them. I don't know why Denny has the face of a perpetually angry man. I don't know why it seems so hard for him to smile, something I've seen him do only a couple of times, and then for only a few seconds in the many hours I've watched him. It's true that I've seen him only when he has appeared as a defendant in federal court, but I've seen many people in worse jams than his who constantly smiled bravely, or nervously, or calmly. What I can say about him has been gleaned from a few records I've found and a few personal, but not very revealing, questions he has had to answer under oath.

He grew up in Brighton, the northwest border territory of Boston, a place indistinguishable from my Dorchester. He went to local parochial schools. He joined the Air Force right after high school graduation in the mid 1950s. His assignment was the Air Force Police. He came out of the Air Force in the late fifties, returned to Brighton, and found a job as a welder. After five years of welding he joined the Police Department. He was married in 1963. Ten years and six kids later, his wife filed for a legal separation. In seeking the separation, Mrs. McKenna accused her husband of subjecting her to "cruel and abusive treatment" and having "gross and confirmed habits of intoxication caused by the voluntary and excessive use of intoxicating liquors." Denny did not dispute the accusations. He'd been drinking hard for years, and had sometimes missed work because of it. He once had to spend two weeks in a hospital to dry out. He had been in and out of Alcoholics Anonymous for two years. Under the terms of the separation, Mrs. McKenna kept the house and the children, and Denny continued to support her and the kids with $153 a week. At age thirty-seven, Denny was living alone in a small Brighton apartment when Dave O'Brian met him. His ten years on the job, eight with the TPF, made him the senior man of the ACU team. The long, scraggly brown hair covering his forehead and ears and hanging over the collar of his green windbreaker made him look like a prematurely aged, wiry junkie. It was an effective look for an undercover cop, but how he could ever fool a purse snatcher when he posed as a woman is beyond me.

Denny McKenna and Eddie Holland had been partners for the eight months since Eddie joined the TPF. At forty-one, Eddie was one of the oldest men on the TPF, but like his younger teammates he had only six years experience behind the badge. When he joined the force, he was thirty-five. He beat the age limit for new recruits by only a couple of months. When asked in a deposition what he had done before becoming a cop, Eddie said, "Basically, I worked construction, and as a salesman." The son of a carpenter, Eddie grew up with his eight brothers and sisters in Billy Dwyer's section of Dorchester. He went to parochial schools. In 1952, shortly after his high school graduation, he joined the Navy. Like Denny, Eddie was assigned to the military police during his three years in the service. He was stationed in Cuba at the Guantánamo Bay navy base. When he returned to Dorchester in the mid 1950s, he moved back in with his parents and presumably began his thirteen years of construction and sales jobs. Eddie has never married. He still lives in his parents' house.

Eddie didn't let his hair grow long the way many TPF men did. "I'm too old. I'm past that stuff," he told O'Brian with an air of regret. He was probably a good-looking guy in his day, but now his short black hair was thinning where it met his high, wrinkled forehead. His eyes were puffy. His small mouth seemed lipless. It was a forty-one-year-old face with some heavy mileage on it. O'Brian thought it "a face like a clenched fist." He was wearing TPF combat boots, baggy pants, a light turtleneck, and a dark three-quarter-length corduroy coat. In the *Phoenix,* O'Brian would report that Eddie and Denny "reeked of street savvy and toughness."

Eddie and Denny and the rest of the cops spoke with heavy Boston accents, which can make anyone sound tough. It's a coarse, slovenly form of speech recognizable by its treatment of the letter *R,* which is pronounced when it is the first letter in a syllable. The rest of the time the *R* is converted to an *ah* sound or ignored. Some of my college classmates considered me something of a tough guy only because of my tendency to call our school Hahvud. A friend of mine familiar with most of the dialects heard from Scotland to Texas maintains that the Boston accent can be the meanest-sounding of all. Eddie's and Denny's voices are about the harshest I've heard. (So to O'Brian and Kobre, neither of whom are native Bostonians, they had to sound pretty tough.)

Eddie and Denny had no more luck cruising the Mission Hill project than Dwyer and Molloy were having back at the intersection stakeout a few blocks away. Nothing happened. Nothing came over the walkie-talkie. Black Roxbury, the most feared section of Boston, was beginning to look to O'Brian and Kobre like not such a dangerous place. O'Brian remembers Eddie busying himself by taking notes on a clipboard of the descriptions of people, cars, and license plates coming over the radio from headquarters. As he squeezed the car along the narrow streets of the housing project, Denny chatted with O'Brian. Careful not to interfere with the reporter's conversation, Ken Kobre kept to himself.

After five o'clock the identical, boxlike, three-story red-brick buildings of the housing project were fading from view in the midwinter twilight. The few working streetlights in the project produced no more than a dim glow. The ACU team's utterly uneventful shift ended at six, and the three cars started back to the TPF office. O'Brian and Kobre were surprised. They had expected action with an Anti-Crime Unit, especially in Roxbury, more especially in the Mission Hill housing project. O'Brian jokingly told Denny his story would be headlined BOREDOM WITH THE TPF. Denny was not amused. No one should think that ACU work was light stuff, he said. He told O'Brian that it was usually not like this, and reminded everyone of the weather, suggesting that even purse snatchers are smart enough to stay out of the rain. Just then, Eddie saw something.

"Hey, that's it!" Eddie shouted. "That's it! That's the car from the Cambridge holdup!"

They were on Smith Street in the Mission Hill project. Eddie was twisting around in his seat to get another look at a car parked to his right beside a SLOW sign. It was a 1973 light-blue Buick Electra with the license plate 4F•6838.

Denny instantly swung the car into an awkward U-turn on the narrow street. A mistake, O'Brian thought. A car with four white guys makes a U-turn on a one-way street and boldly goes back in the illegal direction to get a close look at a parked car—obviously cops.

"Don't blow it, now!" Eddie warned. "Don't give us away!"

"Hey, there's no one in the car," Denny replied, thinking it was okay to go back for a better look.

O'Brian was surprised at Eddie's excitement. *Don't blow what?* he thought to himself. "It seemed to me," O'Brian wrote later, "that if the car had been used in a holdup, it had surely been stolen and surely abandoned."

On the second pass by the car Eddie noticed it had no front

license plate.* He checked the number on the rear plate and said, triumphantly, "That's the number." Denny drove the few hundred feet to the end of Smith Street and went through the intersection with Parker Street to Gurney Street, which is actually just an extension of Smith. Denny turned the car around again on Gurney and pulled over at the corner of Gurney and Parker Streets. From that point they could look straight down Smith Street to the Buick, more than one hundred yards away.

Here Eddie and Denny's version of events begins to differ from O'Brian's. By the time the car came to a stop on Gurney Street, O'Brian says, both cops had drawn their guns. Eddie and Denny say they took out their guns only because O'Brian asked to see them. O'Brian says he had already seen Dwyer's identical gun when he took it out for Kobre and had no interest in seeing Eddie's or Denny's. O'Brian took detailed notes of what was said in the next half hour and reproduced the conversation in the *Phoenix*. Eddie and Denny agree with O'Brian's version of the radio transmissions he heard but claim no memory of what they may have said to each other or to the reporter. They don't deny any of O'Brian's quotations; they simply say they don't remember them, and they don't suggest any alternative lines of dialogue. Here is O'Brian's account.

Eddie got on the walkie-talkie to tell the other ACU cars about his find. Billy Dwyer came over the air immediately to assure Eddie that he and Mark Molloy would take a position at the other end of Smith Street on St. Alphonsus Street. They were ready to block that end of Smith Street if necessary. With that, the Buick was trapped. Loman McClinton came on after Dwyer to tell Eddie and Denny that he and Frank MacDonald were parked a short block away from them on Station Street, just off Parker Street. They would be right behind them if there was any action.

Someone got on the radio to get a description of the robbers. Each car tuned it in as it came over the air: two black males in

---

* Massachusetts stopped issuing two license plates per vehicle and now requires the use of only a rear license plate.

their mid-twenties; one in a blue denim jacket, the other in a blue nylon jacket; both wearing stocking caps; both armed, one with an automatic pistol, the other with a sawed-off shotgun.

O'Brian recalls Denny anxiously holding his .38 in his lap and saying, "Christ, we're no match for a shotgun. They ought to send us a couple of guys with shotguns as long as those bastards have a shotgun."

Turning to the back seat, Eddie said, "Christ, I don't know what to do with you guys if some shooting starts."

O'Brian's right hand was racing across his notebook at this point. Some of what he wrote is not legible, but this note describing his reaction to the shotgun news is clear: "Terror. White kid in back of unmarked cop car in middle of Mission Hill—and all this fucking talk about shotguns."

The radio cracked the mounting tension with a rundown on the license plate: 4F•6368 was an expired plate that was stolen a few months ago from a Cape Cod Volkswagen.

"Definitely a stolen and abandoned car," O'Brian said hopefully of the Buick under surveillance.

"No, they're right around here in the project," said Eddie, who O'Brian thought was "straining at the bit." Eddie's certainty came from "a gut feeling." He wanted to walk down Smith Street to look around. Denny thought that would only advertise the stakeout and talked him out of the idea. Each time a passerby walked near the Buick, Eddie, whose TPF nickname was "Steam" because he overheated easily, would lean forward and say, "Christ, there's someone there! He's at the car!"

"No, no," Denny would reply each time. "He's just walking by."

Denny tried to lighten the atmosphere with stories like the one about the time he was playing a decoy drunk and offered some cheap booze to a genuine wino, who haughtily told him, "I don't drink that crap."

Eddie, on the other hand, kept feeding his guests' anxiety. "I hate this time of night," he said as O'Brian looked at his watch at 6:20 P.M., twenty minutes into the stakeout, "because your eyes haven't adjusted to the dark and there are a lot of kids on the street. All it takes is for one of these kids to make us and the word will spread down that street like wildfire that there are cops up here on a stakeout. Then we're the target." To preserve whatever was left of their cover, Eddie hid the walkie-talkie in a paper bag and put it to his mouth as if it were a bottle every time someone walked by the ACU car.

"Why don't they put up streetlights?" O'Brian asked. "You could walk down that street and vanish."

"They shoot them out," Denny replied. "You can't even keep a window intact on that street."

The walkie-talkie had been silent for several minutes when Dwyer checked in with a plan which assumed that both robbers would return to the Buick: "If they move the car, Mark and I will take the passenger. You and Denny take the driver. That way, we won't be in each other's line of fire."

Denny said over his right shoulder to O'Brian: "Bear in mind, we're going to try to get them before they even get out of their vehicle. We like to stack the odds in our favor. We have the element of surprise, so we should grab him before he even fires a shot."

Eddie got off the walkie-talkie in time to hear Denny's last comment. "If they've got a fuckin' shotgun," Eddie countered seriously, "they could blow all four of us away with one blast." An impossibility, of course, but O'Brian and Kobre didn't know that.

Eddie's mention of the shotgun prompted Denny to order his passengers to hit the floor and stay there if there was any shooting. O'Brian and Kobre nodded obediently. They had no intention of being brave. Nothing in their backgrounds had prepared them for this. Neither had served in the military. Neither had ever heard gunfire.

As his light southern accent suggests, Ken Kobre was born, raised, and educated in Florida, where he landed his first post-college job with the *St. Petersburg Times.* He came to Boston after a few years of free-lance photography in Denver and New York. He was now the photo editor of the *Phoenix* and a photography instructor at Boston University. Kobre had assigned himself to O'Brian's story because he had never been in a police car and it seemed like the best assignment of the week.

O'Brian is from Brockton, a medium-sized Massachusetts city about thirty miles southwest of Boston. He moved to the big city in 1967 to attend Boston University. His first job was at a small-town newspaper published near Brockton. After two years there, he returned to Boston as a political reporter for the *Boston Record American,* then the local Hearst paper. He soon became one of the *Record*'s featured columnists but bailed out of that grind in 1973 for the more agreeable pace at an up-and-coming weekly. O'Brian's move to the relative obscurity of the *Phoenix* was a long step down in the newspaper game, but the shy, soft-spoken reporter has not sought journalistic stardom. For him, the stakeout of that getaway car was not a big chance for a hot story; it just felt scary, and he only wanted it to end. He hoped the TPF night shift would take over soon so he could "get the hell out of there."

It had been a strange winter day for Boston. The temperature had started off in the thirties and had risen steadily. It was in the low forties at six o'clock when the stakeout began and by six-thirty it had made an astounding jump to fifty-one degrees. "Unseasonably mild temperatures" is what television weathermen were saying at that moment on the evening news programs. But it had been raining on and off all day, and at six-thirty in Roxbury, the rain was heavy. Denny had to leave the engine running to keep the windshield wipers going. Visibility was bad. The Buick was difficult to see.

As the excitement gradually ebbed, Eddie's concentration on the Buick did too. His gaze bounced from the piles of garbage in the courtyards to the broken beer bottles on the sidewalks, the boarded-up windows of deserted apartments, the stripped and abandoned cars, the broken streetlights, and the people passing by. He surprised everyone when he began mumbling something about what makes a man an armed robber. "I'm not a liberalist," he said to no one in particular, "but if you had to live in a place like that, how would you make a living?" Eddie's question met silence. By the time he got it out, all attention was riveted on the Buick. After having watched the car so intently for the last thirty minutes, Eddie was the last to notice what was going on. There were no nervous exclamations from him this time. Something was really happening.

A Ford Thunderbird had stopped beside the Buick. It looked as if someone stepped out of the passenger side of the Thunderbird and was getting in the driver's side of the Buick. At that distance, looking through a streaked windshield, in the seconds it took to move from one car to the other, no one could make out any detail of the figure getting into the Buick. When Eddie saw the Buick's headlights go on, he whipped the walkie-talkie out of its paper-bag disguise. The Thunderbird started moving again. It rolled along Smith Street toward Dwyer and Molloy's stakeout position. "We're going in!" Eddie roared into the walkie-talkie.

The Buick backed away from the curb and continued slowly in reverse down the one-way street toward Parker Street. Denny sped across Parker Street onto Smith on a collision course with the Buick. O'Brian and Kobre began to slip to the floor. Denny closed in on the Buick from the rear. When there were only a few feet separating the cars, Denny slammed on the brakes, throwing O'Brian and Kobre against the back of the front seat.

"Go around him!" Eddie yelled.

Kobre was already on the floor. O'Brian stole a last look at Eddie and Denny as they jumped out of the car, guns drawn. They left the doors open. O'Brian dived to the floor.

When the gunfire started, the sound was not the booming explosion O'Brian and Kobre had expected. It was more like a string of firecrackers going off, they thought, but it kept them crouched on the floor. They saw none of the shooting that seemed to be happening about ten feet away from them. O'Brian counted the shots, seven, maybe eight, and scribbled a note of it. Even when the firing stopped, he and Kobre did not look up. They wondered whether Eddie and Denny were still alive. It was not until Eddie and Denny were back in the car that O'Brian and Kobre got off the floor.

"No TPF injured!" Eddie shouted into the walkie-talkie. "Get us an ambulance!"

Denny sped up Smith Street toward the Buick, which was now about a hundred yards away. It had gone forward up Smith Street before it swerved to the left, jumped the curbstone, smashed through a cement light pole, and came to rest only after the left wheels had climbed a three-foot stone wall in front of a school and crushed a small chain-link fence on top of the wall. Denny stopped the car, about twenty yards from the Buick this time, and jumped out again. Eddie was still on the radio calling for help as Denny ran toward the wrecked car. Still sitting in the back seat, Ken Kobre began snapping pictures of Denny reaching in the window of the Buick.

O'Brian got out of the car and headed cautiously for the Buick. Eddie rushed past him with Frank MacDonald and Loman Mc-Clinton, who were already on the scene. O'Brian moved slowly, not knowing what had happened or what might yet happen. By the time he reached the Buick, all six TPF men, with guns in hand, were leaning through the shattered windows of the car. After a minute, Denny stepped away from the car and O'Brian looked inside. There was a black man behind the wheel with blood all over his head and his clothes. He was not moving. On the seat beside him was a newspaper, a pair of gloves, and a pool of blood. More blood was splattered on the back seat. Shattered window glass covered the seats and floor. O'Brian quickly turned away.

It was only when O'Brian saw the water dripping off Denny's long hair that he realized how soaked everyone was getting in the pouring rain. Denny's face was wet, but the hardened look was unchanged. His eyes focused easily on O'Brian without suggesting a trace of what he might be feeling. O'Brian noticed that Denny's right hand was covered with blood.

"Did you get hit?" O'Brian asked anxiously.

"No, it's his blood," Denny answered indifferently as he slipped his gun into his shoulder holster. Then, before walking away, he gave O'Brian the only description of the shooting the reporter would ever get from Denny or Eddie. Holding both hands together to show how he fired, Denny told O'Brian, "As soon as he turned that wheel, I said, 'Fuck him.'" Then Denny squeezed an imaginary trigger.

CHAPTER 3

The twenty-man night shift of the Tactical Patrol Force was lined up for roll call when Eddie Holland's yell for help came over the radio. Sergeant Ed McHale, the night patrol supervisor, ordered everyone over to Smith Street. "We were in a shooting over there," he announced before sending them to their cars. Eddie and Denny had just become the first TPF men ever to fire their guns on duty.

Sergeant McHale jumped into a car with three patrolmen. Sergeant Harry Byrne, the day patrol supervisor, who had been getting ready to go home when Eddie's call came in, squeezed into another TPF car and also headed for Smith Street.

Excitement ran high, recalls Joe Fagone, a patrolman who was sitting beside Byrne. Byrne said that according to Eddie it sounded like he and Denny had made a good pinch. They had gone up against a guy who had pulled a job in Cambridge a few hours earlier. There was some shooting, but they got the bum, and they were okay.

Fagone's partner and boyhood best friend, Joe Raphanella, was carrying a shotgun. He lamented missing the action. "That could have been us," he told Fagone. "We missed it by twenty minutes." At roll call Raphanella and Fagone had been ordered to relieve Eddie and Denny watching the Buick.

"We were so up about this," recalls Fagone. "We all knew that team. We assumed that they had found the car that came over the air and that it was, in fact, involved in the robbery in Cambridge.

And obviously the adrenaline started running and we just wanted to get there. We just wanted to be part of it."

Fagone thinks it took the TPF about ten or eleven minutes of sirenblaring driving to reach Smith Street. By then, a police wagon had taken the bleeding driver of the crashed Buick to the hospital. The street was already filled with squad cars and uniformed men from District 2, the Roxbury police station, and the rain had stopped. More than sixty cops eventually gathered to hold back the curious crowd forming on the sidewalks and to close the street.

John Cullen, who covered the police beat for the *Globe,* was already poking around the Buick when the TPF reinforcements arrived. The thirty-two-year-old Cullen was a street-educated reporter. He had begun working as a *Record American* copy boy when he was fourteen and graduated to reporting for the *Globe* after three years in the Army and two years as a Concord, New Hampshire, policeman. By coincidence, he had happened to be in the Mission Hill project on another story when the police radio in his car picked up the ACU team's call to headquarters to check on the plate number of the still-parked Buick. On his intercity channel—a channel the ACU cars' radios did not have—Cullen heard the Boston dispatcher check with the Cambridge dispatcher, then confirm the number as the one on the Cambridge getaway car and give the ACU team descriptions of the two robbers. About fifteen minutes later, he heard shooting on Smith Street. He was only a block away. He rushed to the scene as O'Brian and the ACU team were looking into the crashed Buick. He tried to talk to Eddie and Denny, whom he had met a few times before. "They were very nervous and very confused," says Cullen. They refused to talk to him.

O'Brian had begun working the crowd, looking for eyewitnesses. Kobre was photographing the Buick. Sergeants Byrne and McHale huddled with Eddie and Denny for a few minutes. Then McHale decided to go to the hospital to check out the guy who was shot. That left Harry Byrne in charge on Smith Street, but not for long. Byrne's first move, perhaps with inquiring reporters in mind, was to get Eddie and Denny out of there. He had them driven to nearby District 2. Next, he ordered the arrest of one Ernest Winbush. (Byrne would later say he could not remember who it was who told him that the Thunderbird, which had dropped off the driver of the Buick, had somehow escaped but had been traced to an Ernest Winbush, who lived a few blocks away in the project.) Byrne sent four men after him.

So, just after seven o'clock, an ACU car carrying four plainclothes patrolmen pulled up in front of Ernest Winbush's building. There wasn't a Thunderbird in sight. The cops assumed their man wasn't home and sat waiting for him and his Thunderbird to return. They weren't sure why Winbush had to be arrested. But they knew it had something to do with what had happened on Smith Street. One of them had heard someone say something about a shotgun being in the Thunderbird.

Back on Smith Street, Byrne was calling the Emergency Service Unit to get a lighting truck to the scene. His men were going to need more than flashlights to find what they were looking for. The ACU team had searched the Buick and its driver for a gun that Eddie and Denny said the guy had fired. They had found nothing. Now the whole area between where the shooting had occurred and where the Buick had finally crashed had to be searched in case the guy had thrown the gun away after the shooting.

From the Brigham Hospital, Sergeant McHale called Byrne to give him what he had on the Buick driver: James Henry Bowden, Jr., twenty-five years old, married, Roxbury address, no warrants, no record, dead on arrival.

John Cullen had followed McHale to the Brigham. "At the hospital," recalls Cullen, "the first thing the cops did was get Bowden's papers out of his pocket. They called Identification and ran him, 'cause everybody figured, as they were saying on Smith Street, that there must be a ticket [a warrant] on the guy for something. And when they found out there was no ticket on the guy and no record, they said, 'Ah shit, it must be a bum name.' That went on for a while."

McHale had one of his men call Cambridge to double-check what they had on the getaway car. Cambridge said it was a Ford or Buick with the number 4F•6368. A check with the Registry of Motor Vehicles showed that plate had been issued to a Cape Cod Volkswagen. The Registry first said it had been stolen from the car months earlier, then said it may have been returned to the Registry. Hearing this, McHale checked the notes he had made on Smith Street and saw that 4F•6368 was not the number on the bullet-riddled Buick. The Buick's number was 4F•6838, and as another check with the Registry's computer revealed, it was properly registered to James Bowden.

"Then, after talking to the wife who showed up there," says Cullen, "they were fully convinced that Bowden had no record and he was 'Mister Legit.' That's when the whole game really got fucked up."

McHale and some hospital personnel led Pat Bowden to an office. McHale closed the door on Cullen. Convinced that the sergeant was going to keep him away from Pat, Cullen decided to return to Smith Street and catch up with her later at the Bowden address that he had overheard from McHale.

When Cullen got back to Smith Street, it was crawling with cops of all ranks. The numbers were split about evenly between the TPF and District 2 regulars. There was a gang of sergeants and detectives. The TPF's captain, Bill MacDonald, and deputy superintendent, Joe Rowan, had rushed there from their homes. There were two other captains and three other deputies on hand. There was enough gold braid on Smith Street for a parade. The man with the most gold on his hat and his double-breasted uniform, Superintendent in Chief Joseph Jordan, had taken charge.

Joe Jordan was the highest-ranking officer in the department. (The commissioner is not a sworn officer.) The busing crisis had made him a familiar figure to any Bostonian who read newspapers or watched television news. He was pictured almost every day at the head of his assembled troops in front of South Boston High School, his alma mater. His appearance was always flawless.

The tall, slim, fifty-three-year-old superintendent never slouched or leaned against a car or a wall. He stood perfectly erect, hands clasped behind his back or tucked into his coat pockets. His silver hair rolled elegantly from his police hat to his white shirt collar, which was set off sharply by his dark-blue uniform. During the day Jordan often wore reflectorized sunglasses that gave him a MacArthur look, and at night he wore steel-rimmed eyeglasses. In the department he was well liked for being an easygoing boss and respected for having worked his way up from patrolman. Standing in the middle of Smith Street near the Buick, he listened attentively to what his deputies told him and had little to say to anyone.

With the lighting truck in place, Ken Kobre's job was much easier. It was like working on a movie set. He had enough light for every shot he wanted and he kept clicking. A detective was also taking pictures of the scene. A ballistics expert, Sergeant Walter Logue, studied the Buick for evidence. Dave O'Brian eventually found someone among the reticent bystanders who was willing to talk to him. A black teenaged boy told him he had seen the whole thing. "The cops just drove up, jumped out, and started shooting as the guy drove off," he said. Wanting to stay uninvolved like the rest of the crowd, the kid scampered off into the shadows after a cop leaned into the conversation and told him that O'Brian was an FBI agent. O'Brian did not get the kid's name. No one else in the black and Hispanic crowd would talk to the reporter.

As he drifted back into a pack of TPF men, O'Brian was startled by the roaring laughter of Billy Dwyer. O'Brian had apparently missed a joke. Still laughing, Dwyer turned to him and asked, "How's this for action? Did we put on a good show for you?" O'Brian mumbled something about never wanting to switch jobs with Dwyer, then went looking for Kobre.

It was 7:30, an hour after the shooting, and Joe Jordan and the rest of the gold-braid set were still waiting for the gun that had to be found.

"Everyone was looking for a weapon," says John Cullen. "Everybody was saying, 'Hey, shit, we gotta find the weapon!' Everybody was conscious that they were in a box. You know, if Bowden didn't have a gun, then why did Holland and McKenna shoot him?"

CHAPTER 4

Why Eddie Holland and Denny McKenna shot James Bowden was the question to be answered by a departmental investigation.

Two months before, Commissioner di Grazia had issued a new rule on deadly force. An internal study he had ordered earlier had revealed that at least twenty-six of the forty-eight people shot by Boston police in the previous three years were unarmed fleeing suspects. Five of the forty-eight were killed. In the study, the twenty-two suspects who represented the "apparently armed" category qualified for that status because they "were reported to have had 'an object' in their hands." In one case, the object turned out to be a beer can; in some others, nothing at all. Shooting at unarmed fleeing suspects violated Massachusetts law. Di Grazia's six-page, seventeen-section rule on the use of deadly force was all but a strict defense-of-life rule. It was modeled on New York City's and the one he had introduced in St. Louis County. The rule described in detail a new procedure for investigating police shootings. In addition to the previously required reports written by the officers involved, the new rule stipulated that all shooting incidents, even seemingly harmless accidental misfires, be investigated by the officer's commanding officer and by a Firearms Discharge Review Board headed by Joe Jordan. If a cop wounded a person, the Internal Affairs Division had to join the investigation. And if a cop killed a person, the Homicide Unit had to come into it too.

At eight o'clock, Sergeant-Detective Robert Hudson of Homicide and Sergeant John Geagan of Internal Affairs were on their way to Smith Street. With them were Denny McKenna, TPF Captain Bill MacDonald, and Sergeant Ed McHale. They had all met at District 2.

Bob Hudson was the homicide man on call that night. A half hour earlier he had picked up the ringing wall phone in the kitchen of the modern home he had built in the woods of a western suburb. He listened for less than a minute, then said, "Call Internal Affairs." He listened a bit more and said, "I'm on my way." He grabbed a raincoat, hustled out the door, and jumped into his car for the twenty-mile drive to Roxbury.

John Geagan got a similar call at his Boston home around the same time. He had only a couple of miles to drive to District 2.

Hudson met Geagan and the TPF guys in the lobby of District 2. They all knew each other. Sergeant Hudson had himself been a TPF patrol supervisor before transferring to Homicide in 1967. With the handshaking out of the way, Hudson suggested that they check out the scene. He asked Denny to come along. After checking with Frank McGee, the union lawyer who was already advising the ACU team, Denny agreed to go, but only to show the investigators where the ACU cars and the Buick had been parked during the stakeout and where the shooting had taken place. On McGee's advice, Eddie and Denny answered no one's questions that night.

The group arrived at the scene a few minutes after eight. Hudson and Geagan took notes and paced off the distances between some of the spots Denny pointed out. The result was a diagram Hudson drew. It showed the placement of all the cars during the stakeout. It indicated that from its parked position the Buick had backed up about 246 feet while Denny had driven forward about 285 feet to the spot where the shooting occurred and that the Buick had then gone forward about 324 feet to its final resting place in front of the school building. Hudson could have figured out where the shooting had happened without Denny's help. The Buick's window glass still covered that spot on the pavement.

Hudson and Geagan shipped Denny back to District 2, and they joined the wait for the gun, which only some of the TPF patrolmen were still trying to find.

Minutes later, Joe Fagone swept his flashlight under an old Chevrolet parked about halfway between where the shooting occurred and where the Buick subsequently crashed. There, under the front of a Chevrolet, was a semiautomatic pistol.

O'Brian and Kobre happened to be just a few feet away from Fagone when he yelled, "Here it is!" Kobre started clicking shots of the grinning young cop shining his flashlight on the untouched gun. Cops ran over and crowded around the car. They made way for the police photographer and the ballistician, Walter Logue. The photographer took a half dozen shots of the gun before the short, heavy Logue eased his weight down on one knee, reached a thick hand under the car, and picked it up. With Kobre following him, he carried it to his car. He opened the trunk, unloaded the gun, and put it in a special case he used for carrying ballistics evidence as Kobre snapped a picture of him. Logue closed the trunk, got behind the wheel, and drove to District 2 to collect the rest of the ballistics evidence.

The lighting truck shut down its powerful beams and rolled away into the darkness. Joe Jordan and the deputies went home. The District 2 squad cars and the ACU cars, one with O'Brian and Kobre in it, started to pull out. John Cullen headed for the Bowden home. Dave O'Brian and Ken Kobre returned to the TPF office in the back seat of an ACU car with two cops they didn't know. From there, they went off in O'Brian's car for a late dinner together. Neither of them finished his steak and beer. They spent the time at the table trying to figure out what had happened on Smith Street when they were hugging the floor of the police car.

Before he left the scene, Bob Hudson paced off the distance between where the gun was found and where the shooting took place. It was about 120 feet. Then he paced off the stretch between where the gun was found and where the Buick crashed. That was about 204 feet. He noted those things on his diagram and, with John Geagan, went back to District 2.

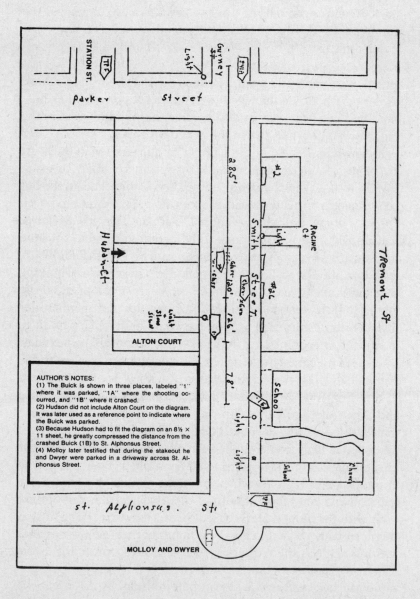

AUTHOR'S NOTES:
(1) The Buick is shown in three places, labeled "1" where it was parked, "1A" where the shooting occurred, and "1B" where it crashed.
(2) Hudson did not include Alton Court on the diagram. It was later used as a reference point to indicate where the Buick was parked.
(3) Because Hudson had to fit the diagram on an 8½ × 11 sheet, he greatly compressed the distance from the crashed Buick (1B) to St. Alphonsus Street.
(4) Molloy later testified that during the stakeout he and Dwyer were parked in a driveway across St. Alphonsus Street.

A tow truck dragged the Buick off the little wall it had been stuck on and began pulling it across town to a police garage. Ten minutes after Joe Fagone found the gun, there wasn't a single cop left on Smith Street.

John Cullen knocked on Pat Bowden's door at about nine o'clock. In the next hour, he managed to get Pat's idea of what her husband had done that day and to borrow the wedding picture the *Globe* would crop and run in the next day's paper.

Meanwhile, at the modern District 2 police station in the heart of Roxbury, Walter Logue collected the six guns of the ACU team. Dwyer told Logue that only Eddie and Denny had fired, but Logue said that the new deadly force rule required him to check the guns of any cop who was near the action. Dwyer's, Molloy's, MacDonald's, and McClinton's fully loaded guns went into the ballistician's case along with Eddie's, Denny's, and the automatic found on the street. Logue then left. The always weary-looking sergeant drove to his downtown office, where he dropped off the guns. He then went home to his row house just around a corner from South Boston High School. He would phone in his findings to Hudson after going over the guns in the crime lab the next day.

Just after Logue left, Sergeant Edwin Petersen, a Cambridge police detective, strode into District 2 with Desmond Callahan in tow. Someone at District 2 had called the Cambridge police and asked them to deliver an eyewitness of the armed robbery that had led to the stakeout of James Bowden's car. There was none better than twenty-eight-year-old Desi Callahan, manager of the small Cambridge store that was robbed. Desi was at one of the two cash registers when the robbers made their move. He had gotten a good look at both of them. When they ran out the door with the money, Desi chased them. He wasn't trying to stop them. He only wanted to get the number of their getaway car. He memorized it as the robbers sped away, then reported it to the Cambridge police.

Ed McHale met them at the counter in the lobby. As soon as he could arrange it, McHale had two of his TPF men drive Desi and the Cambridge cop to the morgue.

At the morgue, Desi looked at James Bowden's body for over thirty minutes. He said that Bowden looked too fat to have been one of the robbers he had seen that afternoon. Sergeant Petersen pressed the stomach, forcing blood and foul-smelling fluids to gush out of the mouth, and said that the body was probably bloated from the shooting. Petersen twisted the head from side to side, showing Desi the profiles. He even offered to have the body raised to a standing position. "It was eerie and disgusting," Desi recalls. "I'd seen bodies before at wakes, but this was horrible." Desi left the morgue telling the cops that he thought Bowden was not one of the robbers.

Henry Nelson, the TPF patrolman who had driven Desi to the morgue, was not surprised. Nelson, a six foot three, 230-pound black man, is a former neighbor of the Bowden family and had known James Bowden for fifteen years. "His father [James Bowden, Sr.] was a hardworking man," Nelson told me. "His mother, Mary, was a helluva woman, a respectable woman. She had her kids in line. I remember her marching James and Walter Lee—they were like two peas in a pod—to church every Sunday. James was never in trouble. I've seen some people do crazy things, but it was hard to believe James'd go and stick up a store. Not James Bowden." Henry Nelson said nothing to Desi.

Back at District 2, Bob Hudson was doing something he hates: hanging around a police station with nothing to do at the ungodly hour of 10:00 P.M. Still red-haired and in fighting trim in his fifties, Hudson (naturally called "Red" by some) is an early-to-bed-early-to-rise guy. He gets up at five every morning and runs five miles before breakfast. In spring and summer, he works up a sweat in his large vegetable garden every evening. And he's no slouch at the office. Everyone at District 2 that night knew that Sergeant Hudson was the hardest-working and sharpest homicide detective on the force. The way Hudson pushes himself, he has to treasure his sleep and it was already past his bedtime.

He had made a deal with Frank McGee over an hour ago that had left him with nothing to do but wait. When Hudson had asked McGee if he could speak to Eddie and Denny and the rest of the ACU team, McGee said no. Since Homicide's role was to look for criminal conduct on the cop's part, Hudson could not force them to talk. They enjoyed the same right to silence that any citizen has when subjected to a criminal investigation. But McGee did agree to give Hudson copies of their reports. Oddly, John Geagan agreed to the same deal, though he could have done better. Since the fruits of Geagan's Internal Affairs inquiry, by law, could never be used in a criminal prosecution of the cops, they had no right to silence with him. Geagan told McGee that he would interview them at some other time convenient to all, and that for now, he'd be content with the reports. So a detectives' squad room upstairs had been given to the six cops to write their reports and consult with their lawyer behind a closed door. Though Eddie and Denny left the room a few times, the team did not emerge with written reports for another six hours.

Standing at the counter in the lobby in one of his conservative dark suits, with his thin hair slicked straight back from his high freckled forehead, Hudson looked more like a lawyer than a cop, but police work is the Hudson family trade. His father was a Boston cop, and so was his brother. In twenty-seven years of varied assignments, Hudson had never fired his gun at anyone. (The last time he did that was as a much decorated tail gunner on Navy planes in World War II.) He had investigated killings by police before, though. "It's a problem," he told me years later when the Bowden case was over. "Nobody likes to investigate their own, but someone has to do it."

Desi Callahan and Sergeant Petersen returned to District 2 a little after ten o'clock. John Geagan and Harry Bryne were waiting for them in the lobby. They led them to a small office, where Geagan set up his portable tape recorder and conducted the first Internal Affairs interview of the Bowden case.

Sergeant Geagan, a gray-haired, square-jawed, soft-spoken

man, had been on the force for over twenty years before he was assigned to the Internal Affairs Division. Investigating the conduct of fellow officers is not the way to win popularity, or respect, in the department. Like everyone else who gets stuck in I.A.D., Geagan had not welcomed the assignment, and he never liked the work he had to do there. Still, he thinks he did his job well.

In his interview of Desi Callahan, Geagan looked for a link between Bowden and the robbery. There were four possibilities: the gun found on Smith Street, Bowden's car, his clothes, and his body. Geagan tried them all, beginning with the gun. Desi told him that the only gun used in the robbery was a small-caliber handgun. Petersen had already told Geagan that the robbers didn't use a shotgun. The false information the ACU team had picked up during the stakeout about a shotgun was apparently the result of a mix-up by the Cambridge dispatcher. (There had been a couple of recent armed robberies in Cambridge in which shotguns were used.) Desi described the pistol to Geagan as a .22- or .25-caliber revolver. The three cops present knew that the gun Walter Logue had picked up was a .32-caliber automatic.

"Do you know the difference between a revolver and an automatic?" Geagan asked.

"Yes, sir," Desi replied confidently. "I do because I have an automatic."

"You have an automatic," Geagan said with some surprise. "So, you're sure that this was a revolver?"

"Yes, a real revolver."

Except for his Army stint in Germany, Desi Callahan had lived all of his twenty-eight years in the blue-collar neighborhood served by the store he now managed. He began helping around the store in exchange for candy money when he was still in grade school. He moved onto the part-time payroll in high school and became a full-timer as soon as he graduated. The Pearl Food Market was the only employer he had ever had. The good-looking black-haired Desi had met the girl he eventually married when she came to work at the store. Amiable and seemingly earnest,

Desi readily admits he's not an authority on many things, but he does know guns. He handled a lot of them in the Army, and for the last couple of years he had been wearing one holstered to his belt while at work. He never concealed it. He wanted anyone thinking about robbing the store to know he was armed. The robbery he was now being questioned about might have ended differently if Desi hadn't forgotten to bring his gun to work that day.

Harry Byrne asked him if he thought the one robber who had appeared unarmed could have had a gun in his pocket. "He had his hands outside his pockets at all times," said Desi in his flat tone. "So, I would surmise that he did not have a gun, because if he did I think that he would have taken it out."

Sergeant Petersen, a tall, heavy, gray-haired man, cut in with a test. He pulled out his gun and asked, "What's that?"

"That's a revolver," Desi answered steadily.

"What caliber?" Petersen demanded.

"The caliber is thirty-eight."

"How do you know?"

"Because I owned one at one time."

With that, Geagan moved to the getaway car Desi had seen. Desi said it was a two-door dark-blue late-model Buick with the plate number 4F•6368. Geagan and Byrne had seen that Bowden's car was a 1973 light-blue Buick, a four-door with the plate number 4F•6838.

Geagan finished the questioning with the visit to the morgue. Desi said he had looked at a body and some clothes: a leather jacket and what he thought was a red sweater. He wasn't sure about the sweater's color because there was so much blood on it. "Did either of the holdup men this afternoon have anything similar to those clothes on?" asked Geagan.

"No they didn't," Desi replied.

When Geagan asked him whether he recognized the "dead person" he had seen, Desi said, "To me, he was not the person that I had seen [in the robbery] because it seemed to me that he was bloated."

The interview ended on a macabre note. Still in a cooperative spirit, Desi said, "Sergeant Petersen said that we may go back there tomorrow. He said that he may have him stand up tomorrow."

"Propped up, you mean," Geagan suggested.

"Yeah," said Desi.

"Okay. Thank you again," said Geagan.

After the interview, Harry Byrne drove Desi and Sergeant Petersen to a police garage in Dorchester. There, they looked at Bowden's Buick. Desi walked around it. The plate number was slightly different from the one he thought was on the getaway car. He remembered the getaway car as a dark-blue two-door, and this was a light-blue four-door. They seemed like minor discrepancies to Desi. He positively identified Bowden's Buick as the getaway car.

At 10:50 P.M., Ernest Winbush, handcuffed and surrounded by the four TPF men who had just arrested him when he stepped out of his Thunderbird in front of his apartment building, walked into District 2. The thin, thirty-one-year-old black man was photographed, fingerprinted, and booked on charges of assault by means of a dangerous weapon, "to wit, a shotgun," and assault with intent to murder Eddie Holland. Winbush's arresting officers turned in four bullets they found in his coat pocket, but no shotgun.

Winbush's one phone call was to his wife, Patricia. She appeared at the station in a few minutes. She was almost hysterical. She swore to anyone who looked at her that her husband had never done anything wrong in his life. No one was impressed. Wives of guys with records a mile long say the same thing. But like James Bowden, Ernest Winbush had no criminal record. Patricia Winbush told the desk sergeant that her husband had a grave kidney condition and needed prescribed pills every few hours. The sergeant let her talk to Winbush for a few minutes in a glass-partitioned booth where visitors met prisoners, but he would not relay any pills to him. Patricia Winbush then returned to the lobby of District 2 where she sat all night, pills in hand, occasionally sobbing.

Bob Hudson doesn't remember what he did at District 2 between ten and eleven, but he says that Desi Callahan was interviewed and Ernest Winbush was arrested, booked, and jailed without his hearing about either event. Shortly after eleven o'clock, with no sign that the ACU team's reports would be finished soon, Hudson decided to go home. John Cullen stopped him on his way out the door. Cullen had just returned from the Bowden home, and had only minutes left to phone in the police version of the shooting for the morning *Globe*.

Cullen says he asked Hudson for the story because he was the best detective on the scene and because he was a longtime friend. (Cullen had more than once been given the grand tour of Hudson's vegetable garden. A few months earlier he had dutifully attended Hudson's wife's wake and funeral.) Hudson led Cullen out of the station. They walked to Hudson's car and leaned against it in the darkness as subway trains elevated on a thirty-foot trestle rattled by overhead. "When he took me outside," Cullen told me recently, "I remember Hudson saying, 'I don't wanna get involved.' I said, 'I understand, Bob.' I could read between the lines that everybody was in deep shit and they were trying to clean up their act. I had been in a lot of tight police situations where there was a shooting and it's bullshit what's said afterwards from what really took place. Hudson didn't know what to say. I said, 'Bob, just give me the official version.'" Hudson quickly recited what he thought was the official version and went home.

Today, Cullen splits blame between himself and the *Globe* for what he admits was cursory handling of the story. "The *Globe* just wanted the official version," he says. "It was just another shooting in the ghetto as far as they [the editors] were concerned. And at that time, with busing, they had us running from one story to another. It was like being a policeman. You finished one call and went to the next."

For his part, Cullen says he was too close to the cops in those days. In print, he was inclined to use whatever they gave him. In private, though, he insists he wasn't so gullible. For instance, he says that he told Hudson what he thought about the gun found on the street: "I said, 'Bob, that's a bag of shit, because he couldn't have thrown that gun out of the car, absolutely couldn't. It would have been a physical impossibility for Bowden to throw that gun out of his car after he got shot."

"As far as I was concerned," Cullen told me, "that gun was a throw-away." In Boston police slang, a "throw-away" is a gun of untraceable ownership planted (or thrown away) by a cop at the scene of a crime. Most cops don't carry throw-aways, but enough do that such guns deserve a special name. (In other cities, other terms—such as Houston's "throw down"—are used.)

Sometime after midnight, Eddie Holland left District 2. Two TPF patrolmen drove him to the Carney Hospital near his home in Dorchester. He told an emergency-ward doctor that a moving car had hit his left knee earlier that night. An X ray revealed no internal damage, but there was a slight bruise on the knee. The doctor suggested that Eddie use crutches to take pressure off the knee. Eddie left the hospital at 1:30 A.M. and returned to District 2. The ACU team was still conferring in its private room and had not yet written the required reports.

John Geagan had given up waiting for the reports and gone home when Eddie went to the hospital. The TPF's Deputy Superintendent Rowan, Captain MacDonald, and Sergeants Byrne and McHale were the only superior officers still at the station.

At about 3:30 A.M., an hour and a half after Eddie returned from the hospital and nine hours after the shooting, the ACU team finally turned in its handwritten reports to Byrne and McHale. For all the time it took to write them, they are surprisingly short. Eddie's is the longest—two and a half pages. Denny's is one and a half pages. The others are each only a page. The six reports do not tell a coherent story of what happened on Smith Street.

Dwyer, Molloy, MacDonald, and McClinton missed all the action, according to their reports. They sped to Smith Street as soon as Eddie yelled, "We're going in!" but when they got there the Buick was already, as Molloy put it, "resting on a wall with a c / m [colored male] sitting behind the wheel and bleeding from the head." None of them had heard any shots fired. The see-nothing, hear-nothing reports of their teammates left everything for Eddie and Denny to explain.

Here is the text of Eddie's report with its original spelling, punctuation, underlining, and crossing out:

About 6 03 PM Wednesday January 29, 1975 Patrols Edward Holland* and Dennis McKenna assigned to ACU Vehicle 841A while on Smith St. Roxbury observed a vehicle a Blue Electra Buick Bearing Mass. Reg. 4F6838 Parked unattended answering the description of a vehicle used in a armed Robbery in Cambridge on 1–29–1975

This vehicle was kept under surviellance by ACU Team 841A, 841 and 842 The turret† was notified also the TPF-ACU office and Sgt. Edward McHale

About 6 35 PM 1–29–75 Ptls Holland & McKenna observed a vehicle a green Thunderbird on Smith at Parker the operator was wearing a Blue Denim jacket and a Blue Denim Cap. also 2 other unknown black males.

This Vehicle pulled adjacent to the Blue Buick whereupon a B / M elighted and entered the Said Buick (Mass Reg 4F6838).

At this point ACU Teams 841 with Ptls William Dwyer and Mark Molloy Team 842 with Frank MacDonald and Loman McClinton were notified of the activity of Both the TBird and Buick

At the same time ACU Team 841A with Ptls Holland and McKenna approached the Blue Buick from the Rear while the operator attempted to remove (Drive) the vehicle from within 2 parked vehicles

Ptls McKenna operator of ACU vehicle #5 and observer

---

* Authors of police reports usually refer to themselves in the third person.
† The communications center on the top floor of Boston Police Headquarters is known as "the turret" in the department.

Holland left the said vehicle and approached the Buick Mass Reg 4F6838 with Ptl McKenna approaching from the operator side and Ptl Holland approaching the passenger Side of the Buick

With Both Badges displayed in a conspicuous Manner Ptls. McKenna and Holland shouted simontaneously "Boston Police Officers" remove yourself from the vehicle.

At about that precise moment the *vehicle sped forward* and to the right striking Ptl Holland and Spinning him around toward the rear of the vehicle Ptl Dennis McKenna again Shouted "Police Officers". the Buick was then put in reverse and with tremendous exceleration moved backward hitting the right rear quarter against Ptl. E. Hollands left leg Knocking him to the ground at that point Ptl Holland got up the vehicle was again in reverse striking Holland again at this Point Ptl Holland was outside of the vehicle looking Directly into the front passenger window the operator was partially leaning over the Passenger side of the vehicle a light shined from the glove compartment and the *operator displayed a long Barrel Fire arm* the vehicle started in Motion forward I heard Ptl McKenna again scream "police Officers Halt" at that precise moment *I heard a loud noise* the passenger side window shattered My service revolver raised I fired 4 rounds into the passenger side window

The vehicle then sped up Smith St. at a tremendous Rate of speed toward St. Alphonsus. The T Bird following. The Buick Struck a light pole in front of the Tobin School also a fence. the TBird made a left turn before the school (Tobin) and Disappeared in Mission project.

Ptl Holland immediately called for a Ambulance the 200 Responded with Ptls. Megnia and Landry who transported the operator to the Peter Bent Brigham Hospital where he was pronounced Dead on Arrival

The operator was Identified as one:

James Bowden 25 yrs of Roxbury.

Patrol Edward Holland was taken to the Carney Hospital where he was treated and released for Sprain, *contusions,* and *severe Bruises* by othopedic DR. Cater Put on Medication and crutches: Dr. Cater ordered ptl. E. Holland from work in writing for one week minimum.

Like Eddie's, Denny's report has an introductory paragraph explaining the reason for the stakeout of the Buick. Then it says:

About 6:35 PM 1–29–75 observed a 1967 Thunderbird Mass Reg# 6S0280 turn from Parker St into Smith St. and stop beside the buick. The right door of the Thunderbird opened, then the left door of the Buick was opened and a c / m entered the Buick and closed the door and turned on the lights and began to back down Smith St. towards Parker St. At this time Ptl Holland radioed to other units that the vehicles were moving. Ptls Holland and McKenna pulled up behind the Buick, got out with their badges displayed and announced "Police Officers" "Get out of the car" Both officers had drawn their Service revolvers. the operator raced the engine and caused the Buick to strike Ptl Holland and spin him around and then knock him down. At this time the operator turned the vehicle sharply to the left and drove the car at Ptl. McKenna; who shouted, "Police officer" "Halt." At this time ptl McKenna jumped backwards and simultaneously heard a gunshot. Ptl McKenna fired two rounds through the left front window, shattering the window, and one round at the rear of the buick as it sped up Smith St., towards St. Alphonsus St. Ptl McKenna ran back to the ACU car and then heard the buick crash further up Smith St. and went to the crash scene and determined that the operator was bleeding from the back of his head, and called for assistance.

The 200 wagon responded & Ptls Megnia & Landry transported the operator two to Peter Bent Brigham Hospital, where he was pronounced Dead on Arrival. Operator identified as James Bowden 25 yrs of Roxbury.

Though Ernest Winbush had been sitting in a cell one floor below the ACU teammates while they wrote their reports, not one of them wrote a word about Winbush or a shotgun attack on Eddie Holland.

Sergeant McHale had the ACU team driven home in separate TPF cars after they gave him their reports. He then sat down to type his own five-page synthesis of the six reports which would become the first official version of the shooting. McHale did not write a word about Ernest Winbush either, or about a shotgun attack on Eddie—even though Winbush had been arrested for firing a shotgun at Eddie by four of McHale's men who were acting under orders from Sergeant Byrne. And McHale took some liberties with Eddie's and Denny's statements. For example, Eddie's "Remove yourself from the vehicle" became "Get out of the vehicle" in McHale's report. And while Eddie said the Buick made *three* threatening moves, hitting him *three* times, and Denny said it made *two* moves, hitting Eddie *once,* McHale said the car made *three* moves and hit Eddie *twice.* He did not mention Eddie's being injured.

McHale made three more changes in Eddie and Denny's story when he wrote his report. The "long Barrel Fire arm" that, according to Eddie, James Bowden "displayed" became "a silhouette of a gun." Neither Eddie nor any of his teammates had seen the gun Joe Fagone found. McHale had seen it. No cop who had seen that pistol would have described it as a long-barrel firearm. Toning down the description of the gun Eddie saw in Bowden's hand to "a silhouette of a gun," left open the possibility of linking the gun Fagone found to Bowden.

Eddie's "The TBird made a left turn before the school (Tobin) and Disappeared in Mission project" became the T-Bird "turned left into an alleyway adjacent to the Tobin School, leaving the scene in the direction of Tremont St." There are driveways on both sides of the Tobin School. If Eddie saw the Thunderbird take a left *before* reaching the school, it would have looked as if the car were disappearing into the project as he described it, since there are project buildings on that side of the school. But that driveway leads to a small school parking lot surrounded by a ten-foot-high cement wall, an impossible escape route. The driveway on the other side of the school opens into a baseball field and playground which stretches from Smith Street to Tremont Street and could have provided an escape route for the Thunderbird. Changing the Thunderbird's turn from Eddie's "before" the school driveway to one ambiguously "adjacent" to the school brought the car's escape that way within the realm of the possible.

Finally, Eddie's "B / M" and Denny's "c / m," their descriptions of James Bowden, became "A black male described as approximately 6–0, with a medium Afro hair style, wearing dark clothing, who appeared to match the description of one of the black males involved in the robbery in Cambridge, as given to the officers." Eddie and Denny did not then, and in the years to come never would, describe Bowden as being six feet tall, or as matching the description of one of the robbers in any way other than his race.

CHAPTER 5

The following morning, John Geagan found copies of the TPF reports waiting on his desk when he walked into the Internal Affairs office at Headquarters. He read them, then typed his first report for the file on Internal Affairs Case #14–75, "Shooting of James Bowden." In one and a half pages Geagan described the shooting and covered Desi Callahan's evening activities at the morgue and the police garage. "Mr. Callahan was unable to identify the dead man as one of the two men that held up his store because, according to Callahan, of the dead man's bloated condition," wrote Geagan. But he "positively identified" Bowden's car "as the car used in the hold-up." Geagan's account of the shooting was an adaptation of Eddie's and Denny's reports. He ascribed to the Buick two threatening moves, one of which hit Eddie and knocked him down. And only Denny was mentioned as doing any shooting. He overlooked Eddie's suggestion that Bowden fired a long-barrelled firearm at him as well as Eddie's straightforward "I fired 4 rounds into the passenger side window." Of course, working from the TPF reports meant that Geagan wrote not a word about Ernest Winbush, who was being arraigned at the Roxbury District Court while Geagan was banging away at his typewriter.

The Roxbury District Court is next door to District 2. It is a low, modern, brick structure that, with the addition of a lawn, could pass for a suburban high school. It is the busiest courthouse in the state.

Eddie Holland was there on crutches to sign, under oath, a formal complaint that Winbush "by means of a certain dangerous weapon, to wit, a shot-gun, did make an assault, with intent then and there to murder him, the said Holland." James O'Connor, one of Winbush's arresting officers was there. Winbush's wife was there too. But since neither O'Brian nor Cullen had learned of the arrest, there were no reporters there. With no prior criminal record and with demonstrably strong family and community ties, Winbush had no trouble obtaining release on bail and left the courthouse with an arm around his wife.

"Yeah," said Ethel Caragianes, "that's him." It was 1:40 P.M. She was looking at James Bowden's body as it lay on a table, ready for the autopsy that was about to begin. It had been instant recognition for Ethel. Sergeant Petersen then walked the short, stout fifty-year-old woman out of the autopsy room and ushered Desi Callahan in. Two minutes later, Desi also identified Bowden as one of the robbers. He told Petersen that the light was better than it had been the night before.

From the morgue Petersen took Ethel and Desi to Boston Police Headquarters, where they met John Geagan. As Geagan wrote the next day in his second report, a half page titled "Identification of James Bowden," the purpose of the stop at Headquarters was to "attempt to identify Ernest Winbush who had been arrested for various charges of assault on Patrolman Holland." Geagan showed Ethel and Desi a bunch of mug shots—including Winbush's, which had been taken the night before. Geagan's subsequent report says, "Mrs. Caragianes looked at a photo of Winbush and said, 'He's too heavy,' and she then picked photo #168902 and stated, 'I think it's this one.' Callahan looked at the picture and said, 'I'd say it was him.'" Geagan's report does not identify whose face was in photo #168902, supposedly the mug shot of the other robber.

Sergeant Petersen's Cambridge report of the same event tells a different story: "The pictures picked out by Desmond & Ethel were of different people." Petersen identified them by name, not photo number. He said Ethel picked out a Mr. Figuratto and Desi chose a Mr. Carter as the robber who had carried the gun. In statements written later for the Cambridge police, Desi said, "I picked out the pictures [full face and profile] of the man who had held the gun"; and Ethel said, "I am positive that the pictures I identified are those of the second holdup man . . . the one with the gun." Neither Ethel's nor Desi's statement identified the mug shots by number or name.

With Bowden positively identified, the Cambridge police had a half-solved robbery to investigate. There was another robber to be arrested, but the Cambridge investigation ended here. Petersen never bothered to question Mr. Figuratto, Mr. Carter, or Geagan's #168902. Nor did any Boston cop. To this day, these suspects do not know that one or more of them was positively identified as the gun-carrying robber of the Pearl Food Market.

In a telephone check with Headquarters that afternoon, O'Brian learned that Ethel and Desi had positively identified James Bowden, but he wasn't told a word about their identifying the other robber.

The TPF reports were addressed to Captain William Mac-Donald, a white-haired veteran of the force, who had been on Smith Street and at District 2 that night. When MacDonald read the reports, he had two more written. He wanted formal reports on finding the gun and arresting Winbush. So Joe Fagone typed a few routine lines specifying where he found the gun, and Jim O'Connor typed a full page on the arrest. O'Connor did not explain what Winbush had done to cause O'Connor and three other TPF patrolmen to make the arrest, but rather only how he was arrested—"about 10:40 P.M. without incident"—what he had to say, and what he had in his pocket:

While on route to District 2, with the subject I advised him of his rights one at a time, each time asking him if he understood what I had said. Each time he (Winbush) acknowledged, that he understood. I further asked him of his whereabouts this evening. He stated that he left his home at about 6:30 PM and went to a PTA meeting at the Edison School. He stated that he went by way of Smith St. Stopping for $1.00 worth of gas at the gas station [on Tremont Street]. He further stated that while on Smith St, he observed noth-

ing out of the ordinary. He further stated that at no time did
he allow anyone to use his m/v [motor vehicle] this evening.

Upon placing the subject under arrest a frisk of his
person was conducted on the street and no weapons were
found. A thorough search of his m/v was also conducted
and no weapons were found. At the booking desk a more
extensive search of the subjects person was conducted and
no weapons were found. However four (4) .38 caliber bullets
were found in his left hand coat pocket.

Captain MacDonald wrote a final TPF report based on all the
others. It was typed single-space on five pages and addressed to
the commissioner. MacDonald obviously used material from the
other reports. He began by reproducing Sergeant McHale's report
word for word in its entirety. Then he threw in the two paragraphs
of O'Connor's and ended with an original paragraph on Ethel and
Desi's identification of Bowden. He did not mention Desi's first
trip to the morgue or his and Ethel's attempts at a photo ID of
the other robber. And Winbush's involvement—how, when, and
where he fired a shotgun at Eddie—was not even hinted at in the
captain's report.

At 3:55 P.M., the end of the first full day of the investigation, Bob
Hudson got the phone call he'd been waiting for. The matter-
of-fact voice on the line was a familiar one, that of Doctor Michael Luongo, the Suffolk County medical examiner. Doctor
Luongo, considered the state's best pathologist, had just finished
the Bowden autopsy. He told Hudson that Bowden had been hit
with three bullets. The entrance wounds were in the left biceps, the
back of the neck, and the back. Two of them were independently
fatal: the one in the left arm, which had entered and exited the
biceps, then continued on a straight line into the chest, and the
one in the back. They both caused massive internal hemorrhage.
Hudson asked Luongo to send the three bullets he had removed
from the body to the ballistics unit.

At about the same time that Hudson and Luongo were talking,

on the street a few floors below the doctor's drab office a hearse was pulling away from the morgue. James Bowden's body was on its way to a Roxbury funeral home for a one-day wake and a Saturday funeral.

The Bowden killing was the least pressing matter on Bob Hudson's desk during the few days that it was an open Homicide file. He had other things to worry about—things that were Homicide's exclusive responsibility to investigate—such as rape-murders, gangland assassinations, robbery-murders, and assorted manslaughters. Knowing Internal Affairs was going over the Bowden case, Hudson gave it low priority. "This was more a thing for Internal Affairs than for Homicide," he told me on a 1981 tour of the vegetable garden, "so I didn't treat it as a regular homicide investigation." Hudson's intention was simply to "make up a case folder and send it upstairs." Nothing he and his men learned would make him want to do more than that.

Just before noon on Friday, Hudson received a phone call from Walter Logue. The ballistician had spent the morning studying the three bullets Doctor Luongo had sent him. Logue told Hudson that the bullet that hit Bowden's left arm came from Denny's gun and the two that hit Bowden's back and neck came from Eddie's gun. Eddie and Denny each fired two additional shots that either ricocheted off the car or missed everything. Logue found no indication that any of the four other TPF guns had been fired. He had already returned them to Dwyer, Molloy, MacDonald, and McClinton. He kept Eddie's and Denny's weapons in his evidence box and saw that they were issued replacements.

Logue said that the gun found on the street was a .32-caliber semiautomatic, Belgian-made Fabrique Nationale. It had been manufactured in 1922; its ownership was untraceable. It was loaded with six bullets and had room for two more. Logue couldn't tell when the Fabrique Nationale was last fired, but he and Hudson knew it couldn't have been fired in the Buick. When an automatic is fired, it ejects a shell as it sends a bullet out the barrel. No ejected shell had been found inside the Buick.

Hudson's eight-page typed summary of the Homicide investigation indicates that he then started his own investigation of the robbery, beginning with a telephone call to Cambridge's Petersen. According to the Hudson summary, Petersen told him about the positive IDs of Bowden and his Buick, but nothing about Desi's first trip to the morgue or Ethel and Desi's attempt to ID the other robber.

Hudson sent one of his detectives, William Smith, the father of the most popular girl in my brother Bill's class at Saint Brendan's elementary school, to Boston City Hospital to run down Bowden's employment history, interview anyone who might have seen him on Wednesday, and check how long it takes to drive from the hospital to the Pearl Food Market.

John Geagan's investigation of the robbery had ended on Thursday with Ethel's and Desi's positive IDs. On Friday, Geagan turned back to what had happened on Smith Street. He scheduled two interviews for the afternoon. For the first, he went to photographer Ken Kobre's apartment in Cambridge. For the second, he met Dave O'Brian at Headquarters. With Geagan during both interviews were TPF Sergeants Byrne and McHale.

Seconds after Geagan clicked on his portable tape recorder, Kobre apologized for not having "a very good memory." Then, responding to Geagan's and Byrne's questions, he told his story of the stakeout and the shooting. Denny parked the car at the corner of Gurney and Parker. Eddie "radioed to the other cars, the other group that was there. He got a description of the men. You want everything I remember?"

Geagan nodded. "Yeah."

"The description of the men said that they were wearing jean jackets, they were wearing dark headgear of some sort, and they were on the slim side."

Byrne asked whether Eddie made a call to check the Buick's plate number. Kobre wasn't sure. Toward the end of the twenty-minute interview, Geagan raised that question again and then Kobre said, "Yes, the car had license plates from the Cape. Yes, so they must have radioed in something. That's right. . . . It had something to do with the plates were a year old and they came from the Cape or something like that and that's about all I know."

Kobre leaned back in his armchair, sipped from a coffee cup, and drawled on about the stakeout: "We're now parked at Gurney and it seemed like an endless amount of time. We've got the description. They had immediately pulled their guns the minute they had ridden by the car. I could see them. They both had guns cuddled in their laps. At one point, Eddie wanted to walk by. We had been sitting there for a while, and at one point, he wanted to walk up and down. Dennis said no. Eddie was the one that said, 'I think that they're going to come back for the car.' He seemed to have some premonition that this was going to take place. It seemed logical that if they [the robbers] had been at all bright they would have abandoned the car, but he seemed to have this second sense to stick it out, to hold it there.

"I assumed that more backup troops were coming. I was rather surprised at that. He seemed to have been radioing. He said it would be very good if they had a shotgun—oh, another thing was that they knew that they had a shotgun and a handgun. That was radioed in to us. I remember that much. He said, 'They have too much firepower. We need to bring up shotguns.' Or something to that effect. I kept expecting to see other policemen or hear about other policemen. We just never did. I don't know why.

"They—at some point during this long stakeout, they described to us the effects of shotgun fire and what to do in that case. I mean what to do basically when the action took place. They said to get down on the floor. They said that they didn't think a shotgun would go through the car door and we would be all right. There was a pretty good assumption that he would shoot and also that he would be shooting from another car. One of the comments was 'We want to take them before they get out of their car. We hope there'll be no shooting.' They also said—I'll be frank, I don't know if this was for our benefit or what, but this is what was said— Eddie also said that he didn't like this time of night because, at this time of night, he was just coming out of daylight and his eyes didn't get adjusted yet and that there were kids around—which was true.

"We sat there. The car was at least a hundred yards up the street. It was about halfway up. You could make out the car, but you couldn't tell what was going on around it. Various people during this period of time came and walked by the car and moved on. It looked like they were going to get in and they didn't get in. . . . You couldn't—anybody at the car—you couldn't basically make out any detail. It just wasn't there to be made out. You couldn't tell what anybody was wearing or anything else.

"Do I remember any other things during the stakeout? Some side points. Eddie was afraid that they would identify that we were there. People did look in our car. He picked up a bag, a Dunkin' Donuts bag, and he pretended like he was boozing it up. That's part of his undercover routine. And they did agree—they did radio, at one point—that one group was going to take the passenger, that is, one car was going to take the driver and the other car was going to take the passenger. I can't remember anything else."

Geagan led Kobre through the action, beginning with the entrance of the Thunderbird. "Did it go down Smith Street?"

"It went down Smith Street."

"It stopped at the Buick?"

"It stopped at the Buick."

"What did you see? Could you see anything?"

"Vaguely," said Kobre. "It was extremely vague, but it did seem that they stopped at the Buick and it did seem that somebody got out. At that point, the two officers I was with radioed and said, 'We're going in. This is it!' And then they took off and pulled up to the car. And, at that point, we got down on the floor."

"After you went down on the floor of the car," Geagan asked, "what did you see next?"

"I think it's what I heard," Kobre replied. And what he heard were gunshots. He said they "sounded like firecrackers."

"Did you hear any words exchanged?" asked Geagan.

"No," said Kobre, "I did not. I did not hear shouting. I didn't hear anything."

Kobre had no idea what the Thunderbird did after stopping at the Buick. He thought that was because he was, as he sheepishly described himself to Geagan, Byrne, and McHale, "a bad witness."

The O'Brian interview, a half hour later at Headquarters, took only half as long as the Kobre interview. Geagan sat at his army-green metal desk. O'Brian took the wooden chair facing Geagan. Harry Byrne stood to O'Brian's left, Ed McHale to his right. O'Brian's account of the stakeout, as it emerged through Geagan's questions, was like Kobre's, though more sharply detailed. And his description of the action was far more revealing by the inclusion of a volunteered bit that neither he nor Kobre was asked about. O'Brian estimated that the elapsed time between the moment Eddie and Denny jumped out of the car and the start of gunfire was "three to five seconds." Enough time only for Eddie and Denny to run to the Buick and start firing. If O'Brian's three-to-five seconds was true, Eddie's and Denny's descriptions of all their and the Buick's jumping around before the shooting were not. There was no time for any of that. No one pressed O'Brian on this point.

"I estimate anywhere from three to five seconds when I heard this quick blast," he continued. "It seemed to me about seven or eight shots in rapid succession—one, two, three, four, five, six, seven, eight, or nine. I would say seven or eight. I was still down, expecting a shotgun blast, when Holland and McKenna returned to the car, got in, and we took off up the road another hundred feet or so. Then they hit the brakes and jumped out again. At this point I got out and saw the Buick on the left-hand side up halfway on the fence and I saw Denny McKenna with his arm in the window on the driver's side holding onto the body, or holding onto Bowden. I got out of the car. A crowd gathered at this point and the action was over."

Geagan asked whether O'Brian heard Holland or McKenna say anything after they got out of the car and before the shooting started. O'Brian said no.

"When you heard the shots fired," asked Byrne, "did they all sound the same?"

"They all did sound pretty much the same," O'Brian replied. "It sounded like fireworks going off to me."

McHale asked, "Do you think that you could judge the distance that you were from the Buick at the time?"

"Yeah," said O'Brian. "Almost on top of it."

"Less than a car length away?"

"Yeah, definitely."

Geagan asked the last question. "After it was all over, did you hear any conversation about Holland being hurt?"

"No."

O'Brian left the Internal Affairs office and made his way through the corridors of Headquarters to the Homicide office, where Hudson then interviewed him.

O'Brian's was the only Homicide interview Hudson personally conducted, and the only one that pertained to what happened on Smith Street. Unlike Geagan, Hudson didn't use a tape recorder. He prefers taking notes. "Tapes can come back to haunt you," he told me years later when refusing to let me tape one of our conversations. Half of Hudson's investigation summary is devoted to the O'Brian interview. The summary indicates that it was essentially a rehash of the Internal Affairs interview. Hudson noted, without comment, the most important thing O'Brian had to say about the shooting: It happened three to five seconds after Eddie and Denny got out of the car. But not even that statement, a complete contradiction of Eddie's and Denny's versions of the shooting, provoked a reaction from Bob Hudson. In fact, the Homicide investigation of what happened on Smith Street ended with the O'Brian interview.

Meanwhile, at Boston City Hospital, Detective Smith had talked to Elsie Pina, one of Bowden's supervisors. Then he drove to the Pearl Food Market and noted that the three miles of city driving took, "on a week-day with normal traffic, between twenty

and twenty-five minutes." Back at the Homicide office, Smith filed
this report.

James Henry Bowden, Jr. was first employed at the B.C.H.
on March 22, 1967, has been a steady employee since that
date. He worked for the housekeeping department, cur-
rently assigned to the children's building, his dutys consisted
of cleaning and mopping of corridors, stairways and clinic
rooms. His regular hours were from 7:00 a.m. to 3:30 p.m.
    WEDNESDAY, JANUARY 29TH IN = 7:09 A.M. OUT = 3:17 P.M.
    Elsie Pina states that on Wednesday, January 29th she
talked with Bowden about 10:30 a.m. She saw him again
about 1:00 p.m. (lunch intervening 11:30 to 12:15) and again
spoke with him about 2:00 p.m. As yet unidentified employees report seeing him in the punch-out line about 3:00 p.m.

Elsie Pina, a slim black woman in her early thirties, left City
Hospital shortly after talking to Detective Smith. She and a few
co-workers went to the afternoon session of the Bowden wake.
The funeral home was jammed with people. There was a waiting line just to get in the front door. Everyone was buzzing about
what they had read in the *Globe*. How could the cops think that
James robbed that store? The robbery was at two-thirty and he
must have still been at work then. Elsie Pina kept telling people
that she knew James was at work then because she last saw him
on his floor of the Children's Building at two-fifteen or two-thirty.
    The theme of conversation at the wake was that James would
never do what the *Globe* had said he did. He would never carry a
gun. He would never rob a store. He would never try to run down
a couple of cops. The mourners told one another anecdotes illus-
trating how timid and law-abiding James was. Pat had the latest
one. Monday night she noticed that the Buick's front license plate
was missing, and she told James about it. He knew he had securely
bolted that plate on, and so was sure it was stolen, not an uncommon fate for a Roxbury plate. James worried that someone using

the plate would collect parking tickets that he would have to pay. He told Pat that he would report the missing plate the next day. He did that at the Registry on Tuesday after work. The Registry gave him a permit to drive with one plate and said a replacement plate would be in the mail in a few weeks. "Who'd bother to rush over there for a missing plate when there was still one on the car?" Pat asked when telling the story. "He just knew he was supposed to do that, so he did. That's the way he always was."

At the wake and after the funeral, there was a lot of grumbling around Pat about getting a lawyer. Pat nodded whenever she heard it. But then, no one was at all sure what a lawyer could do for her.

Monday morning, before closing the Bowden Homicide file Hudson sent another of his men, Detective Thomas Cashman, to City Hospital to try to find out more about Bowden and his last day on the job. Cashman talked to Henry Smith, the head of the Housekeeping Department, who had hired Bowden, and to Donald Webster, another of Bowden's supervisors. The detective returned with this report for Hudson:

> I went to the housekeeping department and talked to the following persons. Henry Smith the manager of the Housekeeping dept. and Donald Webster a supervisor in the same dept. Mr. Smith related to me that he knew Bowden and about a week before his death had given him a steady assignment, up to then he had more or less been given different types of work in different buildings, he was upgraded to Grade 2 and received the Childrens building as a steady assignment. His duties was the cleaning of the stairs and walk in clinics. His working hours were from 7:00 A.M. to 3:30 P.M. daily, he was off week-ends. Mr. Smith further stated that Bowden was about an average type of guy, he was a loner, arrived at work every morning ten or fifteen minutes late but was always one of the first to punch out in the afternoon. Mr. Smith said that Bowden took some kind of

a welding course but never followed it up. Smith thought that Bowden could have made out better than working at the kind of job that he had at the hospital.

Donald Webster the supervisor remembers Wednesday January 29, 1975, at the time clock of the housekeeping dept. He remembers that Bowden was in line that day about 3:20 P.M. actually Bowdens card showed that it was punched at 3:17 P.M. I asked Mr. Webster if he had heard about the death of Mr. Bowden, he replied yes but that it had nothing to do with seeing him that afternoon. He stated that he was the supervisor in charge of watching the employees punch out and that he observed Bowden in the front of the line and at the time a little pushing started about three or four people behind Bowden. Webster also stated that he didn't know of any other employees that were close to Bowden, he stated the same as Mr. Smith that he Bowden seemed to be a loner. Neither Smith or Webster knew anything about Bowdens Car or where he parked, he had no permit to park on hospital property. Mr. Smith and myself checked Bowden's locker and it contained articles of the uniforms they are issued at the hospital. Mr. Smith never saw Bowden wear a hat and even on one occasion suggested that Bowden get a hair-cut, had a large Afro.

Hudson read Cashman's report and added these lines to his investigation summary: "Monday, February 3, 1975, Sergeant Hudson sent Detective Cashman to the Boston City Hospital to find out where Bowden had parked his car. None of the employees knew where Bowden had parked his car. There was no permit for Bowden to park his car on the hospital property, neither." The Homicide investigation was over.

Following the instructions of the new deadly force rule, Hudson sent copies of the Homicide Unit's paperwork—his summary, his diagram of the scene, Detective Smith's report, and Detective Cashman's report—to Bob di Grazia and Joe Jordan. In two sentences on the first page of his summary, Hudson gave the Homicide view of what happened on Smith Street. "The operator of [the Buick] tried to run down Patrolmen McKenna and Holland of the T.P.F., when they went over to this vehicle. These officers fired several shots at this vehicle which continued on down Smith St., and then went up over the sidewalk, knocking down a chain-link fence of the school on Smith St." Nowhere in the Homicide case folder was there a hint that Eddie had been injured, or that Bowden may have had a gun, or that the Thunderbird was somehow involved in the shooting, or that Ernest Winbush fired a shotgun at Eddie. In fact, the name Ernest Winbush never found its way into the Homicide folder.

CHAPTER 6

The *Phoenix* hit the newsstands with the headline A NIGHT OF FEAR AND BLOODSHED WITH THE TPF, on Tuesday, February 4, 1975, the day after the Homicide investigation ended. The cover was a black-and-white photo of Joe Fagone, cigarette in one hand, flashlight in the other, his police badge on his corduroy lapel just under the wings pin his airline stewardess girlfriend had given him. He was crouched at the front end of a Chevy, looking at the Fabrique Nationale pistol on the ground.

John Geagan bought a *Phoenix* that morning. He read it, circled Jessina Stokes's name in O'Brian's article, and left the paper in the Bowden corner of his desk for two weeks. The Internal Affairs investigation was on hold. Everything was waiting for Frank McGee to find time in his schedule of union meetings and court appearances so that Geagan could interview Eddie and Denny, both of whom refused to be questioned without their lawyer being present. Finally, McGee agreed to bring his clients into Geagan's office for interviews on February 13.

Bob Hudson picked up a *Phoenix* that morning, too. He always does when it runs something on one of his cases. But for Hudson, it was hardly more than recreational reading. There was nothing in it that would make him reopen his Bowden investigation.

When someone called Pat Bowden to tell her that the *Phoenix* had something big about the shooting, she went out to get a copy. She sat with it for an hour at her dining room table. She twice read O'Brian's lengthy first-person account of his day with the TPF, underlining and making notes in the margins each time. She underlined the description of the robbers that O'Brian heard over the radio. She underlined Denny's statement: "Bear in mind we're going to try to get them before they even get out of their vehicle. We like to stack the odds in our favor." She underlined O'Brian's "Maybe three, maybe five seconds." She underlined Eddie's "No ACU injured!" She underlined Denny's "As soon as he turned that wheel, I said, 'Fuck him.'" And she underlined Dwyer's "Did we put on a good show for you?"

She bristled as she read the lines about her husband being positively identified as a robber and her family car being positively identified as a getaway car, and at Jim Caragianes's comment: "They got rid of a shit bum."

She drew a star beside O'Brian's quotation of the unidentified teenager who told him, "The cops just drove up, jumped out and started shooting," and O'Brian's accompanying acknowledgment that this description fit his "own mental timetable" of the action. And she drew boxes around the passages where O'Brian questioned the police version.

O'Brian had obtained a copy of Sergeant McHale's summary of the ACU team's reports from Di Grazia's office. He quoted McHale's account of the action, then rhetorically asked, "But could all that is described in that report have really taken place in the few seconds before the gunfire started?" He also asked, "Did McKenna and Holland really shout four warnings before opening fire?" He had an answer for that one. "I was no more than ten feet away," he wrote. "I didn't hear anything." The gun found at the scene puzzled O'Brian. He explained that Fagone had found it "not in or near the Buick, but 150 feet down Smith Street," halfway between where the shooting occurred and where the Buick finally crashed. To the theory that Bowden threw it there as he sped away from the shooting, O'Brian wrote, "I don't know how that could have happened without Denny McKenna, who was blasting away at that side of the car, noticing."

Wait till a lawyer reads this, Pat thought. She didn't have a specific lawyer in mind, but she was ready to start looking for one.

––––––––

"I was scared, confused, hurt, bitter, everything," Pat says of those
first three weeks of February. "I was worried about my children,
too, how I was gonna take care of them. I didn't know what I was
gonna do or what I could do. It was a terrible time . . . worse than
you could imagine."

Years later, in her living room, where James's aquarium still
bubbled silently, I turned on a tape recorder and asked her to tell
me about those days, beginning with the call from the Brigham
Hospital and ending with her appointment with my father. Ever
so reluctantly she dug up a few memories of that time. I empa-
thized but I pressed. As she spoke, she sometimes broke into a
pained smile. "Oh, it was terrible," she kept repeating between
heavy sighs filled with the hope that I wouldn't ask another question. Eventually, I apologized and turned off the tape recorder, but
not before it had captured her recollection of looking for a lawyer.

She began with the lawyers recommended by relatives and
friends, and had no luck. They were Roxbury lawyers, one-man
law offices mostly, specializing in criminal law. Pat soon learned
that she needed someone who could handle a civil case . . . a big
civil case . . . a tough one . . . what the criminal lawyers she met
called a hopeless case. The Roxbury lawyers, mostly young black
men only a few years older than she, sympathized with her. They
told her they had seen this kind of thing before. As always, they
said, the police investigation will quietly conclude, if it hasn't already, that the killing was justified. No one in the District Attorney's office, the Attorney General's office, or the U.S. Attorney's
office will bother to look at this thing. So forget about criminal
charges against the cops. Suing them will be the only thing left,
but it's a waste of time and money. No one has ever won such a
lawsuit, not in Boston—or anywhere else in the country.

Pat would always swear that her husband could never have
done what the cops said he did, that he could never have tried to
hurt anyone. The attorneys would always nod and say they believed her. She would point to her underlinings in O'Brian's article
and ask, "What about the three to five seconds?" The police will
say O'Brian is wrong about that, they would tell her. "What about

that?" she would ask, pointing to Denny's "Fuck him." McKenna will deny that he said it. "What about our niece, Jessina? She saw them just run up and shoot him." Jessina's a relative. No one will believe her. And besides, they did find a gun at the scene and the robbery witnesses positively identified the car and the body. "But he never had that gun," Pat would insist, "and a friend of his told me he was definitely at work at two-thirty." The lawyers would explain that even if it could somehow be proven that he wasn't one of the robbers and that the gun wasn't his, the cops won't change their story about him trying to run them down, which in itself is reason enough to shoot him. And they can always claim that they *thought* he had a gun in his hand. That too is reason enough to shoot. Any jury will accept it, especially a Boston jury. "Don't forget," said one battle-weary black lawyer, "these are two Irish cops against a nigger."

To show how easily defensible the police position is in such shooting incidents, one lawyer told Pat about the case of James Wilds, Jr., who had been killed by the Boston police only six months earlier. Having mistaken Wilds for James Johnson, a black escaped prisoner, two white cops approached him as he sat in a parked car on a Roxbury street late one night. For reasons now known only to himself, Wilds jumped from the car and ran when he saw them coming. The cops each fired two shots, hitting Wilds in the back with one. It killed him. James Wilds was unarmed, but because the cops said he "turned in a threatening manner as if to shoot," the department approved the shooting and a judge found it "legally justified" in an inquest that was closed to the public and the press.

The lawyer was bothered more by the Wilds case than any other like it, because two black patrolmen who arrived on the scene just before the shooting, and saw no need to draw *their* guns, went along with the official version. "There's always a lot of pressure on cops, white or black, to do that," he told Pat. "They're cops first, and that's whose side they'll always be on." The Wilds case had convinced him that it was impossible to crack the cops' code of honor to stick together no matter what, and therefore impossible to win a wrongful-death lawsuit against them. He wouldn't take the Bowden case. Nor would any of the other lawyers Pat had already met.

In the waiting rooms of the law offices she visited every day, Pat had been reading newspaper accounts of a local trial that was competing for front-page space with stories headlined KISSINGER OPTIMISTIC ON MIDEAST; THIEU APPEALS TO US FOR AID, VOWS SOUTH VIETNAM WON'T GIVE UP; BOSTON SCHOOLS PEACEFUL BUT TENSE THIS WEEK. The case involved one Kenneth Edelin, a young black physician who was on trial for manslaughter. The prosecution contended that Doctor Edelin had performed an abortion at Boston City Hospital in such a way as to violate U.S. Supreme Court guidelines for legal abortions and constitute manslaughter. The defense maintained that the doctor had used standard medical procedure and that because the one-and-a-half-pound fetus could not have survived outside the womb, whatever happened to it on the operating table could not be homicide. Pro-choice forces and assorted liberal groups assembled publicly on the side of the defense. The National Association for the Advancement of Colored People condemned the district attorney for prosecuting a black City Hospital doctor for aborting the unwanted pregnancy of a teenaged black girl, while never interfering with identical situations involving white doctors and white patients in Boston's more prestigious medical facilities. Contributions poured into a defense fund that had been established to cover Edelin's trial expenses, including a fee for his attorney, William Homans.

Pat's interest in the trial focused on Homans. Front-page treatment in the *Phoenix* was not enough to spark interest in her husband's death among the NAACP, the American Civil Liberties Union, the Black Caucus of the state legislature, or any of the other groups rallying around the Edelin defense. Pat thought Homans could activate such support for her case if he'd take it.

In Boston, criminal defense is the specialty of the gritty Irish, Italian, and Jewish lawyers who graduate without academic distinction from plebeian colleges and law schools. They could never win employment in the city's high-powered corporate law firms founded a century ago—and still largely staffed—by patrician Harvard Law School graduates like William Homans. But Homans is actually the most prominent exception to this generalization about the legal community. A middle-aged descendant of a distinguished Yankee line that includes the Presidents Adams, he is one of the three or four leading criminal lawyers in Massachusetts. In 1975, he was running an overburdened one-man law office that seemed to catch every liberal-cause trial that came along. The Edelin case was his most publicized yet. In the last week of the trial, a newspaper profile portrayed him, with reasonable accuracy, as something of a legal knight in shining armor, devoted to the pursuit of justice for all and inclined to represent poor people without extracting a fee. Reading that, Pat decided to call him.

Like all good defense attorneys in big trials, Homans was working eighteen to twenty hours a day on Edelin. But, remaining true to his reputation, when his secretary briefed him on Pat's call he had her arrange a meeting at the courthouse the next day. During a trial recess, Homans ignored the noisy crowd of spectators and reporters in the hall and listened to Pat. He slouched his tall, heavy frame against a wall and glanced at Pat's *Phoenix*. The conversation lasted only a few minutes. Homans was noncommittal but plainly interested. He told Pat to call for an office appointment the following week. The Edelin trial would be over by then, he said, and he could give her situation the attention it deserved. Pat left the courthouse uplifted—for the first time since January 29—by the hope that her lawyer search was over.

On Thursday, February 13 (the day Homans made his final argument to the Edelin jury), Eddie and Denny appeared for their interview with John Geagan. At about one o'clock, Eddie, Denny, and Frank McGee walked up the granite front steps of Police Headquarters. McGee led the way to Geagan's office. He'd been there many times representing patrolmen in other Internal Affairs matters.

Internal Affairs interviews are comfortable routines for McGee.

Every patrolman questioned by the I.A.D. has a right to be represented by counsel. Nearly all of them opt for McGee, since his services are paid for by their union. This helps run his hourly billing of the union to something over $100,000 per year. Normally garrulous in public, McGee can be serenely silent in the I.A.D. office. The transcripts of Eddie's and Denny's interviews show that he had nothing to say that afternoon. From an experienced, professionally obstinate labor negotiator and lawyer like McGee, passivity was a sign that his clients were not in danger.

Geagan invited Denny into his bare, fluorescent-lighted office first. That left Eddie pacing the hall alone. Denny and McGee took seats facing Geagan's desk. Geagan introduced himself to Denny, turned on his tape recorder, and said, "This investigation concerns the use of your firearm on Wednesday, January 29, 1975, on Smith Street, Roxbury, when James Bowden was mortally wounded." He dropped his eyes to a piece of paper on his desk and read his standard opening statement: "This investigation is administrative in nature. Answers must be responsive to all questions and directives, and answers must be given to all questions. Your rights will be observed in conformance with pertinent court decisions which provide, in substance, that answers given by you cannot be used in any criminal proceedings against you. This hearing is being conducted in conformance with Rule 54 of the Boston Police Department Rules and Regulations. Pursuant to Rule 54, you have exercised your right to have your attorney present here with you, and Attorney Frank McGee is present."

Geagan's speech droned into another more elaborate assurance that anything Denny might say could not come back to haunt him in "any criminal proceedings." A freezing wind whistled around the air conditioner in Geagan's frosted window. Three snowfalls that week had left little drifts on the outside windowsill.

With the name, address, identification number, and present assignment questions out of the way, Geagan gave Denny a wide-open field by saying, "Tell me what happened on January 29, 1975."

Only the three men in the room know how Denny began his

reply. The transcript of the interview has this to say in the place where Denny's answer should be: "There was a malfunction in the tape at this point and Patrolman McKenna related the events almost exactly as he reported them in his report to Captain William P. MacDonald on the night of the occurrence." The unexplained malfunction was temporary. After a half-page blank spot, the transcript resumes with Denny saying: "Patrolman Holland notified over the walkie-talkie the other Unit that the Buick Electra was now moving." What follows is a two-and-a-half-page uninterrupted expansion of Denny's report, chock-full of the kind of stiff language that cops think sounds authoritative: "I again removed myself from the front of the path of the direction of the car."

In his report, Denny had the Buick making two threatening moves forcing him to jump back only once. To Geagan, Denny described five threatening back-and-forth swerves that forced him to jump back three times. Also in his report he had said he "heard a gunshot" before he fired. Now, to his mention of the gunshot he added, "which I believe came from inside the vehicle." Denny told Geagan that he fired his third and final shot, which missed by no one knows how much, as "the Buick accelerated very fast up Smith Street."

Once Denny got past the shooting, his sentences flowed naturally. He ended his description of the Smith Street scene by saying: "Eddie called an ambulance, and the ambulance responded. And we tried to get the driver out, and it was difficult because the driver had the armrest down. You couldn't see it because of the size of the driver. His bulk was covering it, and at first it was hard to get him out of the car. And then I got into the car with him and I lifted his weight off the armrest and I pulled the armrest out of the way and the uniform men took the upper half of his body and I took his legs and they took him out the passenger door and put him on a stretcher and removed him from the area.

"And right after that, I asked Eddie Holland if he was all right, and he responded that he was okay. And he and I then observed

Sergeant McHale and Sergeant Byrne, Eddie McHale and Harry Byrne, arrive on the scene with numerous other police officers."

Geagan questioned only one point in Denny's description of the shooting: "Now, before you fired, you heard a shot that you thought was from inside the vehicle?" he asked.

"Yes, I did, but the shot was coincidental," Denny explained. "I knew at that time he had struck Patrolman Holland and he was trying to run me down, and if I hadn't heard the shot it wouldn't have changed my action."

Geagan asked about the license plate of the getaway car. He knew that it was a mistake for Eddie and Denny to have thought during the stakeout that Bowden's number was precisely the one that Cambridge was looking for. It seemed an academic point of interest now that Desi Callahan had positively identified Bowden's car, but Geagan was still concerned with who was responsible for the mistake. "Do you know if the number was written down at the time it was given out on the radio that afternoon?" he asked.

"We wrote down his number first as 4-Sam-6838," Denny replied, "and almost immediately, or in a very short time after we took it down as 4-Sam-6838, it was corrected by the dispatcher to be 4-Frank-6838 [Bowden's number]."

Denny was blaming the dispatcher for the error. Of course it was a remarkable coincidence that the dispatcher scrambled Cambridge's 4F•6368 into 4F•6838 instead of some other variation. Geagan didn't think the dispatcher had made an error. He thought the mistake was Eddie's. He figured Eddie wrote down 4F•6368 in the afternoon, when the robbery alert was broadcast, and when he checked with the turret during the stakeout he was reading that number from his notes, so naturally the turret confirmed it. Geagan had already received copies of short reports written by the two turret men involved. Patrolman John Tanous, the afternoon dispatcher, said that at 2:36 P.M. he first broadcast the Cambridge getaway car's number as 4S•6368, and a few minutes later changed it to 4F•6368 after Cambridge added the letter correction. Patrolman Robert Mullen, the evening dispatcher, reported that the number checked during the stakeout was 4F•6368, not Bowden's number.

Geagan asked who wrote down the number when it came over the air that afternoon. "Eddie Holland wrote it down," said Denny, "and I believe I also wrote it down."

"You don't happen to still have that paper you wrote it down on?" Geagan wondered.

"I don't know," Denny replied. "I haven't been able to locate it, so I couldn't honestly say that I have it. I might have it."

"Okay," said Geagan. "When you're riding down Smith Street and saw the Buick parked at the curb, was the number taken from the car then and written down at that time?"

Denny said, "Eddie's response was something to the effect: 'There it is. There's the car that was in the holdup.' He checked it with the number that he had written down. I know that he checked it with the paper that he had, and we turned around to verify that that was the number."

"After spotting the Buick, what was [the plate number] checked from at that time? Was it checked from the paper you wrote it down on at two o'clock or two-thirty or the paper that you wrote it down on at six o'clock?"

Denny hedged at first, then bolstered Geagan's theory: "If it was written down at six o'clock, which I'm not sure it was, it could have been checked from that. I think when Eddie checked it, he was checking it from the original information that we had received early that afternoon."

"Are you telling me that he didn't write it down at six o'clock when you first went by?"

"I don't recall."

"When you checked it—checked the registration—was it checked through the TPF or with the turret?"

"Ah . . . I'm not sure."

"Where were you when you checked it?"

"We were on Gurney Street with the car under observation . . . close to three hundred feet away."

Geagan moved on to a strangely light treatment of the Thunderbird. "Tell me about the T-Bird that came up and made a right turn onto Smith Street," he said. "Did you get the registration number of the T-Bird at that time?" Denny said he did and in anticipation of the next question immediately added, "I didn't write down the registration of the T-Bird at that time. Perhaps I should have—I can't say—but other vehicles had turned up Smith Street prior to this time and none of them had stopped alongside the car."

"Did you remember the number of every car that went up?" asked Geagan.

"Nope, I did not."

"Why did you remember the number of the T-Bird then?"

Denny thought for a moment and said, "I can't honestly say why I remembered it, but I did remember that number."

"Okay," said Geagan, "the T-Bird came up Parker Street and turned right on Smith?"

"Yes, that's correct."

"It stopped at the Buick?"

"Yes, it did."

"Now, where did the T-Bird go?"

"It then proceeded forward down Smith Street towards St. Alphonsus Street."

"And do you know where it went from there?"

"From my own personal knowledge, no," Denny replied. "I was told where it went afterward." Geagan did not ask Denny who told him what about where the Thunderbird went.

Ernest Winbush's name never came up during the interview. But his involvement was alluded to in one simple question and one surprising answer. "Do you know why the operator of the T-Bird was subsequently arrested?" Geagan asked.

"The operator of the T-Bird," Denny began cautiously, "from what I was told, uh, was arrested, if I'm correct in my recollection, uh, he was arrested, uh, I believe that Patrolman Holland observed a firearm. I'm not sure of that. I don't know."

This provoked no follow-up questions from Geagan. Denny's interview was over. It had taken about twenty minutes. Denny left the room and told Eddie it was his turn.

It was 1:30 P.M. when Eddie sat down for his interview. It lasted twice as long as Denny's because Eddie had the Ernest Winbush arrest to explain. Geagan's opening line—"Eddie, for the record, I'll introduce myself. I'm Sergeant Geagan"—indicates that he knew Eddie. The interview started like the previous one: Geagan reading his speech; asking Eddie his name, address, ID number, and present assignment; then saying, "Tell me what happened on January 29."

This time the tape recorder did not malfunction. Eddie launched a five-minute answer beginning with his spotting the Buick between "6:00 P.M. and 6:05 P.M." and ending with his radio call for an ambulance after the Buick crashed. It was no more than a wordier version of his report. "That's about it to the best of my recollection," he said in summation. He had not said a word about Ernest Winbush or a shotgun attack.

Geagan temporarily ignored the curious omission and talked about plate numbers. He asked whether Eddie had made a note of the robbery number when it first came over the air in the afternoon. To the same question, Denny had said, "Eddie Holland wrote it down and I believe I also wrote it down." Now Eddie replied, "I didn't write it down, no." When asked whether he had written down the Buick's number after he'd seen it on Smith Street, Eddie paused and said, "Gee, I don't know. I don't recollect, to be honest."

"Do you keep a stolen-car list in your car?" Geagan asked.

"No, we don't," said Eddie. "I do keep certain numbers down."

"What kind of numbers?"

"Probably cars used in holdups."

"But you didn't write this one down, and it was a car used in a holdup?"

"I don't remember, to be honest about it."

Geagan moved to the other plate number involved. He asked Eddie whether he had noticed the Thunderbird's number. Eddie said he had not. "Do you know who checked the registration list-ing of that T-bird [after the shooting]?" Geagan asked.

"I believe, uh, Dennis put it over the air," said Eddie. "He had the number of the vehicle. He had got that probably, uh, I don't know where he got it from, to be honest, but it was definitely the vehicle."

The only detail of Eddie's version of the shooting that Geagan questioned was what kind of gun he had seen in Bowden's hand. "To the best of my recollection," Eddie said, "it was a large gun, possibly a forty-five. It was big. That's all I know."

Then Geagan introduced a subject that would confuse the rest of the interview. "Do you know why Winbush was arrested?" he asked.

"Yes, sir." Eddie replied.

"For what?"

"He was arrested for assault by means of a deadly weapon."

"On who?"

"On myself."

"What happened?" Geagan asked. Twenty minutes of talk en-sued, but the answer to this two-word question did not emerge.

"When I first approached it," Eddie began, "I remember the 'police officers' was yelled. A light come on in the T-Bird and I heard a 'crack' and a man with what appeared—I thought it was a sawed-off shotgun; it could have been a rifle—it appeared to me to be about that size, eighteen inches, sixteen."

"When you first approached what, the T-Bird?" asked Geagan.

"No, we didn't approach the T-Bird at all. They [Molloy and Dwyer] were notified that there was a T-Bird involved in it."

"Tell me when you were assaulted with a dangerous weapon," Geagan demanded.

"Immediately, right off the bat," said Eddie.

"Where?"

"Right on Smith Street adjacent to the Buick on the opposite side of the street."

"The T-Bird was beside the Buick when this happened?"

"They weren't right alongside of each other," Eddie explained. "They were on opposite sides of the street."

"Where was the operator of the Buick at this time?"

"The operator of the Buick was right in there."

"In where?"

"In the Buick."

"O.K. He was in the Buick?"

"Yes, sir."

"And what happened?"

"And I heard the crack from what I believe to be a—"

"Where were you then?" Geagan interrupted.

"I had just moved and said 'Boston Police officers, open the door!' I had banged it with my left hand."

"Banged what with your left hand?"

"I banged the window of the Electra, the passenger's side."

"Now, when you banged the left side of the Buick, where was the T-Bird then?"

"The T-Bird, uh, that's the Buick there, right there." Eddie pointed out the spot on a copy of Hudson's diagram which Geagan had placed on the table between them. "And the T-Bird was opposite, only it was farther back on the opposite side of the street." Eddie was placing the Thunderbird between the ACU car and the Buick. Geagan couldn't understand how the Thunderbird got behind the Buick, but he tried to keep the interview moving by asking, "Now, when you rapped on the window of the Buick with your left hand, what happened then?"

"I shouted, 'Boston Police officers, get out of the vehicle.' I moved toward the front and out approximately a foot and a half, and there was a hesitation, and the Buick lunged at me and hit me on the left side of my body."

"He's parked at the curb now?"

"What, the Buick?" Eddie asked.

"Yes."

"No, the Buick was out," said Eddie.

"Out where?"

"The Buick was out in the center of the street."

"Where's the T-Bird?"

"It was opposite."

"Behind the Buick?"

"No," said Eddie. "It was not quite parallel. It was on the opposite side of the street but back maybe five, six, eight, maybe ten feet from it at an angle."

"The Buick was in front of the T-Bird?" Geagan asked, still not understanding Eddie's placement of the cars on the diagram.

"Right," said Eddie, "but on opposite sides of the street."

"How many cars can get down Smith Street at one time?" Geagan asked.

"Two," Eddie replied after a pause.

"With cars parked on both sides, two cars could drive down the street parallel?"

"I would say so, yeah."

Geagan had seen cars parked on both sides of the street that night. What Eddie seemed to be saying was that the Buick and Thunderbird backed down the street side by side, something that McKenna, O'Brian, and Kobre did not see and something impossible to imagine happening on such a narrow street with cars parked on both sides. Geagan did not challenge Eddie on this point. Instead, he returned to the beginning of Eddie's Thunderbird story and went through it a second and then a third time. Each version was as confusing as the first. Geagan took an active role in telling the story on the last try.

"You're parked here at Gurney Street?" he began.

"Yes sir," confirmed Eddie.

"The T-Bird came down and parked beside the Buick here at Alton Court," Geagan continued. "The operator of the Buick gets out of the T-Bird and gets into the Buick. The Buick pulls out and backs up to Huban Court where the shooting was. Then, the Buick goes forward and smashes up here at the Tobin School. Do you agree to that part?"

"I'd say that's a fair representation," said Eddie.

"All right, you drive down the street and the Buick is right in the middle of the street?"

"The Buick is more to the right part here."

"Where was the T-Bird when he pointed the gun out the window at you?" Geagan asked. Eddie said that it was on the left side of the Buick. Curiously, though, Eddie had not told Geagan that the shotgun was pointed out the window at him. Actually, he never told Geagan how the shotgun was fired at him.

"You're on the opposite side of the street," Geagan declared. "You're on the opposite side of the car. Your partner is on this side of the street [the spot where Eddie had just placed the Thunderbird]."

"I know that," said Eddie.

"But he makes no mention of the T-Bird or a gun pointing out the window at him," said Geagan.

"Well, maybe he had his back to it," ventured Eddie.

"He said the T-Bird, when it let the passenger out, it came up and went in the school yard here and up to Tremont Street," said Geagan. In fact, Denny had said nothing like that. The only thing he had said about the Thunderbird after it stopped at the parked Buick was: "It then proceeded *forward* [emphasis added] down Smith Street towards St. Alphonsus Street."

Geagan gave up trying to get the Thunderbird story from Eddie. Could Eddie identify Ernest Winbush as his assailant? Had Eddie already fired at Bowden when Winbush fired? Was Winbush in or out of the Thunderbird when he fired? Did Eddie fire back at Winbush? Did Eddie see how the Thunderbird left the scene? None of these questions were asked or answered.

In concluding the interview, Geagan had Eddie concede that it was, as Eddie put it, "a possibility" that the number he had checked during the stakeout was not the number on Bowden's car. Geagan obviously believed the turret man's notes and report rather than Eddie. "You checked 4F•6368 [not Bowden's number]," he told Eddie.

Geagan called Denny back into the room after Eddie left. He briefly went over Denny's observations of the Thunderbird in more detail. "The T-Bird came up Parker Street and turned right on Smith Street," Geagan began. "You were parked here on Gurney and Parker and you observe it come down here to Alton Court and park beside the Buick?"

"Yes," said Denny.

"Was it parked beside the Buick in the middle of the street," Geagan asked, "or did it park over here at the curbing?"

"I believe it parked in the middle of the street," Denny answered. "It didn't park. It stopped in the middle of the street next to the Buick."

"Did the T-Bird move away before the Buick pulled out to back up?"

"I believe they moved about the same time."

"Which way did the T-Bird go then?"

Denny said that it went forward. Geagan suggested that it may have gone "in the driveway here on the side of the school." Denny said nothing.

"You don't know if it went up the driveway or not," said Geagan.

"No," Denny replied.

"All you know is it didn't go to Smith and St. Alphonsus."

Denny said he "was told that it didn't come out the end of this street by Patrolman Dwyer."

"All right," said Geagan. "Then the Buick backed up to about here, Huban Court, where the action happened?"

"Yes."

Geagan said, "There was cars parked on the left side and cars parked on the right side. How many cars could go down the street at the same time, side by side?"

"I think only one car," Denny replied.

"At any time that you saw the T-Bird, did you see a gun pointed out the window of the T-Bird?" Geagan asked.

"No, I didn't," Denny answered.

"O.K.," said Geagan. "That's all. Thank you."

On Saturday morning John Geagan tried to arrange an interview of Jessina Stokes. He telephoned the Stokes apartment from his own house. He was rebuffed, and his first duty on the following Monday morning was to type a report of what happened:

Sergeant Geagan spoke with Mrs. Stokes and she stated that her daughter, Jessina, did see the incident. She then refused the sergeant permission to speak to the girl because she was too nervous and every time that it is mentioned the girl gets very upset. When asked by the sergeant if she, Mrs. Stokes, would tell him what her daughter told her, Mrs. Stokes declined, stating that she would not do so without the permission of Mrs. James Bowden's attorney.

Mrs. Stokes is the sister of the deceased James Bowden.

Iris Stokes had called Pat immediately after Geagan made his request. Pat shared her sister-in-law's instinct not to cooperate with the police without the advice of a lawyer. "I just felt that if we were gonna be suing the cops," says Pat, "then we shouldn't be talking to them."

She had already told Iris about her meeting with Homans, and both women thought it might be only a matter of days before he was on the case.

Hours later, Iris called back to tell Pat that she had just heard over the radio that Edelin had been found guilty of manslaughter. Sunday morning after church, Pat spread the *Globe* out on the dining room table and read its coverage of the Edelin trial. There wasn't a negative word about Homans in any of the stories, but by the time Pat finished reading, she had decided not to call him for the office meeting he had suggested. Her confidence in Homans was gone.

On Monday, Pat started looking for another lawyer. She called friends for more leads. A man who had grown up with the Bowden brothers suggested that she try a lawyer who had once defended some distant cousin of his who had been accused of bank robbery.

"He told me his cousin was found guilty," Pat recalls, "but the lawyer took the case all the way to the Supreme Court and got him out of jail by proving the FBI covered up something in court. I said, 'Well, anyone who can prove the FBI was covering up should be able to prove the Boston Police are liars.' When he told me the lawyer's name was O'Donnell, Lawrence O'Donnell, I said, 'It sounds Irish.' I was sort of surprised at that." Surprised that a Boston Irish lawyer would have a black client.

Pat found the listing *O'Donnell Lawrence F lwyr* in the telephone book and dialed the number. A cordial, though demanding, secretary screened the call, asking Pat about as many questions as some lawyers had, then left her on hold for a few minutes. The secretary came back on the line only to say she would try to call her back before the end of the day. Pat busied herself with housework while waiting for the call. A few hours later, the secretary called back and offered a Friday afternoon appointment. "That would be fine," said Pat. "I'll bring a copy of that *Phoenix* article I told you about."

"You don't have to," replied the secretary. "Mr. O'Donnell just read it."

The day before she was scheduled to meet my father, Pat found another downtown lawyer willing to handle her case. He was a well-known civil rights specialist and a champion of liberal causes. When Pat finished telling him her story, he asked what her financial condition was.

"I told him James took home a hundred and ten dollars a week," she recalls. "We had over two thousand dollars in savings, but I spent that on the funeral. I really didn't have anything then. I told him I had some money on the way, though. James had a ten-thousand-dollar life insurance policy. It was supposed to pay double on accidental death, but the company already told me they wouldn't count this as an accident 'cause he got killed committing a crime. They said I'd get ten thousand in a few weeks, and that's what I told the lawyer." He told her that he would take the case but she would have to cover the expenses, which he estimated could easily amount to $10,000. If she gave him the insurance money as a retainer, he said, he could get the case started. If he won, he would take 50 percent of the winnings as a fee. Pat said she would think about it.

On the subway ride and the walk home through forty-degree

sunlight that was melting the last traces of snow, she considered the proposition. She wasn't surprised. Some lawyers had told her that if anyone took the case, she should expect to be asked to cover expenses and offered a fifty-fifty contingency fee. The standard lawyer's contingency fee is a third of the amount recovered, but on tough cases one half is not uncommon. As one lawyer had explained: If she won, her lawyer would get half the jury award for doing the impossible; and if she lost, the lawyer would get nothing for trying the impossible. She decided to wait and talk to O'Donnell, then maybe have another talk with Homans.

She heard the phone ringing as she turned her front-door key. She knew that her mother, who was babysitting that day as she had been every other day during her search for counsel, would answer it. At the end of the hall that runs all the way from the front door to the kitchen she saw her mother holding the wall phone with one hand over the mouthpiece. "It's for you," she called. "It's Sergeant Geagan again. Should I tell him you're not home?" Pat sighed, shook her head, and took the phone. A few minutes later, Geagan typed this report:

On Thursday, February 20, 1975, at 12:35 P.M., Sergeant Geagan again contacted Mrs. Bowden and asked for the name of her attorney at which time she stated that she didn't have an attorney and she concluded the conversation by saying, "Listen, I have nothing to say to the Boston Police Department so don't call here again." She then hung up.

Pat thinks that is an accurate summary of the call, but has this to add: "When I told him I didn't have a lawyer, I felt terrible. It felt like I was saying 'Don't worry 'bout me causing you guys any trouble. I'm a nobody. I can't even get a damn lawyer! . . . I was crying when I hung up that phone."

That same day, Doctor Kenneth Edelin was sentenced to one year of probation. In criminal trials, with the overwhelming majority of verdicts being guilty (in Massachusetts more than 90 percent), much of the fight is really over what sentence the defendant will get. The defense goes into many trials not so much with the hope of a not-guilty verdict—though that dream, no matter how impossible, eventually captures the imagination—but rather with the hope of convincing the judge that what the defendant did wasn't as bad as the prosecution claims, and that he deserves a softer sentence than the prosecutor has offered as a plea bargain. Even with such a diluted definition of victory, the defense usually loses. So, to criminal lawyers—the weathered ones who have sat on hardwood courthouse benches discussing the timetable of an appeal (which they know will be futile) with grieving families who have just watched their breadwinner being sentenced to "a period of incarceration not less than X years and not more than Y years" and led away in handcuffs—probation is almost always a win. "He was facing five to ten," they'll tell you, citing the maximum sentence for the crime. Then they'll add proudly, "and I walked him out of the building."

One day I watched my father get up and beg for a suspended sentence or probation after a jury had floored him with a guilty verdict in a trial he had convinced himself he could win outright. The D.A. demanded five to eight in Walpole, the state's meanest pen. The judge gave five years' probation. The D.A. congratulated my father on the win. When the story hit the newspapers, congratulatory calls poured into the O'Donnell switchboard from other defense lawyers. So it was now for Bill Homans. My father and the gang called in their congratulations on the Edelin win. And they would call back a year later when Homans won an acquittal for Edelin in an appeal to the state supreme court. But the public had thought Homans was a loser when Edelin was convicted, and so had Pat Bowden.

Homans has told me that he would have taken the Bowden case if Pat had done as he suggested and called his office for an appointment that week. Bill Homans would have been a good man for the Bowden case. But Pat's naïve notion that Homans was a loser led her to my father.

Pat's wait in the plush State Street lobby was long but comfortable. The large crushed-velvet armchair soothed her nervousness and impatience better than the hard plastic chairs she had come to expect in lawyers' waiting rooms. Forty-five minutes passed before one of the three secretaries she had been watching through a glass partition ushered her through French doors, into a short, narrow corridor, and around a corner to a smaller lobby. "This is Mr. O'Donnell's office," the secretary said, pointing to a closed door. "You can take a seat here, and he'll be with you in a minute."

The secretary disappeared around the corner. Pat slipped into one of the two wooden armchairs facing a pale-blue wall crammed with a collection of wood-based laminated and framed certificates. In the middle of each were the words *Lawrence Francis O'Donnell, Esquire.* She leaned forward to read the fine print on the gold-sealed documents. One was a law school diploma, class of 1950. Four were citations: the Suffolk Law School Student Bar Association's Outstanding Alumni award, one from the National College of Criminal Defense Lawyers and Public Defenders, another from American Trial Lawyers, and a small one that Pat did not notice from the Massachusetts Chiefs of Police Association. The rest were certificates of permission to practice law in state and federal courts, the Tax Court of the United States, and the United States Court of Appeals. Hanging appropriately above the three rows of plaques was the largest and rarest. Grandly scrolled across the top of the parchment were the words *Supreme Court of the United States of America.* Pat was reading this one when the door opened behind her.

"Mrs. Bowden."

She turned to see a dark-suited, tall, trim, ruddy-faced man with graying black hair who looked considerably younger than his fifty-four years. He was reaching out to shake her hand and smiling politely. She shyly replied, "Hello." He apologized for the long wait and invited her into his office. Once inside and seated, she was no less uneasy. The leather couch and chairs, the Oriental rug, the massive oak desk, the five hand-carved models of famous sailing ships, the floor-to-ceiling bookshelves holding exactly one thousand law books, the large draped windows, and the framed newspaper and TV sketches and paintings of courtroom scenes all made it an imposing room. The single familiar article she spotted was an 8 × 11 photograph of President John F. Kennedy. The same picture hung in the Bowden kitchen. As she nervously began talking, he took notes on a yellow legal pad. It was the first time she saw a lawyer bother to take notes while speaking with her and the first time she was questioned so closely, beginning with seemingly irrelevant details such as the date of her marriage; her children's full names and birthdates; her husband's and her own birthdates, educational backgrounds, and work experience.

He was sizing her up. He wanted to know if there was anything about this woman that he didn't like, that he would find troublesome in a client. If she was okay and if he couldn't find anything that would alter what the *Phoenix* had led him to believe, he was going to take the case. He sat on the edge of his high-backed swivel chair and leaned over his desk to write:

Patricia and James born in Boston
Patricia graduated Girls High 1966
James finished 11th grade Boys Trade
Patricia met James 1969 at City Hospital
while training for 2 weeks as nurse's aid.
James working there since she met him till
death.
Housekeeping Department.
He had good friends there.
Married in Boston Jan. 23, 1970.
First and only marriage for both.
Ideal marriage.
Eurina Carim Bowden born 1970.
Jamil Sekou Bowden born 1974.
When first married James worked 2 jobs.
Patricia also held 2 jobs. They started
off with nothing.

James grossed $151 per week.
Rent only $70—Patricia's mother owns house.
Car payments $140 per month—already
paid 6 months ahead thru July.
Car in custody of BPD
Spent savings on funeral
Patricia to receive $10,000 life insurance.
James visited mother in housing project
almost every day. Left home to visit mother
1/29/75 about 5:30 or 6PM
Told story to John Cullen of Globe
Talked to Capt. MacDonald 1/29/75 & Capt
said husband was in robbery
Sgt. Geagan BPD been calling

He glanced at his copy of O'Brian's article. Pat noticed there was heavy underlining in every paragraph and notes in the margins. He asked her what she could add to O'Brian's story. "A couple of things," said Pat. "First of all, I know he wasn't in the robbery because he would never do that and a man he worked with told me he was with him at the hospital at the time. The other thing is my niece, Jessina Stokes, did see the shooting like the article says. She saw the two guys run up to the car and start firing."

"Why do you suppose he was going down the street in reverse?" he asked.

"Because he was close to Parker, and it was faster than going up to St. Alphonsus and back down Tremont to our house. And it saved him a red light on Tremont. I saw him do that before—back down the one-way."

"What's the name of the fellow who worked with your husband that day?"

"Adolph Grant," she replied. "He was at the funeral."

"Okay." He wrote down the name.

"Oh, and, uh," Pat said with a grimace, "they shot him in the back. His brother saw the bullet holes when he was at the hospital. They definitely shot him in the back."

"Okay," he said without a trace of surprise. Then, seeing that Pat had nothing to add, he put down his pen, leaned back, fixed his eyes on her, and said approvingly, "You were right not to talk to Geagan." He paused and went on matter-of-factly: "All he wants to do is twist what you or Jessina say into something that fits the official version. Next time he calls, tell him I'm representing you, then hang up on him, and forget about him. He won't call you back. I'll take care of that. I'll have to hear Jessina's story soon. Can you bring her in here next week?" Pat nodded as he continued in the same breath: "Good. What we'll do is sue them for what's called wrongful death. We'll file suit in federal court so we can make it a civil rights and wrongful death complaint. Suing in federal court is faster than in state court, but it'll still take a few years to get a trial. In the meantime, we'll be doing our own investigation of the whole thing."

He reached to his right for the telephone intercom button. Pat was glad his eyes were off her. She wanted to hear it all again. She wanted to say, "That was too fast. This hunt can't end so suddenly and easily. Let's go over that again." Instead she blurted, "How much will it cost?"

"We'll do this on a contingent fee," he replied, holding the phone to his ear. "If we win or reach a settlement, I'll take a third."

"What about expenses?" she asked.

He started speaking legalese into the phone. It seemed he was talking to his secretary. When he put down the phone, he said in the oh-it's-nothing manner of someone paying for a friend's lunch, "I'll cover expenses."

For the next few minutes he discussed his collection of ship models, proudly pointing out the individual planking and functional rigging on the U.S.S. *Constitution* and the *Flying Cloud.* He seemed oblivious to the possibility that after a discussion of her husband's last day alive, a recently widowed young woman—a woman who had lost her husband in a sudden explosion of gunpowder; a woman who was raised in a decent, hardworking, God-fearing family and now faced the indignity of reports that her husband died in disgraceful circumstances; a mother of two small children who would have to grow up saying "He died" every time a new friend innocently asked about their father—might not be fascinated by models of famous sailing vessels. In fact, he didn't expect her to be. He lost himself in the rigging and the planking while he waited for his secretary to type a contingent-fee agreement, because he was desperate to get his mind away from the thoughts that had seized him throughout that first hour with Patricia Bowden.

"What do you think I was thinking about that day?" he said, with a forced smile, to my question years later. He turned and gazed out his office window. I had never before heard him answer a question with a question. To reporters who had inquired about this, he had always said, "I was thinking that it was my duty as a lawyer to take this case." I'm sure that lawyerly duty was one of his motivations in taking the case, but I always believed that something else must have haunted him that day—because the similarities are so striking. Presently I said, "Your father."

He turned back to me and said, "Yeah." His eyes, the most expressive I know, spoke of a long-held sadness. Though he had never discussed it with any of his children, we all knew about his father's death. We put the facts together from bits of information collected over the years, and my mother confirmed the basics. He knew we knew, of course.

It happened in 1932, when my father was eleven and Roxbury was still an Irish ghetto. He lived in a tenement there with his parents, two brothers, and baby sister. One night after dinner, his father, a bank guard and former champion amateur boxer, pulled his gun out and began mumbling something about killing himself. Before anyone else could react, thirteen-year-old Patrick O'Donnell, Jr., grabbed the gun from his father's shaky hand and ran out of the apartment, intending to throw it away. Patrick Sr. chased him. They ran across the street into Franklin Park. My father and his other brother ran after Patrick Sr., crying all the way and begging him to stop. Patrick Jr. stumbled over a rock and dropped the gun. Patrick Sr. picked it up and sprinted past him. The three boys kept chasing their father and yelling pleas to stop.

They lost sight of him in the darkness. Suddenly there was an odd noise. Seconds later they saw their father slumped against a tree trunk. He had put the gun in his mouth and pulled the trigger. The suicide got routine treatment in the newspapers. I've heard that my grandmother couldn't stop crying for a week. And the O'Donnells became a transient welfare family, moving every year or so from one three-decker to another in and around Roxbury.

"I know something about what it's like for a mother to be left alone with children," he told me as he turned to the window again. "So, I couldn't have looked at Patricia Bowden and said, 'Sorry, I can't help you.' Not me. I didn't feel like I even had a choice about taking the case. . . . I wasn't thinking much like a lawyer that day."

A secretary delivered duplicates of a contingent-fee agreement, one to be kept by the O'Donnells and the other to be kept by Pat. My father signed them and handed his thick fountain pen to Pat. She read both pieces of paper, then carefully signed "Patricia Ann Bowden" at the bottom of each.

At home an hour later, Pat put the contingent-fee agreement in a drawer of the small desk in her living room and began to wonder whether she had signed on with the right lawyer. "After a while," she told me, "I decided to stop worrying about it and trust in God that my prayers were answered."

CHAPTER 7

The Bowden file—Lawrence O'Donnell's 4,103rd case file—was on Michael O'Donnell's desk Monday morning. It contained the contingent-fee agreement, the *Phoenix,* six yellow pages of notes, and a memo from LO'D telling MO'D to "work up a civil rights—wrongful death complaint."

Michael read O'Brian's article and underlined something his boss seemed to have overlooked. It was one sentence, just an aside, about Ernest Winbush, "the owner of the Thunderbird," being arrested the night after the shooting "and held on a vague assault charge." Such was the quality of the information that O'Brian had picked up at Headquarters. It was unclear to Michael whether the Winbush arrest was at all related to what happened on Smith Street.

He called a clerk he knew at the Roxbury District Court and found out what the charges were against Winbush; he also learned that his case was scheduled for a probable-cause hearing—a pretrial hearing to determine what caused the arrest—on March 13, and that he was being represented by the Roxbury Defenders Committee, a nonprofit, federally funded corporation that provides counsel for indigent defendants in the Roxbury Court. Next he called Roxbury Defenders and was connected to Patricia Gunn, the young lawyer assigned to the Winbush case. She told him that it was scheduled for a probable-cause hearing but would say nothing else about the case. Michael wasn't surprised. Criminal lawyers don't freely discuss their pending cases, especially one like Winbush's in which the defendant is facing a possible fifteen years. He told her that he could wait until the 13th to see for himself how the evidence unfolded at the hearing. Gunn said she could save him a trip to the courthouse by sending him a transcript. Michael gladly accepted the offer and scratched the hearing off his jammed appointment calendar. Then he took a fresh legal pad into the small law library beside his office.

Still in his first year of working for his father, Michael had never written a complaint. In the past, the paperwork of civil cases had been done by a succession of lawyers O'Donnell had employed before Michael joined the firm. He expected the research and writing to take as long as three or four days. It took four weeks.

A complaint is the cornerstone of a lawsuit. It states in general terms the defendant's alleged offense against the plaintiff, cites both the law allegedly violated and the law that establishes the court's jurisdiction over the case, and asks for "relief" of some sort—usually money. For civil litigation specialists—divorce lawyers, for example—drawing a complaint seldom involves more than changing the names on complaints they've filed in similar cases. But with no civil-rights or wrongful-death complaints in the O'Donnell file room, Michael had to build the Bowden complaint from the ground up.

Most lawyers avoid such ventures into unknown legal territory by developing a specialty and never straying from it. Lawrence O'Donnell, Esq., sees specialization as a retreat from the kind of unbounded field of battle that he finds irresistible. He actually seems to fear specialization as something that can sneak up and rob a trial lawyer of his essence. With a straight face he once told me, "As soon as you start ruling out going to the Tax Court, or the Land Court, or a criminal proceeding, or appeals courts, or federal court, you're losing what it takes to stand up in a courtroom. And you know what's the first thing you lose?" Pause. "The gall to do it." Michael has a rich enough inheritance of gall that he was not a bit reluctant to step into a new area of law. He soon had tall stacks of law books on the oval mahogany library table and was lost in the study of wrongful death law,* civil rights law, and the 922-page Federal Rules of Civil Procedure, a soon-to-be tattered paperback that he would keep in easy reach for every minute of work on the Bowden case.

On Wednesday, February 26, 1975, two days after Michael's work began, the last Internal Affairs interview took place. John Geagan had scheduled it and was present, but the principal interviewer was Deputy Superintendent Francis Schroeder of Staff Inspection. The interviewee was TPF Sergeant Harry Byrne. "Geagan couldn't do this one," Schroeder told me, "because we never did sergeant-to-sergeant interviews. We always had a higher-ranking officer take over when a sergeant had to be interviewed." Schroeder himself was a last-minute substitute for Internal Affairs Deputy Superintendent John Barry, who called in sick that day. He was the logical fill-in for Barry because he had previously put in two years in Internal Affairs.

Francis "Barney" Schroeder, a stocky, balding man, is off the force now. In 1978, he retired to his gray-shingled home in Brighton, Denny McKenna's neighborhood, where he is taking it slow in deference to a heart condition that he developed toward the end of his thirty-two-year career. Nothing in his manner— thoughtful, polite, soft-spoken—suggests his former line of work or position of power in it. As a twenty-nine-year veteran of the force, he brought a web of personal and professional associations, friendships, and memories to the Bowden investigation that could have made him solidly prejudiced in favor of Eddie, Denny, the TPF, and especially cops using deadly force against armed robbery suspects.

In 1962, Barney Schroeder had become the first sergeant as-

---

* "Wrongful death" is a death caused by someone's negligence or recklessness. For example, fatal airline crashes always lead to wrongful death suits which claim the crash was the result of the airline's negligent maintenance or reckless operation of the plane. What is wrongful death in civil law can be, but is not necessarily, manslaughter or murder in criminal law.

signed to the TPF. Subsequently he was a lecturer at the Police Academy for sixteen years. There he watched Eddie and Denny take their initial training and grew confident that they would be "good policemen." He knew Denny long before they met as teacher and student at the Academy; they were neighbors. Schroeder was a longtime friend of Denny's father and mother. And Schroeder's two brothers, whom he had persuaded to join the force, were both shot and killed—Walter in 1970 and John in 1973—when they tried to stop armed robberies in progress. "It didn't make me go for my gun any quicker," says Schroeder, who never fired it outside the target range. Nor did it make him a prejudiced questioner of Harry Byrne. Barney Schroeder hated Internal Affairs interviews: "It's a tough thing to investigate police officers. Anybody who volunteers for Internal Affairs has to be a nut." But he asked good questions.

He scanned the TPF, Homicide, and Internal Affairs reports and asked Geagan a few questions before inviting Byrne to join them in his Headquarters office. Geagan turned on the tape recorder and Schroeder made an opening statement to clarify for the record that Byrne was not suspected of any wrongdoing but was being formally interviewed only to save him from writing a report on what his own investigation of his men's actions had revealed. Then Schroeder went directly to something about the police story that bothered him and had been left unexplained— Ernest Winbush's involvement. He wound up spending the entire interview on that subject.

"What did [Holland and McKenna] say about this Thunderbird that had pulled into Smith Street and then took off?" he asked.

"They said the car went down Smith Street," Byrne replied flatly.

"They gave you the registration of this Thunderbird?"

"Yes, they did, sir."

"From the best of my knowledge in reading all their reports," said Schroeder, "neither Patrolman Holland nor Patrolman McKenna nor anyone else at the time wrote down this T-Bird registration, and yet they gave you the registration of the Thunderbird?"

Byrne wavered. "I believe they did, to the best of my recollection. . . . I know that the number was given to me, and it had already been checked."

Schroeder tried what he thought would be an easier question: "Why were they checking on the Thunderbird?"

"Because Bowden stepped out of that car," Byrne answered.

"Bowden stepped out of this car," echoed Schroeder, looking for something more.

"And got into the Buick," Byrne continued, "and the Thunderbird then sped away."

"The Thunderbird then took off?"

"Yes, sir."

"As a result of this," said Schroeder incredulously, "they arrested this fellow Winbush about ten-forty at night for assault and battery by means of a dangerous weapon—to wit, a shotgun, if I recall it correctly, or some kind of gun. Why did they arrest Winbush? On what information? What evidence did they arrest him on?"

"They arrested him on the information of the car and the description," said Byrne, the man who had ordered the arrest.

"The information on what car—the Thunderbird?"

"The Thunderbird," affirmed Byrne. "And then he was brought to District Two and he was identified by Patrolman Holland, to the best of my recollection, as the operator of that car."

"And the assault and battery was in reference to a shotgun that Holland or McKenna said they saw in this particular car?"

"That I don't know," said Byrne, to Schroeder's frowning surprise. "I know that Holland said in his report he saw the silhouette of a gun."

"That was in the Buick," Geagan interjected.

"In the Buick," Byrne agreed.

"But you're not sure who saw the shotgun in the T-Bird or how they saw the shotgun," Schroeder declared.

"Somewhere along the line," said Byrne, "I think our turret broadcast that information, that a shotgun was used in the holdup in Cambridge. That's the only thing I know about a shotgun."

"Now, in O'Connor's report," Schroeder continued, "it says that he appeared in court with Holland before Judge McKenney [the morning after the shooting]. This is when they charged Winbush with assault with a dangerous weapon, and they also charged him with assault with intent to murder. Do you know what this assault with intent to murder [was] comprised of, by any means? If Holland ever told you why he was putting this charge against him?"

"No," replied Byrne. "Holland hasn't been back to work since."

"What's he, out sick?"

"As a result of that injury," said Byrne.

"As a result of the injury he received when the car backed up and, it's alleged, twice into him?" asked Schroeder, now overtly skeptical.

"Yes, sir."

"Was he hospitalized?"

"No, I don't think he was hospitalized, but I know he was sent home on crutches."

"Was he treated at any hospital that night?"

"I know he went to the Carney."

"Did we take him in one of our vehicles?"

"Yes, sir."

Schroeder turned to Geagan, asking, "Do we have the report of the hospital?"

Geagan said they did not, then tried his own hand with Byrne. "Harry," said Geagan, "you don't know anything about the assault on Holland?"

"Other than what the report says, no, sir."

"The report doesn't say anything about an assault on Holland except by the Buick," said Geagan. Then he asked, "Do you know why Winbush was arrested—on what grounds he was arrested?"

"It seems to me," Byrne haltingly replied, "now I could be mistaken, but, uh, to the best of my recollection it seems that, uh, somebody said something about a shotgun being stuck out a window, but I don't know. It doesn't seem to, uh—"

Geagan cut Byrne off, saying, "We agree."

Schroeder explained to Byrne what bothered him about the Winbush arrest: "This is what we're trying to find out either from you or your investigation or from Sergeant McHale or some superior officer of the TPF: Did they make a full investigation as to why Winbush was arrested? On what evidence he was arrested or what probable cause, I should say. What caused them to arrest Winbush? This seems to be a very important part of the investigation. . . . It seems to me that everything took place at once, and yet they could remember the Thunderbird registration number, and yet they didn't write it down, and this is part of our investigation as to how they could remember that number so vividly. When did they check this number up at Operations? When did they find out who owned that? Who did they pass the information on to? And what other information did they have to have probable cause to arrest this Winbush for what we *did* arrest him for: assault and battery by means of a dangerous weapon—to wit, a shotgun—and assault to commit murder? Can you understand what we're driving at? No one made a complete investigation anywhere to find out from Holland and McKenna where this information came from, how they arrived at this information, who did they give it to, to have probable cause to arrest Winbush. And this is what we're trying to find out."

Byrne just said, "I see."

Schroeder leaned on him. "They go down there [to Winbush's address] and some four hours later they make the arrest of Winbush on these two charges, and the information to substantiate these charges is what we're trying to find out."

Byrne said nothing.

Schroeder says he saw no point in continuing, since Byrne and Geagan, who'd had exactly four weeks to investigate, seemed to know so little. This wasn't Schroeder's investigation, and he didn't want it to be. He told me: "I expected Geagan and Barry [the head of Internal Affairs] to follow through with Harry on the unanswered questions."

In closing, he asked, "No shotgun was found to substantiate

the charges in the courtroom when we say 'A and B by means of a shotgun'?"

"No shotgun was found," said Byrne.

"So it's going on oral evidence alone, on Holland or McKenna's part?"

"Yes, sir."

"Okay, Sergeant, thank you very much," said Schroeder.

So ended the Internal Affairs interviews.

Michael was finding nothing encouraging in his research. He couldn't find a single example of a plaintiff winning a wrongful death case against police defendants who had intentionally shot and killed a person. The few wrongful death cases lost by police defendants involved only traffic accidents with patrol cars. More troubling to Michael was his discovery that there were no "deep pockets" on the other side.

In civil lawyers' parlance, the phrase *deep pockets* means an ability to pay. A doctor defendant in a medical malpractice case has deep pockets, not so much because of his personal income or wealth as because he carries a multimillion-dollar malpractice insurance policy which will pay any judgment against him. Similarly, defendants in automobile accident cases usually have the deep pockets of an insurance company behind them. In other cases a defendant may have the deep pockets of his employer *beside* him. If a bank guard, for example, shot and killed an innocent bystander in a robbery, the bystander's family would sue the guard and the bank. The plaintiffs would go after the bank because an employer is usually responsible for the on-the-job actions of its employees and because the bank has deeper pockets than the guard. Government employers, however, are not so strictly responsible for their employees' conduct. Cities and towns are often immune from lawsuits arising out of their employees' actions. The doctrine of municipal immunity, to use the textbook term, originated in English Common Law, which forbade citizens to sue the crown, back when all governmental entities were considered arms of the monarchy. Boston's municipal immunity meant that Michael could not write the city into the complaint as a defendant, and the hundreds of millions in the municipal treasury were out of reach.

Since Holland and McKenna were to be the only defendants and assuming that the Bowdens were to become the first plaintiffs ever to win such a case, Michael reckoned that a jury would award them a couple of hundred thousand or more, only about $30,000 of which would be easily collectible. (He figured that Holland and McKenna had some money put away. TPF men were making more than $25,000 in overtime alone that year.) Collecting what more they had would require a long, involved pursuit and liquidation of the two cops' assets. As Michael figured it, winning might do little more than cover out-of-pocket expenses.

He laid out the bad news for his father when he handed him a first draft of the complaint. What Michael held back during the brief chat was his belief that Pat Bowden never should have been signed on as a client. Then thirty-one, and still feeling more like a son than the partner he already was, Michael wasn't yet ready to openly disagree with his father.

"I couldn't go in to the old man," he told me later, "and say, 'You never shoulda taken this Bowden thing. Let's drop it.' But I did try to make him see how hopeless it was. I didn't play up the fact that nobody had ever won one of these things, because I knew he'd say, 'That's because I've never tried one'—which he did say. I kept going over the collection problem, no deep pockets. He said, 'If we get a judgment against those cops, the city will have to pay it.' I kept telling him that we couldn't hook the city into the case, but he thought the city would still have to come forward and pay in the end out of some sort of, you know, moral obligation." Michael spoke the last two words as if they were the punch line of a joke. He clearly thought they didn't belong in lawyers' conversation. He's never seen them in a law book.

They are a complementary pair, this father-and-son team. Oddly, it is the son who brings to his work the cool detachment you would expect of a seasoned professional and who sometimes finds himself trying to fasten a leash on the father for fear that he will do something rash. Where the father is instinctive, the son is objective. Where the father is passionate, the son is reserved. Where the father is impulsive, the son deliberates. Where the father boasts, the son is modest. Where the father is sentimental, the son is unmoved. The father's desk is always messy and cluttered with useless items—like paperweights and empty vases—received as gifts. The son's desk, the identical twin of his father's huge hunk of oak, is always neat and has nothing on it or in it that is not related to his job. The father usually keeps irregular office hours. The son usually works nine to five. At the core of their professional relationship is a mutual respect. When they team up on a case, the son is the steady director and the father is the mercurial star. Each is invaluable to the other.

On the morning of March 13, 1975, Philip Tracy, a stern judge in his late fifties who had been assigned to the Roxbury District Court for seventeen years, marched into his courtroom at the stroke of ten. Springing to their feet at a court officer's growled "All rise" command were Thomas Douzaine, a young assistant district attorney at the prosecution table; Patricia Gunn at the defense table; Ernest Winbush and his wife in the front row of benches; three people who were going to testify for Winbush one row behind him; Harry Byrne, Eddie Holland, Denny McKenna, Bill Dwyer, Mark Molloy, and James O'Connor across the center aisle; and together in the back row, Dave O'Brian and John Geagan. The probable cause, if any, for first arresting and now prosecuting Winbush was to be determined.

A probable-cause hearing resembles a trial in as much as witnesses testify, exhibits are produced, and lawyers argue. It is, however, only a prelude to a trial. Judge Tracy's options at the conclusion of Winbush's hearing would be either to find no probable cause and throw the case out of court, or to find probable cause and send the case downtown to Superior Court for indictment and trial. Felonies, such as assault with intent to murder, could not go to trial at the lowly district-court level.

O'Brian and Geagan chatted as the court clerk read the charges against Winbush. O'Brian had liked Geagan when they met for the Internal Affairs interview. Now Geagan's friendly manner was a welcome relief for O'Brian, who minutes earlier had been listening to the angry complaints of Denny McKenna and Billy Dwyer. They had approached him in the hall to tell him what they thought of his shooting story and a follow-up article he had written a week later.

"Billy Dwyer was the most upset," O'Brian recalls. "The thing that really bothered Dwyer the most was my quoting him about putting on a good show. He didn't deny the quote. He said he had gotten shit about it from other cops because it made it look like he was just joking around and having a good time after the shooting and that he wasn't concerned with the loss of life.

"Dwyer kept saying I didn't know anything about police procedure, so who am I to be speculating about what happened. He thought it was terribly unfair to imply that the gun on the street could have been planted." In his second article O'Brian had written, "A cynic might suspect this gun to be a police plant, but there is no evidence to warrant such a conclusion." He had followed that with this statement (which had previously appeared in *The Village Voice*) by former New York City patrolman Frank Serpico: "Some cops carry an extra 'clean' gun, so if he kills a guy, and the guy didn't have a gun, he can place it in the guy's hand; then the killing was justifiable."

Denny implied that O'Brian's articles contained inaccuracies, but when O'Brian asked for specifics, Denny only mentioned that the reporter had underestimated his age. He told O'Brian that he would like to talk to him some time about what happened on Smith Street. "I said I'd like to do that," O'Brian remembers, "and that's the way we left it." They have never again spoken to each other.

Eddie Holland was the first witness called by Assistant District Attorney Douzaine. Eddie testified that as Bowden was trying to hit him with the Buick, the Thunderbird backed into the action.

The prosecutor then used only six questions and answers to try to establish probable cause:

"Would you tell the court what you saw when you looked over to the T-Bird?"

"I observed a man outside of the passenger side with a, uh, firearm in hand pointed in the direction, my direction there. I observed a flash, a crack, and, uh, I would say that he fired. He fired at my direction."

"And at this time now, can you identify the person that you say stepped out of the T-Bird and held the object when you saw the, uh, when you heard the crack and saw the flash?"

Patricia Gunn had instructed her client to stand politely when Eddie identified him, so the judge would be able to see him. The judge would appreciate it, she had said. Winbush sat on the edge of the bench waiting for Eddie to point a finger at him.

"Well, if I was to identify Mr., uh, Winbush, uh," Eddie said, shifting uncomfortably, "I could not be morally certain that it is he. I did get a good glimpse of the driver, and, uh, I know Mr. Winbush was not driving that vehicle."

"You got a look at the driver of the Thunderbird?" the district attorney asked.

"I got a perfect look at him," Eddie replied. "I'd know him ten years from now."

"It wasn't that man that you say was standing outside the T-bird when you saw the flash and heard the crack?"

"No, sir, it wasn't the operator of the vehicle."

"It wasn't the man that got into the Buick and backed it down Smith Street?"

"No, sir."

"Would you tell the court how many men were in the T-Bird when you saw it round the corner of Parker onto Smith Street?" Douzaine asked.

"I observed three people in it," Eddie replied.

"Thank you, Officer," said Douzaine.

Given Eddie's reluctance to identify Winbush, the prosecution's case rested on a process of elimination: If Winbush was not the driver of the Thunderbird, and if he wasn't the man who went from the Thunderbird to the Buick, then he must have been the man "outside of the passenger side" of the Thunderbird with the shotgun.

For Patricia Gunn, Eddie's failure to identify Winbush—after having identified him when he was brought into District 2 and when he was arraigned—was a welcome surprise. She stressed two points in her cross-examination.

The first was what she called a "glaring omission" in Sergeant McHale's official version. (The McHale report was the only one that Gunn had been able to get from the police.) She pointed out that the report "made no mention whatsoever of any shotgun," and asked Eddie: "Will you please tell this court when you decided that there should be a shotgun involved in this incident?"

Eddie answered slowly: "Uh, I, I put it over the air, 'There's a shotgun or a rifle.' I didn't know what, uh, which it was at the time, and uh—"

"And consequently you decided to delete it?" Gunn interrupted.

"I still, I still, uh, maintain it could be either one. I, I still don't know what it was," said Eddie.

"Well, Officer, perhaps I'm hard to understand," said Gunn, as if talking to a child. "For my benefit and the court's benefit, could you please explain why no mention whatsoever was made of any firearm in connection with the Thunderbird?"

Eddie said, "I . . . I don't know."

Gunn's other point of emphasis was Eddie's newly discovered lack of moral certainty in his identification of Winbush. "All right," she said, "could you please tell us what Mr. Winbush's arrest was based on, Officer?"

"Based on, uh, my allegations here that he fired a shot at me," he replied.

"Didn't you state in your earlier testimony that you couldn't describe the person who fired at you?" she asked.

"I could not, no, not morally," said Eddie.

"And the only reason he was arrested was because he drove a Thunderbird. Is that not true?"

"That is, uh, I would assume. I didn't make the arrest."

In Eddie's report he had said without equivocation that the Thunderbird made a left turn before the Tobin School after the shooting. In Gunn's cross-examination Eddie abandoned that description of the Thunderbird's exit. Instead, he said, "After I got knocked down, I didn't see the T-Bird after that. I assumed that it left."

Denny McKenna was the next prosecution witness. At the D.A.'s prompting, Denny delivered a long-winded recital of his story which didn't stray from his report but was congested with nonsensical cop talk, such as: "I stopped the police vehicle in which I was in and dismounted on the left-hand side of the police car"; and "I observed Patrolman Holland spinning and falling to the ground. I didn't see him fall to the ground; I observed him fall." Denny's testimony concerning the Thunderbird was simply that he "did not consciously see the Thunderbird" after the Buick began to back down Smith Street. Nor did he see or hear anyone fire a rifle or shotgun at his partner. When Douzaine finished with Denny, Geagan whispered his prediction of the judge's ruling to O'Brian: "No probable cause."

In Gunn's brief and actually unnecessary cross-examination, Denny showed a wisecracking sense of humor. In making a technical point for the judge, Gunn asked Denny who would have firsthand knowledge of what happened on Smith Street that night besides his partner and himself. She expected him to say no one would.

"At what point, ma'am?" he asked.

"At the point when Mr. James Bowden was shot and killed," said Gunn.

With a smirk Denny said, "James Bowden."

Shocked, Gunn said quietly, "Pardon me?"

"James Bowden," Denny repeated, still grinning.

Gunn recovered enough to say, "Well, he's no longer with us, so—"

"Well, uh—" Denny began.

"Excluding the dead," she continued, "what living person would have firsthand knowledge of this event?"

"I don't know of any."

"Besides you and Officer Holland?"

"That's correct."

After Denny, Mark Molloy took the stand to explain that he and Billy Dwyer were covering the opposite end of Smith Street and never saw the Thunderbird. This was Molloy's only purpose in testifying. But on cross-examination, he was not rock-solid. When Gunn asked him whether he saw the Thunderbird come out his end of Smith Street, Molloy answered, "No." Then, after a pause, he volunteered, "Not that I can recall, anyway." Under oath, an *I don't recall* is always safer than a definite yes or no.

Jim O'Connor, a tall, handsome TPF patrolman, was the fourth and final witness called by the prosecution. Douzaine asked O'Connor to relate a conversation he had with Winbush after arresting him. O'Connor testified: "I asked Mr. Winbush, after informing him of all his rights, whether or not he would say anything to me. He said sure. I asked him where he had been earlier in the evening. He said he had dinner with his family and left about six-thirty to go to a PTA meeting or some kind of school meeting at the school of one of his children, I believe. I asked him what route he took. He said he went by way of Smith Street and stopped [on Tremont Street] to purchase a dollar's worth of gasoline. I asked him if he had seen, or did anything unusual take place while he was on Smith Street. He said he didn't see anything unusual. I asked him if he had loaned his car to anyone that evening. No, he had not."

On cross, Patricia Gunn tried to show that Winbush's admission that he was on Smith Street was not incriminating. "Isn't [Winbush's address] in the same Mission Hill project area as Smith Street?" she asked O'Connor.

"As Smith Street, yes, ma'am," he replied.

"And isn't Smith Street a fairly well traveled route by occupants of the Mission Hill project area?" she asked.

"I don't know, dear," he said. It was an impersonal *dear*—the one post office clerks, gas station attendants, and the like use with female customers. Still in currency with Boston Irishmen—a group not known for feminist inclinations—it was not calculated condescension, just a reflex. It probably went unnoticed by everyone in the room except Gunn, and maybe O'Brian. She returned to her seat infuriated.

Douzaine then asked O'Connor about his search of Winbush and the Thunderbird. "Officer, you testified that you didn't find any shotgun."

"No, ma'am," O'Connor replied, quickly correcting it to "No, sir."

"Would you tell the court what you did find and where?"

"Yes, sir," said O'Connor. "When they had Mr. Winbush at the booking desk at District 2, I conducted, a, uh, conducted a more thorough search of his person than could be done on the street, and in his coat pocket found four thirty-eight-caliber rounds of ammunition."

Patricia Gunn objected: "It is immaterial and irrelevant, Your Honor. They are not shotgun bullets, and this particular incident involves an alleged assault on a police officer with a shotgun, and thirty-eight-caliber bullets cannot be used in a shotgun." Judge Tracy said he would take that into consideration and invited Gunn to cross-examine O'Connor on the bullets. She strode to the witness stand, where O'Connor had just removed the four bullets from an envelope. "Are these the same type of bullets that are used in all thirty-eights?" she asked.

"No, ma'am," said O'Connor.

"And do they differ significantly from any other thirty-eight-caliber bullets?"

"They're shorter than most of the modern ammunition, ma'm. They're called short rounds."

Gunn started speaking faster and louder. "And what type of firearms use short rounds of this type?"

"A thirty-eight-caliber revolver. However, there, uh, there—"

"Aren't police officers issued thirty-eight-caliber guns?"

"Yes, ma'am."

"Were the officers on this particular evening carrying thirty-eight-calibers?"

"Yes, ma'am."

"Thank you," said Gunn. "I have no further questions."

O'Connor's testimony concluded the prosecution's case. Patricia Gunn then called five witnesses for the defense. The nervous and frail-looking Ernest Winbush was not one of them. When Eddie failed to identify Winbush, Gunn decided not to put him on the witness stand. She thought she could win without his testimony. Keeping a defendant off the stand in a probable-cause hearing is a common defense strategy when there are other strong defense witnesses. The idea is to avoid giving the prosecution a preview of what the defendant's testimony would be at trial.

Charles Gibbons, the principal of the Tobin School, where three of Winbush's four children were enrolled, appeared as a character witness. Gibbons, one of the Boston public schools' most respected educators, testified that Winbush had "a reputation for truth and honesty," and that "as far as his dealings with the children and what have you is concerned, yes, he's always been very good. He picks his youngsters up each afternoon and attends each of the Home and School meetings."

Next, Miss Gerry Gardner of the Citywide Education Coalition, a group established to help the school system cope with the introduction of busing, took the stand as both a character witness and a material witness. "He's been very responsive," she said. "He's been interested. He's presently a member of the Biracial Council at the Edison School, and he's the treasurer of the Tobin District PTSA [Parent Teacher Student Association]." More importantly, Gardner said that on the evening of January 29, she saw and spoke to Winbush at the Edison School during a meeting that began at about seven-thirty and ended some time after ten o'clock.

Gunn then called Dave O'Brian, whom she had subpoenaed after reading his article. As she expected, O'Brian flatly contradicted Eddie's testimony, saying that the Thunderbird stopped beside the Buick, discharged a passenger, and then proceeded along Smith Street toward Dwyer and Molloy and away from the shooting scene. In cross-examination, Douzaine emphasized an interesting difference between O'Brian's testimony and that of both Eddie and Denny, who had testified that they were not sure that the man who got out of the Thunderbird when it stopped beside the Buick was the same man who got into the Buick. "Let me ask you," said Douzaine, "was it the same man that got out of the T-Bird that got into the Buick?"

"I would think so," O'Brian answered. "I saw a man get out of the T-Bird, cross the street, open the door, and get into the Buick."

"So there's no question in your mind?" asked Douzaine.

"No question in my mind that it was the same one," said O'Brian confidently.

Gunn called Winbush's wife, Patricia, to testify after O'Brian. She said that her husband left home that evening at about six-thirty to go to a meeting at the Edison School. Because of the traffic pattern of the neighborhood, using Smith Street was "a normal part of our life," she said. Gunn was using Mrs. Winbush's testimony to explain why her husband was on Smith Street at about six-thirty. Then Gunn backtracked to ask her what time her husband had left home that morning.

"He left that morning about quarter to seven," she replied. "I'd say seven o'clock."

"And where did he go after he left the house?" Gunn asked.

"The Babcock—"

Douzaine cut Mrs. Winbush off, protesting to the judge that she couldn't testify as to where her husband went unless she was with him. Gunn maintained that Mrs. Winbush knew where her husband went because it was "part of his daily routine." But even if it was part of his daily routine, Judge Tracy wanted to know, "How would she know he went there *that* day?"

"Because, Your Honor," Gunn replied slowly and emphatically, "if he failed to go to the Babcock Kidney Center, he would die. He's on a kidney dialysis machine three days a week."

That was good enough for Tracy. He allowed Gunn to ask Mrs. Winbush more about her husband's kidney treatment.

"And how often is he treated at the Babcock?" she asked.

"He's treated three times a week."

"And for approximately how many hours?"

"Approximately five hours," Mrs. Winbush sighed. "That's if the run goes good. If it doesn't, it's longer."

"And was he treated at the center on this particular day?"

"Yes, he was."

"And what time did he arrive home that afternoon?"

"I'd say he arrived home about two-twenty, two-thirty, somewhere around there," said Mrs. Winbush.

The last witness to testify was Doctor Theodore Steinman, the director of the Dialysis Unit of the Beth Israel Hospital and an assistant professor at Harvard Medical School. Doctor Steinman had been Winbush's personal physician for a little over three years. He remembered, and his records indicated, that Winbush received a dialysis treatment on January 29. Gunn asked him what the "physical capabilities" are of a person who has been plugged into a kidney dialysis machine for five hours or more. "Usually, after dialysis treatments," Steinman explained, "the patients are a little washed out, feel very fatigued and weak, and are able to sustain minimal activity. You know, he was able to walk, get in the car, and drive. Most patients feel much better the following day, post-dialysis, but feel kind of washed out after dialysis."

"Now, would he, would Mr. Winbush on this particular day, in your opinion, have been capable of running at all?" Gunn asked.

"Uh, no," said the doctor. "I'd find it very difficult for him to run on almost any day, whether it was a post-dialysis day or in between dialysis periods."

With the testimony finished, the lawyers each made five-minute final arguments. As always, the defense argument came first. Patricia Gunn started by reminding the judge that Eddie could not positively identify the defendant, and sarcastically contrasted that with his confidence in the observations he claimed he had made that night. As he had done in his Internal Affairs interview, Eddie had testified in detail about the appearance of the driver of the Thunderbird, who he swore was not Winbush. He testified that he could positively identify the driver "ten years from now." To

Geagan and in court, Eddie had said that the driver never got out of the Thunderbird, but then Eddie went on to describe the man's clothes: a denim jacket and denim pants—precisely what one of the Cambridge robbers was reportedly wearing. "The testimony of the police officer as to the vivid description of the person driving the Thunderbird," Gunn told Judge Tracy, "was the exact description broadcast over the air, which may account for his ability to describe him through the rain, through the windshield wipers, through the poor lighting conditions, at a distance, and yet not being able to identify the person who was allegedly holding a gun on him."

Gunn insisted that if a shotgun was fired, Denny would have heard it. "A shotgun is a very audible sound," she said. "It's not something that would be mistaken for any other sound, and it would certainly not escape the attention of a police officer."

She concluded by highlighting both "the grave omission from the police report that never stated that there was ever a gun involved with the Thunderbird" and Dave O'Brian's testimony that "the Thunderbird had already proceeded down the street" before the shooting. As she sat down she asked the judge for "a finding of no probable cause."

"The Commonwealth suggests," Douzaine began, seconds later, "that it was Mr. Winbush who was the third man in the car, who stepped out of the T-Bird and fired a shot at Officer Holland." He stressed Winbush's admission to O'Connor that he had driven on Smith Street at about six-thirty. It was almost as an aside that Douzaine said, "I'm curious to know why [Winbush] has four thirty-eight-caliber bullets in his pocket when he's arrested at ten-forty."

"Your Honor, I would object," Gunn interrupted. "Thirty-eight-caliber bullets do not go into a shotgun. They are irrelevant and immaterial, having nothing to do with the case." Judges rarely welcome objections during final arguments. At that stage of the proceeding, they prefer to give lawyers as much rhetorical leeway as possible. Tracy told Gunn that he could sort out what was relevant and allowed the prosecutor to continue.

"Your Honor," said Douzaine, "Officer Holland testified to what he thought—he referred a couple of times to what he thought—was a shotgun. But he described it, and at one point, he said it could be a shotgun or a rifle, or an elongated gun. Even if, even if they don't link up, Your Honor, with any shotgun or rifle, the Commonwealth still finds it strange that if [Winbush] did what he, what himself and his witness said he did, why he'd have bullets on him.

"And just one other point, Your Honor," Douzaine said as he headed for his conclusion. "Defense counsel makes a point that Officer Holland was too preoccupied with the Buick to pay much attention to what was happening over in the T-Bird. And the Commonwealth admits that he was very occupied at the Buick, suggests that he did have time to look over and see what was happening. And he did admit that after he saw that shot fired, and he went back to the incident taking place at the Buick, that he didn't see where the T-Bird went. And I suggest, Your Honor, that that's understandable. The Commonwealth asks for probable cause, Your Honor."

Judge Tracy didn't bother to review his notes of the testimony. He immediately leaned forward and whispered his finding to the clerk. Exactly thirty seconds after the district attorney had asked for a finding of probable cause, the clerk turned to face the defendant and announced, "Ernest Winbush, the court finds no probable cause on both these counts and dismisses these charges against you."

That afternoon, John Geagan called Pat Bowden again. This time she said calmly, "My lawyer is Lawrence O'Donnell. You can deal with him." Geagan must have been surprised. Of all lawyers, O'Donnell was probably the last one he expected to find in the Bowden case—on the Bowden side, that is.

O'Donnell was known in the department as a high-priced criminal lawyer. Back when Geagan was a beat-walking patrolman, he and the rest of Boston and most of the country had read newspaper accounts of O'Donnell's first big case. It was the 1956 armed robbery trial of the ten men accused of taking $2,700,000 in cash and securities from the Boston office of the Brink's Armored Car company. The Brink's job was then, and for years to come, the largest theft of cash in American history. Geagan followed the Brink's case closer than most people and with unique embarrassment. Of the three defendants O'Donnell represented, one was Geagan's uncle, Michael Geagan, a Charlestown longshoreman with a string of robbery convictions and a few years of prison time already served. He and his gang pulled life sentences for Brinks.

The family tie never hurt John Geagan's career. In Boston it is well understood that cops and robbers often come from the same stock, and it is assumed—rightly in most cases, including Geagan's—that such relatives keep their professional distance. It is also understood that in the event of an awkward situation, a cop is allowed to give a relative a break. One cop I interviewed for this book told me of the time he happened upon a member of his immediate family in the act of committing a serious felony. The cop let the felon go. When the cop asked me what I would have done under the same circumstances, I told him, without needing to deliberate, that I would have done the same thing. No one from Dorchester would ever consider the alternative.

Five years after the Brink's trial, John Geagan met O'Donnell when they were both involved in a police brutality case. Jackie Washington, then a popular black folk singer, had filed a complaint of assault and battery against some officers who arrested him one night in Roxbury on misdemeanor charges. O'Donnell successfully defended the cops. Geagan was not one of them, but was a member of a patrolmen's association, a precursor to the union, that paid O'Donnell's fee. O'Donnell remembers Geagan as the only cop who complained that the fee was too high.

Geagan knew that in the years since their meeting, O'Donnell had defended many more cops in varied corruption cases— once, an entire police department that was questioned, but never charged, by a grand jury—as well as the entire staff of a jail, several lawyers, the occasional politician, and a few judges who found themselves in trouble. He had become an insiders' lawyer, the one to whom the people running the system turned when the system turned on them. But long before O'Donnell earned the respect of lawyers and judges he had impressed the Boston police. They knew he was a driven man, bold, relentless, and hard-hitting—the kind of guy you want on your side when you're in a jam. They learned that when he was one of them.

After a stint in the Army and bouncing from one odd job to another—the oddest being a door-to-door salesman of Campbell's Soup—at age twenty-three Lawrence O'Donnell was sworn in as a Boston Police Department patrolman on January 6, 1945, along with forty-two other fresh graduates of the Boston Police Academy. His graduation class picture hangs in a corner of his office above a shelf that holds a glass-encased tin belt buckle with the letters BPD stamped diagonally across it. He was a cop for seven years. He worked nights for $38.65 per week. "Somewhere along the line the department had invented the eight-day week," he says. "We worked seven straight days and then had one day off. One day off in eight, and we were all happy to have the job." *

After a year of walking a relatively peaceful beat in Brighton, he enrolled in Suffolk University as a full-time college student. The diploma he had earned less by academic ability than by regular attendance at his neighborhood public high school was Suffolk's only admission requirement. The G.I. Bill of Rights covered tuition. He continued to work nights and went to school days. He told co-workers, friends, and family that he was going to be a lawyer. Everyone thought he was crazy—except his wife.

---

* The supremely effective Boston Police Patrolman's Association unionized the force in 1966. Accordingly, the patrolmen's average annual income has risen to about $25,000. With overtime pay, several patrolmen actually earn well over $40,000 per year. Days off now rotate on the basis of four consecutive days of work followed by two days off, which in effect gives the typical officer sixty-one weekends a year. Boston patrolmen now work an average of 182 days per year, two days per year more than public school teachers and more than 20 percent fewer workdays than the private sector averages.

He had married the former Frances Marie Buckley of Cambridge in 1942 while still in the Army. She was an honors graduate of a parochial high school and was able to help him with his college courses. She edited and typed his term papers, broadened his vocabulary, worked on his diction, tried to soften his Boston accent, and—when she could find a babysitter for Michael—took temporary jobs as a secretary or a model to supplement the $38.65 a week.

In four years of year-round college and law school attendance, my father picked up a Suffolk Associate of Arts degree, a Suffolk Law School degree, and two more sons—Kevin in 1947 and William in 1950. He passed the bar exam on his second try and was admitted to the Massachusetts bar on November 1, 1951. I was born the following week and, a few months later, was the son of an ex-cop who had just resigned from the force, taken his $1,200 retirement fund in a lump sum, opened an office in Dorchester, and hung out a shingle saying LAWRENCE F. O'DONNELL, ATTORNEY AT LAW.

Bob Hudson was a patrolman in the one-day-off-in-eight era. Like everyone else I've met who was on the force then, Hudson still likes to tell the one about Larry O'Donnell and a certain much-disrespected captain called Potato Nose. It seems Potato Nose gave O'Donnell a traffic-directing assignment on busy Commonwealth Avenue early one evening. Oddly, perhaps thoughtlessly, he ordered the patrolman not to leave his post until "I personally relieve you." The captain, who had earned his nickname by damaging his nose with excessive drinking, was always cluttering his sentences with words he didn't mean. O'Donnell, on the other hand, was learning to appreciate the precise use of language from the lawbooks he hid under his uniform and constantly glanced at. He was also dying to tell off Potato Nose.

When midnight came and his shift was over, O'Donnell was still at his post. He had had no traffic to direct for the last six hours. The midnight-to-eight patrol supervisor came by to tell him to go home. O'Donnell respectfully declined, explaining that he was under specific orders not to leave until the captain relieved him. Two hours later, O'Donnell left his lonely post and walked to the captain's house, confident that he had earned the right to give Potato Nose a piece of his mind. He rang the captain's doorbell by kicking it. (His violent streak was always unleashed at things rather than people—outside the family anyway. Without much of a model to hark back to, he was understandably slow at learning fatherly communication skills and disciplined his sons a bit more than they deserved.) Lights went on in the house, and the captain appeared at the door in a bathrobe. Before he could speak, O'Donnell lit into him for issuing a stupid order and forgetting it. Potato Nose seemed to have no idea what the patrolman shaking a finger at him was ranting about. O'Donnell demanded that he call a patrol car to drive him home. Potato Nose muttered, "You're crazy," and closed the door.

Minutes later, a patrol car arrived. The driver told O'Donnell that he had orders to take him home. "On the way home," O'Donnell recalls, "he asked me what I thought would happen to me. I said, 'Nothing. Nobody's ever done anything like this before, so nobody'll know what to do about it.'" He was right. After a series of high-level conferences at Headquarters, nothing happened.

When a cop tells the O'Donnell versus Potato Nose story, you get the feeling that insubordination is about the most admired form of bravery among patrolmen. It earned O'Donnell a permanent place in the folklore of the department.

Little else about Patrolman O'Donnell is remembered today, and for good reason. He never made a big arrest. The night he caught two burglars in a store, he could have made a good pinch, but when his superiors arrived on the scene and discovered that one of the burglars was a BPD sergeant from another district, they let them go. The one fight he had was with another patrolman who started to beat a handcuffed prisoner, over O'Donnell's objection. He never fired his gun after graduating from the Police Academy. He put in his time and got out as soon as he had somewhere to go. Bob Hudson, who still says he likes O'Donnell, never worked with him but believes he couldn't have been much of a cop. "He must've been in dugouts reading law books all the time," Hudson told me. O'Donnell says his beats didn't have many "dugouts"—warm, out-of-sight places, like the back rooms of bars, where cops are welcome to pause and relax—but he did use the few there were as study rooms whenever he thought Potato Nose wouldn't miss him.

"Everyone knew your old man had balls after the Potato Nose thing," a cop told me twenty years later, when my father was defending the cop's son, at no charge, in a drug case. "You know when he started going to Suffolk, some of the guys didn't wanna see him make it. They were hoping that smart-ass O'Donnell would fall on his face trying to reach too high. Mind you, I was always cheering for him, but even I didn't think he could do it. Now look at him. He's the best I've seen in a courtroom." The cop shook his head, chuckled, and said, "I guess Potato Nose was right about him. He must be a little crazy."

So, this was the Lawrence O'Donnell whom John Geagan called on March 13, 1975: an ex-cop, reliable defender of cops in trouble, a lawyer who never caused any problems for the department, an honorary member of the Massachusetts Chiefs of Police Association, and, as Geagan knew, a man with a streak of the unpredictable. It was a short conversation. Geagan asked O'Donnell if he represented Patricia Bowden. He said yes. Geagan asked what he intended to do for her. O'Donnell replied, "Sue the shooters."

"Well, you know Bowden was ID'ed as an armed robber?" said Geagan.

"Yeah, and I know how positive, positive IDs are," said O'Donnell. "And I know he had no record and he was a steady worker."

"Yeah, I know," said Geagan. Not until this moment had O'Donnell been sure that Bowden had no criminal record. He believed that Pat thought so, but figured Bowden could have been arrested before Pat met him. "What about this kid Jessina?" Geagan asked. "I want to talk to her."

"She's my witness," said O'Donnell. Then he set the tone for all that was to follow between him and the Boston Police Department. "When the suit gets started next week," he told Geagan, "the department's lawyers will subpoena her and take her deposition. That's legal process, Sarge. We have to go along with that, and we will. But she's never gonna talk to you, so stay the fuck away from her and stay away from my client."

Geagan's information gathering ended there. He still had some Bowden paperwork ahead of him, though, and something to do the following day that would not find its way into his next report. He visited the Roxbury Defenders Committee office, carrying a handwritten note from an assistant district attorney.

District courts, like Roxbury's, do not maintain stenographic records of their proceedings. Usually nothing important enough to require a transcript happens in district courts. In 1975, the Roxbury Defenders began making tape recordings of probable-cause hearings, which the court allowed them to do on condition that they provide the D.A.'s office with transcripts of the tapes whenever requested to do so. The note Geagan handed to the Roxbury Defenders receptionist said: "Would you kindly supply the Commonwealth with the tape transcript of the hearing on *Commonwealth* v. *Ernest Winbush.*"

The receptionist brought the note to Patricia Gunn and told her that the man who delivered it identified himself as a police sergeant and was waiting in the reception area. Gunn knew that she was under no obligation to provide hearing transcripts to the police. She went out to see Geagan and asked him why he wanted the transcript. He explained that he was conducting an Internal Affairs investigation of what happened on Smith Street and thought the transcript would be helpful. Gunn told him that the four hours of tape (recorded only the day before) had not yet been transcribed. Geagan was prepared for that. He said he had two tape recorders with him and had the time to make copies of the tapes. Gunn agreed to let him do that after having him sign a statement: "The recording I wish to make is to be used only for purposes of an internal police investigation [and not] against Mr. Ernest Winbush."

Dave O'Brian remembers that Geagan had been in the courtroom for every minute of the Winbush hearing and had been taking notes. Nevertheless, Geagan closeted himself in an empty room at the Roxbury Defenders office to listen to the testimony again with one tape recorder and to rerecord it with another.

A few weeks later, when Gunn sent Michael O'Donnell the tape transcript she had promised him, her cover letter said:

> Pursuant to our conversation of last month you will find enclosed a copy of the transcript that was made in the probable cause hearing of *Commonwealth* v. *Ernest Winbush*.
>
> On March 14, 1975, Sergeant Geagan of the Internal Affairs Division of the Boston Police Department came to our office and requested to listen to the Winbush tapes. After signing a statement . . . Sergeant Geagan was allowed to listen to the tapes. . . . large portions of the tapes . . . were found to be blank after the tapes were loaned to Sergeant John Geagan. . . . Consequently, the transcript you have received represents the tapes as they were found to be after Sergeant Geagan listened to them.

The gaps in the Winbush tapes cover much of Eddie's testimony, as well as all of the prosecutor's opening statement and the first half of his closing argument, both of which must have contained his version of the shooting as told to him by Eddie and Denny. If anything Eddie or the prosecutor said in those sections of tape contradicted anything Eddie had said in his Internal Affairs interview, Eddie and John Geagan are the only people who might know.

The day after Geagan called him, O'Donnell had Pat Bowden bring Jessina Stokes into his office. She was a shy ten-year-old who was small for her age and spoke in a barely audible voice. She was intimidated by the surroundings and by the white man who asked her questions and wrote down her answers. Jessina probably would have been more relaxed if O'Donnell, who talks to children of any age as if they are about eighteen (the main reason his own children had little to say to him until their late teens), had let Michael, a father of two young daughters, ask the questions. Of course Michael could have jumped in if he wanted to, but he chose to sit unobtrusively in a corner behind Pat and Jessina and take notes.

Jessina said she had been leaning out her bedroom window talking to her friend Carla Davis that night. Carla was at her own window across Huban Court. Jessina said that she and Carla and other kids in the project, especially those without telephones, talked to each other from their windows "all the time." "It wasn't too cold" that night, said Jessina, so they had been talking for a while before anything happened on Smith Street. She saw a car slowly backing down the street. No, she could not see where the car had begun moving from. The buildings limited her view to the spot where the shooting occurred. Another car pulled up behind the car that was backing up. Both cars stopped. Two men jumped out of the rear car, ran up to the car stopped in front of them, and started shooting. Jessina yelled, "Look!" to Carla. The man on the passenger side of the car, the side Jessina had a clear view of, held on to a door handle. "Little blue fires" came out of the guns. No, she did not hear the men say anything. No, the front car did not move before the shooting started. No, she did not see a "little blue fire" inside the front car. No, she did not realize it was her uncle's car. The car started to move forward and out of sight, then she heard it crash somewhere up Smith Street. She asked Carla, "Did you see that?" and Carla said, "I think I saw a shot."

The last note Michael made during the interview was a reminder to himself: "*Check*—what color flame emitted from Holland-McKenna guns."

On Tuesday of the following week the Firearms Discharge Review Board met to consider what had happened on Smith Street. The composition of the eight-member board was determined by the specifications of the deadly force rule. Superintendent in Chief Joe Jordan was the only regular. He always served as chairman. The rule required that the other members include a district deputy superintendent, the commanding officers of "the officer whose actions are under review," an officer from the Training Division, an officer from Internal Affairs, and two officers "chosen by the officer whose actions are under review." Denny declined to select anyone for the board, but Eddie chose Patrolman Charles Webb, a young union activist, and TPF Patrolman Robert Armstead, a middle-aged black man. Leroy Chase, the commander of District 2 and the department's highest-ranking black officer, was the board's district deputy superintendent. The Training Division sent Patrolman Homer Thibodeaux, a firearms instructor and the third middle-aged black man on the board. Internal Affairs sent John Geagan. And Eddie and Denny's commanding officers, Deputy Superintendent Joe Rowan and Captain Bill MacDonald, were members of the board.

Their meeting began at 11:00 A.M. in a conference room next door to the commissioner's office and lasted an hour. Only the three black men who were present would later agree to tell me what happened. Although it was empowered to "interview any person who can give information pertinent to the inquiry," the review board called no witnesses. The board's report notes that its discussion was based exclusively on "copies of all reports relating to the discharge incident."

"It was a paper investigation," says the firearms instructor, Homer Thibodeaux. He was the Training representative on a few other Firearms Discharge Review boards in 1975 and remembers that their work never amounted to anything else. "The review boards relied completely on Internal Affairs," Thibodeaux says. "If it was alleged an officer was fired at, I would assume it was true." He recalls that Geagan, who did most of the talking, did indeed say that Bowden fired at Eddie and Denny. "No one would doubt that at that stage," says Thibodeaux, who had not read any of the reports before the meeting and glanced at only a few of them during the meeting. His concern with the shooting began and ended in the conference room that morning. He remembers being reluctant to speak. As a patrolman among much higher-ranking men, he told me, "I felt I was not a good voice."

Robert Armstead, the TPF patrolman serving at Eddie's request, also recalls Geagan doing most of the talking. Armstead hardly bothered to listen and read none of the reports. He understood his role to be that of "a character witness for Holland," which is not what the deadly force rule suggests.

"I worked with Holland a few times on ACU decoy stuff," Armstead told me one night at his kitchen table. He was wearing a TPF jump suit as his around-the-house relaxing outfit. "I thought he was okay, and that's what I told the board." When I asked Armstead why Eddie chose him for the board, he shrugged and said, "I really didn't know him well. . . . I could've been chosen because I'm black." Then, putting him back in his character witness role, I asked Armstead—himself a much decorated and widely respected cop—whether he would be willing to rely on Eddie in a dangerous situation. He said, "No comment."

When I interviewed Leroy Chase, the Roxbury deputy superintendent, six years after the board meeting, he said that he had been on so many review boards that he could not "remember much about this one." Chase claimed no memory of what was said at the meeting but was sure that he must have had something to say. "I got a big mouth," he told me. "I don't usually stay quiet."

It was Joe Jordan's duty to write the review board's report, but—presumably because he was so busy with the busing crisis—he didn't get around to doing that until July, three weeks after the end of the school year. In the report Jordan said that it was "the unanimous opinion of the Firearms Discharge Review Board . . . that Patrolmen Holland and McKenna acted within the purview of Rule 303, Section 4 in that at the time of the discharges they were defending themselves from an attack which they had reasonable cause to believe could result in their death or great bodily harm."

The three board members I interviewed said they had never seen the board's report before I showed it to them.

"I don't know why Jordan calls it a unanimous opinion," said Robert Armstead. "He didn't ask me what I thought." When I asked Armstead what he thought of Eddie and Denny's actions on Smith Street, he said, "I don't know whether they were right or wrong. I can't say that. I wasn't there." With a deep breath, he added, "If I was there, it probably would have gone down different."

Deputy Chase, now retired, said, "I don't know if I did approve of that shooting. I was on so many review boards I can't remember them all, but I'm sure I would have written my own report. You don't rely on memory or word of mouth in police work because you're going to hear about some of these things later and you won't remember them. So you take notes. You write all the time. I can't believe there's no report of mine attached to Jordan's, saying I agree. That's Jordan saying the opinion was unanimous, not me. If it was unanimous, why isn't my report attached? I would've had a report attached, saying I agree. Jordan doesn't have anything there showing what I said." Department records do not include anything written by Chase about the Bowden shooting. "Maybe they got rid of my report," he said in what seemed like an unguarded moment, when we were looking at the ocean from the living room of his seaside condominium. He retracted that thought immediately. "Of course, I wouldn't want to say they did. I don't know. I don't understand it."

Leroy Chase, who had been off the force for three years when we met but still slipped into the present tense when discussing his job, offered this reflection on his Firearms Discharge Review Board experiences: "You know, it's hard to be tough on a policeman. Policemen have a tendency to band together. When it comes right down to it, a policeman is going to go with a policeman in most cases like this. Maybe it's sad, and that might be where we make a mistake. I hate to hurt a cop. The camaraderie is a reality. This closeness flows over in making decisions. I don't say it's right, but that's the way it is in a job like that."

The day after the Firearms Discharge Review Board meeting, Geagan wrote his fifth and last Internal Affairs report. It was a one-pager on the Winbush hearing. Geagan summarized Eddie's testimony this way:

Someone then got out of the T Bird and crossed the street. Then someone got into the Buick which then backed up Smith Street towards Parker Street where it was stopped by the ACU car. Holland then stated he went to the Buick with his badge conspicuously displayed on his coat, announced that he was a police officer and demanded that the operator get out of the car whereupon he was struck by the Buick and knocked to the ground. As he was getting up he saw a man outside of the T Bird which was parked about 18' away point a long rifle or shotgun at him and then fire at him. He gave out the registration of the T Bird after getting the numbers from his partner, Patrolman McKenna.

It seems either Eddie or Geagan or both of them were still having trouble integrating the shotgun attack into the action. Here Geagan describes the shotgun incident, but leaves out the Bowden shooting. It was as if only one could be discussed at a time.

A month earlier, Geagan had seen fit to write two reports on such details as his telephone calls to Iris Stokes and Pat Bowden. But he wasn't moved to put anything in writing about his visit to the Roxbury Defenders, nor did he ever have a transcript produced from his copies of their tapes, as he did with all his other Internal Affairs tapes.

On March 20, 1975—the day after Geagan wrote his last report—at the Clerk's Office of the Federal District Court, Michael O'Donnell filed a seven-page complaint with the heading *Patricia Bowden, Eurina Bowden, and Jamil Bowden* vs. *Dennis McKenna and Edward Holland.* The complaint alleged that James Bowden was killed without justification by Holland and McKenna. Its legal grounding was Section 1983 of Title 42 of the United States Code, a 112-year-old act of Congress, which holds that a public official who intentionally causes "the deprivation of any rights, privileges, or immunities secured by the Constitution and laws, shall be liable to the party injured in an action at law, suit in equity, or other proper proceeding for redress." As is customary in civil complaints, the last section was titled "Prayers for Relief." It said:

The plaintiffs pray that: the defendants be adjudged to have violated the laws of the United States and the Commonwealth of Massachusetts as pleaded herein; [and] the plaintiffs have judgment against the defendants for the sum of Five Million Dollars in compensatory damages and Five Million Dollars in punitive damages, plus interest and costs.

CHAPTER 8

The next day, March 21, 1975, the *Globe* carried a short article on page 7 headlined POLICE SUED FOR $10M IN KILLING HERE.* It outlined the circumstances of the shooting and included a statement by the department's press spokesman that Bowden "was positively identified by two witnesses as being one of the holdup men in the store." The article ended with the complaint's allegation "that Bowden's civil rights were violated by the 'willful, malicious, callous and recklessly indifferent' conduct of the police."

The article prompted a few calls to O'Donnell, who was identified in the *Globe* as the Bowdens' lawyer. The NAACP, the Black Caucus of the state legislature, and a Roxbury minister and well-known social activist called to offer their help. O'Donnell was wary. He politely put them off, saying he might need their help in the future when the case started moving toward trial. Later that day he gave Michael his true reaction to the offers. "I don't want them around this case," he said. "I'm not going to make a political thing or a racial thing out of this. What we've got here is bad police work, stupid police work, and that's all it is. There's no big cause here. I try cases, not causes.

"Suppose I asked the NAACP for expense money or to help set

---

* The $10 million was merely an attention-getting device. The Bowden jury was never going to hear the figure because in Massachusetts, lawyers are not allowed to tell juries how much they want. The idea is to keep judgments reasonable. Giant judgments occur in those states where you can ask the jury for anything.

up a Bowden case fund like the cause lawyers do. Then we've got them calling here all the time to see how it's going. We've got fifty people asking why we're doing this and why we're not doing that. We've got a hundred people in the courtroom telling me questions they want me to ask on cross-examination. No, we're not going for that."

Michael nodded and thought to himself that having a fund for expenses didn't sound so bad. As it happened, declining such outside assistance from people practiced in public relations meant that from then on the Bowden case would progress in utter obscurity. Not another word about it would reach the newspapers for three years. (And in the end, the O'Donnells were going to regret not becoming an NAACP cause.)

Gerard Powers read the *Globe* article on his way to work that morning, and so was not surprised to find a copy of the Bowden complaint on his desk in City Hall when he arrived. Powers was the chief trial counsel of the City's twenty-five-lawyer Law Department. A clause of the patrolmen's union contract holds that the City must provide defense counsel for officers who are sued for claims arising out of on-duty events. Gerard Powers was the Law Department's veteran defender of police brutality lawsuits. He had twenty days to file an answer to the complaint for his new clients, Edward Holland and Dennis McKenna.

Two weeks after the suit was filed, the Internal Affairs Division officially reached a conclusion in case #14–75. It appeared in a seven-page typed report signed by "Deputy Superintendent John E. Barry, Commanding Officer, Internal Affairs Division." It was I.A.D. standard procedure to have the investigating officer write a case's conclusive report and have the commanding officer sign it. So Deputy Barry's involvement with the Bowden investigation was probably limited to reading this one report—if he had the time—and signing it. Under oath two years later, John Geagan would not say that he wrote it, but acknowledged that it was based exclusively on his investigation.

The report opened with a one-paragraph account of the shooting. It was the then two-month-old Sergeant McHale version with this one new sentence: "McKenna reported that he then saw Bowden turn towards Holland and point, what he thought was a gun towards Holland." Neither in his report nor his I.A.D. interview did Denny say that he saw a gun in the Buick. At the Winbush hearing, he only went as far as saying he "saw a flash within the Buick." Of course, using the McHale version meant that I.A.D. did not say a shotgun was fired at Eddie by anyone.

The report said that there were "several discrepancies which must be commented on at this time." The first was Bowden's plate number, which, said I.A.D., was not "the registration number of the car wanted for the Cambridge hold-up." Despite Denny's claim to Geagan that he and Eddie both wrote down the robbery number when it came over the air at 2:30 P.M., and Dave O'Brian's observation that Eddie was making notes on a clipboard, I.A.D. now said, "There is no evidence that when the registration number of the wanted car was given out that either officer wrote it down and it was apparently committed to memory. The officers reacted to a number that was similar to one that they had been alerted to look for. It must be remembered that this vehicle was positively identified as the car used in the hold-up by one of the victims although the number was different."

On the question of whether Eddie checked Bowden's number or the robbery number during the stakeout, I.A.D. said, "Department records indicate that Patrolmen Holland and McKenna checked registration #4F•6368 [the robbery number] through the Communications Division and were informed that that was the vehicle used in the Cambridge hold-up." The "department records" that the report referred to on this point were the dispatcher's note pad. Everyone in the department knew that there was a better way to determine precisely who said what over the air during the stakeout. Every radio transmission into or out of the Communications turret is recorded for possible later use as evidence. But, as the I.A.D. report explained, "None of the radio messages from the Communication Division to the sector cars relaying information about the hold-up in Cambridge or the checking of motor vehicle registrations can be verified because the recording system at the Communication Division did not operate properly on January 29, 1975." The twenty-four-hour tape of the date in question was blank. All the stakeout and post-shooting radio traffic—about everything from Bowden's plate number to his identity, his criminal record, his physical description, to the Thunderbird and Winbush's arrest—was lost.

Most of the other items on the I.A.D. list of "several discrepancies" that required comment were points raised by Dave O'Brian in the *Phoenix*. To O'Brian's claim that he did not hear Eddie and Denny shout anything to Bowden before firing, I.A.D. said, "There were two radios in the ACU car, a mobile unit and a portable unit: the car windows were closed due to the inclement weather; and the Buick motor was racing and the tires were screeching. Under these conditions it would have been unusual for anyone crouched down in the rear seat of the car to hear any speaking from the street." But what if, as O'Brian and Kobre remember it, the radios were quiet, the car doors were open, the Buick's engine was not racing, and its tires were not screeching?

I.A.D. did not mention the sharpest inconsistency between O'Brian's and Eddie's and Denny's stories—that the shooting started within three to five seconds.

I.A.D. quoted O'Brian's expression of doubt about how Bowden could have thrown away the Fabrique Nationale without Denny noticing, then said, "It is conceivable that McKenna would not have noticed the gun being thrown from the car as at this time he was returning to his vehicle in order to pursue the Buick."

I.A.D. quoted O'Brian's reference to a "kid in the crowd" who told him—before being scared off by a cop who said O'Brian was with the FBI—"The cops just drove up, jumped out and started shooting as the guy drove off." I.A.D. said, "This kid was unable to be located nor did he come forward to give his version of the incident."

And I.A.D. quoted O'Brian on the Bowden family's claim that Jessina Stokes "was looking out her bedroom window and saw the whole thing," then said, "although entrance was not gained to the Stokes' apartment, [an inspection of the building] revealed that, at best, it would be very difficult to have seen the incident as it occurred on Smith Street on the night in question." I.A.D. did not explain why it would have been so difficult. In fact, Bob Hudson's diagram, part of Geagan's file, shows that Jessina could have had a perfect view of the action.

The final item on the discrepancy list was "the activities of the occupants of the Thunderbird and the route of that vehicle." The report commented on this by asking itself four questions and answering them:

(1) "Was Winbush's car on Smith Street on the night in question?"
Yes, because Winbush admitted it to Patrolman O'Connor when he was arrested.

(2) "Did Bowden get out of the T-Bird and get into the Buick?"
Yes. I.A.D. noted that Eddie and Denny weren't sure and that O'Brian was positive that he did, and then adopted the O'Brian view.

(3) "Where did the T-Bird go after Bowden left it?"
"It sped down Smith Street towards St. Alphonsus Street," I.A.D. answered, citing Denny, O'Brian, and Kobre as sources. "Why it was not stopped by Patrolmen Molloy and Dwyer is open to conjecture," said the report. I.A.D. found no fault with Geagan for leaving this open to conjecture by neglecting to interview Molloy and Dwyer, but it did offer its own conjecture: "More likely than not, then Thunderbird went to St. Alphonsus Street and left the area before Molloy and Dwyer were notified that it was travelling in their direction."

(4) "How and when was Holland assaulted by the occupant of the T Bird?"

He wasn't, I.A.D. concluded. The report said: "There is no corroboration to Patrolman Holland's version of being assaulted by the occupant of the Thunderbird. There is ample proof that the Thunderbird left Smith Street prior to the actual shooting. This is not to say that he was not fired on by some person, but in the confusion of being fired at and returning the fire he mistakenly believed, and *reported* [emphasis added], that it was the occupant of the Thunderbird that fired at him."

Having moved all of Eddie's claim about the Thunderbird backing up with the Buick and getting involved in the shooting into the realm of fantasy, I.A.D. went on to embrace the rest of his story and conclude that because "their badges were conspicuously displayed," because "they announced their office and demanded that the Buick stop," because "the operator drove towards Patrolman Holland and struck him twice," because "Bowden then drove towards Patrolman McKenna," because McKenna "saw Bowden turn and point a weapon in Holland's direction," because Holland "saw a flash from inside the car," and because "there were no other witnesses to the incident to cast any doubt on the officers' versions except the two Phoenix reporters who said that they didn't hear anything said by the officers . . . Patrolmen Dennis McKenna and Edward Holland were justified in the use of deadly force."

Deputy Barry submitted the conclusive I.A.D. report to his immediate supervisor, Superintendent Edward J. O'Neil, Chief of the Bureau of Inspectional Services. Superintendent O'Neil's office had a rubber stamp for inking such documents with the words "Respectfully forwarded to the Police Commissioner with APPROVAL." On April 2, 1975, the same day Barry submitted the I.A.D. report to O'Neil, it got the stamp of approval and was sent on to the commissioner. Di Grazia says he didn't read it. Instead, he waited for the Firearms Discharge Review Board report, which was then three months away from being written.

Answering a complaint is a mere formality—the legal crossing of swords—but it has to be done before a lawsuit can start moving. A sentence denying the allegations of the complaint is all that's expected. The twenty days allotted to the defense to take this action passed without the City of Boston Law Department's filing an answer to the Bowden complaint. Michael hardly noticed. He was, as always, occupied with dozens of other active civil and criminal cases that required research, the writing of motions and briefs, court appearances, client interviews, and the like.

Two weeks after the answer deadline, Michael filed a request that the defendants be found in default. Two weeks later, Judge Walter Jay Skinner, who had won the Bowden case in the federal court's judicial assignment lottery, granted the request and sent Eddie and Denny a Notice of Default. Theoretically, issuing the default notices meant that the judge could declare the Bowdens winners without even having a trial, because Eddie and Denny refused to defend themselves, but in practice, default notices are just a way of prodding the defense into action. Two weeks after the default notices were issued, the Law Department, in the person of Attorney Gerard Powers, officially entered the case by filing a motion to remove the defaults. Judge Skinner routinely did so and gave Powers another twenty days to answer the complaint. Thirty days later, on June 13, Powers filed his answer, which claimed that Eddie and Denny had acted in self-defense. What was supposed to take three weeks took three months. Despite the defense's tendency to similar delay at every turn, the O'Donnells were going to overtake hundreds of slower-moving cases already on Judge Skinner's civil docket and bring the Bowden case to trial in the remarkably fast time of three years.

On April 24, the day Michael filed the default motion, he received the Roxbury Defenders' transcript of the Winbush hearing. When he showed his father Patricia Gunn's letter about the tape erasures, Michael said, "What did she think was gonna happen when she gave Geagan the tapes?"

O'Donnell muttered profanities as he read the letter. Neither father nor son was outraged by the possibility that Geagan had erased the tapes; they were only surprised at what they thought was the Roxbury Defenders' naïveté. "You don't have to be around very long," said O'Donnell, "to know that's where cooperation'll get you."

Michael called a friend with expertise in tape recording. The expert said that trying to recover the erased material could cost thousands and might not produce results usable in court. "You're slipping, Mike," said the expert. "You shoulda got to the tapes first."

Michael laughed. "I thought the tapes were secure, sir," he said.

"You wouldn't have been so trusting in the old days," said the expert.

"This is a different world," said Michael, still laughing.

"Doesn't sound so different."

"I guess not."

The expert was speaking from an office in New York City. It was the office Michael worked in when he was a U.S. Army Counter Intelligence agent.

After graduation from Suffolk College—the alma mater of my father, three brothers, and sister—Michael enlisted in the Army for a three-year hitch. Patriotism was the farthest thing from his mind. He felt the draft blowing his way and figured joining gave him a better chance at the assignment he wanted, which was Intelligence. A friend had told him Intelligence was a gamble. He said that in Vietnam, Military Intelligence agents were getting some extremely dangerous assignments, but elsewhere they were famous for pulling easy ones. Michael took his chance with Intelligence, hoping for anything but Southeast Asia, and he got New York. From 1968 to 1971, he was the Military Intelligence liaison to the New York City Police Department. When the Southern Baptist colonel in charge of M.I. New York made Michael his police liaison, he told him why: "You look like a cop. You walk like a cop. You talk like a cop. And you're the only man I have with an Irish name."

Michael was then and is now a slender six footer with the arms of a blacksmith and a shock of straight brown hair that flops onto his forehead no matter how often he pushes it back. He has blue eyes and movie-star teeth all his own. He is handsome to those who don't mind pale skin. A harsh Dorchester accent colors his every word. Though I don't have his perfect teeth, am eight years younger, and usually have longer hair, we are occasionally mistaken for each other. We are exactly the same size and shape, and our facial features are so similar that I'm never surprised when someone I've never seen looks at me and says, "Hi, Mike." It's not that I look eight years older than I am; it's that he hasn't aged in the eight years since he hit thirty, so now we both look that age.

Michael had learned the ins and outs of big-city police work in New York. In fact, he now knew more about the latest in police bureaucratic intricacies than his father did. He had also learned a good deal about conducting investigations. He began his Bowden investigation after reading the Winbush transcript.

Finding that Winbush did not testify in his own defense was as disappointing to Michael as losing some of Eddie's testimony. The transcript didn't answer the questions he had wanted to ask Winbush: Did Winbush drop Bowden off at the Buick? If so, how long had they been together and why? Eddie and Denny testified that they weren't certain whether Bowden got out of the Thunderbird, while O'Brian testified that he was sure of it. When Michael asked Pat Bowden if she thought James had been with Winbush that night, she said, "What's a Winbush?"

The only Bowden who knew Winbush was James's mother, Mary, who lived across the hall from some of Winbush's relatives. She didn't know him well—where he lived or anything like that—but she did know him as a familiar face seen around her building. She did not think that James knew him. "He mighta known him," Walter Lee told Michael. "And Winbush mighta dropped him off, but so what? If they were together it couldn'ta been for more than ten minutes."

In talking to the Bowdens, Michael learned that James came home from work, as usual, at about 3:45 P.M. on January 29; that he played with Eurina and Jamil for a while, watched *Sesame Street* with them, had dinner with Pat and the kids at about 5:00 o'clock, and left to visit his mother at about 5:45 P.M.; that, at about 6:00 o'clock, he found his mother wasn't home—she was at a Laundromat a block away—and decided to drop in on his sister Edith, who lived in the apartment below his mother's; that he left Edith's at about 6:15 P.M.; that Edith heard the shots and the car crash on Smith Street about fifteen or twenty minutes later; and that no one knew what James did between the time he left Edith's and the time he got into his car, which was parked a two-minute walk away.

Ernest Winbush seemed to be the person who could fill in the gap. Michael got his address from the clerk of the Roxbury Court and knocked on his door in Mission Hill one foggy afternoon in early May. It was a building Michael knew well from his five years as a City of Boston housing inspector. After the Army, he had attended Suffolk Law School nights and become the Housing Inspection Department's lead-paint man in Roxbury. He knew how to walk through Mission Hill with the nonchalance of a plain-clothes cop even though he carried only a housing inspector's ID card. One day when I joined him on his lead-paint rounds we got smiles and greetings of "Hello, Officers" from street corner bad guys—Billy Dwyer's "maggots"—who would have undoubtedly been less hospitable if they knew we had neither badges nor guns. He was accustomed to having to convince people he wasn't a cop before they would open doors for him, but at Winbush's door he didn't have to. There wasn't the slightest stirring inside the apartment. On a business card he wrote, "J. Bowden's lawyer. Call me or Mary Bowden," and slipped it under the door.

The next morning Patricia Gunn called. She told Michael that Winbush didn't want to speak to him, that he didn't want to get involved in the Bowden case. "She told me that he'd never been arrested before," said Michael, "and he was still terrified by the whole thing. He thought he was going to die when he was in jail and the cops wouldn't give him his kidney pills. And he wanted nothing more to do with cops, lawyers, and courts. That left us in a bind. We could subpoena him for a deposition, but that would probably scare him into saying, 'I never saw James Bowden in my life,' whether it was true or not. So we wouldn't learn anything from that. We didn't want to scare him, and he didn't want to talk to us. So I tried to find someone else who might've seen Bowden in those last ten minutes."

Most weekends that spring and early summer Michael canvassed Mission Hill looking for witnesses. He would slip his business card under yet another triple-locked door, promise the voice on the other side that he wasn't a cop, and suggest calling Pat or Walter Lee to prove it. Most of the doors would eventually open, usually because the person inside had a legal problem of his own to discuss. Michael spent hours explaining landlord-tenant law and what to do when a prison suspends your visiting rights, all in the hope that having earned his listener's trust he would pick up something about Bowden's last ten minutes. Just to return his kindness, some people gave him names of neighbors who, they said, saw the whole thing. Invariably these leads turned out to be false. A few of them saw the Buick crash, but that wasn't a helpful observation.

Michael was slowed by false rumors such as: The police had Bowden's body exhumed last week; one cop fired a shot after the Buick crashed; Winbush had a shotgun on him when he was arrested. The rumor Michael most wanted to be true was that TPF Patrolman Henry Nelson, the former neighbor of the Bowdens who took Desi Callahan to the morgue that night, had told someone that the gun found on Smith Street was planted. In a telephone conversation with Michael, Nelson explained that he was on Smith Street for only "a couple of minutes" after the shooting and denied saying or knowing anything about the gun. Whether Nelson had actually told someone the gun was a plant mattered little to Michael. What he wanted to know was what people would say in court, and Nelson had nothing helpful to say.

Though Michael was opposed to taking the Bowden case, it had now become his top-priority work. At the outset he could have happily defended Eddie and Denny, if they were paying customers. He felt nothing for James Bowden, who, as far as Michael was concerned, might well have been an armed robber who deserved what he got on Smith Street. Pride in his craftsmanship was his sole motivation in the hours of tedious research for the complaint. Now, a few months into the case, having met the Bowdens and liking them, he still felt nothing for James Bowden and, as far as I can tell, never would. There is not a trace of his father's sentimentality in Michael, the legal technician. But beneath the Brooks Brothers pinstripes, there is all of his father's street-corner toughness. In his Dorchester days, no one messed with Michael O'Donnell. As a street fighter—everyone in Dorchester was ranked within his own age group according to fighting ability—Michael earned the reputation of a guy who never looked for a fight but never backed down and never lost one. By his middle teens there were no challengers left. Now he felt personally challenged by the Police Department and the Law Department. Two things did it: the erasure—and Michael had no doubt that it was an erasure—of the Winbush tapes and the runaround on answering the complaint. They were *his* tapes. Patricia Gunn had promised him a transcript of them before they had even been recorded, and John Geagan got to them first. And it was *his* complaint that Gerard Powers ignored for so long.

Michael O'Donnell, the pale-faced, white-shirted, suburban commuter, was getting angry.

On July 9, Joe Jordan finally wrote the Firearms Discharge Review Board report. There was nothing original in it, except a few inaccuracies. Jordan had the robbers entering the store at "about 2:50 p.m., Wednesday, January 29, 1975, armed with handguns." As was well documented by the time Jordan began to write, the robbers had left the store by 2:50 and they had had only one gun. "The Buick Electra, Massachusetts registration 4F-6939," wrote Jordan, "was a positive ID by *two* [emphasis added] civilian witnesses as the motor vehicle involved in the armed robbery." Of course, only Desi Callahan saw the getaway car and only he identified the Buick. Presumably, Jordan's version of Bowden's plate number—the nines should be eights—was merely a typographical error. And Jordan said the Buick hit Eddie "several times" causing him "severe injuries." Eddie had said he was hit three times and his medical records show he had nothing more than a bruised knee that night.

The rest of the report was a rehash of others with "a narrative of the incident" lifted verbatim from Sergeant McHale's summary written the night of the shooting. Using McHale's account, which since Eddie's testimony at the Winbush hearing had become rather dated, left Jordan with no description of the Thunderbird's or Winbush's involvement in the shooting. The only interesting thing about the Thunderbird in the McHale-Jordan version was that it left the scene by turning "left into an alleyway adjacent to the Tobin School." Though there is no indication in Jordan's report that he realized it, this put him in marked disagreement with the Internal Affairs conclusion that the Thunderbird left Smith Street via St. Alphonsus Street immediately after dropping off Bowden. Jordan went beyond the McHale summary to mention Winbush's arrest, but not the reason for it or the disposition of the charges against him. Jordan stuck with McHale word for word on the confrontation with Bowden: He tried to run down Eddie and Denny; they both "heard a gunshot"; Eddie saw "a silhouette of a gun in the operator's hand"; then they fired. Jordan said that it was the unanimous opinion of the Firearms Discharge Review Board that Eddie and Denny fired in self-defense and were, therefore, justified in the use of deadly force.

Unanimous or not, the report's recommendation of "no further review of the actions of the officers as regards this incident" reached Bob di Grazia on July 17, 1975. In his deadly force rule Di Grazia had given himself "the authority and responsibility for final departmental disposition of a firearms discharge case." Though the rule requires that "copies of all reports relating to a discharge incident" be sent to the commissioner, the only one that Di Grazia now remembers reading is Joe Jordan's Firearms Discharge Review Board report. "I'll be the first to say I couldn't read all the stuff that came up," Di Grazia told me. The day after he received it, Di Grazia initialed the last page of Jordan's report, indicating that its recommendation was officially accepted.

Bob di Grazia's initials were the Boston Police Department's final stamp of approval on Eddie and Denny's conduct on Smith Street. But even with the police investigation now closed six months after the incident, Eddie and Denny—still doing ACU patrols—knew they had not finished answering questions about what had happened that night.

CHAPTER 9

The next questions Eddie and Denny faced were Michael's interrogatories, written questions that require written, under-oath answers within thiry days. The interrogatories mainly covered indisputable points such as Eddie's and Denny's home addresses, the weather and lighting conditions on Smith Street that night, what they were wearing, how many shots they fired, and the serial numbers of their guns. Michael did not ask for a narrative of the incident. Instead, he posed a series of narrow questions about the shooting, most of them answerable with a yes or no and most of them concerning Winbush's involvement. While waiting for the answers, which Powers would file a month after the deadline, the Bowden case took an unexpected personal turn for the O'Donnells.

Thursday, September 25, 1975, was a parking lot night for me. I was in my last year of college. (I had strayed from the family path to Suffolk and ended up at Harvard.) It was raining and business was slow that night. I was studying for my first Irish exam the next day, doing the kindergarten-style memorizing that language study demands in the early stages. I would stare at a page repeating an Irish phrase and its English equivalent.

Cé chaoi bhfuil túu?

How are you?

Occasionally I would look up and spin around on my stool to make sure nothing was happening on the lot, no cars were being stolen, and no customers were sneaking in without paying.

About ten minutes after nine, while repeating to myself, "*Tá mé go maith*, I'm fine," I saw a taxicab swing into the lot, turn around, and stop so that it completely blocked my narrow driveway. The cab was still on the lot facing away from me toward the Trailways bus station across the street. The driveway was about 150 feet from my booth. I watched the cab, hoping it would move before I'd have to leave my comfortable perch. My supervisor was due to come by for a money collection soon and having the driveway blocked was not something that would please him. In a couple of minutes the cab's lights went off. Then I heard the noisily idling engine go off and knew I had to get over there.

I walked across the lot and approached the driver's window. There was a beefy red-haired guy in his early thirties behind the wheel and no one else in the cab. The windows were closed. I told the driver he was in my driveway and he'd have to move. He rolled his window down a couple of inches, looked at me, and said nothing. I told him again. He looked across the street to the bus station, then back at me, then back to the bus station again.

Suddenly he swung open the door, knocking me back against a car behind me, and jumped out with his right hand over his head. He swung so fast, in wood-chopping motion, that I barely had time to close my eyes. There was no pain at first. My head dropped and my knees buckled. He propped me up against the car and hit me again. In a second he spun me around, slammed my face down on the hood, and pulled my hands behind my back. I knew resisting could only make things worse. I may have gone out for a second or two. His grip on my wrists felt like steel—which, I soon realized, it was. He pulled me off the car, carried me a step, threw me into the back seat of the taxi, and closed the door. I was handcuffed.

Two guys dressed in jeans and Windbreakers appeared and began chatting quietly with the driver outside the cab. Another guy, similarly dressed, walked toward them from the bus station. I recognized him. It was Billy Dwyer. The last time I had seen him was when I played softball against him a couple of months earlier in Dorchester. I was in the outfield for the Atlas Club and he was pitching for Town Field Tavern. It was the night our pitcher, Gooba, drove into a wall on the way home. I knew Dwyer was a cop. He stepped to within a few feet of the cab, looked at me expressionlessly, said nothing, and turned to join the chat outside. That was when I knew I was under arrest.

I was booked at District 1 police station about fifteen minutes later on the charge of disorderly conduct. My arresting officers were William C. Dwyer and his partner, Mark F. Molloy, the taxi driver. They were working as an ACU team with two other plainclothes patrolmen. As I testified later, I spoke only to the booking officer at the station, giving him name, address, and date-of-birth details. All the while Billy kept barking from across the room: "Get your father down here. We wanna talk to him. Get him down here. He thinks he's big stuff. He's suin' our guys. We wanna talk to him right here." (Years later, under oath, Billy Dwyer denied making those statements.)

As luck would have it, for my one and only arrest my father was at Walpole State Prison that night and couldn't be reached. He didn't find out about the arrest until midnight. By then, my brothers—Michael, Kevin, then an assistant district attorney, and Bill, then a Suffolk law student—had me out on bail and admitted to Harvard's Stillman Infirmary, where I was bedridden for the next couple of days until the blinding headache was gone. Diagnosis: concussion. Skull X ray: negative. The tennis-ball-size bump on my forehead near the left temple took weeks to shrink and finally disappear, and there was no permanent damage.

Today, I can scarcely remember how angry I was at Molloy and Dwyer. When we see each other now, we always wave, smile, and say hi. Bumping into them in a restaurant in 1982, I introduced them to my mother—"Mark Molloy, Billy Dwyer, this is my mother"—joked about picking up their tab, and said, "See ya later." And I did see them later—two days later—on my way into another downtown restaurant. From a passing unmarked car Mark yelled, "Stop following us!" I turned to see him and Billy laughing as they drove by. I waved and laughed.

I can't explain what happened to all that anger we aimed at each other in 1975. It's a Dorchester thing, maybe an Irish thing, this ebbing of ill will—but then, so is holding lifetime grudges, something I've been doing with a couple of people who've never even hit me. I've seen best friends slug it out to the point of black eyes, chipped teeth, and broken jaws. As often as not, after some months of awkwardly avoiding each other, they're suddenly friends again. There's never an apology, just the unstated realization that what happened was stupid and no lasting harm was done.

Long after I stopped thinking that Molloy could have done some real damage to me, I saw Billy Dwyer walking down the street near Headquarters. We hadn't spoken since he arrested me. He nodded, broke into a grin, and said with mock formality, "Hello, Mr. O'Donnell." His impish eyes said, "You're not still mad, are you?"

I realized I wasn't, and said, "Hi, Billy." We kept moving. The hi-how-are-yas and the jokes would come in subsequent chance meetings. And our one brief—but most revealing—chat about the Bowden case would come after it was over. Now it's hard to think of my arrest and its aftermath as anything other than rather flat farce, but when I woke up in a hospital bed on Friday, September 26, 1975, it was serious business.

My father was angry, too, but in what for him had to be a great exertion of will, he masked his feelings when he stood beside my bed at eight o'clock that morning, listening to my story. I suppose he didn't want to excite me. When I finished he said calmly, "Okay, pal. I have to get to court. Take it easy. I'll let you know what happens." He was on his way to the Boston Municipal Court for the case of *Commonwealth* v. *Lawrence F. O'Donnell, Jr.* He left his composure in room 21A of Stillman Infirmary.

There is a charitable view of my father's temper, which holds that it often explodes without justification because courtroom behavior demands so much self-control that he has to let go when he can. Given that the old man—we've always called him that—is not all that controlled in courtrooms, there is a competing view: that, occupation aside, he is the type who once every week or two is bound to go off on a tear about something—anything. When he actually has provocation, the explosion is so much the scarier. If you had told Mark Molloy that a gray-haired lawyer was going to walk into the police room at the Boston Municipal Court that morning and push him around, you would have encountered some doubt. But then, Molloy had never met the old man.

"Larry," said a sergeant just inside the door. He pulled the old man aside. My brother Bill made it a three-man huddle. "I just heard about your kid," said the sergeant. "If I was at the desk last night, I wouldn'ta let them book him. You know that, Larry. It was the TPF that grabbed him."

The old man asked him who made the arrest. I had told him Dwyer's name but I couldn't remember Molloy's. The old man had already forgotten the name I gave him. There were at least twenty cops in the small room, about an even split between the TPF and the regulars. The sergeant nodded toward Molloy and said, "His name's Mark Molloy." The name meant nothing to the old man, who then remembered only the names Holland and McKenna from the Bowden case. Dwyer wasn't there. Bill would have spotted him right away. (Michael had thought the names Molloy and Dwyer sounded familiar when the desk sergeant gave him the arresting officer's names the night before at the police station. That morning, Michael was handling an insurance fraud case in a suburban court. At the office later that day, he checked O'Brian's article and reported the Molloy-Dwyer-Bowden connection to the old man, who wasn't a bit surprised to hear it.)

The old man walked across the room to Molloy. Bill stayed with the sergeant. They heard the old man's opening line clearly enough—"Hey, Molloy, you arrested my son"—but they could hear nothing of what Molloy said in a low voice, timid by comparison. The old man boomed, "You fuckin' bastard!" more times than anyone could count. He stood toe to toe, chest to chest, nose to nose with the bigger Molloy. No one intervened. Only Bill was not surprised.

Bill wasn't worried, either. A boyish blond of average height who still kept his high school football muscles in tone, Bill was known for his quick fists during a period of juvenile delinquency which he luckily survived without any arrests. (He was now in law school for lack of anything better to do and, despite the absence of motivation, was the best O'Donnell law student yet.) If it had been Bill instead of me in the parking lot the previous night—he worked there too—Molloy might have run into some resistance.

"Are you outa ya fuckin' mind?" the old man roared to something Molloy said. Without ever raising his hands—just using his chest—the old man was pushing Molloy against a wall. The foul-mouthed yelling ended after a few minutes, with the old man saying, "Hurry up and get in that fuckin' courtroom"—his version of a barroom step-outside challenge. The old man later claimed that Molloy offered to drop my case if the O'Donnells would drop out of the Bowden case. Molloy adamantly denies this.

Walking into the courtroom, the old man underwent one of his Jekyll and Hyde transformations into the very picture of civility. He was going to ask the court for a hearing on the issuance of the disorderly complaint—roughly the equivalent of a probable-cause hearing for a misdemeanor—and a continuance to a later date. Bill was going to establish formally the need for a continuance by testifying that he drove me from the police station to the infirmary, where he saw me admitted as an inpatient.

When a clerk called the O'Donnell case, the old man and Molloy stepped forward. Molloy spoke first to Judge Maurice Richardson, asking that he issue a complaint against me immediately because, as Molloy had typed on the complaint application after the old man had left the police room, I "was a disorderly person, to wit, did use unreasonable, loud, and course speech." The old man outlined my story—without calling Bill to testify—and asked Richardson for a hearing before issuing the complaint and a two-week continuance. The judge gave him both.

A week later a lawyer called the old man from a pay phone

outside the same courtroom. "Hey, Larry," he said anxiously, "I hear the TPF is trying to get an assault and battery complaint against you."

"No, it's only a disorderly and it's against my son. He has the same name."

"No," said the lawyer. "I know about that one, but I'm talking about an A and B complaint against *you*. They're going in front of Judge Nolan with an application right now."

There is no transcript of what transpired in Judge Joseph Nolan's courtroom at the Boston Municipal Court that crisp October afternoon, but the old man told me this story over the phone an hour after it happened: "I hustled over to the BMC and found Joe Nolan's courtroom. Now, Nolan's a terrific guy. I was lucky to get him. Most BMC judges give the cops whatever they want. Lo and behold, there's Molloy and a sergeant, Harry Byrne, who I've known forever, and a bunch of TPF guys, all in those phony jump suits as if they just parachuted in. The older cops think the TPF looks crazy in those getups, you know. So, I walk in there and take a seat. The clerk calls the Commonwealth versus Lawrence F. O'Donnell. They have two A and B complaint applications in. Guess what for? I can't believe it. It's a Three Stooges scene. Molloy is saying I hit him with my chest the day I was in the police room, which is exactly what I did. And a kid named Bradley, another TPFer—his father was on the force with me, a good friend of mine, and I've done big favors for him over the years—the Bradley kid has an application saying I grabbed him by the arm. I don't even remember seeing him that day but I know I did some pushing and shoving in the police room and he probably got in the way.

"Now, Harry Byrne starts us off and I feel sorry for him 'cause he looks sick when he sees me and I figure the young jerks have forced this thing on him. You know the BMC is sort of a police court. The sergeants come on like prosecutors. Byrne outlines the case against me and goes through some Q and A with Molloy. All nonsense. Then I go at Molloy with 'How tall are you? How much do you weigh?' You know he looks massive, for chrissake. And I go on to 'Were you wearing that jump suit that day?' Yeah. 'Were you wearing those storm trooper boots?' Yeah. 'Did you have that club with you?' Yeah. 'Did you have that gun?' Yeah. 'How many other cops were there?' About twenty. 'Well, can you tell me why I wasn't arrested on the spot?' Big pause. He says no. I ask him if he was afraid of me, and he says no. Now, fear is an element of assault. I ask him if he felt pain and he says no. Now, pain is an element of battery. If you don't have fear and you don't have pain, you don't have assault and battery. So I'm finished with Molloy, but before I let him go I have him show Nolan how I assaulted and battered him. I get him off the witness stand. He stands in front of me, puffs up his chest, and bumps me with it. I go back to my seat laughing and Nolan has his hands over his face.

"Then Byrne puts the Bradley kid up there and gives the judge this he-grabbed-my-arm bullshit. I start off with Bradley on the fear and pain, and he says, 'Yes, I was afraid. I didn't know what you were going to do.' And he says, 'Yes, it hurt!' See, someone clued him when Molloy was on the stand that he had to have the elements of A and B. I ask him to describe the pain, and he says he can't. And that was it for Bradley.

"Judge Nolan asks me if I want to testify. I say no. What am I gonna do, deny this stuff? I was proud of it. 'All right,' says Nolan, 'both of these applications are denied. There'll be no complaints against Mr. O'Donnell.'"

The next week, my hearing led to the same result: a denial of the complaint application after a one-on-one credibility contest between Molloy and me. Presiding was Joseph Funari, a judge temporarily assigned to Boston from another county. The old man didn't know him. We—the old man, Michael, Bill, and I—went into the hearing expecting the judge to issue the complaint and send the case to trial, because we were sure that Molloy would widen the charge against me to include something more than parking attendant rudeness. But he didn't. According to Harry Byrne's outline—the old man stopped feeling sorry for Byrne now that he was helping to prosecute *me*—and Molloy's testimony, the confrontation on the lot that night was merely verbal. We expected Molloy to say I grabbed him or shoved him or kicked him or something like that, but he said neither of us laid a hand on the other. He maintained that he had patiently explained to me that he was an on-duty police officer, that he showed me his badge and promised to leave in a minute, and that I then screamed, "Get the fuck out of here!"—which was disorderly conduct, as far as he was concerned, and had to be stopped.

Dwyer testified that he was playing the ACU decoy drunk across the street and didn't see what happened on the lot but "heard the commotion" and came over after the arrest was made. Two other ACU men—not involved in the Bowden case—who were watching Dwyer from dark doorways, said that they saw and heard nothing until after the arrest, when Molloy yelled to them.

There was the implication in Molloy's testimony that I was under the influence of drink or drug that night, a fair enough assumption inasmuch as I was a parking attendant from Irish Dorchester. Indeed, in the rather loosely managed parking company that employed me, attendants usually had a beer or two (or more) on the job—but not me. I had become a Dorchester iconoclast by age thirteen by steadfastly refusing to consume either alcoholic beverages or nonmedicinal drugs. I've remained, like my father before me, a total abstainer from both. I don't drink, because I hated the taste of all things alcoholic when they were first presented to me at about age eleven on our street corner. The taste has not changed. I have no equally good reason for not using drugs. I guess the very eccentricity of abstinence has become its appeal. My father says he doesn't drink just to defy the stereotype of the Irish drunk. Hardheaded people don't need very compelling reasons for what they do. My mother thinks my father drank, and got drunk, once—the day he got fired from his door-to-door soup-selling job. I have never been drunk and never been higher than caffeine can lift me. For the record, the old man asked me at the outset of my testimony whether I was drunk or on drugs that night. Then he led me through my story, highlighting the contradictions with Molloy's version: Molloy did not identify himself; he did not show me his badge; I did not shout at him; and he hit me enough times to hospitalize me. The old man closed with a comment to the judge: Since neither vulgar language nor yelling constitutes disorderly conduct, Molloy's story, even if believed, did not describe a crime.

Judge Funari stared at the complaint application and rubbed his chin. Everyone waited. He reached for a pen. Then he looked up, found Molloy in the bunch of blue jump suits, and said, "Frankly, this exchange that you describe, Officer Molloy—I just don't buy it." I had never known such bliss in the company of men. The judge wrote *Denied* on the complaint application and initialed it.

Molloy, Dwyer, and Byrne watched us as we left the courthouse. Michael, Bill, and I were laughing. As he always does in a courthouse, the old man was smiling, waving, greeting every familiar face, and shaking hands. In a voice that Molloy, Dwyer, and Byrne could easily hear, he boasted to anyone who stopped long enough to listen about his back-to-back victories over the TPF. One lawyer asked him what he thought the TPF would do to him now. "Nothing," he said confidently. "See, they tried their play. They thought they could trade the disorderly for the federal thing I have against them. I was supposed to worry about my son getting a record, right? Okay, so that didn't work for them and they tried the A and B on me. I was supposed to get scared of being convicted, right? I was supposed to worry about what the BBO [the Board of Bar Overseers] would do about a guy convicted of brawling in the courthouse." Pointing at Molloy, Dwyer, and Byrne, he said, "That's the way those crazy bastards think. Well, now they know how I think."

Under another threat of default, Attorney Powers submitted Eddie's and Denny's answers to interrogatories in the last week of October. The answers filled in background details such as the serial numbers of their guns, but did not include what most interested Michael: their version of Winbush's involvement. Both Eddie and Denny said they did not know whether Bowden got out of the Thunderbird and, citing irrelevance, refused to answer Michael's other questions about Winbush, such as: Did he assault you? Did he fire any shots at you? Did you testify at his proable-cause hearing? Michael had expected to get the same answers to these questions that the Roxbury Defenders' transcript had given him. Powers's claim that the Winbush questions were irrelevant led him to believe that Powers regarded the Thunderbird action as unrelated to the Buick action, since, according to Eddie and Denny's testimony, Bowden might not have gotten out of the Thunderbird. The Thunderbird might have coincidentally stopped beside the Buick and dropped off someone who vanished into the darkness at the very moment Bowden walked out of the same darkness and got into his car. In that case, whatever the Thunderbird or anyone in it may have done next was irrelevant to what Bowden did. Hence the refusal to answer Bowden case interrogatories about Winbush.

Of course, Michael had not read any of the police reports yet. He didn't know that Eddie's report said that Bowden did step out of the Thunderbird. And he didn't know that if Powers couldn't see how Eddie's Thunderbird-shotgun story fit into what happened on Smith Street, then Powers was stuck with the same problem that Ed McHale, Harry Byrne, Bob Hudson, John Geagan, and Joe Jordan had had before him.

CHAPTER 10

Discovery began with Michael's interrogatories. Discovery is a lawsuit's pretrial stage, in which each side can question the other with interrogatories and, using court-authorized subpoenas, can obtain copies of relevant documents from one another and conduct depositions (under-oath interviews) of any witnesses.

The day before Thanksgiving, Powers sent Michael a batch of interrogatories to be answered by Pat Bowden. They were routine questions about James and the family: Please state the date and place of birth of James Bowden. Please state when and where James Bowden and Patricia Bowden were married. Please state the names of all children born of James Bowden and Patricia Bowden. Please state where James Bowden was employed as of 1/29/75. Michael sent copies of the interrogatories to Pat, then had her handwritten answers typed and sent to Powers three days before the Christmas Eve answer deadline.

By the end of 1975, the Bowden case had been on the federal court docket for nine months and twelve days, and it had been through only the filing and answering of a complaint and a round of interrogatories. It was proceeding at a normal pace. In 1976, it would move even more slowly.

Michael began the new year with a letter to Di Grazia requesting copies of all the police reports. The commissioner's office forwarded the letter to Powers. It prompted his first quick response: He immediately filed a motion for a Protective Order. Powers's motion claimed that the reports "are not public records but are privileged communications made within a government agency" and were, therefore, "beyond the scope of discovery." Impressed by Powers's motion and fearful that Judge Skinner would protect the reports, Michael withdrew the request. In the following months he tried a variety of legal maneuvers to get the reports, but was stopped short each time by Powers, who had the invaluable advantage of experience in such matters. Michael's partner, whose forte is courtroom work, not paperwork, was encouraging but not actively helpful. At the same time, Michael's load of other cases was growing steadily and reducing the time he could devote to the paper battle over the police reports, which dragged on from winter to spring to summer to fall and back to winter.

About a dozen times that year, Michael found himself in Roxbury checking leads on eyewitnesses. Walter Lee would call to say he had just heard third- or fourth-hand of someone who saw the shooting. Michael would track down the person and find out that he only saw the Buick crash, or that he was obviously inventing an eyewitness account in the hope of getting Michael to help him with a landlord problem, or that he wanted to be paid to tell his story. "They were all useless," said Michael. When I asked whether he was ever tempted to buy eyewitness testimony, he said, "I just figured the people selling it were full of shit. You know, if I gave them money, they would've said, 'Okay, tell me what you want me to say.'" Why not buy invented testimony? "There are guys who do that, but you know if it ever catches up with you, you're at least disbarred and maybe in jail. There aren't many clients worth that risk." It was typical of Michael to explain staying the course of honor simply for fear of being caught in dishonor. I've never heard him frame a decision in moral terms.

In mid-August Michael hit Di Grazia with what he was now certain was an airtight subpoena for the police reports. The commissioner's legal counsel teamed with Powers in an effort to dodge this one. They managed to delay responding to the subpoena long enough so that it became moot on October 3, 1976—the day Bob di Grazia suddenly resigned.

Boston was stunned by Di Grazia's announcement that he

would be starting a new job the following week as chief of Maryland's Montgomery County Police Department. His publicly stated reason for the move was the $10,000 salary increase Montgomery County promised him. He said he could not "afford to send two boys to college and a girl to Catholic school" on the Boston commissioner's $35,000 per year. The truth was more complicated.

Mayor Kevin White—who had burst into Boston politics in 1967 as a handsome, young, articulate, liberal mayoral candidate on his way to beating a field of older, conservative, indiscreetly racist candidates, and who had by 1976 become commander in chief of a powerful political machine devoted to keeping the White star shining over Boston—had nudged Di Grazia out of town. From wanting the best and the brightest on his team, Kevin White had switched to wanting the most loyal and the most servile. Not only was Di Grazia too independent to fit into White's new design, he had for some time also been perceived as a threat to it. A public opinion poll commissioned by the mayor in 1975 revealed that Di Grazia was the most popular and trusted public official in Boston. The poll stimulated City Hall talk of a Di Grazia mayoral campaign, a notion Di Grazia claims he never seriously considered. When, in the spring of 1976, Di Grazia sought White's assurance that he would be reappointed to a five-year term and given a pay raise in 1977, the mayor was noncommittal. Di Grazia knew what that meant.

He started listening to job offers. And after it was revealed that his had recently been one of the names on President Jimmy Carter's long list of candidates for the directorship of the FBI, there were many offers to choose from. The $45,000 post in Montgomery County, a suburb of Washington, D.C., was the most attractive for reasons that no doubt included its clear visibility to Washington power brokers.

The *Globe* went into mourning at Di Grazia's surprise announcement. "The city is losing a police commissioner," it said in an editorial, "the best it has ever had, who was liked, trusted, and admired by a vast majority of the public." Mayor White, in a thoughtless reflex, promised a nationwide search for a replacement. Twenty-four hours later, with the nationwide search presumably complete, the mayor announced his choice. The new commissioner would be the only man ever to hold every rank in the Boston Police Department—the silver-haired Joe Jordan. The *Globe* heartily approved. "Superintendent in Chief Joseph M. Jordan is a good man," said the next day's editorial, "bright, courageous and progressive . . . a worthy successor to Robert di Grazia."

The mayor administered the oath of office to Jordan on November 15, 1976. In a short speech after the ceremony the new commissioner said, "The Boston police force is made up of dedicated, mature officers who work in their city, care about it, and need only leadership and added resources to permit them to do a job that needs doing. I will do my best to provide that leadership, and the first area in which I intend to exercise that leadership is integrity." Everyone applauded. Jordan kissed his wife and smiled for photographers. A few blocks away in the O'Donnells' office Michael was having the name Joseph M. Jordan typed on a subpoena.

It was the same subpoena that Di Grazia had received. It demanded that Jordan hand over the police reports. Powers and the commissioner's legal counsel again tried to protect the reports, but by this time Michael believed he was on the right track and closed in on them with a motion for "an order compelling discovery." In January, Judge Skinner referred the issue to a magistrate, essentially an assistant judge empowered to do everything short of presiding at trials. Magistrate Laurence Cohen scheduled a hearing for February 16, 1977.

The hearing was brief. To the O'Donnells' surprise, Gerard Powers did not attend. In his place, Nicholas Foundas, the commissioner's legal counsel, argued that the reports were privileged communications beyond the scope of discovery. The old man, in turn, delivered a five-minute lecture, backed by Michael's research, on the definition of privileged communication and maintained that the documents in question did not qualify for that status. Magistrate Cohen agreed and wrote an order compelling Jordan to "provide counsel for the plaintiffs with copies of the above-mentioned documents" within seven days.

The O'Donnells later learned the reason for Powers's absence: He had been fired earlier that day. The firing had nothing to do with the Bowden case. Powers was a victim of one of Mayor White's post-election housecleanings. Nonunionized municipal employees risked their livelihoods by not energetically throwing themselves into White's campaigns. Powers had sat out the last campaign, mistakenly believing that sixteen years of Law Department service had earned him that right, and now he was out of a job. He soon established a thriving private practice.

Michael had never met his genial middle-aged adversary. To him, Powers existed only as a signature on papers that had been blocking his path for a year. The old man knew Powers well. "Gerry Powers was the best trial man in the Law Department," he said. "He was treated badly there in the end, but we weren't sorry to see Gerry leaving the Bowden case."

Seven days passed without a response from Police Headquarters. On the eighth day Michael filed a motion asking the court to hold Jordan in contempt for "the willful failure to obey its said order."

"I wasn't gonna wait another day to move for contempt," says Michael. "I could just see them at Headquarters cranking up the paper shredder." The next day in the late afternoon, a uniformed patrolman delivered a package to the O'Donnells' office. Michael opened it and pulled out an inch-thick stack of paper. There were TPF reports, Ballistics reports, Homicide reports, Internal Affairs reports and interview transcripts, the Firearms Discharge Review Board report, and some Cambridge Police reports. It was February 25, 1977, a year after he had first asked Di Grazia for this material. Michael started reading it at about 4:30 P.M. At about 9:30 he called his wife to say he wouldn't be home that night. He could not stop turning pages. He spent the night reading the reports and making notes. The next morning, disheveled and unshaven, he walked into his father's office, dropped the police reports and his notes on the desk, and said, "You gotta read this stuff." He plopped down on the couch, stretched out, and added, "It's a pretty bad cover-up when you take a good look at it. But I guess they weren't expecting anyone to do that."

Michael fell asleep before the old man had finished reading the first page of his notes.

The Bowden case's docket sheet—a log kept by the clerk of the Federal Court—summarizes the action for all of 1976, the year of the police-reports impasse, in seven lines. The log for 1977 is five pages long. Two things prompted the flurry of activity in 1977: the release of the reports, which gave the O'Donnells many leads to pursue, and the hiring of a third O'Donnell partner, who took over much of Michael's case load and freed him to devote about half his time to Bowden.

Unlike Michael, who started working part-time for his father while still in law school and never dreamed of doing anything else, Kevin O'Donnell had worked as a federal magistrate's clerk and then as an assistant district attorney before embracing the inevitable at age twenty-nine. Kevin never resisted the idea of joining his father and brother; he just wanted a bit of outside experience first. Married to his high school sweetheart, who had recently given birth to Kevin O'Donnell, Jr., he was now ready to take his place in the family business. The day he moved a desk into One State Street, the O'Donnell letterhead switched from THE LAW OFFICE OF LAWRENCE F. O'DONNELL to O'DONNELL, O'DONNELL & O'DONNELL. Kevin, of average height and weight and the only O'Donnell with eyeglasses and a constantly sunny disposition, soon became popular with the O'Donnells' clients. He was the one who returned their phone calls. He was the one who seemed to be on top of everything. But then, he wasn't working on Bowden, and never would. Instead, he tended to the income-producing work that kept O'Donnell, O'Donnell & O'Donnell in business, that paid the Bowden case expenses, and that therefore allowed his two partners to have all the fun of mounting a full-scale attack for the Bowdens.

In the police files released to the O'Donnells, there were copies of some Cambridge Police records including statements made by Ethel Caragianes and Desmond Callahan. Two lines of type were deleted from Desi's statement by what was obviously a fold in the original when it was inserted in a copying machine. Rather than protest to Judge Skinner, Michael subpoenaed Cambridge's records. If a complete copy of the statement was not forthcoming, then the O'Donnells would turn to the court. Cambridge did not respond to the subpoena. Michael immediately filed a motion to compel discovery. This time Skinner quickly ruled in the O'Donnells' favor, and Cambridge's Sergeant Petersen showed up at the O'Donnells' office to hand over everything he had on the Pearl Food Market robbery of January 29, 1975. There was a clear and complete copy of Desi's statement, which showed that the lines deleted from Boston's copy contained this sentence about Desi's first trip to the morgue: "I was taken to the morgue and was shown a body of a black man, but could not make a positive identification." Of course the O'Donnells had already learned this from the transcript of Geagan's interview with Desi that night.

With all the police records in hand, the O'Donnells started conducting depositions of potential witnesses, beginning with the two they thought could hurt them the most: Ethel Caragianes and Desi Callahan. They believed that regardless of what they could prove happened on Smith Street, they could never win over a jury if Ethel and Desi were going to testify convincingly that Bowden pulled the armed robbery. They subpoenaed Ethel first.

Ethel Caragianes arrived at the O'Donnells' office, as ordered, on the sunny afternoon of March 1, 1977. Her husband, Jim, accompanied her. Thomas F. McKenna, Jr., arrived minutes later. He was a dark-haired, husky, young-looking thirty-nine-year-old with a thick moustache. He wore a dark suit and high-mileage brown penny loafers, which actually had shiny pennies in them. Tom McKenna had worked his way through Suffolk College and Law School, become a lawyer ten years ago, and was the Law Department's new man on the Bowden case. Michael had sent the

Law Department a standard Notice of Taking Deposition. The opposition had the right to attend and question the witness.

A secretary ushered McKenna and the Caragianeses into the small windowless library where the O'Donnells' twenty-six depositions took place. There was a mahogany table in the center of the room surrounded by seven dark wooden chairs. At one end of the table a stenographer was setting up her stenotype. Without speaking, they took seats on the same side of the table, Ethel between the two men. McKenna pulled a yellow pad out of his briefcase. The O'Donnells entered. McKenna stood up to introduce himself and shook hands with both; it would be his first and last handshake with them. Michael asked whether he was related to "Patrolman McKenna." Attorney McKenna said no. The Caragianeses remained seated and said nothing. The O'Donnells took their places across the table. Michael put some files in front of the old man and nodded to the stenographer, who had Ethel raise her right hand and swear to tell the truth.

"Would you kindly state your name?" the old man began. As in all the depositions, he asked all the questions, many of which were fed to him by Michael in a note or a whisper. The old man had Ethel outline the ownership history of the Pearl Food Market (her parents opened it in 1921 on a Pearl Street corner next door to their home, and it remained a family business until she sold it two months after the robbery), then ran into trouble while still covering the background details. He wanted to know how often Ethel worked at the store around the time of the robbery.

Q: Was it your habit to be at the store daily at that time?
A: Yes and no. It depended on circumstances.
Q: Then, as a general rule, would you be at the store sometime every day?
A: No, not necessarily.
Q: Would you average four days a week at the store?
A: I couldn't say.
Q: Well, tell me, in December of 1974, how many days you were at the store.

A: I don't know.
Q: Were you there once?
A: More than that.
Q: Were you there twice?
A: Yes.
Q: Were you there ten times?
A: I couldn't say.
Q: Were you there twenty days out of the month?
A: You're making me feel—
Q: I'm not interested in how you feel.

Ethel felt she was being grilled by someone who had no right to ask questions about anything other than the robbery she was there to testify about. When she had received the subpoena, she had found it hard to believe that a private attorney could summon her to his office for a deposition. She consulted her son-in-law, a Boston lawyer, who confirmed the validity of the subpoena and told her to show up and give the best answers she could. The subpoena still bothered her. It was something criminals got. And here was this guy O'Donnell, who her son-in-law had said was a respectable lawyer, prying into every little thing about the store and, she thought, trying to twist her answers around. Her usually pallid cheeks were reddening with anger.

For his part, the old man was doing what he instinctively does when he senses resistance—pushing harder. The fiery Ethel Caragianes, who had gone after one of the robbers on the way out the door and kicked him in the groin, was not a bit intimidated by the lawyer glaring across the table at her. But she was in his ball park playing his game by his rules. Eleven questions later, he got her to concede that she was in the store in January of 1975 "on a daily basis." The hostility generated over this unimportant point marked the next two hours of question and answer.

The old man asked one of his standard background questions: "Have you ever been arrested?"

"Objection," said McKenna with a what-a-ridiculous-question roll of the eyes.

Indignantly, Ethel said, "No!" Jim Caragianes fumed.

Then the old man, desperately wanting to think the worst of this woman who identified James Bowden, but having no basis to do so, asked whether the store was really a front for a bookie operation. He knew nothing about the workings or the history of the store.

"Objection!" McKenna said instantly, trying to match Ethel's indignation.

"Never!" cried Ethel.

When I interviewed Ethel after the Bowden case was over, she was too polite to say she hated my father. But after the wild swipe he took at the business where her father, her mother, her brother, her husband, her son, and she had worked over a span of fifty-four years, what was she to think of him? She told me, "I know your father was just doing his job, and he thought Bowden was innocent and everything, but he was callous at the deposition."

Tom McKenna continued to object occasionally to the old man's questions even though objections are essentially pointless in depositions. Michael thought it was a good idea, though. "McKenna gave Ethel the idea that he was on her side," says Michael. An hour into the deposition, after one of McKenna's objections, the old man turned to him and said point-blank, "You say, 'Objection,' we get it on the record, and I totally ignore you. That's the way it goes. I'm not taking any correction from you. You are here as an observer. You are representing some people. This is a witness. You are not her counsel. I'm utterly indifferent to you."

The old man asked whether the store had ever been robbed *before* January 29, 1975. "Twice," said Ethel. One robbery was in 1974 on a day when her twenty-five-year-old son was minding the store. The robbers were never caught. When the old man asked for descriptions of the robbers, Ethel said, "My son said it was two black men, young black men. I don't remember anything about descriptions. All I know is it was a very terrifying experience for him." She recalled that the other robbery occurred "about five years before." In that one, she said, "My brother was killed."

McKenna and the O'Donnells were plainly taken aback. Suddenly soft-spoken and compassionate, the old man told Ethel that he understood how "grievous" it must be for her to be reminded of the loss of her brother.

Ethel's forty-year-old brother, Andy, an immensely popular man in the Pearl Street neighborhood, had been shot in the pelvis in that robbery. He bled to death on the floor of the store. Before the police arrived, neighbors armed with handguns ran frantically through the streets searching in vain for the killers. It was the next day that Desi Callahan began wearing a gun at work.

After the old man's expression of sympathy, still in a soft voice he asked whether anyone was arrested and convicted of the robbery-murder. Ethel said that two men were arrested a few weeks later, ultimately convicted, and given life sentences. "They were two black men," she said when asked to describe them, "young black men."

Leaving nothing to deduction, the old man gingerly asked, "Having in mind the history of running the store on Pearl Street with black people robbing it, would it be fair to say that black people are not your favorite people?"

"I would say it's unfair for you to make such a statement," Ethel angrily protested.

"Would it be fair for us to say," the old man continued softly, "as a result of the occurrence to your brother, that they are people that you have a heavy suspicion of when they come into the store?"

"No," said Ethel. She explained that many of her regular customers were black.

The old man nodded and pulled the *Phoenix* out of the files in front of him and read aloud O'Brian's quotation of Jim Caragianes: "Everyone on the street has been fighting to get the death penalty back. They were right to shoot him. They got rid of a shit bum." He asked Ethel whether her husband, who now looked embarrassed, had said that. McKenna objected.

"I don't know anything about that," she replied testily.

The old man pressed. "Did you ever have occasion to ask your husband whether or not he said that to the reporter for the *Phoenix* article of February 4, 1975, yes or no?"

"I don't have to answer you!" cried Ethel. "I don't know! I don't want to answer you!"

Michael whispered to his father, "Drop it. It's not worth it. You don't want her to walk out." If Ethel walked out on them, it would take Michael weeks to get Judge Skinner to order her to come back.

The old man finally turned to the robbery in question. Ethel's account of it, extracted in a painstaking stretch of detailed questions, was consistent with what she had told the police. Two young black men came into the store at about two-twenty or two-thirty and milled around for as long as ten minutes. She got suspicious of them and hid the big bills under the cash tray. One came to her register to buy cigarettes. The other headed for the door. Suddenly the one at the door said, "This is a holdup." She turned to see him leveling a gun at Desi, who was at the other register. She slowly emptied her cash tray, leaving the big bills hidden underneath. She then contemptuously threw the money on the floor. The guy at her register stooped to pick it up. She got a good look at him. As he headed for the door with fistfuls of cash, she scrambled after him and kicked him "in the good news." Desi chased them to their car and got the plate number. She gave it to the police over the phone when Desi came back in the store. She told the old man that the next day at the morgue, she identified Bowden as the one who scooped up the money, the one she kicked, the one who did *not* have a gun.

The old man went after the between-the-lines details. Yes, she does own eyeglasses. They were prescribed thirty years earlier. She hadn't visited her eye doctor in over ten years. No, she was not wearing her glasses when she saw the robbers. No, she could not describe the clothes on the man with the gun, but she could describe Bowden's clothes. He was wearing a leather jacket, definitely the jacket she was shown at the morgue, and a stocking cap pulled down over his hair. No, she couldn't see any of Bowden's hair when he was in the store and "couldn't tell whether he had an Afro or whether he had a bald head." No, she did not see a hat at the morgue. She can't remember whether Bowden had a moustache. Yes, she read the *Globe* article *before* going to the morgue. She recognized Bowden's picture in the *Globe* immediately. No, she was not wearing her glasses when she saw the picture. No, she did not call the police to tell them she could identify Bowden, but two hours later Sergeant Petersen called her and asked her to come with him and Desi to "see a body." On the way to the morgue, Desi told her that he couldn't identify the body the night before, and she *may* have told Petersen and Desi that she had already identified the robber from the newspaper picture. The face she saw at the morgue "was the same face" she saw in the store. Desi saw the body after she did. No, she was not wearing her glasses at the morgue. At Boston Police Headquarters, she identified the second robber, the one with the gun, from a mug shot. No, she was not wearing her glasses then either.

Michael was more than pleased. He thought Ethel's admission that she read the *Globe* story before going to the morgue was just what his father needed to keep Ethel's testimony out of the trial. He would argue that her identification of Bowden was, in legal terms, a "suggestive identification"—that it was made, or subconsciously suggested to her, as much (or more) by what she read in the newspaper as by her memory of the robbers' faces—and was, therefore, inadmissible in court. Michael passed his father a note saying he had no more questions, and that ended Ethel's deposition.

Desi's deposition, held three weeks after Ethel's, was subdued by comparison. The old man did not clash with Desi as he had with Ethel. The O'Donnell-McKenna antipathy ran as high as before, though. Tom McKenna objected to even more questions in Desi's deposition than he had in Ethel's. After thirteen objections to his last twenty questions, the old man told Desi, "This man keeps saying 'Objection! I want you to know he is abusing the process. He thinks he is getting a message to you to cue you in and that when he says, 'Objection,' for you not to answer the question. So that's utterly a waste of time, because I persist in my questioning."

The old man asked Desi what model Buick was used in the robbery. Bowden's was a Buick Electra. Desi had not mentioned a model in his statements to the police. Now he said, "Buick Century."

"Buick Century?"

"Yes."

"You said a Buick Century?"

"Yes."

"The model was a Buick Century?"

"Right. . . . I don't know if I stated *Century* then or what."

"Now do you want to change the word *Century*?"

"No."

"You're just saying now you don't know if you stated *Century* at that time. But it's clear in your mind that what you saw was a Buick Century?"

"Yes. I don't know if I told [the police] the model of the car."

"But you're satisfied today that it was a Buick Century?"

"Yes."

Desi gave the O'Donnells more evidence of suggestive identification than they had expected to get. Desi told them that before bringing him to the morgue the first time, Sergeant Petersen brought him to District 2 at about 10:00 or 11:00 P.M. Desi said he spent about twenty minutes there and spoke not only to John Geagan and several other officers whose names he could not remember, but also to two TPF men named Holland and McKenna.

Q: When you were introduced to McKenna and Holland of the TPF, they told you that they had shot this man?

A: I believe so.

Q: They told you what had happened on the street when they shot him, the police?

A: Yes.

Q: Did they tell you that before or after you went into the morgue?

A: Before. I believe the first time I was at the station when I met all these police officers.

Q: It's so—before you ever went to the morgue—isn't it, [that] Sergeant Petersen, TPF McKenna and Holland, and Sergeant Geagan had told you that this was a suspect that was in the model car with the number plate on it that you had seen, and they had shot him? You knew all that before you ever walked into the morgue on January 29—that's so, isn't it?

A: I knew everything.

Q: And they told you that they got the guy that robbed you?

A: Right.

Q: And they said, "We'd like you to come down to the morgue and identify him"?

A: Yes.

Q: And looking at him for half an hour as a corpse didn't satisfy you so that you could make an identification that he was in your store?

A: Right.

Desi said that at the morgue he was shown Bowden's Boston City Hospital ID photo and saw no resemblance to either of the robbers in that picture. He did not recognize the leather jacket he saw at the morgue because, he told the old man, the robbers both wore denim jackets.

Desi remembered that on the way to the morgue the next day, Ethel said she had already identified Bowden from the *Globe* picture. They then viewed the body separately, Ethel first. "I positively identified him that day," Desi said.

"And was there some difference between that day and the night before?" the old man asked.

"More lighting," replied Desi.

"Did you complain [the night before] about the lighting conditions?"

"I don't know."

When I talked to Desi after the Bowden case was over, he said,

"When I first walked into the police station that night, it was like being a movie star with all the attention and all these people coming up to me. All the cops were telling me, 'We got the guy! We shot him in Roxbury! We killed him!' When they told me he was dead, I thought it was all over . . . but it was really only the beginning."

The O'Donnells' next deponent was Doctor Michael Luongo, the Suffolk County Medical Examiner who performed the autopsy. The stocky, weary-looking doctor opened his Bowden file on the library table. There were Luongo's report, photographs of the entrance wounds, a lab report showing no trace of alcohol or drugs in Bowden's blood, and a list of Bowden's personal effects at the time of death: two rings, a watch, seven keys, $3 in bills, and $2.72 in coins.

The old man started reading Luongo's four-page report. Well aware of how lawyers can drag out routine testimony like his, the doctor said, "Maybe if you tell me what you are trying to establish, I could help you out."

"All right," said the old man, putting down the report. "There is a witness who viewed the body on January 29, and he used the expression that the body was in a bloated condition."

"I've described the body," said Luongo, pointing to his report, which said nothing about the body being bloated. "And I have seen some twenty thousand or more bodies. I consider myself an expert in the field of forensic pathology, and if there were observations which I should have made regarding the status of this body, I would have made them." He scanned his report and said, "It wasn't puffed up."

"And when he viewed it," the old man added, "he said there were poor lighting conditions."

"I would say in the places where the body is examined in that mortuary the lighting was adequate for its purposes."

The old man's only other concern was whether Bowden's hands were tested for gunpowder residue, which would prove he had fired a gun. "No," said Luongo. "My function in this matter was to determine the cause and manner of death. I'm not a police investigator, so that—let me finish." He saw that the old man was about to interrupt. Indeed, the old man was about to say that he knew Luongo didn't do such tests and that he asked about it only because he thought the doctor would have noticed that the hands had already been tested by the police chemist. He let Luongo continue. "My function was to determine how it was that this man came to his death, which was as a result of the gunshot wounds. So, I ruled it was a homicide, and it's a homicide in the sense that he was killed by somebody."

The police had no record of Bowden's hands being tested for gunpowder residue.

At the end of the deposition Michael made copies of everything in Luongo's file. Twenty minutes later during lunch—his usual take-out tuna sandwich and tomato soup—Michael started reading the autopsy report, and there on the first page was a routine autopsy detail that so powerfully contradicted Ethel's and Desi's positive identification of Bowden that it was enough to shock even Michael. Doctor Luongo, who measured Bowden to the tenth of an inch, reported that he was "64.5 inches" tall and weighed "an estimated 180 lbs."

Forgetting the intercom beside him, Michael yelled to Kevin, whose office is around a corner from his. When Kevin appeared, Michael asked with an uncharacteristic mix of edginess and glee, "What's this in feet and inches?" Michael, a lifelong incompetent in mathematics, didn't trust his own conversion of the Luongo figure—it was too good to be true.

Kevin looked at the line Michael pointed to in the autopsy report and said, without knowing its significance, "Uh, that's, uh, five feet, uh, four and a half inches."

"Holy shit!"

Michael grabbed the phone and dialed Pat Bowden's number for maybe the hundredth time. As the Bowden phone rang he pulled Pat's answers to Powers's interrogatories out of his files and flipped open to the page where he remembered Pat saying that her husband was five feet ten inches tall. His memory was right. That's why the O'Donnells had thought Bowden fit the robber's description. Michael knew that the descriptions Cambridge put in a teletype to Boston were TWO BLACK MALES . . . 6 FT. THIN BUILD . . . 5'10" THIN BUILD. He knew that Boston's description of Bowden, as first reported by Sergeant McHale and still used six months later by Joe Jordan, was "approximately 6–0" and a "match [of] one of the black males involved in the robbery in Cambridge." He knew that in their depositions, Ethel said Bowden was "around six feet tall" and Desi said he was "about five ten, medium build." Now Pat said she wasn't sure how tall he was. "I'm not any good on heights," she said. "When I said five ten, I must've been thinking of myself because that's how tall I am. But he was definitely shorter than me."

Michael was surprised at himself for not having thought to ask about Bowden's height or weight in the conversations he had had with Bowden's mother, sister, and brother, who are all short themselves. He chuckled at the thought of Bowden's tiny mother, a bit less than five feet tall, having a tall son. Then his eyes wandered to the morgue's list of Bowden's personal effects. "I wondered about his driver's license," he recalls. "Why wasn't it on the list? I remembered Pat telling me one of the first times I talked to her that she was surprised that they didn't give her his wallet. She figured it was lost somewhere between Smith Street and the hospital and the morgue. I didn't think anything of it then. Now there was more to it. The license had his height on it." Michael called a friend at the Registry of Motor Vehicles to get a copy of the license. The Registry man ran a computer check and couldn't find a James Bowden in the driver's license files. He wasn't surprised. He said that a lot of people in Roxbury drove without bothering to register their cars or pick up driver's licenses.

"Not this guy," said Michael. "He was a straight arrow. The car was registered to him. He was insured. His wife gave me the papers on that. And he lost his front plate one time and went into the Registry to report it. You know he knew his way around the Registry. He wasn't the type of guy to have two cars registered over five years or so and try to get away without having a license."

"Let me check it again," said the Registry man. He found James Bowden, the car owner. He had registered a used Buick Electra in 1974, which replaced the used Buick Electra he had registered a few years earlier. But the computer still could not find James Bowden, the licensed driver.

An hour later, Michael's father and mother returned from lunch—their usual leisurely paced meal at one of the many nearby restaurants where maître d's greet them by name. She picked up her bookkeeping where she had left it and he dropped into Michael's office to discuss one of their criminal cases. Soon they were working on Bowden conspiracy theory, the initial elements of which could have been confirmed by John Cullen. But because Cullen's *Globe* story of the shooting read as if he had merely spoken to Hudson and Pat Bowden, it had never occurred to the O'Donnells that Cullen had actually touched all the bases that night. They never spoke to him about his night on Smith Street, at the Brigham Hospital, and at District 2, but they shared his view that it was at the hospital that "the whole game really got fucked up."

"Try this," the old man began. "Ed McHale chases the body to the hospital. He has to identify him. He gets the license. First thing he's gonna do is call the name in to Identification for his record. Nothing. Right away he's gotta start wondering about this guy. A Roxbury punk pulling armed robberies has to have a record by the time he's twenty-five, like the license says Bowden is. Now he calls for a check on the robbers' description. The turret— and of course the turret tape of all this has to be erased later on— the turret says they're six feet and thin and five ten and thin. He's looking at a license that says five four, and he's looking at a fat guy on a stretcher."

"And they wanna match everything up with the robbery," said Michael. "What Cambridge gave them was two tall black males with an automatic and a shotgun. And what they have now is one short black guy and no guns. So they gotta make him taller and they have to get a gun for him and a friend with a shotgun. By the end of the night they've done all that."

"Yeah. McHale just declares Bowden to be six feet tall in his report."

"Right. And they get an automatic on the street. During the stakeout the turret said the robbers had an *automatic* and a shotgun. But then Desi Callahan talks to Geagan and screws that up. He tells him the only gun in the robbery was a *revolver*. And you notice Geagan never asks him for a description of the robbers. Here's Desi saying, 'I don't think the guy at the morgue was one of them,' and Geagan never says, 'Well, what did they look like? How tall were they? How much did they weigh?' Standard police description—skin color, height, weight . . .'"

"Then they bring in Winbush. Where are you gonna get a shotgun to stick in his pocket? A throw-away gun is easy enough for cops to come up with, but a throw-away shotgun? So you settle for some bullets in his pocket and go with the idea that he had a few hours to get rid of the shotgun. Should be good enough, but Eddie and Denny can't figure out what to say about Winbush in their reports. And then the whole thing collapses when Winbush turns out to be Mister Clean—no record—and with the kidney thing, he physically can't do what Eddie finally says he did."

"Then along comes Luongo with his tape measure," said Michael. "They know they can't bag Luongo, but they can keep his description of Bowden out of their reports. And that's what they did."

"Did Hudson and Jordan do that?" asked the old man, whose memory of who reported what was always inferior to Michael's. Hudson and Jordan were the only men involved whom the old man really liked. After first reading the police reports, he said, "I'd like to think that Red Hudson and Joe Jordan were just lazy and weren't actually in on all this cover-up, but . . ." Michael reminded him that Hudson's file didn't have any description of Bowden and that Jordan used McHale's.

"Shit," said the old man with a look of disappointment.

CHAPTER 11

—————

Now that they could dismiss the possibility that Bowden was involved in the robbery—something Michael had been reluctant to do, but which his father had long ago done on blind faith—the O'Donnells were ready to start questioning the cops.

They made a list of thirteen cops they wanted to depose in their little library during the spring of 1977. The plan was to get an overview from Hudson and Geagan first, then move in on the TPF men who had firsthand information: Joe Fagone on the Fabrique Nationale pistol; Jim O'Connor, Daniel Sullivan, James Keegan, and Thomas Foley on the Winbush arrest; MacDonald, McClinton, Molloy, and Dwyer on the stakeout; and finally Holland and McKenna on the shooting. Michael scheduled the depositions over a four-week period beginning in the last week of April and inserted Dave O'Brian and Ken Kobre in the final round.

Bob Hudson arrived for his deposition in the company of Tom McKenna. The O'Donnells exchanged pleasant greetings with Hudson and ignored McKenna. Hudson brought his Bowden file and kept it open on the table in front of him. He consulted it before answering each question. "I have to go back over the records," he would say. If an answer was not in his file, he would say, "I don't recall," or "I don't know." He was the most careful deponent in the case. The old man treated him indulgently, never pressing and never asking the potentially embarrassing whys:

Q: Did you talk to Edward Holland that night?
A: I don't know.

Q: Can you remember looking at an injury on Edward Holland?

A: I don't recall offhand.

Q: Do you have any reports regarding a Mr. Winbush who
was prosecuted in the Roxbury court?

A: No, I don't have anything on that. At least I don't recall.

Q: Did you read the autopsy report?

A: No.

Q: Did you get a copy of it?

A: No.

Q: Does your report involve any fingerprints [on the Fabrique Nationale]?

A: No.

The old man wanted to make sure Hudson didn't have anything up his sleeve that was going to help the defense. He didn't.
He stuck like glue to his report throughout the forty-minute
deposition. In closing, just for the hell of it, the old man asked
whether Hudson thought that Bowden had a gun and fired a shot.

"According to Holland's report," Hudson replied, "he saw a gun
with a long barrel. He heard McKenna scream out. And then he
heard a loud noise, and on the passenger side, which would be his
side, the glass broke."

The old man did not ask whether he believed that. Instead he
asked, "Now, having in mind your experience in Homicide, did
you ever hear of the expression in the police department 'throw-
away gun'?"

Hudson smiled, ran a freckled hand over his red hair, and said,
"I've heard it on TV, but not in the police department."

The next day John Geagan was under oath in the O'Donnell
library twice as long as Hudson had been. With Geagan, the old
man felt no compulsion to take it easy. His view of Geagan was
apparent from the start of the deposition. The old man began
with the Roxbury Defenders' tapes of the Winbush hearing. "I
never destroyed any tapes," Geagan said before the old man had a
chance to ask if he did. The old man hammered away at Geagan's

visit to the Roxbury Defenders office, and forty-seven questions later Geagan conceded, "I could have inadvertently erased it."

"That was really your purpose in taking the tape, wasn't it?" the old man snarled.

"No, it was not," said Geagan.

The old man moved to another tape, the one in the communications turret at Headquarters intended to record radio transmissions to and from police cars.

"What caused the malfunction?" the old man asked.

"No one knew," said Geagan.

"Did you entertain the notion that that might have been deliberately done?" the old man asked.

Obviously shaken by the rough treatment he'd just received on the Winbush tapes, Geagan sighed, "Yes, I did." Geagan said that he did not pursue the notion.

The old man asked Geagan for the identity of the other robber positively identified by Ethel and Desi from a mug shot reported by Geagan to be "photo #168902." Geagan said he could not remember who it was. The old man made a note to subpoena the mug shot and left it at that.

Like Hudson, Geagan had nothing to say about the shooting that was not in his reports. The Geagan deposition ended with some cop-to-cop talk. "Doing the job you were doing," said the old man, "living within the police department and at the same time checking their conduct, that's not the most enviable role and easiest role to be in."

"No, it wasn't," Geagan agreed.

"But, nevertheless, you did the job?"

"That's right."

"The old story is 'someone had to do it,'" said the old man. "But did you ever get the impression that the fellas would expect you to help them cover up a situation if they were wrong?"

"I don't think so," said Geagan. "I said I don't think so, because I don't think they'd expect it."

The old man asked Geagan whether he personally agreed with the Internal Affairs conclusion that the shooting was justified.

"That's not fair," said Geagan, "to put me in Holland's shoes that night, when I wasn't there." Not a surprising response from most cops, but from an Internal Affairs investigator and a member of the Firearms Discharge Review Board?

"What if you felt that this story was falsified?" the old man asked. "Being in the Internal Affairs Division, you could make a conclusion different from his. I can look at facts. I wasn't there. I can look at facts and say, 'You shouldn't have used your service revolver.' You are in Internal Affairs. You can look at facts and say, 'You shouldn't have used your revolver.' I'm not saying you said that, but what I am getting at is you can make a judgment different from theirs if the facts indicate it to you."

"I think the Internal Affairs reports show that there was some doubts about it," said Geagan.

"You're right," said O'Donnell.

That afternoon, a constable hired by the O'Donnells was serving eleven subpoenas at the TPF office. He left the subpoenas with Deputy Superintendent Joe Rowan, who said he would distribute them. According to the Federal Rules, that was "good service"—as good as putting them in the individuals' hands. The first two TPF depositions were scheduled for the following Tuesday, May 3, 1977—Joe Fagone at one o'clock and Jim O'Connor at four o'clock. When Fagone's time came, the O'Donnells and a stenographer were sitting in the library waiting for him. They were still waiting ten minutes later. And there was no sign of Tom McKenna, who had always been early for the other depositions.

At one-fifteen a middle-aged, jump-suited patrolman, one of the eldest on the TPF, stepped out of an elevator into the O'Donnells' lobby. He handed the Fagone subpoena to a receptionist, telling her that Fagone was on sick leave and would not be coming to the deposition. He turned back toward the elevators and pressed the down button. The old man, who had overheard the cop, rushed out of the library with Michael trailing behind. Grabbing the subpoena from the receptionist he bellowed, "Hey!"

The TPF man turned to see the old man coming at him roaring, "Don't you try to interfere with a subpoena of mine!"

"Larry, Larry, take it easy!" said the cop anxiously. "You know me. I'm Bob Whalen."

The old man did not recognize the face or the name. Michael recognized Whalen. He was the most feared cop of Michael's teenaged years, when Whalen was stationed in Dorchester. He stepped between Whalen and his father with visions of another BMC assault and battery case rushing to mind.

"This is federal process you're interfering with!" the old man barked.

"Joe Rowan sent me up here," said Whalen, backpedaling. "I don't know anything about this. Rowan sent me up here."

"Well, take this back to Joe, and tell him I'll have him and his whole goddamn TPF held in contempt in Federal Court if they don't show up here when I tell them to."

"Okay, Larry. Take it easy." Whalen took the subpoena. Then the elevator door opened and he left.

In about fifteen minutes Deputy Superintendent Rowan called the old man. The two knew each other well. The old man had once represented Rowan's mother in a civil matter, something Rowan himself had asked him to do. And when the old man was on the force, he worked under Rowan, who was then a sergeant. Now, on the telephone their tones were friendly and jocular. "Larry, how can you expect Fagone to come to a deposition when he's out sick?" Rowan asked.

"What hospital is he in, Joe?" the old man asked. "We'll have the deposition there."

Rowan said that he didn't know where Fagone was, only that he was on sick leave. The old man told him he was going to have Fagone held in contempt of court along with any other TPF men who might not show up at his office when subpoenaed. Rowan said he would give his men the message.

Two hours later Jim O'Connor arrived right on time for his deposition. Tom McKenna was with him. During the next three weeks, the rest of the subpoenaed TPF men appeared as scheduled, too. The four depositions of Winbush's arresting officers kept Michael so busy that week that he was unable to file a motion for contempt against Fagone.

In their depositions, Jim O'Connor, Daniel Sullivan, James Keegan, and Thomas Foley agreed on the basics of the Winbush arrest: O'Connor sat in the back seat of the ACU car on Winbush's left during the ride to District 2. Yes, all four of the cops were carrying extra bullets. O'Connor informed Winbush of his rights to remain silent and consult an attorney. Nevertheless, Winbush answered all of O'Connor's questions. Winbush admitted driving on Smith Street at about six-thirty. He claimed to have been on his way to a PTA meeting. He did have a PTA notebook with him. He said that he noticed nothing unusual on Smith Street and that he then stopped for gas a block away on Tremont Street. No, no one asked him whether he knew James Bowden. No, no one asked him whether he dropped off someone on Smith Street or stopped there for any other reason. No, no one asked him whether he fired a shot at Eddie Holland. No, no one tried to verify his story by checking with the Tremont Street gas station he mentioned or the Edison School Parent Teacher Student Association.

At the Roxbury Court hearing, O'Connor, the only one of the arresting officers who testified, had said that he searched Winbush just after handcuffing him and found nothing. Then at the District 2 booking desk he searched him again and found four bullets in his left coat pocket. In his deposition, O'Connor, perhaps thinking there was no record of what he had said under oath in Roxbury, told the same story with a new wrinkle: It was actually Sullivan who found the bullets. The old man let him think that the inconsistency went unnoticed.

The depositions isolated Sullivan and the bullets. Sullivan took exclusive credit for finding the bullets, and O'Connor, Keegan, and Foley said that they didn't actually see him find them. When he found them, Sullivan said, he handed them to O'Connor, who in turn handed them over to Walter Logue, the ballistician. No, the shells were not dusted for fingerprints. Of course the old man asked Sullivan if he planted the bullets on Winbush. Tom Mc-Kenna objected, and Sullivan calmly said, "No."

The only thing that seemed really to interest—and amuse—the old man about the bullets was how O'Connor could have missed them in the first search of Winbush.

Was it "a careful, meticulous search?" he asked.

"I searched his clothing as best I could," said O'Connor.

"And there is no question about it, you would examine a person's pockets?"

"I would feel them, yes, sir."

"It is so, isn't it, when you are arresting a man for Assault and Battery with a Dangerous Weapon, or Assault and Battery with Intent to Murder Officer Holland, one of your fellow officers, that one of the elementary things you do is put your hands in his coat pockets?"

"Not necessarily, no, sir."

The old man laughed. Michael kept a straight face. McKenna kept his head down, taking notes. O'Connor blushed and glared at the old man, who said, "But it is something you did that night?"

"I don't recall doing it on the street, going in his pockets."

"So you're saying to me, under oath, that you conducted a faulty search of a person who was alleged to have attempted to murder a fellow officer."

O'Connor looked at McKenna and said nothing. The old man taunted him: "With ten years experience, you would conduct a faulty search?"

"No, I am not saying that, no, sir."

When the bullets were finally found—the old man facetiously asked—"Did you say, 'How the hell did I miss it? I had him up against the car. I waited three hours for him. I arrested him pointing my gun at him. I knew he was charged with trying to kill Officer Holland. And how in the heck did I miss those four rounds of ammunition in the coat pocket?'" No answer. "So, having in mind the cooperative nature of this prisoner," the old man continued, "is it your testimony now that no one said to him, 'Now, Mr. Winbush, would you explain these four rounds of ammunition that Officer Sullivan found in your left coat pocket?'"

"No one said anything like that that I know of ... that I remember."

On the following Tuesday, when Michael was writing a contempt motion against Fagone, the O'Donnells received a letter from a lawyer named Michael DeMarco. It was about Fagone. DeMarco had been the Police Department's legal counsel when Di Grazia was commissioner and was well known to the O'Donnells from the struggle over the police reports. He was now in private practice. His letter stated that Fagone had been injured on duty and that DeMarco was representing him in "a petition for disability retirement." According to the letter, Fagone could not be deposed because he was then "under a doctor's care and not ambulatory."

The old man called DeMarco, whom he liked and respected, thanked him for his letter, and told him that he was not giving up on Fagone. The old man said that he was going to ask Judge Skinner for an order to hold the deposition in a hospital, or doctor's office, or Fagone's home, or wherever he had to go to question Fagone. Then he offered a compromise: "Look, Mike, I can see your guy doesn't want to get involved in this case. I can understand that. Let me interview him off the record, and if I think I won't need his testimony, I'll leave him out of the case. Out of *my* case anyway. I imagine the cops'll still need him in their case." DeMarco said he would consider the offer. An hour later he called back to accept and arranged a meeting at Fagone's home for the following week.

The next day the O'Donnells deposed Frank MacDonald and Loman McClinton in brief, back-to-back sessions. As expected, the two cops stuck to their see-nothing, hear-nothing reports of the shooting, which were actually the O'Donnells' favorite police reports. "MacDonald and McClinton were a short block away from Eddie and Denny on the stakeout," Michael explains. "They take off as soon as Eddie yells, 'We're goin' in!' They must've swung into Smith Street seconds after Eddie and Denny. They should've been right on their bumper, but they say the action was over by the time they turned the corner into Smith. It all happened so fast. That corroborates O'Brian and Kobre's three-to-five seconds. So we weren't gonna argue with them, but we didn't believe them."

The O'Donnells thought it was impossible for them to have missed the action. They figured that MacDonald and McClinton had to be rounding the corner of Smith Street by the time Eddie and Denny jumped out of their car, and that they saw the whole thing—which left them with a choice of lies: an easy one (they heard nothing and saw nothing) or a complicated one (they saw Bowden trying to run down Eddie and Denny). The O'Donnells speculated that McClinton, the black cop, may have had some qualms about the latter. McClinton's qualms, combined with the fact that as eyewitnesses they would end up in Internal Affairs interviews, made the see-nothing, hear-nothing position the only mutually acceptable one. There had to be some heavy negotiations among the ACU teammates about who was going to say what that night if it took MacDonald and MacClinton seven hours to write one-page reports saying they saw and heard nothing.

In his deposition, Loman McClinton could not remember anything he had not written in his report. A typical exchange:

Q: How long did you spend on Smith Street [after the shooting]?
A: I have no idea.
Q: When you were on the street, did you have any conversation with Patrolman Holland?
A: I don't recall.
Q: Did you have any conversation with McKenna?
A: I don't recall.
Q: Do you ever remember making a search of that Buick?
A: No, I don't remember making a search of the Buick.
Q: Do you recall Holland saying to you that night that someone tried to kill him with a shotgun?

A: That night? I don't recall. I don't recall if I had a conversation with Holland to be specific.

Frank MacDonald remembered only one thing that was not in his report. It was, however, in Sergeant McHale's summary report. "Upon questioning several people in the area," wrote McHale, "Patrolman MacDonald found one, William Alexander, of 24 Montpellier Road, Apt. #1172, Dorchester, who stated he observed what took place and would be available to testify if needed." There was no indication in McHale's report of what William Alexander saw. Michael had gone to the Alexander address the day after he read McHale's report. It was an apartment in the Columbia Point housing project, an isolated and unfriendly collection of high-rises at the edge of the harbor more than a mile from the nearest residential area. The occupants of the apartment said they had never heard the name William Alexander. Now Frank MacDonald told the old man that Alexander said he saw a flash inside the Buick, presumably from a gun Bowden must have fired. "Did you ask him if he saw anyone there with a shotgun?" the old man asked.

"No," said MacDonald. "I didn't ask him anything else actually."

MacDonald claimed he told Bob Hudson about the eyewitness, and "he said he would have to check the fellow out." There is not a word about this in Hudson's file.

"Are you aware," asked the old man, "by virtue of your conversation with Hudson or anybody else, what the results were when they checked out William Alexander?"

"No," MacDonald replied. "They wouldn't tell me."

It was actually John Geagan who checked out William Alexander. According to one of his reports, Geagan telephoned "the manager of the Columbia Point Housing Project and he stated that William Alexander is unknown at that address." That ended the follow-up on the mysterious—but, according to MacDonald, potentially very helpful—William Alexander.

Mark Molloy's and Billy Dwyer's depositions were held the day after MacDonald's and McClinton's. Molloy was called into the library first. There were no greetings exchanged, no acknowledgment of prior meetings. The deposition began on an unsettling note for Molloy. Along with the standard introductory questions—name, address, age, previous employment, years on the force—the old man asked, "Have you ever been arrested?" The old man knew nothing of Molloy's background. "I just wanted to knock him off balance at the beginning," the old man said later. "If the guy has never been arrested, the question will get him mad. People make mistakes when they're mad. If he has been arrested, it makes him think I already know about it, along with everything else about him, and that scares him."

Molloy replied that he had been arrested twice, once when he was eight years old and again the year before he joined the force. The second arrest was for "carrying a loaded rifle," he said, and he was found not guilty in court.

The old man asked about Molloy's military service—a meaningless point to all but the old man. Army doctors had declared Lawrence O'Donnell unfit for combat duty in World War II due to a childhood bout with osteomyelitis, a bone infection that weakened his skull and hospitalized him for a year shortly after his father's death. Though his forehead was left scarred and vaguely asymmetrical, he was fully recovered by the time he volunteered for the Army. But the doctors took one look at his forehead and his medical history and ruled out combat. So the old man never faced what he thought was the ultimate test of courage and soon was in awe of anyone who did. He had opposed American involvement in the Vietnam War long before it claimed one of his nephews, but if Molloy (or Dwyer) had fought in it, he would grudgingly have had to respect his courage. To his relief he found that Molloy was a National Guard medic who never left Massachusetts (and Dwyer was an "inventory specialist" in the Massachusetts National Guard).

Just when he seemed to be finished with Molloy's background, the old man skipped back to Molloy's arrest to try a hunch that he hoped would contrast nicely with Winbush's arrest: "Just getting back to that arrest on the rifle, isn't it so that the police actually produced a rifle in court as evidence?"

"Right," said Molloy, who favors short answers when questions make him tense.

When the old man finally came to the matter at hand, Molloy seemed confused. Like the McClinton-MacDonald backup unit, Molloy said he and Dwyer did not see or hear the shooting. Molloy was then asked whether he talked to Holland after the shooting. "Yes," Molloy replied. "He said, 'He tried to hit me. He tried to hit me.'" Minutes later, Molloy changed his mind. "That was McKenna," he said. "It wasn't Holland."

"What did Holland say to you?" the old man asked.

"Nothing," said Molloy. He then remembered speaking to Holland at District 2. "He was nervous," said Molloy, "and stated he didn't want to talk about it until he got everything straight."

Molloy said he did not hear Eddie's story until the Winbush hearing, which was the first time he heard of a shotgun attack on Eddie. "There wasn't any talk about a rifle when Winbush was first arrested?" the old man asked.

"Right."

In his report, Molloy had written that during the stakeout "A check with the dispatcher on channel #1 confirmed that this was the vehicle used in the holdup." Now the old man asked, "Who checked with the dispatcher?"

"Myself," said Molloy, insisting that the number he checked was 4F•6838, the number Eddie gave him over the walkie-talkie. The old man told Molloy that that was Bowden's number, but that Bowden's number was not the number the Cambridge police had broadcast, which was 4F•6368. The old man told him of the dispatcher's handwritten notes, which indicate that the number Molloy checked was 4F•6368. "I didn't know it was different until now," said Molloy, even though O'Brian had pointed out the difference in his article, which Molloy had read. He conceded that he could have mistakenly checked that number instead of the one actually on Bowden's car.

"And it just so happened," said the old man, "that the number you put down [in the report] corresponded with the actual number that was on the car on Smith Street."

"Could be."

When Billy Dwyer took his place across the table from the old man, he supported Molloy on every point. He, too, said he had never known of the different plate numbers before the old man brought it up, though he had read O'Brian's story.

The old man read an excerpt of O'Brian's story to Dwyer: "Bill Dwyer spots me and smiles broadly, 'How is this for action? Did we put on a good show for you?'" He asked whether Dwyer remembered talking to O'Brian after the shooting. Dwyer said he did. The old man did not ask him to confirm the quotation. He intended to save that for the trial.

Though Dwyer remembered talking to O'Brian, he claimed no memory of talking to Eddie or Denny after the shooting. The O'Donnells had not yet seen Ken Kobre's photographs. Kobre had three shots of Dwyer talking to Eddie at three separate times after the shooting.

Q: When you were on Smith Street that night, Officer Dwyer, did you talk to Holland?

A: I don't recall so, no.

Q: Did you talk to McKenna on Smith Street?

A: Not that I recall.

Q: When did you first hear of Ernest Winbush?

A: I don't recall.

Q: When you got back to the station house, did you have a conversation with Holland?

A: I don't believe so.

Q: Later that night, how about McKenna?

A: Not that I recall, no.

Q: Have you had any conversation with Holland since January 29, 1975, where you said to him, "What happened?"

A: No.

Q: So, as of this moment [May 12, 1977], you have never had a conversation, an exchange with him, telling you what happened on Smith Street that night?

A: Not that I recall.

Q: And how about McKenna? Did he ever exchange with you what happened on Smith Street that night?

A: At one point. I don't recall when it was, but I remember him relating to me that he was petrified and scared—and he had been on the job awhile—and he thought he was going to die. The guy was backing up at him.

In any court case some of the questions raised can be answered by objective facts, while others are a matter of whom to believe. For example, the question *Did Bowden rob the Pearl Food Market?* was answerable once the objective fact that Bowden was short and fat was discovered. On the other hand, the Bowden case's central question, *What happened on Smith Street?*, was for the most part a matter of whom to believe—O'Brian and Kobre? Eddie? Denny? Jessina Stokes? Here the O'Donnells thought their case turned on the outcome of a credibility contest.

O'Brian seemed credible on paper, but the O'Donnells wondered what he would be like as a witness. Would he be strong on the three-to-five seconds? Or would he say it could have been five to ten, or ten to twenty, or twenty to thirty? Would he back off his *Phoenix* quotations of Eddie and Denny and say he could be wrong on some of them? And what about Kobre? How close would his memory be to O'Brian's? What if they contradicted each other on details not covered in their Internal Affairs interviews? And then what about Eddie and Denny? After two years, would they tell their story with authority and make it sound believable? Would they finally be able to integrate the Thunderbird and the shotgun into the action or would they drop that stuff completely? Would they insist that Bowden fired a shot or settle for his just trying to run them down? Would they be better than O'Brian and Kobre on details?

O'Brian and Kobre were deposed on the same afternoon in May. O'Brian spent two hours and fifteen minutes in the library. Then Kobre went in for forty-five minutes. Neither the O'Donnells nor Tom McKenna had ever seen or spoken to either man before their depositions. From the muscle of his prose, the O'Donnells had pictured O'Brian as a tough Boston Irish type. They were surprised to find themselves sitting across the table from a short, soft-spoken guy who exuded all the toughness of a poet. But not for a second were they disappointed. O'Brian was a better witness than the old man had hoped for. And Michael was as impressed by the reporter as his father was. "He remembers what kind of pencil he was using, for chrissake," Michael told me weeks later.

O'Brian affirmed all the major points in his *Phoenix* story. He said that he had been taking notes constantly and that every quotation in the *Phoenix* came from his notes. He was sure about the three-to-five seconds, not hearing Eddie and Denny shout at Bowden, not hearing the Buick's engine racing or its tires screeching, and hearing about eight rapid-fire shots, all of which sounded alike.

Kobre, in turn, was also sure about all these things with the exception that he thought he heard only three shots. Not having taken notes or written an article about the incident, Kobre was understandably softer on details than O'Brian, but everything he did remember corroborated O'Brian. Both were true to their normal personalities in the depositions. O'Brian was reserved and deliberate; Kobre was engaging and expansive. Where O'Brian would limit an answer to exactly what he saw or heard, Kobre, a former psychology student, would include atmosphere and intuitions:

> O'BRIAN: McKenna had advised us that if there was shooting, we should hit the floor.
> KOBRE: There was a fear that they had a shotgun, and they warned us to stay down. . . . They said, "Get down low in back." They expected shooting. . . . The tension was tremendous at this point . . . and the thing had been kind

of building up. . . . We had spent this entire day . . . and basically nothing had happened all day, and I had this sense that now they were kind of showing off, which was one of the problems.

In O'Brian's and Kobre's deposition, Tom McKenna for the first time asked questions. His brief cross-examinations reviewed details already covered by the old man, except for one: Did Bowden get out of the Thunderbird? O'Brian was certain of it. Kobre thought so, but was not sure.

The next day the O'Donnells deposed Eddie, and the day after that, they deposed Denny. Their depositions lasted three hours each. To the O'Donnells' great delight, the defendants turned out to be worse witnesses than had been indicated by their reports, Internal Affairs interviews, and Roxbury Court testimony.

"First of all," Michael told me weeks later when I began reading the transcripts of Eddie's and Denny's depositions, "they look pretty bad. Denny's got the long hair going down his neck and they both have hard-guy mugs. Their nonsense might be all right for Internal Affairs, but when the old man gets them on the stand, he's gonna kick the shit out of them." As an afterthought Michael said, "You know, the old man really hates these two. I had to pull him away from Denny. The old man was gonna go at him in the library. . . . It's a fuckin' gang war now—our guys against their guys. We may lose it, but at least we're gonna knock some people down."

The old man began both depositions with personal background questions. Eddie admitted to having been arrested twice, both times while visiting relatives in Miami before joining the force. His first arrest, when he was in his early twenties, was, as Eddie remembered it, for "swimming with a girl." The old man would normally pick at information like that for all the fun he could find, but he was so deliberately heading for a confrontation with Eddie that he ignored it. Nothing amused him in Eddie's or Denny's depositions. Eddie said his second run-in with the Miami police was for being a "suspicious person under the old SP law." When pressed Eddie added that he was also charged with larceny that time.

"How long did they hold you?" the old man asked.

"They held me seventy-two hours and released me."

"Was anyone with you arrested at the same time?"

"No. I went to see a friend of mine from Boston that was locked up at the time," Eddie explained, "and they said, 'Grab him too.'" His friend, who was not later released, had also been arrested for larceny, according to Eddie. The old man left it there, preferring to let Eddie think that he already knew all about it. With Denny, the old man was so anxious to get on with the fight that he forgot to ask him whether he had ever been arrested.

Eddie and Denny gave the old man their by-now-familiar accounts of the action on Smith Street. Inconsistencies with each other and with their own previous statements developed when the old man had them describe each move the Buick made. Both said the Buick had come to a stop when they jumped out of the ACU car. According to Eddie, the Buick then made three threatening moves, hitting him twice. He had always previously claimed to have been hit three times. According to Denny, the Buick made four moves, forcing him to jump back three times. He had previously told Geagan of five moves and in his report wrote of only two. Eddie told the old man that the first Buick move was forward, "maybe forty feet." Denny said the first move was a swerve backward toward him.

Eddie unwittingly corroborated a detail of Jessina Stokes's story. Jessina had said that the man on the side of the car that she could see grabbed one of the door handles. When Eddie said, "Then I grabbed the handle of the door," the old man emphasized it:

"You grabbed the handle of the door?"

"Right."

As in the Geagan interview, Eddie made it all the way through his story of the shooting without mentioning the shotgun attack. When the old man asked about it, Eddie said that as he was being hit by the Buick the second time, a man stepped out of the Thunderbird and fired a shot at him. "This happened just before I went down," he said.

"Did you yell, 'Dennis, watch out! There's a guy with a rifle behind you!'?" the old man asked.

"No, I didn't. . . . No."

"Did you shoot at the guy with the rifle to protect McKenna?"

"No, I did not," said Eddie. "It all happened so fast."

Denny stuck to his simpler claim of not having seen the Thunderbird again after it pulled away from the still-parked Buick and not having heard shotgun or rifle fire. He also continued to maintain that he memorized the number of the Thunderbird when it turned onto Smith Street before it was at all suspicious. When asked, Denny said that about "two dozen" cars turned onto Smith Street during the stakeout. "Now," said the old man, "you didn't write down the numbers of all the cars that turned from Parker Street into Smith Street?"

"No, I didn't," replied Denny.

"Because you would have no reason to write it down as it made that turn," said the old man.

"No."

"In fact, your only interest in the Thunderbird was when it stopped parallel to the Buick."

Denny agreed: "It became more prominent in my concern with the car under surveillance when it stopped next to the car that was under my surveillance."

"Now," said the old man, "when it stopped next to the car that was under surveillance, you could not read the number plate of the Thunderbird."

"Not then," Denny replied. "Not from that distance. I had already made a note in my mind of the number of the Thunderbird as it went by me."

"Can you suggest any reason that you would take such particular note of this Thunderbird?"

"I don't recall it doing anything erratic," said Denny, "but when I was sitting there, I was taking in as much as I could observe, and I made a note in my mind and was able to recall it as the case necessitated."

"Isn't it a fact," the old man asked with a straight face, as if expecting an affirmative answer, "you created that story for Geagan—that you just mysteriously somehow or other remembered that number of the Thunderbird—because you didn't want Geagan to know that Molloy and Dwyer copied down the number?"

"That's not true."

"All right. Now you said you spoke to Molloy and Dwyer [after the shooting] and you asked them, 'Where's the Thunderbird?' "

"They said it never came out that end of Smith Street," said Denny.

"You remember that very clearly, don't you, that they said it never came out the end of Smith Street?"

"I remember that very clearly, yes."

"You remember very clearly," said the old man, "because you contrived that answer and it is false. The Thunderbird went by Molloy and Dwyer, and they recorded the number."

"Objection," said Tom McKenna.

"No, that's not true," said Denny.

The O'Donnell theory on the Thunderbird agreed with Internal Affairs in that the car did pass Molloy and Dwyer when it left Smith Street. The O'Donnells believed there were two possible reasons that Molloy and Dwyer did not stop the car: They were parked in a driveway across St. Alphonsus Street, the busy street Smith emptied into, and could not move in fast enough to block Smith Street; or, they had no idea that the Thunderbird was involved in the action. According to O'Brian, Eddie shouted only, "We're going in!" over the walkie-talkie, and not a word about the Thunderbird. So, the O'Donnell theory had it, when Molloy and Dwyer saw the Thunderbird, they let it go. One of them—probably Molloy, since Dwyer was driving—made a note of the plate number, just in case it meant something later on. Then they sped down Smith Street, where they knew they would be needed and where they probably already had heard shooting. The story of the Thunderbird going through the school yard instead of passing Molloy and Dwyer was, the O'Donnells believed, concocted for the Roxbury Court to make Winbush look like a fleeing criminal. Of course, insisting that the Thunderbird left through the school yard meant someone had to get the number before that, which, in that scenario, could have been done only by Eddie and Denny. In the O'Donnell view, Denny's claiming to have remembered the number coincidentally was simply his way of lending a needed hand on Eddie's Thunderbird-shotgun story. "Once they saw what a bad case they had against Winbush," said Michael, "they probably regretted the whole Thunderbird story, but by then the case was already in the Roxbury Court, so they were stuck with it."

In the Geagan interviews, only Denny had said he remembered the Thunderbird's number. He told Geagan that he gave it to Eddie after the shooting and Eddie called it in to the turret for a listing. But Eddie had told Geagan, "I believe Dennis put it over the air. He had the number of the vehicle. He got that probably, uh, I don't know where he got it from, to be honest." But now, in his deposition, Eddie said that he also noticed the number when the Thunderbird turned the corner and he also remembered it.

The O'Donnells were happily surprised by other points of conflict between Eddie and Denny's deposition testimony and the transcripts of the Geagan interviews. "Either Tom McKenna didn't give them the Geagan transcripts to study before the depositions as he should have," said Michael, "or they just didn't do their homework." Like Molloy and Dwyer, Eddie and Denny insisted that they had never heard of the difference between the reported getaway car's number and Bowden's plate number, through they did admit reading O'Brian's article, where the difference is made clear. Eddie even told the old man he had "never discussed it" with Geagan, when in fact he had, and Geagan plainly told him of the difference in the numbers.

The most striking contradiction of the Geagan transcripts came in answer to the question "Did you ever talk with Attorney Frank McGee about this matter?" The old man put the question to Eddie at three different points in their three hours together and got three different replies: (1) "I talked to him, yes, one time." (2) "I haven't talked to him about it." (3) "I don't recall talking to him."

Denny, when asked the same question, told the old man that he spoke to McGee only when the Bowden lawsuit was filed. "I had been directed to go to the Law Department, and I asked him his advice. He said that I should go to the Law Department and that they would act as my counsel in this regard."

"Did you have any other conversation with him?" asked the old man.

"Other than that," said Denny, "I can't recall no discussions with Frank McGee regarding this matter."

But the tapes and transcripts of each of their Internal Affairs interviews show that McGee was there. And evidence of a previous consultation with McGee came from Bob Hudson, who, in his report and in his deposition, said that he spoke to McGee the night of the shooting at District 2, where McGee was already acting as the ACU team's attorney. "When they denied talking to Frank McGee," the old man said later, "I didn't mention the Hudson and Geagan stuff because I wanted them to think they could get away with things like that in court. I wanted them to get used to taking long leads off base."

The old man's contempt for Eddie and Denny was apparent throughout the depositions. For example, in questioning Eddie about the gun that he claimed to have seen in Bowden's hand, he asked, "You killed him for firing the gun at you; that's so, isn't it, Mr. Holland?"

"I killed him for pointing it at me," said Eddie, "and trying to run me over."

"Didn't you enter into a scheme with your fellow officers to frame this up as though he had a gun in his hand?" the old man growled.

"Objection," said Tom McKenna.

"No, sir!" Eddie protested.

"You know it's a throw-away gun, don't you?"

"Objection," said McKenna.

"No, I don't!" said Eddie.

"And wouldn't you like at this time, Mr. Holland, while you're under oath, just to say, 'Mr. O'Donnell, it's been a burden on me for a long time. He didn't have a gun'?"

"Objection!"

"No, sir!"

"'That I am making it up to defend myself for being reckless and killing him,'" the old man continued. "Isn't that what you really want to say to me?"

"Objection!"

"No, sir."

The old man's final question to Eddie was: "Mr. Holland, insofar as the testimony that you have given here this afternoon on this date, would you consent to taking a polygraph test in relation to that testimony?"

"Objection!" said McKenna.

"No," said Eddie.

Denny's three hours in the library ended in a near-violent clash started by a soft-spoken taunt from the old man. Leaning over the table with an icy stare, he asked Denny, "Did you ever think of yourself as a killer?"

"Objection!" Tom McKenna barked with more indignation than ever.

"Did you?" the old man continued in a shout. "How do you like being called a killer?"

"Objection!"

Startled, Denny began saying, "Would you like—"

The old man cut him off: "Don't you rate being called a killer? You killed a fellow, didn't you?"

Michael grabbed his father's arm to calm him.

"Objection!"

"No, I don't like being called a killer!" Denny replied excitedly.

"Would you like to be called a killer?" Tom McKenna yelled at the old man.

"He is a killer!" the old man roared as he jumped out of his chair. Then, jabbing a finger at Denny, he yelled, "You never got hit by a car! You never got fired on! You went up against the wrong car, and you phonied up this story!"

"Objection!"

"Isn't that a fact?" the old man asked as Michael wrestled him toward the door.

"Objection!"

"That's not true!" cried Denny.

Kevin, having heard the commotion through the closed door of the library and the closed door of his office, had come running into the room. He read the scene instantly, and helped Michael get the old man out into the corridor.

Realizing that the O'Donnells were leaving, a flabbergasted Tom McKenna protested: "Just a minute! I might have some questions!"

McKenna had not posed one question to any of the cops yet deposed.

"So, go ahead and ask them," snarled the old man. And, as the deposition transcript notes, "Mr. L. O'Donnell left the room."

The McKennas sat in stunned silence for a moment. Then Tom McKenna turned to the shocked stenographer and said, "That will be it."

That night, after a working dinner, the O'Donnells drove to Nahant, an affluent suburb on a narrow bootlike peninsula jutting into Boston Harbor from the North Shore. The old man pulled his rusting Cadillac—he buys a new one every ten years—into a tree-lined side street a few hundred feet from the beach and parked in the wide driveway of a modern, picture-windowed house with a good-sized front lawn. It was Joe Fagone's house. He and his lawyer, Michael DeMarco, were waiting inside for the O'Donnells.

DeMarco greeted them at the door, ushered them into the large, comfortable living room, and introduced them to Fagone. Everyone shook hands and used first names. It had taken several hours after Denny's deposition for the old man to calm down. But he had made the switch from brawler to deal maker, and now here he was smiling and shaking hands with the guy who he figured had planted the Fabrique Nationale on Smith Street.

Fagone, thirty-five, looked healthy, but said he was suffering from a painful back strain that would require surgery. Michael noticed that he did seem to move awkwardly.

After a few minutes of small talk, Michael turned on a tape recorder and directed the conversation to the night in question. "Did *you* discover the gun while you were flashing around your flashlight," he asked, "or did someone say, 'Joe, look what I found'?"

"I found the gun," Fagone replied. He said that he began searching as soon as he arrived at the scene about twenty minutes after the shooting. The search took "about an hour, an hour and a half." And he found it after Harry Byrne directed him to look under some parked cars.

In his report Fagone had not said how long it took to find the gun. Nor did he mention Sergeant Byrne's suggestion of where to look. "When Fagone told us that," said the old man later, "I knew what was going on at the TPF. They didn't want a Fagone testifying because all those sons of Erin couldn't trust him to carry the ball.*

"Dave O'Brian thought it took an hour to find the gun, but he wasn't positive on the time. Then Fagone comes along saying it was even longer than that, and that Harry Byrne told him where to look. The TPF wasn't trying to protect Fagone. They were trying to protect themselves. That's why Joe Rowan sent back the suppoena [*sic*]."

The O'Donnells reviewed for Fagone an abbreviated list of the weaknesses in the police story, which prompted Fagone to say, "There's so many things that don't fit."

---

* *Sons of Erin* is the old man's favored expression for men of Irish ancestry. With the exception of Loman McClinton and Henry Nelson (both black) and Joe Fagone (Italian), all the TPF men involved in the Bowden case, as well as Bob Hudson, John Geagan, and Joe Jordan, are of Irish ancestry.

In thirty minutes, the conversation came full circle back to the Fabrique Nationale. Michael told Fagone what he thought was the most persuasive proof that Bowden did not fire the automatic. As everyone present knew, when an automatic is fired, at the same time that a bullet is flying out of the barrel, the bullet's shell casing is being ejected sideways from the firing chamber, and the shell falls a few inches or feet from the firing position. "According to Holland's testimony," said Michael, "Bowden is holding the gun right in the middle of the car. All the windows are closed. He takes a shot at him. It's an automatic. The shell is going to pop into the back seat or onto the floor. Logue goes over the car with a fine-tooth comb. No shell."

"Logue brought in extra lighting," the old man added, "super lighting to do this."

"They never matched up any ballistics evidence with that gun you found," said Michael.

"It seems to be your contention," Fagone said quietly, "that it was planted."

The O'Donnells nodded. "They didn't know then that the Cambridge gun was a revolver," said Michael.

"Am I going to have to appear [in court]?" Fagone asked. "From what I hear, I don't want to get involved."

The old man said he would not call him as a witness if Fagone would give him an affidavit stating when and how he found the gun. DeMarco and Fagone readily agreed.

The O'Donnells' work was done for the day. A few weeks later, when I started asking Michael questions, I wondered why the old man had agreed to let Fagone avoid testifying. "The only reason to put him on the stand," Michael said, "is so the old man can accuse him of planting the gun. But that could backfire. He's not like the rest of them. He's an honest-sounding guy. Some jurors could like him and believe him. We accuse him of planting the gun. He denies it, strongly denies it, the jury believes him, and thinks we're just taking a wild shot at him, which we would be. We don't want to look like we're taking any wild shots. This way we get the hour-and-a-half search from his affidavit and leave the jury wondering why this mystery man Fagone doesn't come in to testify. We're better off all around."

Both sides left Fagone out of the Bowden case after the O'Donnells obtained his affidavit.

Later that year, with Michael DeMarco as counsel, Joe Fagone left the force with a disability retirement pension. In 1981, I found him living in a recently built house five miles from the nearest paved road in the Green Mountains of Vermont. It was a warm Sunday afternoon in September. He and his wife showed me more easygoing courtesy than I deserved after showing up unannounced at their front door. We sat on his porch for a few hours. Forest noises filled what would have been some long silences on my tape recording of our conversation. Fagone had a couple of beers. I eventually got around to asking if he planted the Fabrique Nationale. He smiled. A few days before, a former TPF partner of his, who had refused to speak to me, had told him that I was looking for him. Fagone knew then that I was going to ask this question.

Presently he shook his head and said, "I couldn't possibly even imagine planting a gun in a situation like that. Why should I? For who? Because of what?" He shrugged and warned me that what I was about to hear would sound "corny." Mistakenly slipping into the present tense for a moment, Fagone, now a bearded woodsman, said: "My attitude about being a cop is probably different than anybody in the department. Always has been. I don't like to see a lot of bullying because you have a badge. Perhaps I said that once too often. . . . In my eight years on the job, nothing ever happened that I intentionally hurt anybody and went against the oath I took as a police officer."

Did he know police officers who would plant a gun in such a situation? "Yeah, oh, yeah, there are police officers who would do that. There are police officers in any department who are capable of that."

Fagone insisted that he still could not accept the notion that the gun was planted, but conceded, "I think maybe I could've been used. I think maybe some sergeants on that job, specifically the

TPF, were more than capable of doing that and a lot worse . . . and have." There were only two TPF sergeants involved in the Bowden case. Of Ed McHale, Fagone said, "We used to call him 'Shaky' McHale. That was his nickname. He was just shaky in every situation. I would've picked a lot of other sergeants to lead me." Of Harry Byrne, he said, "He was painted blue. He's a typical Irish cop. Man, I'll tell you, he's a cop from the word go."

Fagone admitted that he had considered the possibility that the gun was planted by the police. In fact, he said that he thought of that the moment he found it. "What I couldn't understand at the time and what I don't understand now is where I found the gun," he told me. "It should've been found immediately. I mean they had a lot of police officers there. . . . You could see the gun very clearly. It wasn't hidden like behind a wheel or lodged up under anything. It was obvious. . . . In fact, it's funny, walking up searching for the gun, I saw another team sitting parked on the side of the road in a car—all sitting in the car—and I thought that was very odd. Obviously they were there before we got there. And we were given the orders to search, and that's what struck me wrong. I said to myself, 'Why the fuck don't these guys search for it? What are we? Niggers?' You know, we're given all the crazy jobs. And then I walked by after the gun was found and I was gonna say something to them, but Byrne pulled us off and told us to go back to the barn. He said, 'You're all through. Go ahead home.' So, I never did ask them what their situation was."

Had he asked such questions, Fagone thought, "I just would've been sent down some place directing traffic in the middle of Frog Pond [a manmade pond in Boston Common]. I mean, you just do what you're told. You don't question anything."

CHAPTER 12

Depositions are expensive. There is a constable's fee for serving the deposition subpoena—about $30 if he doesn't have to travel beyond the suburbs. There is a mandatory witness fee of $21 plus travel expenses for the deponent. Stenographers charge by the page of deposition transcript. The ninety-four-page transcript of Denny's deposition cost the O'Donnells $251.59. And the three hours they spent with Denny could have been spent on one of their corporate client's cases, such as Sentry Insurance Company's, for which Lawrence O'Donnell then received $120 per hour and Michael O'Donnell recieved $60 per hour. So O'Donnell, O'Donnell & O'Donnell's real cost—including the missed billing hours—of a long deposition like Denny's was more than $800.

The bills for depositions poured in as the transcripts were delivered in the late spring and summer of 1977. Michael and the old man rarely saw the bills. Their secretaries opened them, stamped a date received on them, and put them in an overflowing accounts-payable tray in a small office in the middle of the O'Donnell suite. They became my mother's worry.

Frances Marie Buckley O'Donnell was trained in classical bookkeeping—paying bills on time—in her uncle's jewelry store, where extreme conservatism prevailed in financial matters. Uncle Ed Reagan, a quiet, even-tempered man, never miscalculated how much inventory to stock, never had a cash flow problem, never borrowed money, never overextended himself in any way, and never got rich. But he lived comfortably and had something to leave his children after he sold the store and died. He was a model businessman in the eyes of his niece Frances, who fondly remembers her days at Uncle Ed's store.

In 1975, my mother started working in my father's office, where she soon discovered that her financial training was useless. She adopted the pseudonym Miss Frances, because her job sometimes involved as much bill juggling as bill paying. When a creditor called, she wanted to be able to say things like: "Mr. O'Donnell is in court this week, but I'm going to try to speak to him next week about expediting this payment." She didn't want creditors asking, "Why don't you mention it to him at dinner?" Cash flow problems can be acute in an unpredictable business like the O'Donnells'. All too often in 1977, my mother found herself making painful decisions about when and how to pay the $2,055.84 monthly office rent bill, the $788 monthly employee health-insurance premium, the $600 monthly telephone bill, as well as countless other bills for law books, stationery, and miscellaneous items. The main reason for the cash flow problems was the Bowden case. Not only was it pulling Michael and the old man away from income-producing work, but it was now generating bills of its own—top-priority bills. The old man had told Miss Frances to pay the Bowden bills as soon as they came in. He didn't want to have trouble getting stenographers or constables just because he owed them a thousand or two.

Kevin, the only business-minded lawyer in the firm, often looked over his mother's shoulder at the Bowden bills. In irregularly scheduled Friday afternoon partners' meetings, he would complain about what a drag on the business the case had become. "A third of nothing is nothing," he would say, reminding his partners of the unlikeliness of victory and the apparent impossibility of collecting a judgment. Kevin never suggested to the old man that he should drop the case, but he often did to Michael. Kevin never created acrimony. He just talked wistfully about how much richer and less harried the partners would be without Bowden cutting into their profits and their time. Michael always told him that he was right, promised never to let the old man take a case like Bowden again, then went back to work on it.

I joined the team in June and made the matter $200 per week worse. I was glad to be finally out of the parking lot, but Kevin was none too pleased by my presence. It was nothing personal—just the money. To mollify him, I gave him a hand with the paperwork on his desk whenever the Bowden action slowed down—which wasn't often, because trial preparations were beginning.

The old man wanted an architectural model of the Mission Hill housing project made for use in court. A man who had built some of his ship models agreed to do it. The model builder asked for and received $500 to get started.

We were going to need an actuary to give the jury an idea of how much money Bowden would have earned in the rest of his working life—one of the law's ways of putting a price on wrongful death. We hired the best in Boston, Jack Marshall, senior actuary of the John Hancock Insurance Company. All communication with Marshall was left to me. Though Marshall's explanations of economics and actuarial science are designed for elementary school graduates, he could never make himself understood to Michael or the old man, both of whom tune out automatically at the sound of anything mathematical. Marshall's services in the Bowden case cost $1,100 in the end.

The old man wanted an independent ballistics expert to review Walter Logue's work. He hired Massachusetts' best, Carl Majeskey, formerly the Massachusetts State Police ballistician. In a motion filed in May, Michael had persuaded Judge Skinner to order the department to allow Majeskey to examine all the ballistics evidence. For $49 an hour, Majeskey began by studying Logue's report, as well as Eddie's and Denny's reports, I.A.D. interviews, Roxbury Court testimony, and depositions. Then on June 10, he spent the day in Logue's ballistics lab.

On June 24, 1977, Majeskey sent us a report, followed by bills amounting to $1,336.58. Majeskey agreed with Logue on the basics but offered three important clarifications concerning the Fabrique Nationale:

1. "The five (5) cartridges reportedly removed from this pistol *are not correct for this weapon.* These 5 cartridges are .32 S&W shorts and they are rimmed and designed for revolvers." The automatic could reliably fire these revolver bullets only if "manually loaded one at a time."

2. "On page 3 of the Ballistics Report there is mention of 'foreign material' in the bore of the pistol that is 'consistent in appearance to powder residue.' This statement would lead one to believe that the weapon had been recently fired." But nothing in Logue's findings indicated that. Powder residue can be found in guns that have not been recently fired because "even after cleaning, a barrel will sweat out additional residue." And since Logue did not do chemical analysis of what he thought looked like powder residue, "it could have been anything such as lint, rust, etc."

3. "There was no discharged cartridge case or projectile recovered that would indicate the .32 A.C.P. Fabrique Nationale Model 1922 semiauto pistol was fired."

After reading Majeskey's report, I still had one unanswered ballistics question. I asked Michael, "Has Carl Majeskey told you what color flame comes out of Eddie's and Denny's guns?"

"No, I meant to ask him that."

As Michael dialed Majeskey's number, I said, "Jessina says blue."

"Yeah, I know. . . . Hello, Carl, this is Michael O'Donnell. . . . Good. How ya doin'? . . . Listen, on those two TPF guns, I meant to ask you, would flame have come out of the barrel when they were fired? . . . What color? . . . Okay, that's it for today. . . . Yeah. Thanks, Carl." Michael hung up the phone and said, "Well, I guess Jessina's for real."

"Blue?"

"Blue."

During John Geagan's deposition Michael had made a couple of notes to himself about subpoenaing more material from the Police Department. He wanted whatever reports and records the department had that explained how the turret tape malfunction occurred, as well as anything—a bill for repairs or parts, for example—that indicated how, when, and by whom the taping system was repaired. He also wanted mug shot #168902, the one Geagan said Ethel and Desi had agreed was that of the second robber. And he wanted the two other mug shots that Cambridge's Sergeant Petersen reported Ethel and Desi had chosen as depicting the second robber. He subpoenaed these items in June. In July the department's lawyer, Nicholas Foundas, in a written response said that the department had no documentary evidence of the turret tape breakdown or of its repair—which was exactly what we expected to hear. And Foundas refused to turn over the mug shots because, he said, doing so "would constitute an illegal dissemination of a criminal offender's record." Michael filed a Motion to Compel, and Foundas filed a Motion to Protect. Judge Skinner referred the matter to Magistrate Cohen, who eventually scheduled a hearing on the motions for the first week of October.

In the meantime, we held seven more depositions. Intrigued by Eddie's and Denny's refusal to admit that they had consulted Frank McGee at District 2 that night and that he represented them during the Internal Affairs investigation, we deposed McGee one sweltering August afternoon. With McGee, a courthouse acquaintance, the old man was at his courteous best. We expected McGee to claim, rightfully, that he was bound by the confidentiality of attorney-client communication and could tell us nothing about having represented Eddie and Denny. Instead, he flatly denied representing Eddie and Denny: "I have no memory—and this is a fact—of speaking with McKenna or Holland about this." He said he knew Eddie and Denny well and saw them frequently in 1975 because the TPF office was "right next door" to the patrolmen's union office where McGee spent most of his workday. "We would quite often go right around the corner and have beers together," he said. Confronted with Geagan's transcripts of the I.A.D. interviews, McGee shrugged. "If it says I was there, I was there." Nevertheless, he continued to claim no memory of being there or ever being consulted on the matter.

McGee did remember trying to prevent O'Brian and Kobre from riding in the police cars that afternoon but claimed "no recollection of being contacted by anyone that night." In reaction to Hudson's report of speaking to him at District 2, McGee said, "I have no recollection of being at District Two in connection with this incident." Nor, said McGee, did he have a "recollection of even a telephone conversation" with Hudson.

When he first heard of the shooting, he considered it a routine incident, he said, because "there was no civil rights lawyers, like Bill Homans, out there knocking the doors of District Two down."

McGee readily admitted that on-scene consultation with patrolmen involved in shootings is "part of my job." For such consultations, he said, "I am and must be available around the clock." He explained that he could always be reached at the union office during business hours and at other times through "the communications division in police headquarters, to wit, the turret."

After the deposition the old man was the first to say what we all were thinking: "There must've been a lot of good stuff on the turret tape, huh?"

In a final round of depositions, we looked at the possibility of Bowden's participation in the robbery from the Boston City Hospital perspective. We began with the three hospital employees whose names surfaced in the Homicide Unit's reports: Henry Smith, the head of the Housekeeping Department; Elsie Pina, Bowden's supervisor that day; and Donald Webster, the supervisor who saw him punch out that day.

The first one deposed, Henry Smith, a heavy, bald black man, had hired James Bowden in 1967. In eight years, though Smith never saw Bowden outside the hospital, he thought he came to know him well. The old man asked whether there was anything "in his demeanor, conduct, or manner that would suggest to you that he was an armed robber?"

"Objection," said Tom McKenna.

"No," said Smith.

As Michael had ordered in Smith's subpoena, Smith brought Bowden's personnel file to the deposition. It contained Bowden's last time card, punched in at 7:09 and punched out at 3:17. Smith said he was sure that Bowden always punched his own time card because supervisors watch the workers punch in and out.

Knowing that Desi had told the Cambridge Police immediately after the robbery that both robbers were wearing sneakers, the old man asked Smith whether he ever saw Bowden wear sneakers at work. Pat Bowden had told us that he never did. Smith said that he never saw him wearing sneakers and added that he always recommended wearing substantial shoes that could withstand water from the mops. "If I saw they wore sneakers," said Smith, "I would call their attention to it."

At the end of Smith's deposition, I made photocopies of a few things in his Bowden file: the time card, payroll records which the actuary needed, and a one-paragraph typed report to Smith from Elsie Pina. Pina's report concerned Bowden's last day at work. It said:

On January 29, 1975, James Bowden worked with me, Elsie Pina. I saw and spoke to him at 10:30 a.m. After lunch I again saw James Bowden and spoke to him as he did not do a good job on the third floor clinic. At approximately 2:15 I again saw James Bowden in front of the House Officers Building on the A corridor. He spoke to me saying "hey, Elsie, are you looking for me?" I replied, "no Jim—I am not looking for you."

Pina's report was the big news of the Henry Smith deposition. It was a robbery alibi for Bowden. If he was at the hospital at 2:15, he couldn't possibly have walked into the Pearl Food Market five or ten minutes later, as the robbers did. Bill Smith, the Homicide detective who interviewed Pina, had accurately reported that the driving time between the hospital and the store is "between twenty and twenty-five minutes" in afternoon traffic. But Detective Smith had also reported that Pina last saw Bowden "about 2:00 P.M."

The old man began Pina's deposition by handing her a copy of her report and asking her to read it. She complied and said, in a shy voice: "That is just what I said." Then looking back at the paper, she began shaking her head and said, "This, now, two-fifteen—"

The old man pounced: "Is that your signature?" He wasn't going to let her say another word about the time. She obviously wanted to change it. We had anticipated trouble getting an alibi out of Boston City Hospital. Everyone we subpoenaed from there was a City of Boston employee who, we thought, could be easily influenced by a highly placed City Hall operator like Tom McKenna. When Pina wanted to change 2:15 in the first minute of her deposition without even being asked about it, we were all certain that McKenna had reached her.

"It would've been easy for him," said Michael, experienced in the ways of City Hall influence from his years as a housing inspector. "He leaves her a message to call him at his City Hall office. She's never spoken to anyone that high in the White machine. She's already nervous when she calls him. He says, 'Elsie, I notice your report says two-fifteen but you told the police two o'clock. The police don't make mistakes on things like that. Do you know the penalty for perjury?' He wouldn't have had to imply that her job was in trouble. She'd know that." Now, with Michael, the old man, and me on the edge of our seats, and McKenna leaning back contentedly and not bothering to take notes, Pina affirmed that it was her signature on the report. Then—again without being asked about it—with an air of bewilderment she said, "Two-fifteen?"

The old man sprang again. "How long a period did James

Bowden work for you?" Anything to keep her away from two-fifteen.

"It just so happened just that day because the regular man was out sick."

"How long had you known him by that time?"

"I had known him, I guess, since he had been there. I would say hello to him. That's about it, you know, just a fellow worker."

"You read this before you signed it?" he asked, warily returning to her report, hoping to lock her into it without going over the details.

"Yes," she said, "I am almost sure I did."

"Your memory was fresher at that time?"

"Definitely, yes."

"At the time you wrote your name in ink on there, you agreed with the facts that are contained therein?"

"Yes."

The old man left it at that. And even though Pina was so clearly ready to change two-fifteen, Tom McKenna asked her no questions. We took that as proof that he already knew she was going to move it back to two o'clock.

Hatred became our unanimous feeling for McKenna that day. Actually, it was *my* getting the feeling that made it unanimous. The old man had been ready to strangle him since the day they met, at Ethel's deposition. And even Michael had begun to boil at the sight of him. I revised my opinion of McKenna—and years later had a pleasant chat with him—after we learned that in fact he had never tried to influence Elsie Pina.

After the Pina deposition, we expected that Donald Webster would not be as strong in person as he was on paper. In the Homicide report he was positive that he saw Bowden punch out that day. The old man began Webster's deposition by asking whether he had already met and spoken to Tom McKenna, who was sitting beside him. Webster said McKenna had come to the hospital "a couple of months ago" and asked him about seeing Bowden punch out. To our surprise, Webster then testified that he did see Bowden punch out at the usual time that day. He said he also saw him punch in that morning and "assigned him to the Children's Building" to work for Elsie Pina.

I later learned that Donald Webster, a middle-aged Southie resident, was no friend of James Bowden's. In 1969, Bowden's third year on the job, Webster complained to Henry Smith about Bowden's disrespectful attitude and occasional outright insubordinate refusal to do certain messy jobs. Smith warned Bowden that his conflicts with Webster could lead to disciplinary action. That warning apparently ended the problem. Smith continued to give Bowden good work-performance ratings, and neither Webster nor any other supervisor complained about Bowden again.

We deposed three more hospital workers, whose names Michael and the old man had received from Pat and Walter Lee Bowden. At the wake, Adolph Grant, a co-worker of Bowden's, had told Walter Lee that he had been with James at work that day. Grant also told him that a friend of James's named Johnny Barnes saw him at work too. From another hospital employee Walter Lee had heard of a Mrs. Coakley, who seemed to be the only person at the hospital receptive to the idea that Bowden was involved in the robbery. The old man wanted to question Mrs. Coakley first.

Eileen Coakley, a thirty-year employee of the Housekeeping Department, did not show up for her deposition. Late that afternoon Michael filed a motion asking Judge Skinner to order Mrs. Coakley "to show cause why she should not be held in contempt of Court for failing to comply with the subpoena served upon her." Skinner, in turn, issued an order summoning Coakley to come to his chambers a week later. Coakley showed up this time and told the judge that she had ignored the subpoena because she didn't "think it was valid." Skinner told her it was and suggested that the deposition get under way immediately in a room adjacent to his courtroom. Then he left to conduct a hearing.

The old man started Coakley's deposition by asking her why she had thought our subpoena wasn't valid. "Did you read what was on it?" he asked.

"No, I did not," she replied.

He pressed the point until, minutes later, she blurted out, "I have a son, a policeman, who told me I did not have to appear!"

"Tell me what your son's name is," the old man demanded in a soft but menacing tone.

"I take the Fifth Amendment on that," said Coakley.

"What police department is he associated with?"

"I'm not answering it."

"Where is your son a policeman?" The old man's face was reddening now, but he was still speaking quietly so he wouldn't be overheard in Skinner's courtroom.

Coakley folded her arms and said nothing.

"Where does your son do police work?"

"It is not related to this case," said Coakley defiantly.

"Where does your son do police work?"

"I don't think it's related to this case!"

The old man took a deep breath. Michael knew that he was doing all he could to suppress his instinct to punch the answer out of her.

"We'll suspend here," the old man said with feigned calm. "I'm going to the judge and ask him for an order to get that question answered. Excuse me for a while."

The deposition resumed thirty minutes later and Coakley testified—after Skinner ordered her to, of course—that her son, Joseph, was a ten-year veteran patrolman of the Boston Police Department.

"Did your son ever discuss James Bowden with you?" the old man asked.

"Never," said Coakley.

He asked whether she saw Bowden on his last day at work. She said she did not. He asked whether she ever heard from anyone or told anyone that Bowden "was engaged in any kind of criminal conduct." She said no.

Satisfied that Coakley had nothing relevant to say, the old man—for no particular reason—asked her for a physical description of Bowden, something the homicide detectives neglected to ask anyone at the hospital. "He was about my height," she said, "not much taller. Maybe an inch taller than I. He wasn't very tall, and he was stocky."

"What is your height?"

"About five four."

Tom McKenna had no questions for Eileen Coakley.

We deposed Johnny Barnes and Adolph Grant back-to-back on the afternoon of September 22, 1977. Johnny Barnes, the only hospital worker who said he was a close friend of Bowden's, had nothing illuminating to say. He testified that he was not working with Bowden that day and that the only time he saw him was at lunch, "around eleven-thirty."

Adolph Grant, a black man then in his late fifties, looked as work-weary as anyone mopping floors at that age would. When he took his seat in the library, his body seemed to drop instantly off to sleep, but his eyes were alert and he held his head back a bit as if listening to some distant sound that none of us could hear. He was by far the most relaxed and straightforward deponent in the case. He testified to having seen Bowden "early that morning . . . before seven o'clock" and once again in the basement of the House Office Building "around two-thirty." He said that he and Bowden then punched out together.

Grant's alibi testimony roused Tom McKenna to his first spirited cross-examination. "You didn't work with him up until two-thirty?" he asked in a challenging, fast-spoken thrust, as if the very speed of his questions would trip up this janitor.

"No," said Grant, "because he was in one building and I was in another building."

"Where had Bowden worked that morning?"

"In the Children's Building."

"So, you saw him before seven, and then the next time you saw him was at two-thirty?"

"Sure."

"And that was in the basement of the House Office Building?"

"That's right."

"What was he doing at that time?"

"Duckin' work," said the imperturbable Grant, "just like I was."

"What does that mean?"

"Stayin' out from where the boss would hang," Grant lazily replied, impervious to McKenna's glare.

"How long were you with him in the basement of the building?"

"Until we went up to the time clock."

"During that period when you weren't working, between two-thirty and the time you checked out, what were you doing?"

"Talkin'."

"Just talking?"

"Yes."

"I have no further questions," said a flustered Tom McKenna.

So ended the pre-trial depositions. We had expected McKenna to depose Jessina Stokes and Ernest Winbush, but he never ordered a single deposition. We didn't depose Jessina, because we already knew what her trial testimony was going to be, and we were still at a standoff with Winbush. Because he didn't want to get involved, we thought a deposition would scare him into saying he wasn't with Bowden that night, no matter what the truth was.

On October 7, 1977, Magistrate Cohen held a brief hearing on our motion to compel discovery of the mug shots chosen by Ethel and Desi, and the department's motion to protect them from discovery. The old man explained the photographs' relevance to the case. He stressed that we only wanted to see who else Ethel and Desi positively identified and that we had no interest in obtaining the criminal records of the people in the pictures. Arguing for the department, Nicholas Foundas did not dispute the mug shots' relevance but insisted that turning them over to us would be "an illegal dissemination of a criminal offender's record." Cohen saw it our way and ordered the commissioner to give us the photographs. Foundas sent us the mug shots a week later.

We always knew why Cambridge never went after the second robber. Petersen obviously thought Ethel's and Desi's mug shot IDs were useless because, according to his report, they picked out "different people [as the] person holding the gun." When we saw the mug shots, we were staggered by how different the two people were. If Petersen's version of the photo selection was true, Desi chose a thin sixteen-year-old black boy, and Ethel chose a forty-eight-year-old man who was *white*. And they were both positive about their choices.

Desi told me that he and Ethel looked at the mug shots separately. When they finished, said Desi, "It was like the sixty-four-thousand-dollar question. I asked Petersen, 'Who is it?' And he said, 'You drew a blank. You picked two different guys.'"

But John Geagan, who also watched both of them go through the mug shots, reported that Ethel and Desi agreed on a positive ID of "#168902," whom he did not identify. Mug shot #168902 turned out to be a picture of a twenty-four-year-old black man who was five feet nine inches tall and weighed 170 pounds—one Wardell Washington, Jr. If Geagan's version was true, then why not arrest Washington, who fit the description of the robber reasonably well? We were happy with the fact that the police didn't bother to question Washington. That seemed to be evidence enough of the real value the police attached to Ethel's and Desi's positive IDs. It was only by chance that we found out why Geagan couldn't name Washington as a positively identified suspect.

Our head secretary, Nancy McGillivray, my sister Mary's childhood best friend, put the mug shots in a folder and found a spot for them in the four-drawer filing cabinet that had been moved into Michael's office to house the mass of paper we called the Bowden file. Hours later, in the middle of another research assignment that Kevin had given her, she began reading the case of *Commonwealth* v. *William Harry Simpson*. Simpson had been convicted of first degree murder after his partner in the crime confessed and testified against him. When Nancy read the Supreme Judicial Court's preliminary statement of facts in its opinion affirming Simpson's conviction, she forgot what Kevin had asked her to do. She was back in the Bowden case. "Around sunrise on the morning of March 17, 1974," said the court, "the defendant [Simpson] and one Wardell Washington broke into an apartment ... with the intent to rob the occupant, [who] died from knife wounds inflicted by Washington while the defendant was also striking him repeatedly with a baseball bat and a hammer. . . . Washington was allowed to plead guilty to murder in the second degree."

Nancy walked into Michael's office, where he and I were preparing quick-reference indexes of the deposition transcripts. Grinning, she said, "I know why Washington wasn't such a good suspect." She started reading the case she'd just found.

In minutes Michael was on the phone with the lawyer listed as having represented Washington. Michael explained his interest and asked the lawyer three questions that sent the man looking for his now-closed Washington file. He came back on the line with the answers Michael wanted. Nancy and I listened in. "My guy was born on October 5, 1950," said the lawyer.

"Okay," said Michael. "Same guy. That's the birth date I have on the back of the mug shot. Now, what did he get for a sentence?"

"Life."

"And when did they lock him up?"

"December 3, 1974."

There was no chance of Wardell Washington, only two months into a life sentence, having been out on a furlough or work-release program on the day of the robbery. But Michael, ever true to his instinct to leave no stone unturned, wanted an official confirmation. The Massachusetts Department of Correction at first refused to give us any information on Washington, citing the law on confidentiality of criminal records. Michael outlined the problem in a quickly drawn motion to Judge Skinner, who referred it to Magistrate Cohen. In what proved to be the fastest run through this discovery routine, Cohen soon held a five-minute hearing and ordered the Department of Correction to tell us what we wanted to know. And on the last day of 1977, the Department of Correction gave us an affidavit saying: "Wardell Washington was incarcerated in unit B-6, a maximum security section of MCI-Walpole . . . on January 29, 1975, [and] said Wardell Washington was not absent from the institution."

The same day we received that affidavit, we received a routine notice from the clerk of the Federal Court telling us that *Bowden* v. *McKenna and Holland* would come to trial in thirty days.

Before we went to trial, however, Judge Skinner held a hearing on January 9, 1978, on a point of law raised when Michael had filed a motion to include the City of Boston as a defendant. It was a desperate last-ditch effort on our part to bring in the deep pockets. Michael's supporting brief contended that because the Massachusetts Supreme Judicial Court had recently suggested that the legislature reduce the scope of municipal immunity, Judge Skinner could—in the spirit of things—eliminate municipal immunity in civil rights cases. We were on thin ice with this proposal. The City's opposing brief, filed right on time by Tom McKenna, argued that the state court's recent halfhearted suggestion about municipal immunity could have no effect on the Bowden case. McKenna cited a long string of cases that backed him up.

At the hearing, we were surprised by another abrupt Law Department personnel change. Tom McKenna wasn't there. In his place was John L. Keefe, a boyish twenty-nine-year-old with tortoiseshell glasses too big for his thin face, a rumpled suit, a well-worn white shirt, and all the poise of an altar boy suddenly called upon to give a sermon. Keefe told Judge Skinner that he was taking over the Bowden case from McKenna, who that very day had quit the Law Department to begin private practice.

Having read the briefs, Judge Skinner, as expected, summarily denied the motion to include the City. Then he turned to something else in front of him: John Keefe's Motion for a Continuance of the fast-approaching trial date.

Lawyers coming into a case at the last minute always ask for continuances. They almost always get them. Keefe told Skinner that he had joined the Law Department only a month before and said he needed more time to study "the complex factual case, including the police investigation of the subject incident and the numerous depositions." Keefe also mistakenly added that since *we* had already been granted a continuance a few months before, he should now be allowed one.

The old man rose to correct Keefe: "We have never asked for a continuance. As you know, Your Honor, we have always tried to advance discovery as quickly as possible while the City has dragged its feet and had to be threatened with default at every turn before complying with standard discovery procedures. Most respectfully, Your Honor, I see no justification for delaying the trial, and the timing of Mr. McKenna's surprise resignation is surely nothing more than a transparent contrivance to do exactly that."

Keefe objected to the swipe at the integrity of the Law Department. He stressed that he simply would not be able to prepare a defense on such short notice.

Through his rimless spectacles, Judge Skinner fixed sympathetic eyes on Keefe and said that he understood the problems of being assigned to a case when it was so close to trial. "But, Mr. Keefe," he added, "that is one of the hazards of public employment."

Skinner knew the hazards of public employment better than anyone in the room. After graduation from Harvard Law School in 1952, he had worked for a prestigious Boston law firm for five years, then left the firm to become an assistant district attorney. Six years later he was chosen by then Attorney General of Massachusetts Edward Brooke to head his criminal division. Skinner remained there for three years.

The old man had always thought of him as a tough but fair prosecutor. As Skinner wrote in the Twenty-fifth Anniversary Report of his Harvard College graduating class, he found criminal prosecution "very exciting, educational and occasionally bruising." In that same class report, he cited Lord Kenneth Clark's comment on post-revolutionary French leaders ("They suffered from the most terrible of all delusions. They believed themselves to be virtuous.") and went on to say that a prosecutor or judge should never lose "sight of the common thread of fallible humanity which links him to the defendant."

Skinner was back in private practice in late 1973, when Edward Brooke, then the state's Republican U.S. senator, persuaded President Richard Nixon to make his conservative Republican friend a federal judge. Walter Jay Skinner had been on the bench for four years when Keefe stood before him asking for a continuance. His docket held a backlog of hundreds of pending criminal and civil cases. Many of the civil cases had been filed years before he had become a judge and were still crawling through the discovery process. Readying a major lawsuit for trial in only two years and ten months, as Michael and the old man had done, is unusual and something a judge anxious to reduce his case load wants to encourage. Skinner denied Keefe's motion for a continuance. "All the depositions have been taken," he said, smiling at Keefe. "All you have to do is read them."

On the way out of the courtroom, Keefe formally introduced himself to us. We all shook hands with him—for the first and last time—and made easy small talk. By the time an elevator had carried us from the fifteenth floor of the John W. McCormack U.S. Post Office and Court House to the lobby, we learned that the affable Mr. Keefe had been a classmate of Kevin's at Catholic Memorial High School. Later, from Kevin, we learned that Keefe had been a high school track star and the smartest kid in his class, that he graduated magna cum laude from Harvard, and took his law degree at Boston College Law School.

Keefe walked along Devonshire Street with us through a freezing wind. He and the old man chatted away about nothing the old man could remember a few minutes later. Michael and I dropped back a few paces and whispered about Keefe.

"How can the City give this case to this kid?" Michael wondered. He answered his own question before I could: "It's gotta be a bluff. They have to have somebody else lined up."

"Yeah, definitely."

"But nobody else in the Law Department would want to take this case."

"Maybe he's the guy, then. Maybe they think the old man'll come on like a bully against him and the jury'll feel sorry for him."

"I don't know. A week before trial the City will probably hire outside counsel to try it. Then they'd have to get their continuance."

"Yeah, that's gotta be the play."

We parted company with Keefe at the corner of Devonshire and State in the shadow of the Old State House. We turned left to One State Street, and Keefe, wearing a rather nonlawyerly woolen ski hat, heavy briefcase in hand, trudged across the street to City Hall to start preparing for his first federal trial.

Lawyers accustomed to billing by the hour keep work diaries. For the month of January 1978, Michael's diary has the same entry for each day up to and including Sunday the 29th: "Bowden—Review of files, records and depositions." The old man's diary says the same thing from the 16th to the 29th. Michael's had additional entries on some days: the 16th, "Measurements taken at scene"; the 18th, "Preparation of request for instructions to the jury"; the 19th, "Preparation of memorandum on liability and damages"; the 20th, "Preparation of memorandum on pendant jurisdiction"; the 25th, "Preparation of special questions to prospective jurors"; the 29th, "Visit to scene with photographer." I didn't keep a diary of those final weeks preceding the trial, but if I had, it would have been nearly identical to Michael's.

They were days of steadily mounting tension—like the weeks of study before final exams. Imagine studying for the final exam of a course that lasted three years instead of three months and cost about $10,000. I remember events better than the anticipation of them or the preparation for them. I know I was hunched over police reports and depositions for most of that month, but I remember clearly only my trips out of the office.

In the first week of January, I went to Ken Kobre's office at Boston University, where he was teaching photojournalism. I spent a couple of hours there studying his 144 negatives of the scene at Smith Street after Bowden had been shot. I picked out 24 shots that would be good exhibits. For $170, Kobre agreed to turn them into 8 × 10 glossies suitable for passing around a jury box.

On Thursday the 12th, I went to the Registry to check again for Bowden's driver's license. The Registry computer still drew a blank on the name James Bowden.

On Monday the 16th, a gray afternoon, Michael and I went to

Smith Street armed with a surveyor's tape measure. Not trusting Bob Hudson's paced-off estimates of the relevant distances, we put the tape to the pavement and found them to be reasonably accurate. Eddie and Denny were sitting 349 feet away from the Buick during the stakeout. The 18-foot-long Buick backed up 78 feet from its parking place beside a SLOW sign to the spot in front of 20 Smith Street where the shooting occurred. That spot was 199 feet from Jessina Stokes's window, which was 23 feet above street level. The Buick traveled 257 feet from the shooting spot to its crash scene. The Fabrique Nationale was found 53 feet away from the shooting spot and 204 feet away from the crash scene. Smith Street is 1,110 feet long. As we were making these measurements, we received several pleasant greetings of "Hello, Officer" from the locals. One tiny black boy, who had obviously seen more than his share of Boston police detectives in their zipper-front jerseys and leather jackets, said to his even tinier friend, "They're wearin' ties. They gotta be FBI."

At 9:00 A.M. on the 29th, a bright and very cold Sunday, the day before the trial was to start, we were back on Smith Street with a photographer who took a series of shots that became 8 × 10 black-and-white glossies that afternoon. We got the view of the shooting site from Jessina's window. Then we moved Michael's Plymouth Valiant into the middle of Smith Street and showed that with cars parked on both sides of the street, only one car could pass between them.

After the photographer left, Michael and I spent an hour cruising around the block. After a third or fourth look at where the three ACU cars had been on the stakeout, where the Buick had been parked, where the shooting had occurred, where the gun was found, where the Buick had crashed, and Jessina's window, I felt as if we were visiting the family cemetery. On our last swing through Smith Street, Michael said, "Exactly three years ago today, 'at about six-oh-three P.M.' . . ." He swung his car into the U-turn that Denny had made. He followed Denny's path back to Gurney Street and we took up the stakeout position. We sat there silently for a few minutes. Then Michael said nonchalantly, "Look who's here." A Dodge Dart was making the turn the Thunderbird had made from Parker onto Smith. Behind the wheel was a white face, eyeglasses, and a ski hat. When the car straightened out on Smith, we could see the rear plate. It was all letters: J•KEEFE.

"I don't believe it," said Michael. "They're not gonna let him try this case. He's gotta be doing the legwork for someone else."

During the last two weeks of January the old man and I drifted into Michael's office every day after five o'clock for long strategy sessions. I would sit on a windowsill at the same altitude as the gold weather vane that spins atop the 270-year-old Old State House across the street. Michael would lean back in his swivel chair. We'd have the latest version of our witness list in front of us. On Thursday the 26th, the old man looked at his list and said what he'd said several times in the last week: "The jury'll want to hear from Winbush."

I did what had become Michael's line for him: "Yeah, but what'll he say?"

There was the usual glum silence that came up when we got into this subject. "All right," the old man finally said, "let's do this much: subpoena him for trial. Maybe that'll smoke him out over the weekend and we can find out what his story is. Course, we won't put him on the stand if he doesn't talk to us beforehand."

Michael nodded slowly: "I guess that's the best we can do with him."

"Well, let's do it right now," said the old man. "Let's get the subpoena in his hand tonight."

It was 6:30 P.M. Michael's secretary, a pretty twenty-one-year-old named Carol Ryan was still at work on Bowden stuff. She put it aside to type the Winbush subpoena. It was already too late to get a constable. Michael wanted to use someone who didn't look like a process server anyway. At seven o'clock Michael drove to Winbush's home himself. With him, subpoena in hand, was Carol Ryan, taking on one of those non-secretarial missions that O'Donnell secretaries always have to be ready for. We figured Carol could catch the Winbushes off guard.

She knocked on the Winbush door, and in seconds a friendly teenaged boy opened it.

"Is your father home?" she asked.

"Yeah, come on in."

She followed the boy into a living room where the family was gathered in front of a television set. To the only adult male in the room, she said, "Mr. Winbush, this is a subpoena for you," and she handed him an envelope. He slumped back in the couch. Carol immediately turned to leave. Closing the door behind her, she heard him calling after her, "Hey, what's this all about?"

Minutes later, Michael called the old man from a phone booth. "She got him in hand," he said.

"Great! Give Carol fifty bucks and take her to dinner. I'll stay near the phone."

Like all our trial subpoenas, this one had the office telephone number and the old man's home number on it along with the suggestion to call him at any time to be "advised as to the exact time and date your testimony will be needed."

At 11:05 P.M. the old man's phone rang. A nervous voice on the other end said, "Hello, Mr. O'Donnell?"

"Yes."

"This is Ernest Winbush."

An hour of talk ensued.

When the old man finally hung up, he dialed my number. It was a little after midnight and he didn't want to risk waking Michael's wife and children with a phone call, but he knew there was no one to wake at my place except me. I was indexing the Roxbury Defenders' transcript when the phone rang.

"Well, we got him in hand," said the familiar voice, too excited to bother with the standard greeting.

"I know. Michael called me a couple of hours ago."

"And we're gonna use him."

You let the old man tell his stories his way. So I put down the transcript, stretched out on the bed, closed my eyes, and listened to what I think was the only bedtime story my father ever told me.

"I started off with 'Thank you very much for calling.' You know,

I'm Mr. Polite. 'As that subpoena indicates, I represent the widow and children of James Bowden . . . ba, ba, ba.' I tell him who I am, that I've been practicing law thirty years [then a four-year exaggeration], where my office is, where I live. I don't want to be some mysterious voice in the night. He asks me if I'm involved with the Kennedys. For once, I said yeah."

It was a lie. President Kennedy had two prominent aides named Lawrence O'Brien and Kenneth O'Donnell—who was not related to us. For over twenty years now, the elision of those two names—Lawrence O'Donnell—has mistakenly rung a bell in many people's memories. The old man has always clarified the confusion—except for this one time with this man whose confidence he had to win.

"After all," he told me, "I met Jack when he was a congressman and I was directing traffic. I defended guys that Bobby targeted for prosecution. I met Ted when he was an assistant D.A. and a few times since then. I've gotten Christmas cards from him. That's 'involved,' right?"

"Definitely."

"So now I get around to the case with him. I say I'm not sure exactly what day he'll have to testify. I ask him if he's got a job. He says he used to be a draftsman until the kidney thing knocked him out of work. 'Are you still on dialysis?' 'Yeah.' I promise to schedule around that. Then he says, 'Why do you want me? I never really knew Bowden.' I knew that second that we were right not to depose him. He would've sworn he didn't drop off Bowden. And I knew that wasn't true. His first impulse was to distance himself from Bowden. That's what always happens in this kind of thing. A guy you know gets in trouble, gets arrested. The cops ask you about him: 'Were you with him last night?' 'Who? Him? I don't know him.' That's a good reaction most of the time. As far as Winbush is concerned when he's reading the *Globe* the next day and then the *Phoenix,* Bowden's an armed robber who tried to kill the cops. You can't blame him for thinking that. I figure he probably still thinks that. So I know I have to unload everything we've got.

"I said, 'Let me tell you about James Bowden.' And I go on for half an hour. You know—no criminal record, never committed a crime in his life, didn't rob that store, was at work, didn't fit the description, didn't do anything wrong on Smith Street, didn't have a gun, O'Brian, Jessina—the whole story. And I end up telling him why the cops tried to frame him, that they wanted to get all of what they thought were the robbery elements involved in the shooting—a guy with an automatic and a guy with a shotgun.

"Then I stop there, hoping Winbush will jump in. He says, 'I see.'

"He's still not ready to tell me anything, and I know he's too smart to fool around with, so I just go to it. I said—you know, very respectfully—'Mr. Winbush, I know you remember Dave O'Brian testifying in the Roxbury Court. Patricia Gunn called him in your defense, and his testimony helped you out of that jam. I believe every word he said that day. And you and I both know that he said Bowden stepped out of your car. Now, O'Brian is my star witness in this case. And I'm telling you right now, the jury's gonna believe him. All I need from you—and no one else knows this—is how and why and when and where you and Bowden got together that night.'

"I stop again. I hear him taking a deep breath. He says nothing.

"I come back with: 'I have every minute of Bowden's last day accounted for except the last ten. I know you couldn't have been together for more than those ten minutes.'

"I stop. All I get is another deep breath.

"I says, 'Ernie, you were lucky. You know it could've happened the other way around. Suppose James had pulled his car away first. Then Holland and McKenna would've been coming up behind you. And believe me, they would've gone after you the same way they went after him. And you know what? Knowing James Bowden as I do now, I can tell you that if I was going to trial for your widow and children next week, I'd have no trouble getting the truth out of *him*.'

"Another deep breath and he says, 'Mr. O'Donnell, you gotta understand my position.' He tells me he'd never been arrested before. Scariest night of his life. Thought he was gonna die in the cell at Station Two. They wouldn't let him have his kidney pills. When he saw Holland and McKenna in court, he thought they were the most terrifying people he's ever seen. I mean this is one scared guy. And no wonder.

"I'm in there step for step with him: 'I understand . . . of course . . . I understand. . . .' He goes on and on about how bad it was. Cops following him for weeks. I can hear his wife in the background reminding him of this stuff.

"He starts telling me about his arrest. He says, 'I thought they were gonna kill me right there. I was on the parents' Biracial Council [established by the Federal Court to smooth race relations in the first year of busing] and there was a lot of talk about guys from South Boston wanting to get us. I thought this was it.'

"Nobody told him why he was under arrest, but he figured it had something to do with guns because they planted bullets on him. He's not sure which one of them did that or when it happened.

"I tell him I know all about TPF tactics. I go into them arresting you in the parking lot. I tell him about the A and B charges against me. I tell him I was guilty, but I beat it. Now I get him laughing during this stuff about me and Molloy 'cause it sounds like a real circus. Then I tell him, 'I've got the bastards on the run now. They're scared shit of me. Everybody thinks cops take no shit from anyone, but these guys took it from me.' Naturally, Winbush has never heard of anyone pushing around cops.

"After that, I tell him how safe he'll be in Federal Court. 'You're gonna be a witness in a federal trial. You walk in there with all the protection of the federal government: U.S. marshals, FBI. The cops won't dare to even look at you the wrong way.' I promised him complete protection from retaliation. I didn't say exactly what kind of protection I could give him, but coming from a guy who's in with the Kennedys and pushes cops around, it must've sounded good enough for him.

"Okay. So now he tells me his story. Fact is he hardly knew Bowden. Just knew he was Mary Bowden's son. He didn't even know his first name. He used to see him around the project. Winbush has relatives living across the hall from Bowden's mother. That night, he's driving along Parker Street on his way to the PTA thing in Brighton. It's raining like hell. It had just really opened up. He sees Bowden coming out of a variety store on Parker. Bowden's holding a newspaper over his head for an umbrella. He recognizes Winbush's Thunderbird and flags him down. He asks for a ride around the corner to his own car. 'Sure.' Winbush swings him around the corner and drops him off. They rode a few hundred yards together. They were together two minutes at most. They talked about the rain. That's it."

"So," I said, "that fills in Bowden's last ten minutes. He left his sister's apartment and went to the store. He picked up a paper. Maybe he hung around the store a minute or two, hoping the rain would let up. By the way, the Kobre pictures do show a *Globe* on Bowden's front seat."

"Oh, good."

"Well . . . I guess discovery is over."

CHAPTER 13

"I hate jury selection," Michael whispered. "You work on a thing like this for three years. Then you come in here, pick names out of a hat, and leave it to them." We were in Courtroom No. 6, Judge Skinner's demesne, looking at a panel of sixty prospective jurors. They were scattered about the spectators' benches wrapped in an assortment of winter coats, waiting, as we were, for the judge. It was 10:07 A.M. on Monday, January 30, 1978, and Michael was noticeably nervous. Since jury selection struck me as an awfully dangerous game, I, too, was full of apprehension. The old man, of course, was serenity itself.

The previous week, Skinner's clerk had told both sides that the judge intended to impanel two juries this morning: one for a criminal case and one for us. Skinner would then hold the criminal trial, which he expected to run two or three days, and have us back on Thursday to get the Bowden trial under way. Neither the plaintiffs nor the defendants were present for jury selection. The lawyers on the criminal case occupied the counsel tables, since they were going to get first pick. We were in the first row of the spectators' section. Across the aisle were John Keefe and none other than Tom McKenna. The defense had not filed a last-minute motion for a continuance.

Michael read the play this way: "McKenna wanted to go into private practice. So he resigned from the City on the eve of a big trial. He knew no one could learn the file in time to try the case. He probably hoped that the City would hire him as outside counsel and pay him a good hourly." Which it did.

We had to wait well over an hour for the criminal jury to be selected. The freshly sworn jurors and everyone else involved in the criminal case then went off for a coffee break, and the old man, Michael, McKenna, and Keefe took over the counsel tables.

Needless to say, there is more to jury selection than picking names out of a hat, though that's about how it began. The court clerk blindly picked eight names out of a small wooden barrel that sits on his desk. Federal civil trials use only six jurors. Two more are usually empaneled as alternates, ready to step in to replace a first-string juror who has to be excused for illness or the like. The clerk called the eight to the jury box: "number fifty-nine, Mr. Zoba; number thirty-one, Mr. Kroll; number forty-five, Mr. Lynch; number fifty-seven, Mr. York; number twenty-one, Mrs. Gallo; number four, Mr. Bentley; number twelve, Mr. Cohen; and number nine, Mr. Cederholm."

Their numbers referred to their alphabetical position on the jury pool list. Once in the jury box they were referred to as jurors number one through six, the first alternate, and the second alternate. Number one sat in the front-row corner closest to the judge. Two through six filled out the front row, and the alternates sat behind them. It was, as expected, an all-white group.

The jurisdiction of Boston's United States District Court includes all of eastern Massachusetts. The most recent census of that area showed that its population was only 4.6 percent black. The sixty-person jury pool was supposed to be a cross section of that population. In fact, the black segment was overrepresented in our pool: there were four, making the pool 6.6 percent black. If by slim chance the clerk were to call a black person's name, then Tom McKenna and John Keefe would probably use one of their peremptory challenges to knock him out of the box—as would any sensible trial lawyer in their situation. We knew there was little chance of getting a black juror.

Judge Skinner's job was to ferret out the plainly prejudiced, if any, in the jury box. He leaned into his microphone and explained that the case was a civil rights–wrongful-death lawsuit against two police officers for shooting and killing a man while on duty.

He read the names of the plaintiffs, the defendants, the lawyers, and all the prospective witnesses and asked whether any of the jurors knew anyone he had just mentioned. None of them did. Then he asked a long list of questions. A sample:

> Have you or has any member of your family or any close friend ever held a job in a law-enforcement agency?
>
> Does your job cause you to work with any law-enforcement officer or agency?
>
> Have you or has anyone close to you ever been the victim of a crime?
>
> . . . would you believe [a] law-enforcement officer simply because he was a law-enforcement officer?
>
> Do you think that because the police live with so much risk and danger every day that they should be excused if they occasionally overreact in a situation and use excessive force?
>
> Do you think that law and order should be maintained at all costs, even if it means sacrificing someone's constitutional rights?
>
> This case concerns allegations that the plaintiffs' decedent's civil rights were violated by the defendants. The plaintiffs' decedent was black and the defendants are white police officers. Is there anything in this set of circumstances that would make it difficult for you to decide this case fairly and impartially, without bias or prejudice?
>
> If you were selected as a juror in this case, do you know of any reason why you could not sit as an impartial juror?
>
> Would you be willing to have jurors of the same mind as you now have sit in judgment of you and your case if you were the plaintiff?
>
> Are you a member of the Hundred Club?

The Hundred Club is a charitable organization that provides financial support to families of Massachusetts police officers killed in the line of duty. The old man had become a Hundred Club member in the early 1960s.

The questions Skinner was asking were written by the old man, Michael, and me. In Massachusetts, lawyers are not allowed to question jurors, but they can submit questions they want the judge to ask. Skinner accepted and used nearly all of ours. Keefe and McKenna did not submit any. "The most we'll find out," Michael had said, "is that someone is related to a cop. No one is gonna raise his hand and say, 'I hate niggers.'"

Of course, more times than we could count we had heard Boston friends of ours who looked just like these jurors say exactly that. But even the stupidest racist I know wouldn't reveal his passion to a federal judge while seventy strangers looked on and a stenographer captured his every word. Hence, the danger of jury selection. Biased people can and often do lie their way on to a jury.

Because lawyers don't trust prospective jurors' answers to their *voir dire* questions and because lawyers often believe that by the time the jury is sworn in, their case has been decided, a small industry has developed to take the guesswork out of jury selection. A new breed of high-priced specialists called jury researchers use public-opinion surveys and computer analyses of the results to give a lawyer profiles of who he or she should be on the lookout for in a particular case. They say things like "Try to get white, Catholic, married women age thirty-five to forty-five," and "Challenge white, blue-collar, Baptist men over thirty." Such information is available in the $20,000 to $250,000 price range. It is therefore used almost exclusively by corporations in their antitrust trials and socialites in their murder trials.

Psychiatrists have found an opening for themselves in jury selection. They sometimes sit at counsel tables and whisper instant readings of the empaneled specimens. David Cohen, our first alternate, had been bumped from the criminal jury selected before ours when a psychiatrist at the defense table picked up something threatening in his body language.

Old war horses, who have had to make decisions about thousands of prospective jurors, naturally scoff at the pseudo-science creeping into their game. When a jury research firm found widespread racism in a Boston jury pool, the old man remarked, "Imagine paying someone to tell you that." Successful trial attorneys, almost all of whom are extraordinarily conceited, generally seem to think that pollsters and psychiatrists cannot tell them a single thing they don't know. Not just coincidentally, conceit can be a superb defense against nervous breakdowns during jury selection. "I don't give a shit if they're all in the Ku Klux Klan," the old man had said on the way to court. "I'll win them over."

Three jurors raised their hands when Skinner asked if they, their relatives, or friends were employed in any branch of law enforcement. Number one, it turned out, was a suburban dog warden. Skinner asked, "Would your role as an officer of the law affect your judgment in this case?" He said no. Number six, a husky auto mechanic in his early twenties with long blond hair pulled back into a ponytail, explained that he coached a kids' football team that was sponsored by the police force of a distant suburb. He said he was friendly with some of the officers he knew through the football team. Skinner asked whether that would affect his judgment in this case, and he said no. Number five, a middle-aged housewife who was the only woman on the panel, told the judge that her brother-in-law was a police officer in Revere, a town on Boston's northern border with a reputation as perhaps the most corruption-ridden municipality in the state. When Skinner asked whether that would affect her judgment in this case, she said, without hesitation, "No." That got them all past the judge's test, and it was now up to the lawyers to challenge the ones they didn't like.

The Federal Rules of Civil Procedure allowed each side only three peremptory challenges. The defense used none. Keefe stood and said, "The defendants are content, Your Honor." After much whispering with Michael, the old man rose to challenge only number one. The dog warden dejectedly returned to the spectators' section and the clerk reached into the barrel for a replacement: "Number fifty-six, Mr. Wright." The judge went through the questions again with this new, white, middle-aged number one, who, as it happened, did not have the vaguest connection to law enforcement. Now both sides were content.

Judge Skinner swore in the jurors and appointed Mrs. Gallo, the only woman on the jury, to be foreman. He told everyone to be in his or her place at nine o'clock Thursday morning, and adjourned.

As soon as we were out of the courtroom, I asked why we used only one challenge. "Remember," said Michael, "when you challenge somebody, someone else has to replace him, and the new guy can turn out to be a lot worse. Suppose we used another challenge and we got someone really scary. What do we do? Use our last challenge to get rid of him? Then, what if we get someone even worse?"

"I had to get rid of the dogcatcher," the old man happily explained. "For us, the only thing worse than a cop is someone who's almost a cop or wants to be a cop. Now the kid who coaches the football team, I love him! Did you see the ponytail on him? He looks like a Hell's Angel, for chrissake. He's got no illusions about cops. I can't believe McKenna didn't challenge him. And the lady? I'm glad her brother-in-law's a cop. She knows what they're like. You know, she might hate her brother-in-law. And besides, Revere cops don't like Boston cops. Revere cops do the same work, get paid less, and the Boston guys act like they're the only *real* cops around here. And, you know, I gotta have a mother in that jury box. She'll love the kids."

The criminal trial before Judge Skinner ended on Wednesday.

At 8:30 A.M. on Thursday, February 2, 1978, Pat Bowden arrived at the office with Eurina and Jamil in tow.

I was in the lobby overseeing the transportation to the courthouse of our twenty-square-foot model of the Mission Hill project, and the four heavy cardboard boxes that contained the Bowden file. Pressed into service for this Thursday morning task were brother Kevin, brother Bill, sister Mary, and a friend of mine named Kim Patrick Bonstrom, a Harvard undergraduate with an eye on law school. Bill and Mary were happily skipping classes— he at Suffolk Law School, she at Suffolk College—to lend a hand with the logistics. Kim, on the other hand, had to be carefully cajoled into missing his nine o'clock class. Knowing he had never been in a courtroom, I had told him that anyone contemplating a career as a lawyer should get a look at a good one in action and this was his big chance. He agreed to show up, but only for the first morning when I needed help carrying and setting up the model. His plan was to watch the first half hour of the trial and rush back to Cambridge in time for his ten o'clock. As it happened, and as I had hoped, he was mesmerized by the old man's opening state- ment. He stayed for every minute of the trial and helped carry boxes and briefcases to and from the courthouse each day.

I had never met our plaintiffs. I introduced myself and the rest of the task force gathered around the material in the lobby. Then I took them into the old man's office, where he and Michael, already in their overcoats, were closing their briefcases. Eurina, now quite a ladylike seven-year-old, shook hands with them, and Jamil, now three and a half, managed a *hello* after some motherly coaxing. Minutes later the entire entourage was shivering its way along Devonshire Street. The old man and Michael, each carrying two briefcases, were in the lead. A step behind them with one of the file boxes was Kevin, a mite worried that box-carrying was beneath his lawyerly dignity. Bill, the strongest of us, was carrying two boxes, one on top of the other. Mary was beside him with the lightest box. Then came the Bowdens—Pat carrying Jamil and holding Eurina's hand—followed by Kim and me at the rear with the very hard-to-carry model.

We walked into the empty courtroom at quarter to nine. Kevin dropped his box on the plaintiffs' table and returned immediately to the office, where he spent the day on his own cases and fielding calls from irate clients who hadn't been able to get the old man or Michael on the phone for weeks. Kim and I set up the model. Michael arranged the file boxes to his liking on and underneath the table. The Bowdens sat in the front row to the left of the center aisle. Bill and Mary sat behind them. The old man wandered aimlessly around the room from the jury rail to the witness stand to the bench. He studied the floor and nervously snapped his fingers. He came over to me at the model and said, "The kids are great, huh?"

"Yeah," I said, "the jury'll love them."

The old man had insisted, over Pat's reasonable objections, that Eurina and Jamil come to court every day of the trial. Naturally Pat didn't want to put them through one minute of this grim reminder of their father's death. She also worried about Eurina's missing school and Jamil's being hard to control for hours on end in a courtroom (he could be trouble enough for forty-five minutes in church). But the old man has a way of wheedling clients, and by the time he takes them to trial he is running their lives and often their family's lives as well. His client's family is always in plain view of the jury, drawing what sympathy it can. "Sure," he says, "sometimes the testimony is pretty painful for the family, but losing your husband or your father or your brother to Walpole is a lot worse."

Children have sometimes been the main reason the old man has gone to trial. He's talked more than one client out of pleading guilty by saying, "Come on. If you go to trial, at least you can give your kids a chance to say you were framed. If a jury finds you guilty, your kids can always say the verdict was wrong. But if you plead guilty, well . . ." He knows what a father's public disgrace can do to children.

The professional in him was thinking of Eurina and Jamil as props when they took their front-row places that first morning. But in the trial, though I doubt he realized it, their presence was as important to him in its unique way as Michael's. When he mentioned them by name in his final argument, he came as close as he ever has to crying in a courtroom.

We were all in our seats with no one else in the room when the defense arrived. John Keefe was the first man through the leather-covered swinging doors, followed in single file by Tom McKenna, Eddie, and Denny. Each carried a briefcase. The one in Keefe's hand was especially thick. Eddie and Denny dropped the brief-cases on the defense table, whispered to Keefe for a few seconds, then took up positions in the front row across the aisle from me. I had never seen either of them but recognized them instantly from the Kobre pictures. They slipped out of their coats and draped them over the bench. Eddie was wearing a leisure suit, shirt, and tie of matching sky-blue. Denny had on a dark-brown sport coat, a shirt and tie of matching light-brown, black slacks, and what we used to call, for reasons unknown, "engineer boots," something like cowboy boots but made of plain black leather with roomy rounded toes and low heels. In the late 1950s and early 1960s they were the footwear favored by motorcycle gangs and Dorchester's most troublesome juvenile delinquents. Denny's hair was still the long ear-and-collar-covering mane that he thought disguised him well for Anti-Crime Unit assignments. Eddie looked like a Combat Zone bouncer, and Denny . . . well, Denny just looked dangerous.

The old man likes, and many times has had to force, his cli-ents to come to court wearing conventional hairstyles, conser-vative suits, white shirts, plain ties, and sensible shoes. Once he had an alleged Mafia assassin cut and degrease his hair, shuck his sharkskins in favor of Brooks Brothers tweeds, and, despite the man's perfect eyesight, wear tortoiseshell glasses. When this defendant (who, incidentally, then lived across the street from Eddie Holland) took the witness stand looking like a prep school headmaster, it was difficult—and the jury ultimately found it impossible—to picture him pumping three bullets into Rocco DeSeglio's skull at close range.

Pat Bowden presented no sartorial problems. The old man had suggested she wear a cloth coat and simple dresses. She owned nothing else. Now he shot a glance at Eddie and Denny, and winked at me. The wink said, "Don't they look perfect?" I winked back. Eddie and Denny wore the same outfits to court every day.

Pat Bowden, seated a foot to my left, had never seen the men who killed her husband. They were now sitting fifteen feet away from her and her children. She did not look in their direction. She said nothing.

Courtroom No. 6, commodious and high-ceilinged, still had acres of spectator seating available, but no one arrived to claim it. To accentuate Pat's image as a lonely widow, we had asked her to keep her in-laws and friends away. This was especially hard on James's brother, Walter Lee, and his sisters, Iris and Edith, but they said they understood. The old man had never called the NAACP or the other groups that showed a supportive interest when the complaint was filed, and the press hadn't given the Bowden case a thought since then. Only the *Phoenix* knew the trial date because we had subpoenaed O'Brian and Kobre. But even the *Phoenix* didn't bother to send a reporter. (O'Brian could not cover the trial, since, at our request, the judge would not allow witnesses other than the plaintiffs and defendants to watch the trial.) We had filed a pre-trial motion to keep witnesses out of the room when not actually testifying, because, as the old man had said, "It's a lot harder for cops to get their stories straight when they can't hear each other testify."

Tom McKenna, looking intense, had been in the room five minutes now and still hadn't taken his overcoat off. He had been studying the model. It was obviously a surprise to the defense. Mounted on a plywood base, with four-foot-high front legs and seven-foot rear legs that inclined the model toward the jury, were Styrofoam versions of the project buildings, painted brick-red, as well as all the essential streets, painted black and labeled with white letters large enough to be legible from a hundred feet. Every detail was in place: trees, streetlights, fences, sidewalks, the SLOW sign, Jessina Stokes's window, Carla Davis's window. On the corner of Parker and Prentiss—the lower right corner of the model— was Paul's Food Land, labeled STORE. McKenna had never heard mention of a store on Parker Street having anything to do with the case. Pointing to it, he looked over his shoulder to Keefe at the defense table and asked, "What happened there?" Keefe shrugged and turned to Eddie and Denny, who returned the shrug.

At that moment, from a door behind the witness stand, the jurors entered, led by a plainclothes U.S. marshal. They crossed the maroon-carpeted floor between the counsel tables and filed into the jury box, two rows of swiveling black leather armchairs surrounded by a waist-high oak partition, on the window side of the room, on the audience's left. The old man—boldly, I thought—gave the jury a smile. The jury—rightly, I thought—ignored him. Michael, Keefe, and Tom McKenna busied themselves with their files. Bill popped out to the hall to make sure our first witnesses were on hand. A young, moustachioed clerk of court appeared and settled into his large desk, the front of which abutted the front of the plaintiffs' table. About fifteen feet behind the oak plaintiffs' table was the oak defense table. And a few feet behind that was the swinging gate through which no one other than lawyers could pass, unless to take the witness stand.

At 9:09, as the clerk intoned, "All rise," Judge Skinner—a small, gray-haired man in a black robe that revealed an inch of white shirt collar and the knot of his tie—entered through a door leading directly onto his dark marble perch that propped him a good eight feet above all he surveyed. He seemed anxious to get under way, though he knew as well as the lawyers did that nothing gums up the works of our judicial system like a trial.

Judges with huge backlogs of cases (Skinner had more than eight hundred on his docket) have to encourage plea bargaining and its civil equivalent, out-of-court settlement, just to keep things moving. If every case had to be tried, each would have a pre-trial waiting period of at least fifty years. In fact, only a tiny portion—typically less than 5 percent—of the cases on a judge's docket ever get to trial. And often when they do go to trial, a plea bargain or settlement deal is struck in midstream and the case doesn't get to a jury verdict.

Due to backstage judicial dawdling or who knows what, I had never before seen the curtain go up on a trial this side of ten o'clock. Once in his chair, Skinner smiled at the jury and said, "Good morning." He was chipper; his charges were uneasy. They gave him smiles, nods, and half-spoken good-mornings in return. Still facing the jury, Skinner adjusted the tilt of his microphone and, in the manner of a tour guide, explained what was to come: "We'll begin with an opening statement by plaintiffs' counsel, after which defense counsel may also make an opening statement or choose not to make one until the beginning of the defense's case. In fact, the defense need not make an opening at any time. Further, the defense need not cross-examine any witnesses nor call any witnesses on its behalf, and that's because in this case, as in all civil cases, the burden of proof is entirely on the plaintiff." He stressed that opening statements are not evidence but merely attorneys' outlines of what they expect the evidence to show. "After the opening," he said, "Mr. O'Donnell will call the plaintiffs' witnesses." He nodded to the old man and said, "All right, I guess we can proceed with the opening statement."

The old man carried an armful of paper to a light wooden lectern that was midway between the defense table and the jury rail and directly in front of me. We had moved it to that spot so that, with a stretch across the bar enclosure, I would be able to leave notes on it. The old man twisted it a bit to face the jury. He hastily positioned his papers on the thing, then abandoned it. He hates to work with notes. He stepped into the space between the counsel tables, glanced at the clock on the back wall—9:16—and began speaking in a steady lecture tone that filled the room better than Skinner's amplified voice. "Madam Forelady, members of the jury," he said, "this case involves a shooting of a citizen by two members of the Tactical Patrol Force. We are in the federal court because of a law of the United States—Title 42, Section 1983—which was passed after the Civil War. In essence, it says that any police officer who, through wrongful conduct, hurts anyone in any way—in this instance they killed the plaintiff's husband, James Bowden— can be brought into this court."

A good beginning. He hit a nice note of authority on "Title 42, Section 1983." But working without notes means the old man has a tendency to slip off into tangents, which he did immediately.

The jury got a few long minutes of more than it ever wanted or needed to know about the federal laws and Massachusetts statutes cited in the plaintiffs' complaint.

The problem was twofold: He was nervous, and he was thinking about something else—how to lay out our case. Though we had been talking about it for days, we had not settled on what belonged in the opening. We wanted the jurors to have the basics about the shooting, and we wanted to tantalize them some, but we didn't want it to get too complicated too soon. Should we go right into all the Winbush business? What about the Fabrique Nationale? The plate numbers? Adolf Grant? The turret tape? As the old man rambled on about pendent jurisdiction, he was actually trying to find the place to begin the real story.

Presently he meandered into it, but only to make a few false starts. He said Bowden was "at work on Wednesday, January 29, 1975, and he checked out around three o'clock." Good enough. But then he slipped back six years to say that James and Patricia Bowden first met at Boston City Hospital when she worked there as a nurse's aide. "They had a happy marriage. It produced two lovely children." Next he turned to the model and explained that it was "something to help you understand the facts and it shows the setting of where the killing occurred." Again he went off on to something else. The jury had to be getting as frustrated as I was.

Finally, after mentioning the Cambridge robbery and the similarity of the reported getaway car to Bowden's car, he started to make sense. The story he told was short and simple. His speech was uncharacteristically slow, giving it an air of calm credibility and an edge of sadness. "So, what happened on Wednesday, January 29, 1975? You will hear testimony that Mr. Bowden left his house at six-thirty in the morning to report to work. People from the City Hospital, his bosses and supervisors, will be in here with the records of when he punched in his time card in the early morning and when he punched out in the afternoon.

"Now, he has a mother, sister, all kinds of relatives that were then living on Smith Street in the project. He would go there. His mother didn't have a car. He would take her shopping. He had the one car. And evidence will show it was his habit after work to get over there at some time to see if his mother needed anything.

"Interestingly enough, his daughter, Eurina, usually went with him. But on this day, she didn't go with her dad because she wanted to watch the baby get a bath.

"So, he came over here [pointing to the model] and he parked his car on Smith Street. And he was in this area.

"And on that day, it was raining.

"At a time of rather heavy rain, he was at a store by Prentiss Street here. And he received a lift in a Thunderbird and went up here and turned onto Smith Street, was dropped out of the Thunderbird, and went for his own car.

"The two defendants in plainclothes in an unmarked police car had his car under surveillance. They were parked on Gurney Street. They had in this unmarked police car a reporter by the name of David O'Brian and a photographer by the name of Ken Kobre. They had partners in an unmarked car up here at the other end of Smith Street by the name of Dwyer and Molloy. They also had another unmarked car down around Station Street. So, they were flanked and backed up by two other unmarked vehicles, in radio communication with them, and in radio communication with Boston Police Headquarters.

"Another interesting thing. For the first time, the system that tapes the radio stuff that goes over the air in Boston broke down.

"But we will overwhelmingly demonstrate from the police in Cambridge that the number plate on the car that was used in the robbery was not the number that was on Bowden's car.

"They had it under surveillance about a half hour.

"When Bowden got into his car and pulled out on Smith Street and apparently backed up, the two defendants came up, came right up practically to his car, and swung open the doors of the police car, and jumped out with service revolvers in their hands, went up to Bowden's car, and *never*—according to plaintiffs' testimony—yelled 'Halt' or 'Get out' or 'We're police.' Within two or three seconds, both fired bullets and killed him.

"He got shot through the back of the head.

"And his car then was moving and went down and crashed into the fence at the Tobin School.

"So our position for recovery in this case is they approached the wrong number, the wrong man. They ran up—no warning, no nothing—shot and killed him. Our witnesses will show negligence. And not only negligence, they will show gross negligence. They will not only show gross negligence, the witnesses will show willful, wanton, reckless conduct."

The old man headed for his chair. Skinner raised an eyebrow to the defense table. An invitation to make an opening. Tom McKenna shook his head. Skinner nodded to the old man, who was still on his feet. The old man broke the somber silence he had created by turning to the marshal and saying, "We will call Mr. Sheehan."

The marshal went into the hall and returned with John Sheehan, a civil engineer and nineteen-year employee of the Boston Public Works Department. We had sent an open subpoena to the department ordering a civil engineer to come to court with the plans of Smith Street and the housing project. We wanted to show that our model was, in legal terms, "a fair representation" of the scene. In ten minutes on the witness stand, Sheehan said it was.

When, to our surprise, Sheehan testified that he had "grown up in that general area" (back when it was a predominantly Irish neighborhood) and knew the territory well, the old man decided to reach for a detail that he could use later.

"Now, between Smith Street and Tremont Street it's uphill, isn't it?"

"That's right."

The old man pulled from his vest pocket what appeared to be a silver pen but was actually a telescoping twenty-five-inch pointer. "What happens when you go from here on Smith Street to there on Tremont Street?" he asked, using the pointer to trace on the model the Thunderbird escape route that we expected would be suggested by Eddie.

"You have got to go up steps," Sheehan replied.

The day we took our measurements on Smith Street, Michael

and I had checked out the Thunderbird's proposed escape route along the edge of the school playground. It was a cement path that was uphill all the way and led to a small granite staircase. A tough trek for a big, eight-year-old Thunderbird with sagging suspension, even assuming it swerved around the stairs and made the rest of the climb over rain-pummeled mud.

Happy to have gotten more than expected from Sheehan, the old man let him go after offering—and having Skinner accept—the official plan of Smith Street as an exhibit.

We next wanted to establish that Bowden was shot and killed by Eddie and Denny. The combined findings of Doctor Luongo and Walter Logue would do it. Both of them were under our subpoena. Bill had let me know that Logue was standing by, but there was no sign of the doctor yet. I knew the old man's preference was to call Luongo first. I dropped a note on the lectern as he was finishing with Sheehan, and when the time came, he called Walter Logue.

I nodded over my shoulder to Mary, who, according to plan, proceeded to take Eurina and Jamil for a long walk around the courthouse. There was some gruesome stuff coming up about tracing bullets taken from their father's body.

Sergeant Logue carried a case full of ballistics evidence to the witness stand, settled into its comfortable black leather swivel chair, and snuggled up to the microphone on its oak counter. Like all the police witnesses who were to follow, he was not in uniform. He was dressed the way Eddie and Denny should have been: a dull, dark suit and tie and a white shirt. In his direct examination, the old man had Logue spread out Eddie's and Denny's guns and ammunition in front of him. With methodical and somewhat tedious questioning, he showed: (1) that two of the bullets removed from the body had entered the back and the back of the neck, and had come from Eddie's gun; (2) that the other one removed from the body had entered through the left arm and chest and had come from Denny's gun; and (3) that each gun had fired two other bullets which were not found anywhere. The old man submitted as exhibits the two guns, the three bullets removed from the body, and the unfired rounds removed from Eddie's and Denny's guns. Skinner accepted them. The clerk applied exhibit stickers to each item and numbered them. Then John Keefe rose to cross-examine.

We were stunned. We had assumed that Tom McKenna was chief trial counsel and Keefe was *his* assistant. Now we saw that the reverse was true. When the old man saw Keefe moving toward the lectern with a legal pad, he nudged Michael, who turned around, saw Keefe, and turned back to his files. Over his right shoulder, so the jury couldn't see it, the old man gave me a can-you-believe-this-is-happening look. Later, during the lunch break, we settled on a two-track theory of why Keefe was leading the defense. First, McKenna did not have the, shall we say, manliness to take the floor against the old man; and second, the Law Department hoped that the mild-mannered Keefe would make the old man look like a bully when the old man lit into him, as he was sure to do. In the event, though, the old man was always courteous to Keefe in the presence of the jury. "Do you want to see this exhibit, John?" "Here, John, use my pointer." "Thank you, John." "You're welcome, John."

Once at the lectern, Keefe clung to it. He spoke in a reticent, cloudy voice which became all but inaudible when he was looking down at his notes and holding back his constantly slipping eyeglasses. He began by going after what the old man had intentionally left for him: the Fabrique Nationale.

"Now, you testified that you were present on the scene on Smith Street on the night of the twenty-ninth, and that you conducted a search?"

"Yes."

"What did you find in your search?"

"We searched the area for spent bullets, discharged cartridge cases, and anything of a ballistics nature, and . . . we recovered, or . . . I recovered . . . Officer Fagone with me . . . we recovered—"

Skinner interrupted for clarification: "Who discovered what it was that was discovered?"

"Uh, I discovered it," said Logue.

"What did you find?" asked the judge.

"A thirty-two Fabrique Nationale pistol."

Logue took the gun from his case and held it up for all to see. Keefe asked whether it was loaded when found. Logue said that it had six rounds in it. Keefe asked whether he examined it closely. "I broke it down, made it safe," Logue replied. "I examined the barrel and firing chamber and found residue adhering to each area of the barrel consisting of powder residue."

"Could you tell the court and jury what is the meaning of the finding of the residue inside the barrel?" asked Keefe.

"It's possible it could have been fired recently."

Skinner raised a hand to stop Keefe and asked Logue, "Is there any way to determine how long since it had been fired?"

"No."

"Now, when that pistol is fired," Skinner continued, with his prosecutor's knowledge of guns, "the spent cartridge is automatically ejected, is it not?"

"That is correct."

"Now, anywhere in the area did you find a spent cartridge shell?"

"No."

The old man looked at the jury as if to say, "Get it?" Michael whispered to him, "Skinner is really sharp."

Skinner gave the witness back to Keefe, who then submitted the Fabrique Nationale as defendants' exhibit number one.

"Objection," said the old man.

"Sustained," replied Skinner without hesitation.

Keefe looked dumbfounded. He stood motionless, looking at the floor for a moment, then went to the defense table for a conference with Tom McKenna. In a minute he returned to the lectern and asked Logue whether the gun had been in his exclusive custody since he found it, as a strict view of the rules of admissible evidence would require. Logue said it had. Keefe tried again, saying, "Your honor, at this time I offer defendants' exhibit number one in evidence."

"Objection," said the old man, more confidently this time.

"The objection is sustained," said Skinner. "I take it your objection is not based on custody."

"No, Your Honor," said the old man, "not at all."

Skinner told Keefe that custody was "not the problem" and asked whether he had "anything further for this witness." Keefe had nothing and sat down in visible bewilderment as to why the gun had not been admitted into evidence.

The old man got back up for redirect examination. He had previously treated Logue as he had John Sheehan—as a preliminary witness here to establish a few objective facts. Now it was time for some pushing and shoving. He began by emphasizing the points already drawn out by Skinner: No ejected shell was found, and it was impossible to tell when the Fabrique Nationale was last fired. Next he asked whether the bullets found in the automatic were actually designed for revolvers. Logue said, "No," at first, then checked the bullets and said, "Oh, yes."

Skinner interjected: "Was this pistol capable of firing the ammunition that was in it?"

"Yes, Your Honor," said Logue. He did not say, as Carl Majeskey had told us, that each bullet would have to be loaded separately before each firing, or the gun would jam.

"Now, sir," said the old man, eager to get to something else, "in examination by Mr. Keefe you said *you* found the Fabrique Nationale." He gave these two French words a ring of deep intrigue.

"I did," said Logue.

The old man sped through the next questions: "At what time?"

"I would say probably at seven-twenty, seven-fifteen."

"And who is the first person you told that *you* found the Fabrique?"

"I believe it was a sergeant in the TPF."

"What sergeant?"

"I don't know his name offhand."

"Now, when you were first testifying about finding it, you had occasion to mention the name Fagone."

"Yes."

"And that was Joseph J. Fagone, Jr., a TPF man?"

"That's right."

The old man turned to Michael, who was holding out the Fagone affidavit, which the defense had not yet seen. He placed it on the witness stand in front of Logue, who hunched over to read it. The old man started walking toward the jury and let silence take over. Then, with his back to the witness and his eyes on the jurors, he rumbled: "Now, would you change your testimony if I said to you that, under oath, Mr. Fagone said *he* found it at eight-fifteen P.M. after he was directed to look for it in a particular area by a Sergeant Harry Byrne? Would *that* make you change your testimony?"

Logue reread the affidavit, which had just been accurately summarized, and said, "As I say, I wasn't too sure of the, uh—"

The old man cut in: "Well, no, would you change—"

"It was confusing there," Logue said, stopping a repetition of the question. "There was a lot of investigative work going on. It was confusing."

"Now, will you say, under oath, you are not certain of the time you found it?"

"That's right. I said approximately."

"It could have been eight-fifteen?"

"It could have been."

"Are you saying [Fagone] was with you when you found it?"

"Yes. We both found it."

"Now, you both found it?" The old man was still facing the jury.

"Well, as we approached it . . . we had a search team out, and we seen it, and . . . we both viewed the firearm under the vehicle, and we both walked up to it, and Officer Fagone . . . all he done was reach down and pick it up and handed it to me."

"Oh, he picked it up?" The old man was smiling now and turning back toward Logue.

"Yes."

"So *now*, Mr. Logue, you wouldn't, under oath, disagree with Officer Fagone saying *he* found it at eight-fifteen, would you?"

"No."

Joe Fagone, of course, was safely out of the case. He was not on the defense's witness list and the old man had no intention of reneging on the deal he had made for the Fagone affidavit. However, had he testified at the trial, Fagone told me, he would have contradicted Logue by saying, "Logue wasn't there until a couple of minutes after I found the gun."

The old man finished with Logue by taking him a half step out of his expertise and asking about fingerprints on the Fabrique Nationale. We believed the gun was never dusted for prints, since there was no fingerprint report. To our mild surprise, Logue testified that it was examined for prints and none were found.

"And, sir, were you told that James Bowden did not have any gloves on?"

"Objection, Your Honor," said Keefe.

"Sustained," said Skinner.

It was a leading question that called for a hearsay answer. The old man throws around thoroughly objectionable questions like this all the time, not really caring whether they're answered. The point is to get a bit of information to his jurors. Here he was telling them that Bowden was not wearing gloves on Smith Street, and so, by implication, would have left fingerprints on the gun if he had touched it.

The old man had Logue dismantle the automatic and show the jury how to load bullets into the smooth steel magazine inside the handle.

"The person who put the bullets in there would have to handle [the magazine], wouldn't he?" he asked.

"Yes," said Logue.

"Then, that's a fertile area for latent fingerprints."

"Objection, Your Honor," said Keefe.

"This man's a ballistic expert, not a fingerprint expert," said Skinner, probably so the jury would understand the objection. "I will sustain the objection."

"All right," said the old man, content that he had made his point.

Walter Logue's squirming on the witness stand was over. As he started out of the room, Tom McKenna signaled him to the defense table, where, apparently at McKenna's request, he handed over the Fabrique Nationale. McKenna positioned the gun for prominent display on top of his files. The Fabrique Nationale, around which jury suspicion already had to be swirling, was not, for reasons the defense plainly couldn't fathom, allowed a place on the clerk's desk with the exhibits, but McKenna wasn't going to let anyone forget about the gun.

Instead of calling another witness, the old man requested "the court's permission" for the jury to examine the ballistics exhibits. "You can pass those items around," Skinner said routinely.

The old man took one of the guns from the clerk, checked the little yellow sticker on it, and announced, "This is the gun fired by defendant Holland, submitted as a plaintiffs' exhibit." He handed it to the foreman, who had moved into the number one spot. She took it, with some reluctance, in both hands, glanced at it, and passed it to juror number two. The old man watched the gun move through the jury box.

At moments like this, spectators visit the bathrooms, lawyers check their notes, judges confer with clerks, stenographers yawn, and marshals step outside for a cigarette. Not this time. All eyes were on the gun—largely, if not entirely, because the old man's were. Although Skinner was and would remain firmly in control of his court, the old man had—two and a half hours since he had spoken his first word to the jury—taken control of the mood. He had made a bid for it with the strong finish of his opening, and had won it with his run at Walter Logue which forced Logue to change his testimony about finding the Fabrique Nationale. Witness recanting of that sort is a far more unusual event than fictionalized trials in movies, television, and novels suggest. Logue's forced switch hinted not only that the police were up to something here, but that the old man was on to it. He was, therefore—especially by comparison to the colorless Mr. Keefe—the man to watch.

When the gun reached the second alternate, the old man walked the length of the jury box to retrieve it. Without a word he took the gun and returned it to the clerk. He picked up the other

revolver, checked the sticker, and before handing it to the foreman, announced, "This is the gun fired by defendant McKenna,
submitted as a plaintiffs' exhibit." The gun passed through the
jury box, creating discomfort at each stop.

"You give them the guns," the old man explained half an hour
later back at the office. "I mean, you put the goddamn things right
in their laps because most jurors have never touched one. And
when they do, they all think the same thing: *Imagine what this
thing can do to you.* You know, TV is always glamorizing guns.
Now you've got one in your hand and you find out it's a cold,
heavy, ugly thing. And when you know this one has killed somebody, well . . ."

With the second gun back on the clerk's desk, the old man took
four small envelopes, checked the stickers on them, opened one,
and announced, "This is the one unfired bullet removed from defendant Holland's gun, submitted as a plaintiffs' exhibit."

He started it through the jury. Its smallness and simplicity
made it seem hardly lethal, more like an internal part of a typewriter or an engine, the kind of thing mechanics point to when
explaining why your car won't start. As soon as the foreman
passed it to number two, the old man opened another envelope
and said, "These are the two unfired bullets removed from defendant McKenna's gun."

The unfired bullets were a setup. When the jurors had had a
good look at them, felt the smooth roundness of their gray lead,
the old man gave them a shocking comparison. He opened another envelope, handed its contents to the foreman, and said,
"These are the two bullets fired by defendant Holland and removed from James Bowden's *back* and the *back* of his *head*."
Pause. "Submitted as plaintiffs' exhibits."

The foreman cradled them in her palms and looked at them.
They were mangled little chunks of lead no longer of an identifi-
able shape. Dirty-yellow and dark-brown traces of tissue, blood,
and bone were cemented to the cracks, crevices, and ridges that
formed in the lead after it hit Bowden's skin at 1,300 feet per second. She quickly passed them to number two, as the old man said,

"This is the bullet fired by defendant McKenna and removed from James Bowden's chest." Pause. "Submitted as a plaintiffs' exhibit."

The foreman took it without looking at it and immediately passed it to number two.

The old man collected the bullets at the other end of the jury box and returned them to the clerk. Minutes later we were all off to lunch.

Waiting for us back at the office, along with a big box of sandwiches my mother had just had delivered, was a telephone message from Doctor Luongo. He couldn't make it today because of an emergency but promised to show up tomorrow. Courts (and the old man) are understanding of doctors' scheduling problems. We would take Luongo whenever we could get him.

My mother played luncheon hostess to the Bowdens in the library. Bill, Mary, Kevin, and Kim Bonstrom crowded in there, too, for sandwiches and about forty minutes of fun with the kids.

In the old man's office, Michael and I went over our plans for the afternoon and finalized our checklist of what we wanted to cover. There was no point in trying to include the old man in the discussion. In a trial, his adrenaline keeps pumping right through the lunch hour, and actually he thinks more clearly on his feet than he does during breaks in the action, when all he's usually good for is complaining or gloating. Between occasional bites of a Swiss cheese on pumpernickel and gulps from a carton of skim milk, the old man, always the first to admit he's doing a good job, was saying, "How about the way I hit Logue with the Fagone affidavit? His eyes popped out of his head for chrissake. . . . That fingerprint stuff went over good, didn't it? . . . Oh, and did you see Keefe's face when Skinner wouldn't take the Fabrique? I thought he was gonna cry. And McKenna was dying. They never dreamed they'd have trouble making that goddamn thing an exhibit."

Michael laughed. I didn't get it. "Why didn't Skinner take it?"

The old man put his feet up on the desk and said, " 'Cause it's not related to anything in the case—not yet anyway. See, right now there's no accusation that Bowden had a gun, and there won't be until Holland or McKenna takes the stand. It was as if Keefe asked Logue what, if anything, he found anywhere on the street and Logue says, 'Well, I found this beer can and this hubcap and this pile of dog shit,' and then Keefe tries to make 'em all exhibits. What do they have to do with this case? Keefe should've waited till we finished our case-in-chief, then call back Logue *after* Holland and try to get it in. But even then he might have problems with it if Skinner demands any kind of linkage beyond them saying Bowden had a gun."

Already it was time to get back to court. The old man dropped his half-eaten sandwich and, with a wave toward City Hall, said, "They're sitting over there right now looking at that gun and wondering why Skinner won't take it. And our jurors are wondering about that too. They hear from the affidavit that it's not found till an hour and forty-five minutes after the shooting and they see the judge won't admit it into evidence. What's going on here? Without me saying a word about it, the jury's gotta already be thinking *planted gun.*"

The communications division is, in virtually every police department, a dumping grounds for the infirm. Patrolmen with bad backs, weak hearts, or failing eyesight find it an agreeable assignment. It's also a safe place to tuck away the known alcoholics. No confrontations. No tension. No guns. Denny was a good prospect for transfer to the turret in the early 1970s when his drinking problem became acute, but then there are never enough inside jobs for every cop who would be better off, off the street.

Boston's turret men are almost never called to testify in court, but we had two—Patrolmen John Tanous and Robert Mullen—scheduled for the afternoon.

We hadn't deposed them, but from their reports we knew that Tanous could testify about the first robbery information Boston received from Cambridge and what he, in turn, relayed to all Boston cars; and that Mullen could show the jury that during the stakeout the ACU team mistakenly checked the plate number that Tanous had broadcast, not the number on Bowden's car. A welcome feature of their testimony would be the turret tape malfunction. And more or less as a footnote to Tanous's testimony, we would bring on Cambridge's Sergeant Petersen to introduce the teletype of robbery information that Cambridge sent Boston after the initial radio alert.

The old man first called the short, thin, nervous-looking John Tanous—twenty-seven years on the force, the last ten in the turret. He handed Tanous a copy of his report and told him to feel free to refer to it. Not surprisingly, Tanous's testimony agreed with his report. He testified that at 2:36 P.M. an intercity alert from Cambridge had said: "to be on the lookout for two colored males. They were thought to have fled in a blue car—a car blue in color, I should say—and the registration was thought to have been Mass. registration 4, S as in Sam, 6368. . . . On an all-city transmit, I alerted every cruiser in the entire city." A few minutes later, Cambridge "alerted us to change the registration to now read 4, F as in Frank, with the same digits, 6368," and again "I went out on an all-city [to] every unit and every district." Tanous said he made notes on "a memo pad" as the Cambridge information came over the air.

It took about ten minutes to bring that much out through narrow question and answer. Tanous seemed a credible witness and a competent dispatcher. Then the old man said, "Let me ask you this: When you broadcast that type of information, is some recording made of it?"

"All our transmissions," said Tanous, "is recorded on a tape."

"Now, you have frequently played back broadcasts from the tape?"

"Yes."

"Did you do it on this particular incident?"

Tanous considered the question and, instead of the flat no we expected, said, "Not that particular day, no, sir."

"What day did you do it?" the old man asked innocently.

"I believe it may have been the third of February." (That was the day he wrote his report.)

"So on the third of February, in order to check, you went back and played the tape?"

"Yes, sir."

Keefe objected, but not in time to prevent Tanous's very surprising answer.

"Leading question, Your Honor," said Keefe.

"The objection is sustained," said Skinner.

You cannot ask leading questions of your own witness, and since the old man had called him, Tanous was technically his witness. Although Skinner had to sustain the objection, he must have thought the question and answer were important. He did what judges can always do in such a situation: He asked the question himself. "Let me interrupt just a minute," he said. "Mr. Tanous, did you ever play the tape back?"

Tanous shifted uncomfortably, glanced at the defense table, turned to Skinner, and said unsteadily, "I, uh, don't recall, Your Honor."

Skinner gave the witness a hard look. He probably hadn't seen such a fast testimony switch in a long while—except for Walter Logue's, of course.

"Thank you," said the old man to the judge. Walking toward the jury, with a knowing smile he asked, "Have you made an inquiry as to that broadcast tape?"

"No, sir," Tanous replied weakly.

"Well." Chuckle. "Do you think it's still in existence?"

Pause. "I have no idea, sir."

"Did you ever hear that that tape got destroyed?"

"No, sir."

The old man submitted Tanous's report as an exhibit, and Skinner accepted it.

Keefe did a ten-minute cross-examination that covered all aspects of turret operations—except tape-recording the transmissions. It was boring and revealed nothing of significance. For example:

KEEFE: Could you explain for the jury what the all-city covers?

TANOUS: All-city transmit. By activating that one button, every unit in the entire city, whether it be a walkie-talkie or a vehicle, would receive my broadcast, as opposed to my normally operating on Channel Two. Only my vehicles would hear me on Channel Two, and not the others.

Following Tanous to the stand was Edwin Petersen, recently promoted to lieutenant. Once the introductory name, rank, and "Were you working on January 29, 1975" were out of the way, the old man put a copy of the Cambridge teletype in front of Petersen, with the intention of making it a plaintiffs' exhibit. It was the tedious but mandatory approach:

"I ask you to examine that paper I placed in front of you. . . . Have you had a fair opportunity to read it and examine it, Lieutenant?"

"Yes, sir."

"Would you—if you know—state to the court and jury what that is?"

"It appears to be a copy of a teletype sent out on January 29."

"From the Cambridge Police Department?"

"Yes, sir."

"And what's contained thereon?"

"Objection, Your Honor," said Keefe. "This witness has not authenticated the document."

Keefe was objecting on the grounds that it was a photocopy instead of the original. It is one of many objections that slow down the already slow process of making documents exhibits. Skinner didn't welcome it. Nothing seemed to bother him more than wasting time.

"Did you ever see that before?" Skinner asked.

"Yes," said Petersen.

"Where?"

"In the folder of that holdup."

Skinner plodded through fourteen more questions, the last of which was: "Is what Mr. O'Donnell showed you an accurate copy of that original?"

"Yes, Your Honor," said Petersen.

"What do you say, Mr. Keefe?" asked Skinner. "Do you want to press your objection?"

"I withdraw my objection, Your Honor," Keefe replied.

The objection had cost everyone fifteen minutes.

The old man read the teletype to the jury, putting vocal emphasis where he wanted it: "Wanted for armed robbery of a food store in this city. Two black males. One black male *six feet, thin build,* light-skinned, wearing a dark-blue denim cap, light *nylon jacket,* brown pants, black turtleneck sweater, white *sneakers.* A small *black revolver* was shown. Second black male *five-ten, thin build,* dark-skinned, wearing blue peaked hat, short whiskers, *denim jacket* and pants, white *sneakers.* Both fled on foot to a blue Ford or Buick, Mass. registration 4S•*6368* or 4F•*6368.*"

Keefe tried a few minutes of meaningless, barely audible cross-examination on the layout of Cambridge's communications room.

Patrolman Robert Mullen, an eighteen-year veteran of the turret who had relieved John Tanous at 4:30 P.M. on January 29, 1975, took the witness stand next. Following another of Keefe's time-consuming objections, Mullen's report became a plaintiffs' exhibit, and the old man read it to the jury: "About 6:30 P.M., Wednesday, January 29, while working as a dispatcher on Channel 1 and monitoring Channel 8, I received a radio message from ACU 841 unit to check Mass. registration 4F•*6368* that they thought was involved in a holdup in Cambridge earlier in the day. A check with teletype unit confirmed the above information, and ACU 841 said they had the car under surveillance on Smith Street, District 2.

"About 6:55 P.M., the ACU 841 unit on Channel 8 requested assistance at above location. Several units in District 2 on Channel 3 responded to the scene.

"A short time later, some unit that I cannot recall requested a stolen car listing on Mass. registration 6S*0280 because while [this] vehicle was moving, a *shotgun* was *pointed out the window* and vehicle fled from the vicinity of Smith Street.

"This is all the information and knowledge I can recall of the incident.

"P.S. Attached is a record of car checked by ACU 841 unit."

Attached to Mullen's report was his handwritten log of thirty plate numbers he checked during the tour of duty, including the two mentioned in his report. "That's called the hot sheet," Mullen said.

The old man wanted to have some fun with Mullen on the mysterious turret tape but didn't have time because we were in a hurry to get our next witness on the stand. He had already scored enough points on that with Tanous, anyway. Keefe's cross-examination of Mullen was mercifully brief, and the old man called Ken Kobre.

Our plan had been to bring on the City Hospital people next to show that Bowden was at work at the time of the robbery, but we changed that to accommodate Kobre, who had told Bill that he had an important out-of-town free-lance assignment the next day. It was 4:15 P.M. when Kobre took the stand. I had never seen a court stay in session after four o'clock. There was little chance of finishing with Kobre before adjournment. Just getting all his photographs admitted was probably going to take more time than we had.

The old man raced through Kobre's story in twenty minutes. "I spent the day with the Tactical Patrol Force," said Kobre. "We started around two o'clock in the afternoon, I believe. We rode in the back of a car and participated in a stakeout [with Officers] McKenna and Holland. . . . Dave O'Brian, also from the *Phoenix*" was also "in the back seat" on the left side.

"We were watching a Buick, which was near a yellow sign. . . . They thought that the license plate was the same one that had been involved in a robbery earlier in the day in Cambridge."

"Holland talked about—as it got darker—the problem was dangerous because there were children around and shooting might hurt children. And it was extremely dark there."

"The thing I remember most strongly was the idea that a shotgun had been involved in the robbery, and these men might have a shotgun. Therefore, we should get down."

"They radioed to the policemen that we were with earlier. And one group talked about taking the driver and the other talked about taking a person on the other side of the car."

"They had guns in their hands."

"A car drove up, and someone got out. At that point, the car that I was in, the police car, drove up near the Buick. I got down in the back seat of the car at that point."

"They said, 'Here we go!' or 'We're goin in!'"

"Holland and McKenna got out. . . . I do not remember them closing the doors of the car."

"Then, very quickly afterwards, we heard gunshots. . . . I agreed with Dave O'Brian it was between three and five seconds."

"I'm not sure of the exact number [of gunshots]."

"I did not hear them say anything on the street."

"I did not hear any engines [racing, or] tire squealing."

"Now, sir," said the old man, with an eye on the clock, "I show you these photographs and ask you to look at them and tell the court and jury whether or not they're a fair representation of what they portray."

"Yes, they are," said Kobre before looking at them.

Keefe objected, and Skinner, rather than suffer a set of boring questions and objections before admitting each photograph, summarily cut through the nonsense and told the clerk to "get those things marked and numbered."

Then he said, "Why don't we suspend. It's now twenty minutes of five." He turned to the jury and, with a smile and a slight hint of severity, said, "Nine o'clock tomorrow morning." The marshal led the jurors across the room and through their special door behind the witness stand, where Ken Kobre sat, looking as if he had just been robbed—which, in effect, he had.

We had him under subpoena, so he had no choice of whether he would be in the witness chair the next morning or jetting off to wherever it was he had promised to be.

"I want to see counsel at the side bar," said Skinner as he stepped to his left. He slid into the small chair he keeps at the side of the bench farthest from the jury box. It is the spot where he holds bench conferences—whispered discussions with lawyers which for one reason or another must not be heard by jurors. All four lawyers approached the bench.

Kobre, realizing he could leave, did so. He cornered Bill in the hall and told him how angry he was at us for not putting him on sooner. Bill apologized and explained that we had to establish some background points with the police witnesses before getting to him. Kobre was not appeased. "Well," said Bill, "trials are hard on everyone."

Meanwhile, at the side bar, in an off-the-record chat, Skinner was taking both sides to task for how bogged down things had become at certain points. He told them to be prepared to go from nine to five tomorrow—with, of course, morning and afternoon recesses and a lunch hour—and to try to pick up the pace. To Keefe he offered some friendly advice: He would have to speak more clearly and a good deal louder. Everyone had been straining to hear him. With a fatherly smile, Skinner suggested a vocal exercise he had used at the beginning of his career: "Take your wife to some windy, deserted beach and try talking to her at progressively greater distances. Don't be afraid to shout if you have to." Keefe received the advice with good humor. The lawyers were all smiling now.

Skinner asked the old man whether he had a secret for keeping his volume up so high all the time.

"No." He shrugged. "I guess I just like to yell."

CHAPTER 14

When the jury filed in the next morning, the old man offered them a big good-morning smile, which to me seemed as improper as it had the previous day. This time the first alternate nodded, and his eyes, at least, seemed to smile.

Ken Kobre resumed the stand for an hour. The old man spent a few minutes having him explain that the photographs of Joe Fagone finding the Fabrique Nationale were taken in front of 26 Smith Street "about halfway down the street" from the crashed Buick. Then he asked him to look at one of the pictures and read the "number plate of the Buick Electra."

"I can make out F6•838," said Kobre.

"Four-F•*6838*," said the old man.

He passed the stack of photographs to the foreman and watched as the jurors eagerly examined each photograph.

The jury's study of the photographs took fifteen minutes, during which, at Skinner's invitation, Keefe began cross-examination. When Skinner noticed that none of the jurors was paying attention to Keefe, he told him to "wait until the jury is through."

Once Keefe's cross did get going, we were charmed by its timidity. Here was our second-most important witness on the stand. The time had come for the defense to show some spirit. We thought Keefe would surely take a run at Kobre's "between three and five seconds." After all, that time estimate was the most powerful contradiction of what would be the defense's account of the shooting. But, presumably having decided that Kobre was too surefooted a witness, Keefe stayed away from the shooting itself.

Instead, he concentrated on Kobre's "conversations with the officers" and his memory of the radio traffic. It was all rehash, but it
elicited an extra detail here and there that was helpful to us. For
example:

KEEFE: Did you hear any calls while you were with Molloy
  and Dwyer?
KOBRE: Yes.
KEEFE: Can you recall what the call said?
KOBRE: That there was a robbery in Cambridge; that there
  were two men involved; that the men were thin . . .

Kobre's testimony about no shouting at Bowden, no racing engines, no screeching tires, and the three-to-five seconds remained
unchallenged when he stepped down from the witness stand.

The old man turned to the marshal and, with the verve of a
Las Vegas announcer introducing Frank Sinatra, said, "David
O'Brian, please."

The hospital witnesses had to wait, because we wanted to have
Kobre and O'Brian testify consecutively.

O'Brian entered, found his way to the witness stand, took the
oath, and sat down. He adjusted the microphone downward to his
own chin level and answered the old man's questions, beginning
with his employment history and leading to January 29, 1975.

"I was assigned to spend the afternoon and evening riding with
members of the Anti-Crime Unit of the Tactical Patrol Force," he
told the jury in his careful, unassuming way. "I had a photographer with me—Ken Kobre."

"The car I was first in was a car operated by Billy Dwyer and
Mark Molloy. . . . At some point that afternoon we were trans-
ferred to another car with Officers Dennis McKenna and Edward
Holland."

Officer Holland "was carrying a clipboard, and he was using it
to write down information that was coming over the police radio
all afternoon."

"A little before six, we had taken a turn down Smith Street into the Mission Hill project, and Officer Holland, who was in the passenger seat, recognized the license plate on a Buick . . . as a license plate that he had heard come over the police radio that afternoon [and] had been reported involved in a robbery in Cambridge. So we stopped, made a U-turn, and went back [to] Gurney Street within view of the Buick."

"By the time we were on Gurney Street [with] the Buick under surveillance, it had started to rain. . . . It was already pretty dark, and there were no streetlights that I remember right on Smith Street. So, Smith Street was very dark."

"Officer Holland had a walkie-talkie, and he was radioing to the other cars, two other cars also involved in this stakeout. . . . I heard Dwyer's [voice]."

"We heard a report over the police radio that a shotgun had been used in the Cambridge robbery, and there was some conversation and some concern on all our parts about what was likely to happen if we were confronted with someone carrying a shotgun. . . . Officer McKenna advised Ken Kobre and myself that if any shooting occurred, we were to get down on the floor."

"I was very frightened."

"A dark-colored Thunderbird came around the corner. . . . it was six-thirty, six-thirty-five or so. . . . It came up Parker Street and took a right turn onto Smith Street and stopped parallel to the Buick. And a figure got out of the passenger side of the Thunderbird and walked over and entered the Buick on the driver's side. . . . Officer McKenna started the car, and we began to go across Parker Street onto Smith Street . . . moving fairly slowly. . . . Officer Holland radioed to the other cars, 'We're going in. We're going in.'"

"The operator of the Buick had started the car and had put it in reverse and was backing up in our direction. . . . The car I was in came to an abrupt stop. . . . We were almost on top of [the Buick]."

"The two officers jumped out of the car. . . . They were carrying handguns."

The doors "were opened."

"At that point, I dove to the floor. I didn't see anything more."

"After a period of a few seconds—from three to five seconds—I heard a series of gunshots. . . . They were rapid fire. Seven or eight."

"I didn't . . . hear Officer McKenna's or Officer Holland's voice . . . [or] any screeching tires."

"After I heard the shooting, there may have been another—I don't know—thirty seconds or so, and Officer Holland was the first to return to the car. . . . I remember him calling for help and saying that there had been a shooting. The only specific thing I remember hearing him say was: 'No ACU injured.'"

"At that point, they drove the car . . . further down Smith Street to . . . where the Buick . . . had apparently collided with this utility pole and was up against . . . a chain link fence [in front of] the Tobin School."

"I got out of the car . . . The first thing I saw was Officer Mc-Kenna approach the Buick. He was . . . reaching . . . through the window on the driver's side, and he appeared to be holding the man behind the wheel."

"Dwyer and Molloy . . . appeared on the scene, and a series of other police officers, who I did not recognize, came onto the scene very shortly."

"No, I didn't [speak to Officer Holland], although I did see him walking around."

"Yes, I did [speak to Officer McKenna]."

"After I had seen him reach into the Buick . . . I noticed there was blood on his right sleeve, and I asked him if he had been hit in the gunfire. And he responded, 'No, it's his blood.' . . . And then he said, 'As soon as he turned the wheel, I said, 'Fuck him.' And he made a gesture with his hands indicating to me that that was when he opened fire."

"At least five police officers [searched the Buick for] anywhere from a half to three quarters of an hour."

Eventually, a "gun was found under the right front fender of a car that was parked . . . on the even side of Smith Street. . . . It wasn't . . . in the vicinity of where the Buick crashed."

The old man had O'Brian step over to the model. He pulled out his fancy pointer, which Skinner had taken to calling "that collapsible wand," handed it to O'Brian, and asked him to show the jury where the Buick was originally parked, where it finally crashed, and where the gun was found. O'Brian complied, then resumed the witness stand.

Only one O'Brian item that we tried to get in was stopped by a defense objection. At the old man's request, O'Brian began to recount Dwyer's post-shooting remarks: "Officer Dwyer said to me—"

"Objection, Your Honor," said Keefe.

"That is awful slow," said Skinner, shaking his head, "after the answer is started. The objection is sustained."

It was classic hearsay. Generally, witnesses are allowed to quote only what plaintiffs or defendants have said to them, not what anyone else—no matter how involved—has told them. With Dwyer on the stand, however, the old man could, on cross-examination, hold up the Kobre picture of Dwyer laughing and ask, "When that picture was taken, did you say to Dave O'Brian, 'How's this for action? Did we put on a good show for you?'" For that, we would have to wait until Keefe called Dwyer.

A few minutes later, when Keefe was again slow to object—this time to an insignificant but leading question—Tom McKenna popped up and said, "Objection."

Skinner sternly sat him down. "Just one trial counsel, please."

"I'm sorry," said McKenna, sitting back in his chair.

"Decide who's going to try the case," Skinner snapped.

Keefe then made the objection and Skinner overruled it.

The old man's last question was: "Prior to them getting out of the car, did you ever see badges on them?"

"No."

"Thank you."

Skinner said, "Cross-examination, Mr. Keefe?"

"Yes, Your Honor," replied Keefe, slowly rising.

After O'Brian had given forty minutes of wholly credible testimony, Keefe squared off with our star witness. He began with questions about "the processes by which" O'Brian and Kobre "got to have permission to go in these [ACU] cars," and proceeded to questions about "the nature of [O'Brian's] handwriting . . . on the portion of [the reporter's] notes that dealt with . . . waiting on Gurney Street," and many more about overheard "radio communications."

Having skipped over the shooting, Keefe thought he caught O'Brian in self-contradiction with his deposition when he said the Fabrique Nationale was found about an hour later.

"Now," said Keefe, "did you attend a deposition in Mr. O'Donnell's office on May 18, 1977?"

"Yes."

"Was your testimony different at that time?"

"I pray Your Honor's judgment," said the old man softly.

He was objecting to only the most blatantly improper stuff, and this qualified. Keefe was supposed to show O'Brian his deposition before asking him if his previous testimony was different.

Skinner sustained the objection, but not wanting to stop Keefe on a technicality, he asked him, "Do you have anything you want to show him?" Keefe didn't understand. So Skinner said, "That is not the right way to do it, counsel. Come on up here."

In a bench conference, Skinner told Keefe how to impeach a witness with a deposition. The old man and Michael listened in unalarmed. Then Michael handed the judge O'Brian's deposition. He read the relevant lines, shook his head, and said, "He said an hour. . . . There is nothing inconsistent with that." Skinner told Keefe to go to something else.

Finally, Keefe approached the shooting. "After you started to move in on Smith Street, at some point you ducked down behind the seat?"

"That's true."

"Could you tell us what position you were in behind the seat and where you were?"

"I was on the left, on the left-hand side behind the driver. And when I ducked down, I was like, I was on my knees with my head down."

Keefe slipped over to the defense table to confer with Mc-Kenna. Thirty seconds later, he looked up and said, "No further questions."

Toward the end of the fifteen-minute recess that followed O'Brian's testimony, Doctor Luongo arrived and we agreed to put him on next. I told the City Hospital witnesses, who had been waiting without complaint since yesterday afternoon, that we would call them right after the doctor.

The two waiting benches in the hall were filled now. Harry Byrne, Billy Dwyer, and Mark Molloy were on one; Adolph Grant, Elsie Pina, Donald Webster, and Henry Smith on the other. The Bowdens stayed in the courtroom during this and almost every other recess. Eddie and Denny came out and joined the police section. Eddie immediately lit a cigarette. He and Denny so enjoyed the chance to chat, joke, and smoke that, from then on, they would only intermittently leave their friends to subject themselves to the tensions of the courtroom.

On the way to the men's room the old man asked, "Did you see Cohen's face when O'Brian went through the 'Fuck him'?"

"No," said Michael. Almost everything happened behind Michael's back. To his sides he could see the witness stand and the foreman. To see the rest of the jury or whichever lawyer was on his feet, he had to turn around—something he did only to get messages to the old man.

"You should've seen him," I said. "Cohen's definitely with us."

"Too bad he's not in the front row," said Michael, unencouraged by the news that we had won the first alternate, who would have no say in the verdict.

David Cohen was the only juror we referred to by name because he was the one we talked about the most. He earned the distinction by being so expressive. When Walter Logue had to change his story, Cohen's eyebrows jumped with surprise. When the old man was tying up John Tanous with the turret tape, Cohen, an engineer, smiled knowingly. He hung on every word of Kobre's and O'Brian's testimony, and when O'Brian calmly said,

"Fuck him," and, in imitation of Denny's accompanying gesture, gripped both hands on an imaginary gun, Cohen, perhaps unconsciously, sighed, lowered his eyes, and shook his head.

Immediately after Doctor Luongo took the stand, Keefe, in a bench conference, objected to the anticipated introduction of the autopsy photographs. "Perhaps Your Honor would like to see them," he said.

"Sure," said Skinner.

Michael handed them to the judge, saying, "They show the entry wounds."

The old man chipped in: "They were taken by the doctor." Tom McKenna said, "The doctor can [simply] *explain* where [the bullets] entered."

"I feel, Your Honor," said Keefe, "the showing of the photographs would be prejudicial to my clients and it would be inflammatory and go to the emotional factor as opposed to—"

"Oh, heavens, no," said Skinner. "It seems to me quite relevant where the wounds are. . . . These don't strike me as being at all inflammatory. You just haven't seen inflammatory pictures."

"I suppose I haven't," Keefe replied.

Skinner told him about pictures he had once seen of "some woman worked over with an axe." Prosecutors, he said, always "bring those pictures in."

At lunch that day, the old man said, "You can never leave out pictures of the body in a murder trial. And even if the boys from City Hall still don't know where they are, you can bet your life that the Honorable Walter Jay Skinner knows we're really in a goddamn murder trial."

And that night, Michael explained to Bill and me: "The standard routine with a medical examiner is to get his report into evidence and ask what the cause of death was. Most guys would've had Luongo on and off the stand in five minutes. You know, a little technical interlude. Nothing interesting about it. But what the old man did with him . . . that was . . . that was magic."

What the old man did with Luongo—while Bill kept Eurina and Jamil occupied with coloring books out in the hall—was first to make his report plaintiffs' exhibit number 14A, then to read selections of it to the jury, applying emphasis where he wanted it. Luongo sat with nothing to do as his report, the only heavily technical one in the case, got a caring and compelling reading in spite of itself.

The old man spoke slowly and softly, occasionally stressing a few words: "The body is that of a young black man." Pause. "Who appears to be about twenty-five years of age, measuring *sixty-four and five tenths* inches in length and weighing an estimated one hundred and eighty pounds." Pause. "The hair is black and kinky with an Afro-style hairdo." Pause. "The only external evidence of recent injury consists of gunshot wounds." Pause.

"There is a gunshot entrance wound in the *left upper arm*. This wound is oval in shape, measuring six tenths of an inch. [It] passes through the musculature of the left arm straight towards the left upper chest . . . with a perforating tract of destruction." Pause. "The tract thence is into the wall of the esophagus where the bullet lies." Pause.

"There is [a] gunshot wound in the left upper *back*." Pause. "This entrance wound measures one inch by five-tenths of an inch. [It] passes through the skin and subcutaneous tissue [with] a perforating tract through the left scapular." Pause. "The bullet lies lodged near the parietal pleura here at the end of the wound tract." Pause.

"There is a gunshot entrance wound in the right *posterior neck*." Pause. "This is nearly round, measuring four tenths of an inch in diameter. Exploration of this tract shows a destructive path through the subcutaneous tissues and muscles of the neck. The track ends just below the right jaw, the bullet lying here just beneath the skin without exit wound."

Pat Bowden was as stoically expressionless as she always was during the trial.

The old man had Luongo leave the stand and join him in the middle ground between the counsel tables. Offering the doctor his pointer and himself as a model, he asked him to point out the locations of the wounds. Luongo put the pointer on the old man's left biceps, then on the back of his neck at the hairline and on his back, while the old man fixed a mournful look on the jury.

He took the autopsy photographs from Michael and led Luongo to the jury rail. Holding the pictures for him, the old man had the doctor point out the bullet holes for one juror at a time. The foreman squinted and cringed. Cohen grimaced angrily.

The old man thought he was finished with Luongo, but Michael pushed him back out on the floor with a few more questions.

"Was James Bowden in any way in a bloated condition?"

"No, sir."

"Are the lighting conditions at that part of the morgue where people make [identifications] adequate for a person to make an identification?"

"I think so."

"Have you seen people identify bodies there?"

"Oh, yes, many times."

"Thank you," said the old man, as he sat down.

Working without notes has its price. The old man had forgotten to ask the two standard questions always put to medical examiners: "Did you form an opinion as to the cause of death?" and "What is that opinion?" With the old man in his seat, Skinner asked those two questions, and Luongo said, "The deceased came to his death as a result of gunshot wounds" and consequent "massive internal hemorrhage."

"Cross-examination?" asked Skinner.

"I have no questions," said Keefe.

Henry Smith, the head of City Hospital's Housekeeping Department, was our next witness. Through him, the old man showed that Bowden had been working at the hospital since 1968.

Consulting his file, Smith testified that Bowden's income rose from $4,352 in 1968 to $6,927 in 1974, his last full year on the job. He said that Bowden's "work performance" was "satisfactory" and he never had to "penalize him or suspend him or anything."

"Do you have a time card for Mr. Bowden regarding January 29, 1975?" asked the old man.

"Yes," said Smith, handing it over.

The old man offered it as an exhibit, and Keefe objected. Skinner called a bench conference to find out what Keefe's objection was. At the side bar, the old man gave Skinner the time card and Keefe said, "Some other person besides Mr. Bowden [could] have punched the card out."

"You can get into that on cross-examination," said Skinner. He handed the card to the clerk and said, "That is admitted."

Keefe soon made his point in a succinct cross-examination:

"What time was the end of the shift for the housekeepers?"

"Three-thirty. Normally, they have to punch out at three-twenty, around that time."

"How many people are usually punching out at that time?"

"Roughly about a hundred and twenty-five."

"As the people are punching out, is it possible for a person to punch out the wrong card?"

"It's possible."

Keefe resumed his place at the defense table without, I think, noticing that his clients had missed his first moment of triumph. They hadn't yet returned from recess.

The old man bobbed up for two more questions:

"Do you make any provisions to guard against a person punching out someone else's card?"

"Yes . . . several supervisors, as a rule, are in the same room, plus the office clerks, and they would know if an individual makes a mistake [and would] so note it."

"And was anything called to your attention about Bowden's check-out time on January 29, 1975, by any of these supervisors?"

"No."

"Thank you," said the old man. "That's all."

That made for a neat transition to Donald Webster, who passed Henry Smith in the doorway. Webster testified that he was one of the supervisors at the time clock that day and that he saw Bowden punch in "at seven o'clock in the morning" and punch out "at twenty minutes past three."

"That's all," said the old man.

Skinner invited cross-examination with a simple "Mr. Keefe?"

Keefe listened to a minute or two of agitated whispering from Tom McKenna before going to the lectern. Once there, he asked, "Mr. Webster, did you assign Mr. Bowden somewhere that morning?"

"Yes."

"Where did you assign him?"

"Children's Building," replied Webster.

"I see," said Keefe. "No further questions."

So much for the someone-else-punched-out-for-him theory.

The old man tried one more question. It was an objectionably leading one which reminded Webster that he clearly remembered Bowden punching out because there was some jostling in the line near him. Keefe was slow to object, and Tom McKenna jumped up in his place. McKenna caught himself before objecting, though, and sank back in his chair, saying, "I'm sorry, Your Honor. I apologize."

Keefe finally said, "Objection."

"Sustained," said Skinner. To McKenna, he added, "If Mr. Keefe is going to try the case, he is going to try the case, and you stay out of it."

The old man turned to me and rolled his eyes in ecstasy.

Enter Elsie Pina. The old man was ready for trouble. If she tried to move the last time she saw Bowden back to two o'clock, he was going to hit her with her report saying it was two-fifteen. The old man, report in hand, got to the point of confrontation in less than two minutes.

"Will you kindly state your name?"

"Elsie Pina."

"And where do you work, Miss Pina?"

"At the Boston City Hospital."

"What are your duties at the Boston City Hospital?"

"I'm a supervisor in the Housekeeping Department. . . . I'm in charge of the Children's Building."

"And were you working there on Wednesday, January 29, 1975?"

"Yes, I was."

"Did you know one James Bowden?"

"Yes, he worked with me that day."

"And do you recall what assignment you gave him?"

"Oh, yes. He was in charge of the clinics, to take care of the clinics."

"What time did you first talk to him?"

"I talked to him in the morning, and then after coffee break because he didn't do such a good job. And then I saw him in the afternoon."

The old man had been leaning against the jury rail. Now he moved slowly toward Pina, and looking at what she could tell was her report, he asked: "And what time was it in the afternoon that you saw him?"

"Well . . ." Pause. "I would say about two-thirty."

The old man spun on his heel. "That's all, Miss Pina."

My mind was so set on getting her to say two-fifteen that I didn't, for a minute, realize that two-thirty was better. I wondered why the old man wasn't up there stuffing two-fifteen down her throat and putting her report in evidence. By the time the shock passed and I caught on, Keefe was at the lectern.

Keefe could have introduced Pina's report and tried to push her back to two-fifteen. But for what? That would be as good an alibi as two-thirty. Keefe ignored the two-thirty and asked how often Bowden worked for her.

"He only worked for me about three times," said Pina. "It just so happened that the steady man I had called in sick."

"Who was that?"

"Donald Shaw."

"So the day Mr. Bowden worked for you, that was the day Mr. Shaw called in sick?"

"That's right."

"No further questions, Your Honor."

The Donald Shaw stuff sounded like more Keefe-elicited trivia. It would turn out, however, to be a seed Keefe planted for the defense case.

It was twelve-fifty-five when Pina left the stand, and Skinner said it was time for lunch.

As soon as judge and jury left the room, the old man came over to me and said, "Think we should use Adolph Grant?"

"Why not?"

"Well, Elsie already put our guy in the hospital at two-thirty."

"Yeah. And Adolph Grant can corroborate."

"But she was solid. And he's just gonna add that our guy was duckin' work with him."

"So what? Everybody'll believe him. He's good."

"So, I don't want the jury thinking James Bowden wasn't exactly the hardest worker in the joint. And I really don't want them to know he could sneak out of sight like that."

"Hiding in the basement isn't the same as driving to Cambridge."

"Yeah, but what good does it do us now that we already have our guy in the hospital at two-thirty?"

I told Adolph Grant he wouldn't have to testify. "We've already proved James was at work," I said. I thanked him for his patience and released him from our subpoena.

I then raced out to collect our lead-off witnesses of the afternoon: Jessina Stokes and Carla Davis. Jessina had moved from Mission Hill to another project, and Carla had moved to a two-family house on a tree-lined street in a black section of Dorchester. They were still best friends. I picked up Jessina first. She directed me to Carla's house. As the three of us rolled past Dorchester Avenue's unair-conditioned movie theater, its pizza places, liquor stores, gas stations, and its from-here-to-the-horizon array of bars, the girls exchanged favorable judgments of each other's clothes. They were in tasteful pantsuits—just what we, if consulted, would have suggested. Both of these thirteen-year-olds were, to say the least, nervous. They were on their way to speak, for the first time in their lives, under oath, through a microphone, to a roomful of adults—white adults—two of whom they had seen kill someone.

They were worried about what the police would try to do to them in the courthouse. I told a double lie: The cops were afraid of us O'Donnells and the FBI would be there to protect them. They seemed to go for the FBI part, but they still didn't like the idea of having to give their new addresses in court. The cops would know where to find them. I told them that we'd always protect them. They weren't impressed.

Toward the end of Dorchester Avenue, Carla whispered to Jessina, "Are we in Southie?"

I lied again: "No, this is the South End."

We would have cleared this corner of Southie in a minute with the girls none the wiser were it not for the unofficial welcome-to-Southie sign coming up. Carla saw it first. It was spray-painted by a shaky hand on the lower right corner of a billboard advertising cigarettes. Big black letters. Two words: KILL NIGGERS.

This is not uncommon Boston graffiti. In Southie it's about as common as the street signs. In the six months that I once spent as a substitute teacher, I saw it inside many Boston public schools. The white janitors in the school system are reasonably quick to remove anti-white graffiti but seem to have trouble finding the time to get rid of the anti-black messages. For over four months in 1980, a toilet stall in Boston Latin Academy, the city's second-best public high school, carried these gems, all written by the same excited hand:

WHITE PEOPLE (A) ARE SMART (B) ARE RICH (C) ARE
PRETTY (D) ARE NOT BLACK (E) EAT GOOD FOOD (F) DON'T
HAVE DISEASES (G) DON'T THROW SPEARS (H) DON'T
LIVE IN ROXBURY (I) LIVE IN SOUTHIE (J) KILL NIGGERS

REMEMBER, NIGGERS, THE KKK IS AND
ALWAYS WILL BE HERE TO STAY!

IRISH POWER

Plaintiff's exhibit 16: Identification card of James Bowden, Jr.

Plaintiff's exhibit 135: Patrolman Billy Dwyer, moments after the shooting of James Bowden, Jr., asking reporter Dave O'Brian: "How's this for action? Did we put on a good show for you?" (PHOTO © KEN KOBRE)

To Captain William P. MacDonald
from Ptl Dennis M. McKenna
Subject. Discharge of Service Revolver, Ptl on Ptl.
        Edward Holland, Death of James Bowden

Sir: About 6:05 PM WEDNESDAY 1-29-75 while assigned TO ACU patrol and in the ACU 8-41A CAR w/ptl Edward Holland + two (2) civilian report in the rear of the ACUCAR, #1 Dave O'Brien, Ptl. #2 and while on Smi

St. Roxbury observed a Buick Electra Mass Reg # 4F6838 in the vicinity of Smith St, AT Huban Court. THIS vehicle was involved in an armed Robbery in Camb AT THIS time we placed the car under observation and notified by Radio other members of ACU + ACU Base, who notified above officers, that the hold men were two colored males, armed with pistol + Shotgun About 6:35 PM 1-29-75 observed a 1967 Thunderb Mass Reg # 650280 turn from Parker St into Smi St. and stop beside the buick. The right door of the Thunderbird opened, then the left door of the Buick was opened and a c/m entered the Buick and closed the door and turned on the lights and began to back down Smith St. towards Parker St. At this time Ptl Holland radioed to other UNITS that the vehicles were moving. Ptls Holland and McKenna both pulled up behind the Buick, GOT OUT WITH their badges displayed and announced "Police Officers" "Get out of the car" Both officers had drawn their Service revolvers. the operator raced the engine and caused the Buick to strike Ptl Holland and spin him aro and then knock him do

Report by Patrolman Dennis McKenna

Patrolman Dennis McKenna walks around the left front of James Bowden's crashed Buick. The smears on McKenna's right hand are Bowden's blood. (PHOTO © KEN KOBRE)

TO   CAPTAIN William P Mac Donald

FROM   PATROLMAN Edward J. Holland Badge #1599

SUBJECT. Discharge of Service Revolver
         A & B By Means of a Dangerous Weapon
         on Patrol Edward Holland
         Injury To Patrol Edward Holland.
         Death of James Bowden

SIR: About 6:03 PM Wednesday January 29 1975
Patrols Edward Holland and Dennis McKenna
assigned to A.C.U. Vehicle 841A while on Smith
St. Roxbury observed a vehicle a Blue Electra
Buick, Bearing Mass. Reg. 4F 6838 Parked
unattended. Answering the description of a vehicle
used in a armed Robbery in Cambridge on 1-29-1975

This vehicle was kept under surveillance by ACU
Team 841A, 841 and 842 The turret was notified
also the TPF. ACU office and Sgt. Edward McHale.

About 6:35 PM 1-29-75 Ptls Holland & McKenna
observed a vehicle, a green Thunderbird on South
at Parker the operator was wearing a Blue Denim
jacket and a Blue Denim Cap. Two 2 other unknown
Black males.
This vehicle pulled adjacent to the Blue Buick
where upon a B/M alighted and entered the said
Buick Mass Reg 4F 6838.

At this point ACU Teams 841 with Ptls William Dwyer
and Mark Malloy, Team 842 with Frank MacDonald
and Lomax McClinton were notified of the activity
of Both the T Bird and Buick
At the same time ACU Team 841A with Ptls Holland
and McKenna approached the Blue Buick from
the Rear while the operator attempted to remove
(move) the vehicle from within 2 parked vehicles

Ptls McKenna operator of ACU vehicle #5
and observer Holland left the said vehicle
and approached the Buick Mass Reg 4F 6838
with Ptls McKenna approaching from the
operator side and ptl Holland approaching the
Passenger side of the Buick

Patrolman Edward Holland shakes a cigarette out of a pack after the shooting. Bystander with back to camera in foreground is unidentified. (PHOTO © KEN KOBRE)

Upper left, Dennis McKenna. Center, Edward Holland. Right, Mark Molloy. Note license plate number on Bowden's car. (PHOTO © KEN KOBRE)

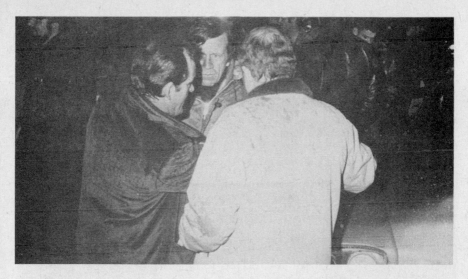

Edward Holland, Billy Dwyer (center), and unidentified officer confer after the shooting. (PHOTO © KEN KOBRE)

Ballistician Walter Logue unloads the pistol found by Patrolman Joe Fagone. (PHOTO © KEN KOBRE)

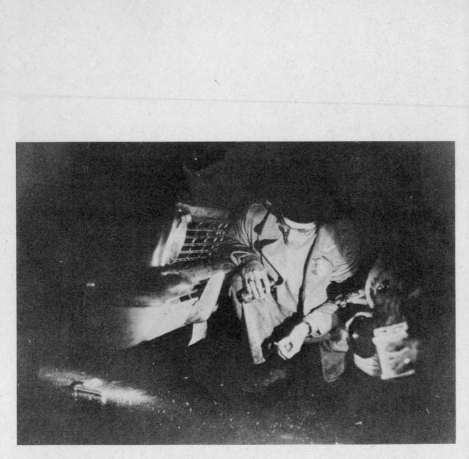

Patrolman Joe Fagone discovers the pistol under a parked Chevrolet. (PHOTO © KEN KOBRE)

Jessina and Carla, both ninth-graders then, must have seen such stuff before. Nevertheless, they spent the next five minutes on the floor of the car in O'Brian-Kobre style and wouldn't get up until we were downtown. I don't recall being much concerned about how an experience like that would affect these girls' lives; I just remember worrying that it might affect their performance on the stand.

We put Jessina on first. Bill and Mary stayed with Carla out in the hall. Eddie and Denny were in their front-row seats.

The old man began by having Jessina point to her window on the model. Then, over Keefe's objection, he introduced a photograph of her building taken from the shooting spot and had her identify her bedroom window in the picture. He handed it to the foreman and got to the point:

"On Wednesday, January 29, 1975, were you in your home in the early evening?"

"Yes."

"And where were you?"

"I was looking out my bedroom window."

Jessina blushed at the sound of her amplified voice.

"Were you talking to anyone?"

"Yes."

"With whom?"

"To my friend Carla Davis."

"And where was Carla Davis?"

"She was at her home looking out the window."

"Did you observe something?"

"Yes."

"Tell the court and jury what you observed."

"I observed two men jumping out of a car. And they was running toward another car. And one was holding on to the handle of the car. And they started firing at the person in the car. And I saw the flames of the bullets."

"And did you hear any voices from the two men that were firing at the car?"

"No."

Thus, the ball rocketed into the defense's court, where Keefe had to return it with the utmost delicacy. He couldn't aggressively cross-examine a little girl without looking like an awful bully. He had to be friendly and gentle, *and* he had to attack her story. And since she hadn't been deposed, he had to ask questions whose answers he didn't already know. Considering the circumstances, he did a fine job.

His opening was predictable: "Are you related to the Bowden family?"

"Yes . . . James Bowden was my mother's brother."

Then he picked at details: "What was the temperature outside?"

"It was like a spring night."

"Was the sun out? Was the sun down?"

"It was dark."

"What were you talking to your friend about?"

"I don't remember."

"Did you do this often?"

"Yes."

"What were you wearing?"

"A pair of pants and a shirt."

"What kind of shirt?"

"I don't remember exactly what kind of shirt I was wearing."

Keefe was smiling and calling Jessina by her first name, but she knew she was being tested. Her voice became softer.

Skinner told her, "The jurors can't hear you very well. . . . I tell you what: You talk to them just as loudly as you would talk to Carla. Pretend you're leaning out the window and shouting to these people, okay?"

"Okay." Jessina smiled.

Keefe asked Jessina to point to the spot on the model where the shooting occurred. The old man handed his pointer to Keefe, who passed it along to Jessina. She pointed to the right place. With Jessina still standing uncomfortably at the model, Keefe asked for more details and stumbled into something very helpful.

"Could you tell us what the men were wearing?"

"No."

"Did you see the color of their car?"

"No."

"Did you see them get out of the car?"

"Yes . . . I just saw like—I looked at the car while I was talking, and then I turned back and started talking. I didn't pay no mind. But I did see them jump out, and then I saw them run up to this car."

"How long did you talk to Carla Davis after you first saw the men on the street?"

"A minute. I don't know."

"Then, you turned back to the street, and you saw the bullets?"

"Yes."

Skinner intervened to tell Jessina she could go back to the witness chair.

Keefe huddled with Tom McKenna, then sat down. They glowed with delight.

Eddie and Denny smiled.

Had we based our case mainly on Jessina's testimony, we would have been in trouble.

Since Jessina had not told us that she took her eyes off the action at any point, the old man thought she was confused and tried to get her straightened out with a simple question: "What did you observe the men do?"

"Run up to this car," she said, "and start firing bullets."

"Did your eyes stay right on them while they were doing that?"

"Yes."

"And you had something to say to Carla?"

"Objection, Your Honor," said Keefe.

It was a leading question, but the tradition and the federal rules allow you to lead "the child witness." Skinner said, "Overruled," and asked the question himself.

"I asked her did she see the bullets," said Jessina, "and she said yes."

"What do you mean by seeing bullets?" Skinner asked.

"I saw a blue flash."

"Did you hear the sound of a gun?" he continued as the old man sat down.

"Yes."

"How many bangs did you hear?"

"About six, seven, something like that."

"Recross, Mr. Keefe?"

Keefe conferred with Tom McKenna for a minute before getting up again.

"Jessina, when you first saw the men," he began, "you saw them get out of their car."

"Yes."

"And they were in the street about a minute."

"I don't know," said Jessina. "All I know is I saw them get out of this car and start running towards this other car."

And so it was left.

Carla Davis, whom we called just to confirm that Jessina was at her window, had an easier time on the stand. After a minute of preliminaries, the old man asked, "While you were talking to Jessina, did something happen on Smith Street?"

"Yes."

"What happened?"

"Well, one car, you know, came zooming down Smith Street and was going kind of fast, you know. We weren't paying no attention to it. Another car came, and it stopped and a bullet fired, and Jessina saw it and she asked me if I saw it, and I said no. And she told me to look over there and I saw another shot and I got out of the window. We were both scared and got out of the window."

"That's all," said the old man.

"Mr. Keefe?"

"One moment, Your Honor," said Keefe. Tom McKenna was whispering something to him.

Keefe tried a couple of detail questions. Carla did not remember what the temperature was or what she and Jessina were talking about. Then he asked only one question about the action: "You heard Jessina say she saw a bullet?"

"She didn't say she saw a bullet," replied Carla. "She said, 'Look.'

And I looked at her, and we both saw another bullet. She saw one and she told me to look at it."

The old man thought that that clarified the girls' testimony.

Our next witness was a man who, when asked about his occupation, said: "I'm the Assistant Deputy Commissioner of Fiscal Service for the Department of Health and Hospitals of the City of Boston." Through him we introduced some City Hospital payroll records which Henry Smith had not been able to provide. They included the kind of fine points of Bowden's income history that Jack Marshall, our actuary, was going to mention in his testimony.

After a five-minute recess, the old man called the last witness of the day: Patricia Bowden. Our shy, private plaintiff was, she told me, "terrified" by the thought of testifying, though she had known for months that it would come to this.

"I don't want to talk about James," she told the old man during the recess. "I still can't do it without crying."

His response was false: "We're just going to introduce exhibits, and I'm going to ask you a few things about the kids. You know, we'll show that they're plaintiffs, too, and they've got a claim here."

We had three things to cover with Pat. First, that the Bowden license plate was 4F•6838 and that the front plate had been stolen two days before the shooting. Second, that the Bowden family was a legal entity with the right to sue on James's behalf. Third, that Patricia, Eurina, and Jamil had lost not only James Bowden's financial support but also the intangibles that the wrongful death statute allows compensation for: his "services, protection, care, assistance, society, companionship, comfort, guidance, counsel and advice."

Wrongful death plaintiffs always cry—sometimes spontaneously and sometimes on the advice of counsel—when testifying about the intangibles. A nice, dignified cry, nothing hysterical that would interrupt her testimony, just an occasional stream of tears—that's what we were hoping for.

Exhibit introduction went smoothly. Keefe made no objection.

"I show you that piece of paper and ask you to examine it."

"This is our marriage license."

It was admitted into evidence, as were James's, Patricia's, Eurina's, and Jamil's birth certificates, and James's death certificate. Then came the Buick's certificate of registration, the permit James obtained on January 28, 1975, allowing him to drive with one license plate, and finally the replacement plate the Registry sent two months later.

After the exhibits were in, virtually all of the old man's questions were leading, but Keefe wisely did not object. The moment belonged to Patricia Bowden, and Keefe knew that no one would welcome his interference.

"Now, it's so, isn't it, that you are the unmarried widow of James H. Bowden, Jr.?"

"Yes."

"During the five years of your marriage, did Mr. Bowden support you?"

"Yes."

"Did he work continuously at Boston City Hospital?"

"Yes."

"Did he have a criminal record?"

"No."

"Did you live together during that period as husband and wife?"

"Yes."

"And you both had, as a result of your union, these two children?"

"Yes."

"And during that period of time, did he give you any help with your daughter, Eurina?"

"Oh, yes."

"What did he do that you can tell the court and jury about regarding your daughter?"

"Well . . ." Pause. "He used to take us to movies and to the circus and different things." Pause. "He was a good father."

"Did he give her guidance and care?"

"Yes."

"What time would he generally get home from work?"

"About four o'clock."

"Would Eurina be home from school then?"

"Yes."

"And what, if anything, would your husband do with his daughter at that time?"

"Well. He would play with her. Talk to her. They would sometimes watch cartoons for a little while."

"Your husband had relatives living on Smith Street in Roxbury?"

"Yes."

"Did he have a custom regarding visiting there?"

"Yes. Mostly everyday he would go over after supper."

"Because who was living there then?"

"His mother."

"And when your son was born, what, if anything, in care and help and society did your husband do regarding your son?"

The old man was standing behind Michael now with a hand on the back of his chair.

"Well," said Pat, "he helped me a lot with him."

The old man looked at the floor and took a deep breath. Pat's composure was flawless, but he was on the edge. He kept his back to the jury.

"On Wednesday, January 29, 1975, did he come home after work?"

"Yes, he did."

"Was Eurina there?"

"Yes, she was."

"And did any conversation go on between your husband, James, and Eurina?"

"Well. James wanted to take her—you know—she wanted to go over to Ma's. That's what I call my mother-in-law. But I was getting ready to bathe the baby, and she wanted to help. So I told her she didn't have to go; she could stay with me."

The old man nodded and, still looking at the floor, asked, "At some time in the evening, did you go to the Peter Bent Brigham Hospital?"

"Yes. I did."

"Did you receive some information there?"

"Yes. I did. I went into the hospital. I was directed to the emergency ward. And I saw my husband." Pause. "He had just passed away."

Long silence.

"Now . . . with James Bowden, you offered one another love and affection?"

"Yes."

The old man looked at Pat as he sat down. "And did that continue up until the time he was killed?"

"Yes."

From his chair, with eyes closed, in a weak voice the old man asked, "Does it continue to this day?"

"I still love him," Pat whispered.

Into the stillness, Keefe mumbled, "No questions, Your Honor."

Skinner said quietly, "Thank you, Mrs. Bowden."

Pat left the stand without having shed a tear.

A few minutes later, she was able to recall very little of her testimony.

CHAPTER 15

Day Three—Monday, February 6, 1978—began with the old man's customary smile to the jury. This time, Cohen and the foreman smiled back.

Jack Marshall took the witness stand. The old man went to the lectern and stayed there. He had done no homework for the actuarial evidence. On the lectern was a stack of forty-seven large index cards. On each I had written a question and its expected answer. For the first time in his life, the old man worked with a script. He made no attempt to hide it or to sound as if he understood his lines. In a boring, twenty-five-minute run through the index cards, he showed that Bowden, assuming he was never promoted, would have taken home $1,058,722.69 in the projected remainder of his working life. Marshall told the jury: "The present value of [that] amount would be $285,888.31."

The "present value" was the compensation figure the jury would be instructed to consider if it found in our favor. Marshall explained: "Present value is a mathematical technique of determining what something you will receive in the future is worth to you [today]. . . . For example, [instead of giving] you a dollar at the end of the year, I could give you something less today, say ninety-five cents." It would be the same thing, "because you could put it in the bank, and it will earn interest and be worth a dollar at the end of the year." So $285,888.31 was, at current interest rates, the equivalent of $1,058,722.69 spread over the next forty years.

Keefe's cross-examination of the actuary was, by far, his longest of the trial. For close to an hour he had Marshall tinker with his figures. Eventually he exposed something we had glossed over: A large portion of Bowden's income would have been spent on his personal expenses. Therefore, the present value of his lifetime income that would have been devoted to his wife and children was only something between $183,389.51 and $164,133.61.

Watching more than a hundred thousand dollars being lopped off our damages scarcely troubled us, because the loud-and-clear message of Keefe's cross—his one tenacious effort at the lectern—was that the defense was very worried about money, which is to say worried about losing.

Of course, for Eddie and Denny there was no difference between getting hit with a judgment of $160,000 and a judgment of $280,000. They couldn't pay either one. But if the City intended to pay it for them, Keefe was serving his employer well—if not his clients—by taking on our money man.

"Your Honor," said the old man when Jack Marshall left the stand, "the plaintiffs rest."

"I would like to see counsel at the side bar," said Skinner. He wanted to clarify a ruling he had made concerning a minor aspect of Marshall's testimony. Keefe rushed into the bench conference with a motion to strike the actuary's testimony. Skinner ignored it and made his little speech on "the inflationary factor," which sailed right over my father's and brother's heads.

Then the old man, in anticipation of the defense case about to begin, requested that Keefe not be allowed to introduce any "statements made by the two victims of the robbery concerning Mr. Bowden."

"I don't understand this," said Skinner.

"All right, Your Honor," said the old man, "this is what actually happened. After Bowden was killed, one victim of the robbery is brought into the morgue that night to look at him and he says, 'That's not him.' He comes back the next day and says it's him.

"The other victim of the robbery—the female—says when she saw his picture in the *Boston Globe* the next day, she knew it was him."

Skinner asked Keefe whether he was going to call Ethel and Desi and bring out their IDs of Bowden.

"I certainly will," said Keefe, "and I intend to speak to it in my opening."

"I think," said Skinner, "you would be well advised to keep it out of your opening. . . . I don't say it's going to be out of the case, because I don't know how the case will develop. There's enough likelihood it will be kept out, so you better not put it in your opening. But I don't see that that's going to spoil your opening any."

I could never hear what was said in bench conferences. (The quotations here are from the trial transcript.) But from the looks on the O'Donnell faces, I knew that this one was certainly going our way.

As the gathering broke up, Keefe reminded Skinner: "I made a motion to strike the actuary's testimony."

"It's denied."

"I would like to renew it."

"It's denied again," said Skinner. "We will take the morning recess."

When court resumed, Keefe asked for another bench conference. Once at the side bar, Skinner sighed, "Now what?"

"A motion for a directed verdict," Keefe replied, handing the judge a six-page request that he immediately order the jury to return a verdict in favor of the defendants because the plaintiffs' case-in-chief had not even supported, not to mention proved, the allegations in the complaint. The defense always opens with a motion for a directed verdict. It always brings out the judge's assessment of the evidence.

Skinner flipped through the motion, saying only: "*Allegation* is spelled wrong." He borrowed Keefe's pen to correct the spelling.

Tom McKenna offered a one-sentence summary of the motion. "If this case were to go to the jury without us putting on a defense," he said, "they would have to [be instructed], as a matter of law, to find these men not guilty."

"To hell they would!" said Skinner. "The motion is denied." He added, "There is no evidence that Bowden did anything that would have warranted the police officers' firing."

"The man shot at them and they shot back," McKenna protested.

"That is not the evidence at this point," said Skinner. "We have only that they immediately, within five seconds, started shooting. . . . Furthermore, when the newspaper reporter asked McKenna what happened, he didn't say he was fired upon. He said, 'When I saw him turn, I said, "Fuck him." ' And he made a motion like shooting.

"Now that's enough to carry [the plaintiffs] through [a motion for a directed verdict]. I'm denying it now in its entirety."

Shaking his head in wonder, Skinner said to McKenna: "I don't know why you people—have you people got any money to offer on this thing?"

McKenna said, "There has never been any discussion of it, Your Honor."

"I should think," said Skinner, "the time has certainly come."

Frequently, when a judge knocks down a motion for a directed verdict, the defense makes a settlement offer or increases what it has already offered.

The old man, arms folded, smiling gleefully, looked down at McKenna. No one spoke. The lawyers headed back to their tables. Skinner stopped Keefe and returned his pen to him. "It's too much to deny your motion," he told him, "and steal your pen."

With everyone seated, Skinner announced, "Now we will proceed with the defense, starting with Mr. Keefe's opening statement."

Keefe pulled away from McKenna's last-minute whispering and went to the lectern. A light snow flurry had just begun, and wet flakes were hitting the windows behind the jury and turning to water on impact.

"Madam Forelady and gentlemen of the jury, my name is John Keefe. . . . In this case, I represent Dennis McKenna and—"

Skinner interrupted. Pointing to Cohen, he told Keefe: "The

chance that this gentleman over there in the corner will hear you is not what I call good."

Keefe began again and after a long-winded preface on the TPF and "what is called anti-crime work," he settled into a reasonable-sounding outline of what he promised to prove: "The officers had occasion to drive down Smith Street. . . . They notice a blue Buick Electra [and] wonder whether it was the one involved in the Cambridge robbery. So they turn around on Smith Street and come back. At this time they look at the number closely, but they do not stop, because they are doing undercover work and they want to take up an unnoticed surveillance position. So, they continue down Smith Street until they get to Gurney Street. They again turn around so they are facing Smith Street—at such a distance that they can no longer read the plate. . . .

"They call in the vehicle description and the plate to the team members, and they call it in to the TPF base. The vehicle is confirmed to them as the vehicle involved in the Cambridge robbery. Additionally, they are told from the TPF base, by a superior, that they are to keep it under surveillance. . . .

"There is a series of radio communications, of which you have heard something already. . . . There is a report to them that the Cambridge robbery involved armed persons and . . . that a shotgun is involved. . . .

"A Thunderbird comes down Parker Street and turns right on Smith Street. The officers see it. They notice it. It has three occupants. And they look at the number plate. The Thunderbird goes down in the vicinity of the Buick. Stops. The person gets out next to the Buick. Starts to get into the Buick. The officers call to their team to say that they are moving in, and they start down Smith Street. . . .

"The Buick is backing down Smith Street. The officers stop. The Buick stops. The officers jump out.

"Officer McKenna approaches the vehicle with his gun drawn—two hands—announces his office: 'Get out of the car. Police officers.'

"The car moves. Officer McKenna jumps back.

"Again he approaches the car. Still has his gun pointed. Shouts to the person. Again the car moves. Still has his gun pointed.

"During this time, Officer McKenna has a large badge hanging on his chest, a special badge designed for the Anti-Crime Unit. It has a reflector in the middle that can be seen from a distance. It has a picture of the officer on it. This is a three-piece badge, approximately eight inches long, hanging down.

"McKenna again approaches the car. This time he sees Officer Holland at the rear of the vehicle, going down. The vehicle comes forward at McKenna, and he thrusts—he hears a pop and thrusts his weapon forward and he fires.

"Officer Holland got out of the car, went up to the passenger window, banged the window, announced his office: 'Police. Get out of the car.' He proceeded to the front of the car and stood.

"The car comes forward, strikes him, and he spins to the side. As it goes past him, now he is behind it, getting up. The vehicle comes back, strikes him, and he goes down. And starting to come up, he grabs the handle. Gets up. He sees the silhouette of a person beyond the Buick and he makes for the Thunderbird, pointing a rifle or a shotgun, and he hears a loud noise.

"He then looks in the front of the Buick. He sees an outstretched hand. He sees a weapon. The Buick window blows out in front of him, and he returns fire.

"The car speeds up the street—the Buick.

"The officers run back to their police car.

"The radio calls in aid concerning the incident, concerning the Thunderbird.

"The car crashes shortly up the street, and the officers proceed to the crash.

"Officer McKenna goes into the front seat. Tends to the person there. And shortly the remaining officers and people are around.

"By the testimony of these officers," Keefe concluded, pointing to Eddie and Denny, "and other officers, we intend to show that the officers' conduct was reasonable in a dangerous situation. . . . the vehicle struck one of them; the person inside fired a gun on them.

"Thank you."

The first witness Keefe called was TPF Patrolman Ronald Monroe. As Monroe, a plump, black-haired fellow in his thirties, climbed into the witness stand, I had the sinking feeling that we had missed something in discovery. Michael turned to me with an anxious who-is-this-guy look. I frowned and shook my head. The name hadn't surfaced in a single police report. His direct testimony turned out to be brief and insignificant.

He said he was manning the radio at the TPF office at "approximately six P.M.," when "Patrol Officer Edward Holland [called in] a request to identify a motor vehicle [and to check whether] it was used in a robbery in Cambridge earlier in the day.

"I called the Cambridge Police Department," Monroe continued. "I received the confirmation. . . . I relayed that immediately [to] the 841A car—Officers Holland and McKenna."

Monroe said he spoke to Harry Byrne and radioed another message to Officer Holland: "Sergeant says to remain by the car. Stand by that car."

We didn't believe Monroe. His relaying Byrne's order to set up the stakeout sounded likely enough, but his story about checking on the Buick was absurd. Eddie knew that calling the TPF office to check out the car made as much sense as calling the public library. It didn't have the information he needed; the turret did. The turret had the Cambridge teletype and an intercity channel to Cambridge that the dispatcher on duty, Robert Mullen, could use with the flip of a switch. So the first call after spotting the Buick would have been to Mullen to check out the car. The next call would have been to the TPF office to get Byrne's thoughts on what to do. Monroe's testimony seemed pumped up to show a vigilant Eddie Holland double-checking on the Buick. The old man deflated it a bit:

"You regarded that call on January 29 around six P.M. as important?"

"Yes, sir."

"As a serious, conscientious police officer, you would make a memorandum of that, wouldn't you?"

"Yes."

"May I see your memorandum?"

"It was a note, that's all."

Skinner interjected: "What did you do with the note?"

"I left it on the desk. Stuff like that is thrown away."

Skinner said, "You threw away whatever note you made?"

"I don't know if I did it or the man that relieved me did it."

Skinner leaned back and let the old man resume cross.

"Did you make a report?"

"No, sir."

"What have you got today in front of this court and jury to verify that the call came in?"

"Nothing."

"Can you recall ever being questioned about it?"

"Just recently by the attorneys."

The old man asked Monroe how he could remember details like Eddie and Denny being in the 841A car "with *all this time* that has passed."

"It was in my mind," replied Monroe.

The old man was about to sit down. Michael whispered something to him that kept him up. He strolled toward the jury, hands in his pockets, smiling, and asked, "When you called Cambridge, how did you do that?"

"By telephone."

"What part of the Cambridge Police Department?"

"Their main number."

"Who did you talk to?"

"I don't have any recollection of who I talked to."

"You would regard that as important?"

"Yes."

"But you don't know whether you were talking to a captain, lieutenant, patrolman, sergeant, or prisoner?"

Cohen wanted to laugh.

"No," said Monroe.

Keefe's second witness was the turret man Robert Mullen. The snow was sticking to the windows now as Keefe went through a tiresome repetition of what Mullen had said when the old man had put him on the stand: During the stakeout he received a call from the "ACU 841 unit," asking for a check on the Buick. Mullen consulted the teletype and confirmed that the Buick was the getaway car. After the shooting Mullen received two more calls from the "ACU 841 unit," requesting assistance at the scene and a run down on 6S*0280, Winbush's plate number.

The funny thing is that, according to the TPF reports, Dwyer and Molloy were the ACU 841 unit. Eddie and Denny were 841A. Why Dwyer or Molloy would have been making Eddie's turret calls for him remains a puzzle. We always figured that Eddie had actually made the calls, and later that night, to distance himself from the mistake made in confirming Bowden's plate number, he got Dwyer and Molloy to take the 841 designation while he and Denny added a handy A to theirs. Anyone checking the turret log would then find it was Dwyer or Molloy who called in the wrong number. Of course, if there were a turret tape there would be no doubt about whom to blame for that carelessness.

The old man had just asked Ronald Monroe, whose extraordinary memory still pinpointed Eddie and Denny as 841A, "why the 'A' was used. Shouldn't [the ACU team] be 841, 842, 843?"

"It should be," Monroe had replied, "but it wasn't."

Now, with Mullen on the stand again, the old man didn't much care who 841 really was; he was too excited about having another chance to discuss the turret tape—something he hadn't covered with Mullen before, because he was rushing to get Kobre on the stand.

The old man facetiously asked Mullen whether he listened to the turret tape when he wrote his report.

"No, I did not," said Mullen.

"Didn't you go right to the tape and listen to it?"

"No."

"That would be the type of situation where you'd check and play back the recording to verify everything, wouldn't you, sir?"

"Not necessarily."

The old man grinned and he cozied up to the witness stand.

Suddenly he stuck his head in front of Mullen's and out of the corner of his mouth breathed into the microphone: "It doesn't miss a whisper, does it?"

"It's not supposed to," said Mullen meekly.

Moving back into the middle of the room, the old man asked, "Can you now say whether or not the recording device on that night broke down?"

"I have no idea."

"Could you explain to this court the reason you didn't bring in the recording?"

"I have no explanation for it. . . . I don't know if it exists or anything else."

"Would you go down and find out and let me know?"

"I'll ask the deputy, yes."

"Thank you."

It was a rhetorical exchange. The old man didn't expect to hear from Mullen again. The point was to whip up more suspicion about the tape and give the defense the burden of explaining why it wasn't being played for the jury. Keefe offered no such explanation.

It was one o'clock when Mullen left the stand, and the snow was swirling furiously. The clerk passed Skinner the word that we were in for a major storm. There were a few inches of snow on the ground already. Downtown businesses were closing so that their employees could make it home before roads became treacherous. Skinner, reluctantly it seemed, decided to go along with the idea of winding up early.

"In view of the storm situation—" he announced, "this storm is very definitely with us and getting worse—I'm going to excuse this case until nine o'clock tomorrow morning."

To the jury he said, "I hope you will make an effort to get an early start because transportation tomorrow morning is apt to be very bad. . . . Tomorrow, we will go all day, fairly late in the afternoon, later than usual to see if we can't catch up this lost time. . . . Good luck, both getting out and getting back."

We didn't want to take any chances in either direction. I made reservations for the three of us at the Parker House, a hotel around the corner from the courthouse, and we spent the day at the office getting ready for Eddie or Denny to take the stand.

When we set out for the Parker House that evening, the storm was raging at hurricane force, but we didn't mind trudging down Washington Street and up School Street through a foot of snow. We were winning.

CHAPTER 16

O ne hell of a storm," was how the *Globe*'s front page described it the next morning. Snow emergencies had been declared in every East Coast city north of Washington, D.C. New England governors had declared full-fledged states of emergency. Public transportation was shut down, and with virtually all roads impassable, non-emergency use of cars was banned. Boston was snowbound as it had never been before, and the snow was still falling. The radio said that the U.S. Army and the Massachusetts National Guard were on the way to dig us out. We had the day off.

In the late morning in the lobby of the Parker House, a place where Emerson, Hawthorne, and Longfellow used to bump into each other, we came upon Eddie Holland. We reckoned that he and Denny had spent the night in City Hall with John Keefe and Tom McKenna. Feeling like a gracious winner, the old man said, "Hi, Eddie. What's the forecast?"

With a halfhearted smile Eddie said, "I don't know," and kept moving.

The snow stopped falling that afternoon, but with the state of emergency remaining in force, we spent the rest of the week in the hotel. It was yet another week before Boston was fully operational again. Our day off became two weeks off, thanks to what is now remembered as "The Blizzard of '78."

In the second week of the recess, on Valentine's Day, a messenger delivered an envelope from Keefe. He was, as required, notifying us that he was going to conduct a deposition the next day and inviting us to attend. The deponent was going to be Francis V. Creeden, M.D., the physician who gave Eddie ten weeks' paid vacation after the shooting by finding him "totally disabled" from the knee injury.

The deposition was scheduled for one-thirty at the doctor's office. We arrived at one-fifteen. Keefe arrived a few minutes late. Tom McKenna didn't show up. Keefe explained that because Doctor Creeden had a troublesome heart condition, testifying in court would be too much for him. To spare him the ordeal, Keefe wanted to take his deposition and read it to the jury. "Well," said the old man, "let's go ahead with the deposition, but I'm not gonna agree to let him skip taking the stand."

A secretary showed us into Creeden's examining room, where the portly white-haired doctor was waiting for us. Creeden, we knew, was not the doctor who saw Eddie at the Carney Hospital the night of the incident; he was the one Eddie visited for follow-up treatment a month later. Keefe's direct examination lasted about twenty minutes.

"I am a graduate of Holy Cross College, 1936; Georgetown University School of Medicine, 1944," said Creeden. "I interned at the Mercy Hospital in Springfield and the Carney Hospital [in Dorchester]. I started practice in 1945—general practice. . . . I have been in practice in orthopedic surgery since 1959."

"Did you have occasion to see Edward Holland in your professional capacity?" asked Keefe.

"Yes, I did."

"When was that, Doctor?"

"On the 28th of February, 1975."

"Where did you see him?"

"At this office here."

"And did you examine him at the time?"

"Yes, I did."

"Could you tell us what you found?"

"He had residuals of medial collateral ligament strain, and . . . he had a good bone bruise of the lateral femoral condyle. . . . He had considerable ecchymosis, or black-and-blue, on the lateral aspect of his [left] knee. . . . He was disabled from performing his duties as a police officer."

Keefe asked "whether or not there was a casual connection between [that] diagnosis [and Eddie's being] struck on the left knee by an automobile on January 29, 1975." Creeden said there was.

He testified that he examined Eddie every two weeks until April 14, when he found him "physically able to return to work."

Cross-examination was a rough ride for Creeden.

"Doctor," the old man began, "during the course of your testimony, I noticed that you had a file on your desk and you referred to various reports. . . . May I look at that file?"

Creeden handed it over. It contained his notes as well as the letters he sent to the Department after Eddie's first three visits, certifying that he was "totally disabled" and the one sent after the fourth visit, certifying that he was fit to "return to full duty." The old man flipped through the file and asked, "Now, Doctor, are you board-certified in orthopedics?"

"I am not certified in orthopedics."

"[Whom did] you bill for these services?"

"The City of Boston."

"So, you've examined other police officers besides Edward Holland?"

"Yes."

"For the City of Boston?"

"Yes . . . Every year in my practice I have examined and treated Boston policemen."

We were willing to believe that Eddie's knee was black-and-blue when he walked, without assistance, into the Carney Hospital five hours after the shooting. He could have gotten the discoloration—that's all the Carney record shows—three ways: (1) by stumbling into the Buick through no fault of James Bowden's; (2) by inflicting it on himself after the incident; (3) by banging his knee the day before, when, as Molloy and Dwyer had told O'Brian, an ACU team that included, among others, Eddie, Denny, Molloy, Dwyer, and Frank MacDonald collared a whole gang of purse snatchers—Dwyer's "maggots." The third possibility was the richest.

When Michael had requested by subpoena that the Police Department provide whatever documentation it had on Eddie's knee injury, the Department gave us a Personnel Division form showing he returned to duty on April 16, 1975, plus a TPF report co-signed by Captain Bill MacDonald and Deputy Joe Rowan on January 29, 1975. It told of the arrest of "the maggots" the day before and of how, in the chase, Eddie was "injured on duty."

Patrolman Edward Holland . . . with Patrolman William Dwyer . . . as observer, in chase of the [5] youths . . . drove the cruiser in LaMartine Street towards Heath Street when one of the pursued subjects . . . ran directly into the path of the police vehicle. Patrolman Holland, in attempt to avoid striking the youth, swerved the vehicle to the left of the roadway and struck a steel dumpster, several ash cans and into the wall of #24 Heath Street. The collision caused the police vehicle to be damaged to the left and right front end. . . .

Patrolman Holland alighted from the vehicle and gave chase on foot and when the officer apprehended him the youth turned on the officer, struggling violently, and slashed out at him with a silver-studded, razor-sharp, sheet metal bracelet being worn on the black youth's wrist. The slashing of the youth caused a laceration on the upper right front thigh of the officer and tearing his trousers. This assault caused the officer to lose his grip on [the suspect] and the pursuit of this fleeing subject was taken up by Patrolman McKenna. . . . While engaged in this foot chase the officers observed the fleeing subject fall heavily, headfirst, into the rear brick wall of #24 Heath Street . . . at which time he was apprehended and handcuffed by the two officers.

Patrolman Holland sought no medical for the injury he received and remained to complete his assigned tour of duty.

What happened to Dwyer's "maggot"? When the thirteen-year-old arrived at the Youth Service Board, he was rushed to the Carney, where, according to the TPF report, he received ten stitches in the scalp and "was held for treatment" because of a "question of skull fracture."

So Eddie did enough things on the 28th, such as smash a car into a dumpster and a brick wall, which could have left him a fairly fresh knee bruise to bring into the Carney's emergency ward on the 29th. But we could find no reason to believe that he was totally disabled or had even a trace of a knee injury when he walked into Creeden's office a month later. The doctor's testimony did nothing to change our minds.

Two tests done at the Carney, an X ray and an arthrogram (which examines cartilage), showed "no evidence of injury." Creeden said he found the "acute strain" of the ligaments and the "bone bruise" by feeling the knee with his fingertips.

"Now, what is the treatment for a severe strain, a very severe strain of a ligament such as you observed here?" asked the old man.

"Heat, rest, crutches, medication for pain," replied Creeden, ". . . an Ace bandage, a Jones dressing, or even a cast if necessary."

"This acute ligamentous strain that you found didn't rate crutches when you looked at it on February 28, 1975, right?"

"No."

"It didn't rate a Jones dressing?"

"No."

"It didn't rate a cast?"

"No."

"You never recommended as much as one aspirin?"

"I prescribed no medication."

"There is nothing in your report to show that you said to him, 'Go home and keep off your knee,' is there?"

"No."

"So, it wasn't a severe strain of a ligament?"

"I said an acute—may I see my first report there, please?"

The old man gave it to Creeden, and the doctor, who clearly didn't like being challenged, quoted his report as if it were a textbook: "'On examination today, he still does show . . . ligament strain and also apparently . . . a good bone bruise. . . .' Now, I did not make that up, sir, on the twenty-eighth of February."

"When did you make it up?" the old man asked softly.

"Objection," said Keefe.

"I beg your pardon," Creeden huffed. "I did not make that up! I put it down on the record, and I did not lie! . . . I am an orthopedic surgeon who treats patients. I treated this man properly . . . and I did not keep that man out of work one day more than I thought was justified. I do not practice medicine that way."

The old man was having a good time. He asked what Creeden knew about how Eddie was injured. The doctor said he knew only that Eddie "had been struck by a car."

"He never said anything to you about being knocked down by the car?"

"Objection," said Keefe.

"No," said Creeden, as if the question were pointless. "I treated an injured knee. Whether he got hit by a Buick or Thunderbird or by what, I could care less."

A miraculous choice of hypothetical cars for someone who knew so little of Eddie's story.

"Did you know that on January 29 he shot and killed a twenty-five-year-old man on Smith Street in Roxbury?"

"No, I did not, sir."

"So you have no knowledge, outside of what he told you, as to how he was injured; that's so, isn't it?"

"Yes."

"So, obviously, we can agree that that bruise could have been caused by other things?"

"I can only take his history," Creeden snapped. "If I knew, sir, that I was going to face you, I would have taken a five-page history."

"Wouldn't the objective signs you found on February 28 also be consistent with an injury [suffered] on January 28?"

"Yes, sure," said Creeden in exasperation. "If you want to make things up, go ahead."

When Creeden added, "You and I are just running around wasting a lot of time," the real fun started.

"I don't think so, Doctor," the old man said with a smile. "I think you are giving us some vital information." Then he asked, "Did you think this Edward Holland was a faker or a malingerer?"

"Sir, to be perfectly honest with you, right at this very moment I can't even picture an Edward Holland."

Referring to Creeden's file, the old man tried to refresh his memory: "Now, he didn't come in here on crutches?"

"No, he did not."

"As a matter of fact, you don't have anything in here that he limped when he came in here."

"I did not say he limped, no."

"You are going to say now that he was not limping when he was in here," the old man said, with the confidence of a hypnotist.

"He was not limping, no."

"A limp, to an orthopedic surgeon, would suggest something, wouldn't it?"

"Yes. Injury."

"All right. So . . . he is not limping. The X ray shows no fracture. The arthrogram shows no injury to any cartilage. Isn't he clearly a malingerer?"

"Objection," said Keefe.

"No, sir!" cried Creeden. "You would not want that man, with his knee the way it was, [to] go down into an alleyway and try to protect your wife or my daughter or anything like that!"

"I wouldn't want him—if I had any choice—out loose on the street under any circumstances," the old man coolly replied.

Needless to say, Keefe objected, but only the stenographer and I heard him.

Creeden continued: "I will send a policeman back to work when I think he can handle the job. . . . I want a policeman in uniform who will protect my wife or my daughter if they are in trouble."

"You wouldn't want Edward Holland," the old man said, with a grin to Michael and me.

Keefe objected again.

"Well," said the old man, "would you conclude, if Edward Holland was lying to you, that he was a malingerer or a faker?"

"Objection."

"I told you, sir," Creeden answered wearily, "I can't picture Edward Holland. I can't see him. I have no conception of Edward Holland, and I am telling you the truth, sir. . . . Mr. O'Donnell, please! I am not a shyster doctor or whatever the hell you're looking for! God damn it, you ought to know that!"

Referring to his heart condition, he added, to all three of us: "You wouldn't give a goddamn if I ended up in the Carney Hospital tonight! Jesus Christ, thanks a lot."

"I think you're an able doctor," said the old man, as if he'd just walked into the room. "But I think your diagnosis miscarried in this case because he lied to you."

"Objection."

"He did not lie to me," Creeden now assured us, despite having no memory of Eddie. "I've been in the game too long. He did not lie to me."

"Fine," said the old man. "Thank you."

"But I don't put up with this kind of nonsense," Creeden went on, "and if I go into the courtroom, if I am subpoenaed, I will tell the judge what I have been put through this afternoon by you. I think it's unfair."

The old man explained: "This is my responsibility to a young widow and two minor children."

"Yes, yes, yes," said Creeden.

In the spring of 1982, a diverting scandal hit Boston, coming, as most of them do, in the form of a series of articles by the *Globe* Spotlight Team. This one was about City Hall's disability-pension system. The *Globe* discovered that some City employees had retired at rather young ages with full pensions by claiming to have been totally disabled by injuries sustained on the job in circumstances worthy of suspicion. The series' lead article concerned the retirement of forty-year-old Bobby Toomey, formerly a Department of Public Facilities employee and Mayor White's political organizer in South Boston.

It seems that in the summer of 1981, while driving through Southie in a City car provided him by the mayor, Toomey had a collision with a van. "The only witnesses to the accident," the *Globe* article later reported, "were close friends of Toomey's [including] the driver and passenger of the other vehicle." Toomey claimed that he injured his back in the collision and immediately applied for a disability-retirement pension. To win it, Toomey had to convince three doctors of his total disability. He did so, and the City swiftly granted him $32,000 per year for the rest of his life.

Toomey didn't have such luck with the nine accidental-injury insurance policies he had purchased in the weeks preceding the car accident. None of the insurance companies holding them believed his claim.

As a result of the *Globe*'s exposé, before the year was out Bobby Toomey was examined by a specially appointed panel of doctors that found him "not physically disabled," and his pension was revoked.

Among the reputations marred in the months of the Toomey scandal was Doctor Francis V. Creeden's. He was one of the three doctors who had supported Toomey's total-disability claim. Once in the *Globe*'s spotlight, Creeden allowed that his assessment of the extent of Toomey's disability might have been different had he known just how physically undemanding Toomey's job had been.

Boston feels like a pretty small town sometimes.

CHAPTER 17

Day Four began at 9:10 A.M. on Tuesday, February 21, 1978, with Judge Skinner's announcement of a blizzard-caused tragedy that was welcome news to us: "Juror number two was a victim of the flood situation in Nahant," he said sadly, "and has lost his home. He apparently has various arrangements to make and he asked to be excused. . . . I have no objection to excusing [him] under the circumstances."

"I certainly go along with the court on that," said the old man.

"What do you say, Mr. Keefe?" asked Skinner.

"I have no objection to that."

Turning to the jury, Skinner said, "Mr. Cohen, as the first alternate, you will drop down there and sit in the number two seat."

Cohen looked as if he'd just been handed tickets to the World Series. As he scrambled into the front row, the old man gave him a welcome-aboard nod.

Assuming that the two-week recess had dimmed his jurors' memories, Skinner told them: "I'm going to just review with you the names of the witnesses that we've heard so far, so that perhaps that will help you get back into this case."

Looking down at his notes, he continued: "The first witness was John Martin Sheehan, a civil engineer from the Boston Department of Public Works. . . .

"The next witness was Walter Logue . . . and he told you about the spent bullets and . . . the revolvers of the two defendants [and] a thirty-two-caliber Fabrique Nationale automatic. No fingerprints.

"Then the next witness was John R. Tanous [who] talked about the broadcasts . . . from Cambridge . . . and a broadcast that he made.

"Lieutenant Petersen of the Cambridge Police Department identified a teletype that was put out by his department. And then Robert Mullen, who is stationed in the turret, . . . told about a report that he got from a car and what he did about it.

"Then, the next witness was Ken Kobre, who was . . . riding in the back of the police cruiser.

"The next one was David O'Brian, who was . . . riding in the back of the cruiser at the time of these events.

"The next witness was Henry Smith, who was Mr. Bowden's boss . . . and he talked about his income and the time that he checked out on January 29.

"Then Doctor Luongo . . . gave his opinion as to the cause of death.

"Then Donald Webster from Boston City Hospital, who saw Mr. Bowden sometime that afternoon.

"The eleventh witness was Elsie Pina, who was a supervisor at the Housekeeping section . . . and assigned Mr. Bowden to certain tasks that day and saw him in the afternoon.

"Then the next witness was Jessina Stokes, a thirteen-year-old girl, who was talking across the courtyard there to her friend and looked out and saw these events.

"And Carla Davis, who is another thirteen-year-old girl—who I guess was ten years old at the time—who was in another window in conversation with Jessina.

"Then there [were] Mr. Bowden's employment and salary records. . . .

"Then the fifteenth witness for the plaintiffs was Patricia Bowden, the widow of the deceased. And she testified about their life together.

"The last witness for the plaintiffs was Jack A. Marshall, the actuary. . . .

"So far, we have had two witnesses for the defendants. Ronald

Monroe . . . talked to you about calls in and out [of] the Tactical Patrol Force headquarters.

"Then Mr. Mullen . . . was called by the defendants and testified again about the calls that he received and sent out. . . .

"So, we are still progressing with the defendants' case, and we will now proceed."

Keefe called Lieutenant Henry Gallagher of the Cambridge police. The defense was still concentrating on radio traffic. Gallagher brought a tape recorder to the stand. He said he was "in charge" of Cambridge's radio tapes, which are recorded "on a twenty-four-hour basis." At Keefe's request, Gallagher played five minutes of the tape of January 29, 1975, "starting at approximately two-thirty P.M."

Somewhere in the middle of heavy static and a bunch of unrelated messages, Ethel's voice crackled into the air, saying "6368." Nothing else of her call over what Gallagher identified as the "emergency line" was audible. Seconds later, the dispatcher could be heard saying something about a car headed for the Charles River.

Skinner allowed Gallagher to identify Ethel only as "the lady that called from the Pearl Food Market that day."

We welcomed the introduction of the Cambridge tape. It confirmed that the reported plate number was not Bowden's and made the absence of Boston's turret tape all the more conspicuous. On cross, the old man asked Gallagher only a few insignificant questions about how Cambridge's taping system worked.

With his next witness, Keefe apparently wanted to show that what we had just heard was the intercity broadcast about the robbery. He called the Cambridge dispatcher John McCann. Keefe was in for a two-minute exercise in futility.

After establishing that McCann's was the voice on the tape, Keefe asked, "Do you have any recollection concerning whether you made any broadcast concerning that incident?"

"Yes, I did."

"And do you have a recollection of making a broadcast over the intercity?"

"No."

Keefe was knocked off stride by the answer. He had to revert to a hypothetical: "If you were the person to put the broadcast out over the intercity, what would be your practice or procedure concerning relaying . . . the information you received?"

Keefe was leading his witness, and the old man decided to put a stop to it: "I pray Your Honor's judgment."

"Sustained."

Keefe led again: "Certain of the information concerned a blue Buick with a black vinyl top headed towards Boston?"

"I pray Your Honor's judgment."

"Sustained."

Keefe gave up and called John Tanous for a quick rehash of the testimony he had given about receiving Cambridge's intercity and relaying it "to all our units throughout the entire city." By now, Keefe and McKenna should have realized that this would only give the old man yet another chance to hurt them with the turret tape, which he proceeded to do.

The old man began by asking Tanous how long he'd been assigned to the turret.

"At that time," said Tanous, "I was up there seven years."

"In seven years, did you ever get curious about listening to a tape?"

"Never had occasion to."

Michael held out Tanous's report. The old man took it, plopped it in front of the witness, and asked: "When you say you never had occasion to, it is so, on February 3, 1975, you were asked to submit a report to your boss, Deputy Bradley?"

"Yes, sir."

"You submitted it, and on the last line you said, 'All this information is to the best of my recollection.' Now, would you tell this court and jury why you'd be depending on your recollection when you had a tape?"

"Objection."

"Overruled."

"This here was from my notes," said Tanous.

"Now, [in] giving this to your superintendent, that was a time to turn on [the tape] and listen to it, wasn't it?"

"I suppose so."

"Did Deputy Superintendent Bradley say to you when he got your report, 'I don't want your recollection. Get the tape and we'll both listen to it'?"

A hearsay question if there ever was one, but Keefe let it go.

"No, sir," said Tanous. "He accepted my report as is."

The old man tried the same finish he had used with Mullen: "Officer Tanous, would you go up to Headquarters, find out, and let us know this afternoon whether or not [there] is a tape for January 29?"

This time Keefe was ready with an objection, which Skinner sustained. You can't send witnesses on errands.

The old man sat down and Tanous left the room. Keefe turned toward his clients and nodded. Denny whispered something to Eddie, and in a second Eddie was sliding through the bar enclosure on his way to the witness stand. Mary led Eurina and Jamil out of the room as Eddie was taking the oath. She took them back to the office, where my mother had their coloring books and a few toys ready for them, since we expected Eddie to be on the stand for a long time. I grabbed a fresh note pad. Michael did too. And I think Skinner did too. The old man pushed his chair back from the table and twisted it to face Eddie. Apparently he wasn't going to bother taking notes—a signal of supreme confidence. Pat Bowden sighed and said nothing. A rustle went through the jury box. Everyone studied Eddie in the long seconds of charged silence before Keefe asked, "Would you state your name, please?"

Keefe quickly moved Eddie through the resumé preliminaries: age, address, education, military service. The fourteen years between the Navy and the Department were covered with: "Basically, I worked construction and as a salesman."

Eddie's style of speaking was disconcertingly slow, full of *uhs* and punctuated by his wrinkled-forehead pauses. It seemed to me to be the speech of a man trying too hard to be sincere and it came in a voice that was hard as a curbstone. As Michael had promised, demeanor was going to be a problem for Eddie.

In twenty minutes Keefe had Eddie "patrolling the area of Mission Hill, Tremont Street, Gurney Street, Smith Street," with O'Brian and Kobre in the back seat, having heard John Tanous's alert "concerning the Cambridge robbery" a few hours earlier. At that point—11:05 A.M.—Skinner called for the morning recess.

In the men's room, the old man, who had been staring at Eddie for every second of direct examination, said, "He's great, isn't he?"

"He was just like that in the deposition," Michael affirmed.

"Now, Holland wasn't the driver, right?" asked the old man. "Or was he?"

I was so shocked by the question, I couldn't speak.

"He was the radio man," Michael said.

"Oh, yeah," said the old man.

We never expected the old man to know the case as well as we did, but this lapse of memory was frightening.

He's a crammer. He was as a student and he is as a lawyer. He does his homework at the last minute. He usually knows what he has to know for as long as he has to know it, and not a day longer. Ask him about a case a week after he's tried it, and he won't even get the names right. It had seemed like he was ready for Eddie and Denny two weeks ago, but that was two weeks ago. That morning my mother told me that he was up most of the previous night apparently studying depositions, but she said she heard the television going at a few points. Michael, who was never any kind of studier in school, does his lawyerly homework well in advance and retains the minutiae of a case forever. Cramming isn't the way to prepare for anything important, I kept telling Michael. He kept saying that the old man would be ready when he had to be.

"How do you know?"

"Because he always has been."

Infuriated now, I pulled Michael aside as we walked back into the courtroom. Before I could say anything, he said, "Okay, so he won't have every detail straight, but he'll get almost everything in."

"What do you mean, *almost* everything?"

"He'll get everything that counts. He'll be jumping all over the place and he'll hit a lot. That's the best you can hope for. He's not gonna start working with notes now. I'll give him one of our Eddie checklists, but once he's on his feet, he won't remember to look at it. We'll get in what he has in his head, and that'll be good enough."

"What's this 'good enough' shit?"

"Hey, just keep feeding him questions. He'll ask them."

Almost every time the old man examined a witness, I had been writing suggested questions on index cards and handing them to him when he was close enough to me or leaving them on the lectern for him to pick up on his next swing by. He had used all of them.

I took up my front-row position again and pulled some extra index cards out of my briefcase. Suddenly, the old man was leaning over the bar enclosure whispering in my right ear so that Pat wouldn't hear him: "Don't worry. I'm gonna knock him out of the fuckin' ring."

It was as if I were six years old again and he was tucking me in, telling me that Santa Claus was on his way or that the Brink's guys were innocent.

I believed him.

At 11:25 Eddie was back on the stand and Keefe was back at the lectern. In half an hour of asking "What next did you observe or what next did you do, Officer?" Keefe took Eddie all the way through his story without offering a single exhibit, such as his report or a medical record, to back it up.

Eddie: "Parked on the right-hand side of the street was a blue Buick with a black vinyl top. As I passed the vehicle, I took a glance to the right and noticed the front plate was missing. . . . I asked Dennis to stop the car. . . . He made a U-turn, and I made mention that that vehicle fits the description of the one put out over the air, used in the Cambridge Pearl Street Market robbery. We stopped just beyond the rear of the vehicle and glanced over at the plate, 4F•6838. At that point, we went to the corner of Gurney Street. I surmised there that perhaps this was the vehicle used in the holdup."

"As I best recall, to my memory, I had conversation with the TPF office, and I don't know who was on the other end. . . . I remember a communication coming back saying that that's the car, 'Sit on it,' [and] to be careful, that there was a shotgun and a gun used in the holdup."

"Officers Molloy and Dwyer in the 841 car said they would station themselves on St. Alphonsus Street at the [other] end of Smith Street."

"The next thing that I recall was a T-Bird . . . making a very slow turn to Smith Street. . . . I observed the operator of that vehicle had a Levi jacket on and a Levi hat, blue in color, denim type, dungaree type, whatever you would call it."

"I observed the Thunderbird pull alongside of the Buick or just opposite it."

"It appeared to me that a person alighted from the—stepped out of the passenger side of the Thunderbird and went to the operator's side of the Buick. . . . He appeared to me to be a black male."

"I observed the T-Bird back up. . . . I observed it back up and . . . back into a parking spot with about perhaps a foot or foot and a half of his taillight sticking out."

"I observed the Buick start in motion backwards. At that point—I believe it was myself, I'm not sure—but I can hear a voice saying that we're moving in and there's a T-Bird involved in it."

Keefe asked, "Can you recall at this time, Officer, where your weapon was?"

Eddie replied, "My weapon, at this time, I really don't know."

"What next, Officer, did you observe or do?"

"The vehicle I was in moved down to the rear of the Buick that was backing up. The Buick came to a stop. Dennis got out the operator's side of the vehicle. I got out the passenger's side. Dennis went to the operator's side of the Buick, front door. I went to the passenger's side of the Buick with my badge displayed and my gun in hand. I banged on the window, announcing my office, stating, 'I'm a Boston police officer. Get out of the vehicle.' I then moved to the front of the vehicle, offset to the right side approximately two, perhaps three feet. I placed the gun in my pocket and kept my hand on it. The next I recall the vehicle took a sharp right toward me, striking me, knocking me off balance. . . . It just grazed me . . . and spun me around to the rear of the vehicle."

"What next did you observe, Officer?"

"I observed the vehicle. I was perhaps three or four feet to the rear and directly in back of the right rear fender. At tremendous acceleration, the vehicle came backwards, striking me and hit me on the left side of the left knee. I went to the ground. I got up. As I got up, there was a shot fired from across the street. Whether it was fired at me or not, I don't know, but there was a figure standing outside of what I believe to be the T-Bird with a rifle or some type of a gun with an elongated barrel on it. Again, still in reverse, the Buick moved in reverse just a short distance as if he was trying to get it out of gear into another gear. I was knocked down again. I grabbed ahold of the door handle. I pulled myself up. I was confronted with a man in that vehicle holding a gun directly at me. At that point, the front passenger window blew out of the car. I was struggling. I still had my gun partially out and I returned the fire into the vehicle."

"What next did you observe, or what next did you do?"

"Well, I was stunned at the time. When I got hit in reverse the first time, there, it actually brought tears to my eyes it hurt so bad. It was like hitting a crazy bone. I was actually stunned at that point. The next thing I knew the Buick had left down Smith Street . . . and I got back to the vehicle somehow."

"What did you do then after you got back to your vehicle?"

"Well, the next I remember is calling for an ambulance. That is the next thing I remember doing there. I believe I put the number out over the air."

"And where did you get the number of the T-Bird from?"

"I don't know. I don't know whether I made a note of it going around the corner or whether I got it off of Dennis or what."

"When was the last time you saw the Thunderbird?"

"The last time I saw the Thunderbird, it was making a left just before the Tobin School into an alleyway. . . . I believe it was just after the Buick had left. I don't know. Maybe I'm wrong on that, but that is to the best of my recollection."

"After you got back to your own vehicle, Officer, what next did you do?"

"I believe we went right to the scene, right to the crash scene. . . . I observed several people. And they just seemed to come out of hallways and everything down there. And they were all around the car. There was what appeared to me to be a young Spanish man. And he had on a sequin jacket. He was inside the car going through the glove compartment of the car. I yanked him out of there and told him to get the hell out of there."

"I visually observed the inside of the vehicle . . . and the only thing I can remember was that there were two packages—Zig-Zag and a package of cigarette paper—right on the door itself. There was a black man in there in an upright position, and Dennis was attempting to give him first aid, help of some type."

"I walked around to the rear of the vehicle, and the trunk of the vehicle was open. . . . I observed inside of the trunk the number plate, a Massachusetts Registration 4F•6838, lying right point-blank in front of me in the trunk of the vehicle."

"So what then did you do, Officer?"

"We went to District Two. . . . We went to the Detectives' Room."

"Approximately how long were you there in the Detectives' Room at District Two?"

"I don't recall the exact time, but it was quite a while."

"What were you doing up there?"

"Well, I was sitting in a chair. . . . I sat in a chair up there most of the time. . . . I had a conversation with, as best I recall, Sergeant McHale. . . . I gave Sergeant McHale a brief report of what had happened. . . . I then went down to the Carney Hospital.

"I was taken into the emergency room . . . examined and treated, given a pair of crutches, and told to stay on them.

"Perhaps between one and two o'clock [in the morning] I was making a written report of the incident."

"What, if anything, occurred the next morning, Officer?"

"I really don't recall."

"Did you have occasion to go to court that day?"

"I don't recall going to court that day, sir. . . . As I best recall, when I did go to court, it was perhaps two weeks later, sir. It was much, much later."

"What was the nature of the court proceeding?"

"Well, apparently some police officers—after the number of the T-Bird was put out over the air—they traced the vehicle to some address on Annunciation Road and apprehended the operator of the vehicle. . . . I believe it was [for] assault, A and B, assault by means of a dangerous weapon, and assault with intent to murder. I may be wrong about that, but that is the best of my recollection. . . . I gave testimony in the case, and I could not identify that person as being in the vehicle."

"Did you have occasion to seek medical attention again?"

"Yes, sir. I went to Doctor Creeden."

"How did your knee feel at that time?"

"I was still shaky."

"Do you recall how many times you saw Doctor Creeden in connection with this?"

"I don't recall, sir."

"Did you return to work at some time?"

"I did, sir. . . . It was about three months after the incident."

"During those three months . . . why didn't you work?"

"I was unable to."

"Why?"

"I was an invalid."

"Why were you an invalid?"

"From being struck by the Buick."

"No further ques—"

Before Keefe could finish the line, the old man was in the middle of the room, booming, "Now, Officer Holland."

"—tions, Your Honor."

"Do you recall that at the Carney Hospital they took an X ray and found you had no evidence of a fracture?"

After a pause even longer than usual, Eddie replied, "No, sir. I don't recall that."

"And do you remember," the old man continued, as Keefe scurried back to the defense table, "they checked your leg—an arthrogram—and they found everything normal?"

"They didn't tell me anything, sir."

"I see." The old man nodded. "And you weren't curious enough to ask?"

"No, I did not, sir."

"You never walked into Doctor Creeden's office on February 28, 1975, with a pair of crutches, did you?"

"As I best recall, I did."

"I see." The old man winked—actually winked—at the jury. Skinner missed it, as did Keefe, who had just begun taking notes. "Now would you change your testimony if I told you Doctor Creeden, under oath, said you didn't?"

"I, I don't—I say I don't recall whether I did or not, sir."

It was a splendid opening minute. Three hours of cross lay ahead.

When the old man was in law school, he found, buried in heaps of dull, assigned reading, a passage on cross-examination that he has never forgotten. It is in Volume 5 of the Third Edition (1940) of John Henry Wigmore's *A Treatise on the Anglo-American System of Evidence in Trials at Common Law:* "Cross-examination . . . takes the place in our system which torture occupied in the mediaeval system. . . . it is beyond any doubt the greatest legal engine ever invented for the discovery of truth. . . . cross-examination, not trial by jury, is the great and permanent contribution of the Anglo-American system of law."

The old man didn't then read, and hasn't since read, anything about *how* to cross-examine. He just took Wigmore's thought and his own genetic inheritance of a boxer's instincts into the courtroom and started bobbing and jabbing and slugging. Had he consulted the how-to books, as most lawyers do, he might have been influenced, as most lawyers have been, by such warnings as: "In cross-examining the hostile defendant, counsel must be extremely calm, extremely courteous, and above all, show no signs of hostility towards the defendant [because] the sympathies of the jurors are ordinarily with the person on the witness stand." * When he squared off with Eddie in Courtroom No. 6, the old man was a wild-eyed, snarling eruption of hostility.

Leaning on the jury rail: "Now, you told this court and jury that it was days afterwards—a long time afterwards—that you went to the Roxbury District Court regarding a Thunderbird and a long rifle pointing out at you on Smith Street?"

"That is to the best of my recollection, sir."

Running to the witness stand, grabbing a document from Michael on the way: "I show you this piece of paper dated January 30 and ask if your signature is contained thereon?"

"Yes, sir."

"Now, sir, isn't that an application for criminal process against one Ernest Winbush [and] didn't you sign that on January 30?"

"Apparently I did, sir."

"You did sign that *in the Roxbury Court* on January 30, didn't you?"

"I perhaps did, sir. I don't recall. . . . I just don't recall the next day, sir."

"You were over there the next day getting this application for criminal process against Mr. Winbush," the old man declared.

"I don't recall, sir," said Eddie weakly.

"And furthermore, in March . . . the case was thrown out, right?"

"That's right, sir."

The old man offered the Roxbury Court record as an exhibit. Keefe made no objection. When admitting it, Skinner asked for "the name of the defendant on that."

"Ernest Winbush," said the old man, sneaking another wink at

---

* *American Jurisprudence, Trials,* Volume 6 (Jurisprudence Publishers, Inc., 1967), page 309.

the jury. He meant, "Be patient. I'm going to put Winbush on the stand in my rebuttal case." Of course, no juror could guess that.

Next, the old man showed Eddie his report, had him identify it, had it admitted as an exhibit, and asked, "Officer Holland, do you have *one word* in this report . . . about a Thunderbird with a gun firing at you?"

"No, sir," Eddie replied quietly.

"Keep your voice up," the old man ordered.

Eddie dutifully moved closer to the microphone. It was now fifteen minutes into cross, and the old man already had Eddie on puppet strings.

"Do you have *one word* in this report about a Spanish man at the [glove] compartment of the crashed car?"

"No, sir."

"Do you have *one word* in this report about Zig-Zag papers being [in] the smashed-up Buick?"

"No, sir."

"Do you have *one word* in this report regarding the trunk of the Buick being open and your looking in and seeing a plate?"

"No, sir."

"Did you talk with Dennis McKenna before writing this report?"

"No, sir. I didn't even see Dennis."

The old man let ridiculous answers like that go when he was already zooming in on something else: "It is so, isn't it, [that] at no time did he ever back you up about a rifle pointing out of the Thunderbird [and] shooting at you?"

"I don't know, sir."

"Have you ever discussed that aspect of your experience on Smith Street that night with Dennis McKenna?"

"No, sir."

"To this day, under oath, you say you went out on that street January 29, 1975—you on the passenger side, McKenna on the driver's side—and as to the Thunderbird firing at you, you never discussed it with Dennis McKenna."

"No, sir. I have not."

"Dennis McKenna was in the Roxbury Court . . . when they found no probable cause. Did you see him there?"

"I don't recall at this time."

The most telling aspect of Eddie's testimony had become the ever longer, ever more awkward silences he was leaving between the question and his answer. Sometimes he appeared to be searching his memory, but most often he just seemed lost.

From the lectern, after reading one of my index cards, the old man asked, "Incidentally—when you talk about your knee—isn't it a fact that you had an accident with a police car on January 28, 1975, wherein you smacked it against a dumpster, ash barrels, and the wall of Twenty-four Heath Street?"

"Would you repeat that, sir?" Eddie requested. The old man did so, with obvious pleasure, and Eddie said, "I remember hitting a dumpster that night, yes, sir."

"And you damaged the police car?"

"There was some damage, yes, sir."

"How about your left knee?"

"There was no damage to my body whatsoever, sir."

"Wasn't there damage to the left side of the car?"

"There was damage to the left and to the right, as I recall it, sir."

"All right."

Standing in front of the defense table, blocking Tom McKenna's view of the witness stand: "As you approached the [Buick], you had in mind that you were approaching the car of an armed man, right?"

"Yes, sir."

"You couldn't identify anything specific about him, could you?"

"Just one thing."

"What is the one thing?"

"That he was black."

The old man let that answer float through the air for a while. He looked at Skinner, who was scribbling furiously.

"It is a fact, when you aimed your gun at Mr. Bowden and squeezed off four bullets . . . you intended to kill him."

"I intended to kill him or stop him any way I could."

"All right."

The old man pulled his chair into the center of the room, sat on it, and said, "Assuming I'm Mr. Bowden sitting here behind the wheel, would you get down and show how you placed yourself?"

Eddie stepped off the stand and took a position near Michael that indicated he was in front of the car.

"Were you within the headlight rays of the Bowden car?" asked the old man, still sitting.

Eddie nodded and said, "I wasn't directly in front, though."

Michael reached into a box and pulled out a toy car about eight inches long and a tiny policeman doll. The old man put them on the witness stand and had Eddie use them to show exactly where he stood. Eddie placed the car and the doll thus:

● DOLL

The old man kept Eddie on his feet for the remaining twenty minutes before the lunch break.

"You were in full view of this man you eventually shot and killed?"

"I imagine he could see me, yes, sir."

"Would you give this court and jury an explanation of how you would come to expose yourself to being killed by walking in front of a car that you feel is occupied by a robber with a gun?"

"Well, it has been my experience that there is no definite way to approach a vehicle, and this has been proven many, many times over. No matter what angle you approach a vehicle from, it is not safe. You take the safest precautions that you feel. You use prudence in it and the best things that work out. And this has worked for me many, many times. And I've never had a problem with it."

"Yeah," the old man grunted. It was a devastating one-word review of the answer.

"Now, where you have yourself stationed in front of the Buick . . . you make an excellent target for the person in the Buick."

"No, sir. I wouldn't say that."

"Would you even concede that if you crouched by the side of it, you would be less of a target than standing in front of its head-lights?"

"That may be so."

"While you were standing [in front of the car, Bowden] didn't point a gun at you, did he?"

"No, sir. He did not."

"Isn't it a fact, Mr. Holland, that what you did was immediately shoot?"

"No, sir. It is not."

"Within about five seconds?"

"No, sir. It is not."

"For what purpose would you ever leave the side of the car and walk up in front?"

"So I could see the operator, see what he was doing."

"How about looking through the window you banged with your hand? You're closer to him."

"I just went to the front. I had a better view of him from there."

"Isn't that just a contrivance that you made up to extricate yourself from killing this man for no good reason?"

"Would you put it in simple words?"

"Isn't it a lie?"

"As God is my judge, I was standing in the front of that vehicle and that man drove it directly at me."

"Why didn't you shoot him?"

"I perhaps would have if I didn't lose my balance. . . . I got hit good enough to knock me off balance."

The old man had Eddie step off the stand and demonstrate what happened to him when he lost his balance. Eddie did a pirouette and demi-plié.

"You're not knocked down?"

"The first time, no, sir."

"All the time you had a gun in your hand?"

"I did not. . . . I had it in my hand and I put it in my pocket. . . . I was fumbling for my gun."

"What was McKenna doing when this car was doing these things to you?"

"I had no idea what Dennis was doing."

"You could see him?"

"Dennis was the last thought in my mind right then."

"What do you mean, 'the last thought'? He was right there in the street separated by the width of the car!"

"Mr. O'Donnell," Skinner interrupted, "just ask questions."

"I'm sorry," said the old man. Turning back to Eddie, he said, "Dennis McKenna, a man with a gun—was he there?"

"I don't know where Dennis was."

"And is it your testimony that the operator put the car in reverse and came back and hit you?"

"Yes, sir. He did . . . with tremendous acceleration."

"You got hit on the knee?" The old man got down on his left knee.

"That is when I got struck, yes, sir."

"Having in mind something coming at you with tremendous force, you move, don't you?" The old man did a quick sidestep.

"You try to get out of the way," Eddie agreed.

"What do you mean try? You jump!" And the old man jumped.

"I was trying to get out of the way," said Eddie.

"I want to see how you stepped. You stepped to the right?"

Eddie bent his left knee, stuck his left foot out to the side, and said, "I stepped to the right." He hopped to his right, pulling his left leg along, and said, "I brought my left foot to the right. I just got out. Otherwise, he would have cut me right in half."

The old man spent the next ten minutes going over each of

the Buick's moves and each of Eddie's corresponding moves in inch-by-inch detail. Then he asked, "There wasn't anything to stop the Bowden car from going right up to St. Alphonsus Street, was there?"

"No, sir."

"But your testimony is that it stayed to put itself in reverse, go forward, then back up at you again?"

"Yes, sir."

"I see."

The lunch break came as usual at one o'clock, but this time it lasted two hours because Skinner needed some time to rule on motions pending in other cases. Back at the office, Michael and I didn't try to stuff the old man with facts to use in the afternoon session. He was doing just fine with what he knew. The long lunch hour raced by and at three o'clock Eddie was back on the stand and the old man was two feet away from him holding out his hand and asking, "May I have the plate that you saw that night in the trunk?"

"I don't have it, sir."

"What did you do with it?"

"I never touched it."

"What happened to it?"

"I don't know, sir."

"You didn't tell me about it when I took your deposition."

"You never asked me about it."

"Who is the *first person* you told about the plate?"

"I mentioned the fact to Mr. Keefe."

The old man gave Keefe a suspicious look, pointed to him, and said, "*He's* the *first person* you ever told about it."

"Yes, sir," replied Eddie.

We weren't sure how Eddie and Keefe thought this new claim helped the defense. Keefe looked down at his notes.

The old man put three toy cars on the stand and asked Eddie to place them in the positions of the Buick, the Thunderbird, and the ACU car during the shooting. Eddie's arrangement of them can be seen on the next page.

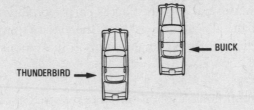

"When did the Thunderbird appear in there?" asked the old man with a face full of confusion.

"The Thunderbird, to the best of my recollection, was there all the time, sir."

"That's just to the best of your recollection?"

"That's correct, sir."

"You can't positively say it was there all the time, can you, Mr. Holland?"

"No, sir. I cannot."

"At what point in the sequence of events where you are getting whacked by the car did the person in the Thunderbird fire a rifle at you?"

"Just after being hit there the second time."

The old man took Eddie's gun from the clerk's desk and said, "You had ammunition in this."

"Yes, sir. I did."

Springing into a firing stance, aiming the gun at the front wall, the old man barked, "Did you smack this revolver right at [the Thunderbird] and squeeze off a couple?"

"No, sir."

Holding the firing stance, the old man asked, "Now, in your police training, they did enlighten you [that] if someone shoots a rifle at you, you can shoot back?"

"Yes, sir."

"But you elected not to shoot at this individual?"

"I didn't have my gun out."

The old man put the gun in his coat pocket, saying, "You had it in your pocket." Whipping it right back out, he said, "You take it out and shoot him." Wanting a demonstration from Eddie, he put the gun on the stand and told him, "Just stick it in your pocket, the right-hand pocket."

"I don't have pockets."

"You don't have pockets in that jacket?"

I counted four pockets in Eddie's jacket.

"I do," said Eddie, blushing, "but they're sewn up."

The old man sighed and shook his head. Cohen smiled. The old man had to skip the demonstration, but he stayed with the rifle fire: "You didn't shoot at the Thunderbird because your gun was in your pocket?"

"That's right. Plus the fact that I was injured."

"That's your *knee*! Your hand is really working! It can keep you alive! If someone points a rifle at you out of a Thunderbird, you just fire back!"

Keefe should have been up objecting to the old man arguing his case instead of asking questions. But the old man had the momentum of a freight train.

He asked, "Are they gentle and only fire one shot at you [from the Thunderbird]?"

"I don't know."

The old man growled, "You never saw a Thunderbird firing at you, did you, Mr. Holland?"

"Yes, sir. I did."

"You just contrived that story to get away with the killing of James Bowden!"

"No, sir."

"All right. . . . Did you note the number of the Thunderbird [after] seeing someone in that Thunderbird shoot at you?"

"Somehow I had it in my mind. I don't know where I got it from."

"You just happened to have it in your mind. Okay."

Emphasizing the preposterous answer was probably more effective than what someone with an encyclopedic command of the details would have done—i.e., confront Eddie with what he had told John Geagan: Dennis "had the number of the vehicle. He got that probably, uh, I don't know where he got it from, to be honest." Of course, you're not allowed to do that—repeat a witness's answer for purposes of ridicule—unless you do it in the form of a question. Ordinarily, Skinner would have rebuked the old man, even without an objection from Keefe. But perhaps thinking Eddie deserved a hard time, Skinner let the old man get away with whatever Keefe didn't protest.

"When the Thunderbird pointed the rifle out at you and shot, did you say, 'Dennis, duck! There's a guy with a rifle behind you!'?"

"No, sir. . . . I don't know where Dennis was at the time."

"He was on that side of the street! He was on that side of the Buick! Did you try to help him? Did you say, 'Watch out for the guy with the rifle! He just shot at me!'?"

"I don't recall saying anything, sir."

"You never warned him, did you?"

"I don't recall ever saying anything."

"Having in mind your testimony [that] you don't know where Dennis McKenna was, how tall do you say Dennis McKenna is?"

"I would say approximately my height . . . five eight."

"You know you were both higher than this car—about fifty-five inches, the height of the car."

"I would say so."

"So, did you take any step at all to guard against shooting Dennis McKenna?"

"No, sir."

The old man picked up Eddie's gun again. "Did you hold it in one hand?"

"That is all I had a chance to do, sir."

"You grabbed ahold of the handle of the car?"

"Yes."

"And what did you do then?"

"I was fumbling for my gun."

"What do you mean, fumbling? It was in your pocket!"

"Yes, sir."

"Then you put your hand in and take it out." The old man was putting the gun in and pulling it out of his pocket repeatedly.

"I just couldn't get it out of there," said Eddie.

"This is a recessed hammer. There is nothing to catch on your clothing, right?"

"Yes."

"That's why it was designed that way."

"Right."

"Now, what did you see the driver of the Buick do?"

"I saw a silhouette of a man leaning over with what appeared to me to be a forty-five-caliber, a very large, automatic."

"Did you shoot him?"

"No, sir."

"What were you waiting for?"

"I was getting my gun out."

"What did he do? Wait until you got your gun out?"

"No, sir. The window of the car blew out."

"You know Dennis McKenna shot through from the driver's side?"

"No, sir. I don't."

"So, when he's pointing this gun at you, you didn't fire?"

"I didn't fire because my gun was still in my pocket."

"Nothing wrong with your right hand?"

"I was stunned."

"Do you mean unconscious?"

"It brought tears to my eyes."

"No—I understand there are tears in your eyes. There's a fella pointing a rifle at you, shooting at you, another fella pointing a forty-five at you. Did you lose consciousness?"

"I had tears in my eyes not because someone was pointing a gun or rifle at me, but because I was injured."

"The question is," Skinner suddenly intoned, "did you lose consciousness?"

"I was stunned. I don't recall, Your Honor. Honestly. I could have for a second."

"Next question," said Skinner.

"How much time would you say elapsed," asked the old man, "between the time you got hit the third time and firing your gun?"

"Perhaps twenty seconds."

"*Twenty seconds* goes by, and when you started to squeeze off your four bullets, he still was at the wheel of the car pointing that forty-five at you?"

"Yes, sir."

"You can squeeze off a lot of bullets out of an automatic in twenty seconds. . . . Could you give this court and jury any reason why you weren't dead on that street—why you didn't get hit with about six bullets out of the magazine of that gun?"

"God only knows, sir."

"How close are you to [Bowden] when you squeeze off four shots?"

"I can't honestly say, sir."

"Two feet?"

"Close."

"What happened to the man when your bullets went into him?"

"I don't know what happened to him, sir."

"Did you see him fall over the wheel?" The old man was in his chair now, falling over an imaginary steering wheel.

"No, sir. . . . The vehicle sped off."

"And went down to the Tobin School and smashed up?"

Eddie nodded. The old man rose and wandered around the floor.

"And at that time, did you look in the car for the gun?"

"I visually observed."

"When you say 'visually observed,' you mean you just looked?"

"A quick glance, yes, sir."

"Wouldn't it be very helpful for you to search that car to see if you could find a gun?"

"No, sir. It would not be."

"Well, assuming you found one and had it on the witness

stand today, with Bowden's prints on it, would that be of any use to you?"

"At a shooting scene, sir, we are taught not to touch anything."

"Do you want the jury to understand you didn't take a thorough look, you didn't take a policeman's look, you didn't take an interested look in there for a forty-five?"

"I just visually glanced."

"Does 'visually glanced' mean you looked?"

"I did, sir."

"Did you find any discharged cartridges that would hold a bullet?"

"I didn't go in the vehicle at all, sir."

Strolling by the lectern, the old man found Eddie's Internal Affairs interview, which I had placed there half an hour earlier.

"Now, you gave a statement to Sergeant John Geagan on Thursday, February 13, 1975."

"I did."

"When you gave that statement to Geagan, you were accompanied by Mr. McGee as your attorney."

"I don't know if he was representing me or not, sir. I imagine he was there for a reason."

"How did he happen to be there with you?"

"I have no idea."

"If you look at this, you'll see it says you elected to be accompanied by your lawyer, Frank McGee."

"Where does it say that, sir?" Eddie looked mystified.

The old man put the transcript in front of Eddie and quoted Geagan saying: "You've exercised your right to have your attorney present here with you—Attorney Frank McGee, sitting at your right."

"Like I say," said Eddie, "I admit he was there."

"You talked this matter over with Mr. Frank McGee?"

"No, sir. I did not."

"Now, when you gave your story to Sergeant Geagan of Internal Affairs, you never said *one word* about seeing a plate [in] the trunk."

"No, sir. I did not."

"You never said *one word* about a Spanish fella fishing through the glove compartment."

"No, sir. I did not."

"And you never said *anything* about Zig-Zag papers."

"No, sir. I did not."

"Now, having in mind that you are looking for a gun down there in the Buick . . . it is critical as to who is putting their hands in that car, isn't it, Mr. Holland?"

"Well, I don't know what the boy was doing, sir, whether he was trying to help the victim or what."

"Did you mean to leave the inference he was probably taking the gun or bullets out of there?"

"He didn't have that much time in my opinion, sir."

"You did nothing but say, 'Get the hell out of here'?"

"That's correct, sir."

"So, when did you first tell anyone on the planet Earth about this Spanish person rifling the glove compartment?"

"I made mention to Mr. Keefe there." Eddie looked at Keefe, as did the old man and everyone else. Keefe looked at his notes.

"Now, when you mention Zig-Zag papers . . . is that the type of paper you would roll marijuana in?"

"It could be used to roll cigarettes," Eddie said innocently.

"Didn't you want the jury to think there was probably a pound of marijuana on the front seat of the car? You never used that before?"

"I don't recall saying it, sir."

"What would make Zig-Zag papers stick in your mind?"

"Just that it was there and I did see it. I tried to visualize everything I did see at the scene there."

"And one thing you would want to have in mind, you would look at Bowden to see if he was wearing any gloves, wouldn't you, Mr. Holland?"

"No, sir, not necessarily."

"Would you think of fingerprints? 'I wonder if he left fingerprints on the gun.' Now, can you say whether or not Bowden had gloves on?"

"I don't know, sir."

Toward the end of the day, the old man closed in on Eddie's version of the stakeout.

"When you observed the number on that car—4F•*6838*—you wrote it down. That's so, isn't it?"

"I don't recall, sir."

"Did you have a pencil, pen, a piece of chalk, *anything* with you . . . to write down numbers and information?"

"I don't recall."

"You trusted everything to memory?"

"I just don't recall whether I had a pencil or not."

"Did you have a piece of paper?"

"I don't recall, sir."

"You wanted to verify the number 4F•6838, didn't you?"

"Yes, sir."

"You wouldn't want to shoot anybody in that car without verifying that number?"

"Positively not, sir."

"Did you call in to the turret?"

"I don't believe I ever called the turret, sir. . . . I believe it was the TPF office."

"Isn't it a fact you were 841?"

"To the best of my knowledge, we were 841A."

"Isn't the 841A designation something you adopted for the purposes of covering up your error?"

"No, sir."

"Well, when you called the TPF office, did you give them 4F•*6838*?"

"I can't recall at this time, now, sir, but I believe I did."

Eddie had sounded sure about this during direct examination.

"Did you hear that number come in on your walkie-talkie or radio earlier that day?"

"I don't recall, sir."

"When you took the number off the plate, did you check it against numbers you had written down earlier?"

"I don't recall writing anything down, sir."

"Aren't you supposed to write down numbers of cars involved in robberies?"

"Not necessarily, sir."

"Would you tell this court and jury when it would be necessary to write down a robbery number?"

"I can't answer that."

"Now, can you think of any occasion, with your background and training as a police officer, when it would be necessary to write down a number of a robbery car?"

"I've never had occasion to, sir."

The old man arched his eyebrows to the jury and gave that answer some time to sink in.

"Did you hear David O'Brian testify?"

"Yes, sir, I did."

"Did you hear him say you had a pad with you, making notes?"

"I heard him say I had a clipboard, yes, sir."

"Isn't it standard procedure to have a pad there to write down this type of information, the number plate of a robbery suspect car?"

"No, sir."

"You had no memo to look at to verify that that was a number used in a Cambridge robbery?"

"I don't recall, sir."

At this point, Eddie's memory was completely gone. Things he had said hours and even minutes earlier eluded him now.

"Now, when you observed the car, and you picked up this number, and you have it in your head, before shooting anyone in that car, did you check with *anyone* to get the number used in the Cambridge robbery?"

"I don't recall, sir."

"So that when you shot Bowden, you had no way of knowing whether or not 4-Frank 6838 was the plate on the car in the robbery?"

"No, sir."

"Did it come over the air? The number of the car used in the robbery?"

"I don't recall, sir."

"So *now,* according to your testimony, when you approached the Bowden car . . . you didn't know *anything* about the number!"

"I don't recall if I did or not, sir."

Eddie wasn't squirming anymore. He had clearly given up the fight. Elbows on the counter, both hands holding his head, he stared glumly at the floor. He seemed beaten. The old man finished him off with a setup and a question that I had given him on an index card an hour earlier.

"Finally, Mr. Holland, this is the last question."

A very chancy announcement. It promises the jury something big.

"When you shot Mr. Bowden, he was looking at you and pointing a gun at you?"

"Yes, sir."

Turning to Eddie with his arm extended, as if aiming a gun at him, the old man whispered, "Can you tell me how your bullets went through his *back* and the *back* of his head?"

Eddie took his longest pause of the day, and the old man still held the imaginary gun on him. Perhaps hoping for an objection, Eddie looked to the defense table. Then to the floor. To the old man. To the floor again. Sitting eight feet from Eddie, Michael could see his lower lip quivering. Finally, looking bewildered and pained, Eddie groaned, "I have no idea."

The old man fell into his chair.

I heard what sounded like voices coming from another room. It was Skinner inviting redirect, Keefe declining, and Skinner adjourning.

CHAPTER 18

O n Day Five, George Washington's birthday, 1978, the old man's good-morning smile was returned by three jurors: Cohen, the foreman, and number six, the ponytailed mechanic. The old man figured he had their votes now, but Michael and I were sure only of Cohen. We thought that he guaranteed us a hung jury at the very least. Even if the other five turned out to be cop lovers and racists, we believed Cohen could hold out against them.

Instead of starting the day as we had expected—with testimony from Denny—Keefe tried to support parts of Eddie's testimony with two other witnesses: Doctor Creeden and Jim O'Connor, Winbush's arresting officer.

The day before, Keefe had requested Skinner's permission to read Creeden's deposition to the jury. He gave Skinner a letter from Creeden explaining that his heart couldn't bear "the strain of court testimony." Skinner said he wouldn't "take his word for it," but if Creeden's cardiologist certified his heart condition, he would allow the reading of the deposition in lieu of in-person testimony. "I've had two people die in this courtroom," said Skinner, "and I don't want any more." Now, Keefe produced the suggested letter from Creeden's doctor and we had the reading of the deposition.

Skinner told the jury: "A deposition has been taken and it's going to be read [because the witness] is not available to come into court." As Keefe headed for the lectern, Skinner said, "I suggest, in order not to make this utterly boring, that Mr. McKenna go over there [to] the witness stand and read Doctor Creeden's answers rather than have Mr. Keefe read both questions and answers. It's very hard to follow if one voice takes both parts. Mr. McKenna, you will be Doctor Creeden."

Tom McKenna looked delighted to have landed a speaking role in the trial. Keefe and McKenna read only the eighteen pages of direct examination. Then the old man got up to read his fifty-seven pages of cross. Seeing that Tom McKenna was about to leave the stand, he said, "Would you do me the honor, Mr. McKenna?" McKenna nodded and opened his transcript to the old man's first question.

The reading lasted two hours. Skinner seldom took notes. Instead, he busied himself with a few law books. The signal to the jury was unmistakable: This testimony is not important.

Patrolman O'Connor took the witness stand in a tan suit and an orange turtleneck. He breezed through direct in twelve minutes.

O'Connor: At the 6:30 P.M. TPF roll call, "we received word that officers of the day platoon had been watching a motor vehicle out on Smith Street in Roxbury that was used in an armed robbery in another city and that they were in trouble."

"Myself and other officers got in a marked police car and went to Roxbury." On the way, "we received a radio transmission relative to a green Thunderbird that had been on Smith Street. The officers who were on the scene wanted the car for assault on the officers. . . . They gave the registration of the vehicle, and the occupants were armed, possibly with a shotgun."

"We arrived at Smith Street. . . . At that time there was general conversation between all the officers there. [Officer Holland said] that he had been run down by the blue Buick."

"I went to the corner of the school building and observed some tire tracks going up beside the school, going out toward Tremont Street."

"As a result of Sergeant Byrne's direction, I went to Thirty-eight Annunciation Road with other officers. . . . We sat waiting for the green Thunderbird. At approximately ten-forty P.M., the green

Thunderbird entered the parking lot at that address. . . . The occupant was taken into custody. . . . He was taken to District Two and booked. [On the way to District 2] I advised him of his rights and asked him several questions. . . . He told me he left his apartment at Thirty-eight Annunciation Road at approximately six-thirty P.M. and went to a PTA meeting for one of his children. He went by way of Smith Street. I asked him what was the route, and he told me he went by way of Smith Street stopping [on Tremont Street] for a dollar's worth of gasoline. I asked him had he noticed anything unusual that evening on Smith Street. He stated that he had not. I asked him if he allowed anyone that evening to use his car, anyone other than himself to have his automobile. He stated no one used the automobile but he himself."

At District 2, "I was present when a search was conducted. . . . There were four rounds of thirty-eight-caliber ammunition found in his coat pocket."

"The following morning . . . Officer Holland [and] I . . . went to the Roxbury Court and obtained . . . complaints."

"The probable-cause hearing was conducted in March. . . . The judge found probable cause against the defendant prior to hearing defense counsel's case. After hearing defense counsel's case, he ruled no probable cause."

At this point Keefe sat down.

Impatient to get on to the new claim about tire tracks, the old man moved to the lectern and passed lightly over the impossible double ruling just attributed to Judge Tracy. He merely looked at O'Connor, as if the strapping patrolman were claiming to be Napoleon, and said slowly, "You stated, under oath, to this jury that the judge found probable cause and then he found no probable cause."

"He did, yes, sir," said O'Connor, looking away from the old man, who heaved a sigh, shook his head, and moved on. He put O'Connor's report on the stand and walked toward the jury, asking, "Now, in that report do you have *anything* about tire tracks next to the Tobin School?"

"No, sir. None that I see."

"The Mission Hill playground and park next to the school would [have] some tracks in there from trucks—Park Department trucks going into the playground."

"Possibly."

"The tire tracks never made such an impression on you that you [had the police photographer] take a photograph of it?"

"No, I didn't, no, sir."

"You couldn't say how wide they were, could you?"

"No, sir."

"Trucks could have made them?"

"I don't know what made them."

"Why would you tell this jury about them? Did you want to connect those tracks to the Thunderbird? Who told you to say that?"

The old man glared at the defense team. Keefe could have objected—one question at a time, please—but didn't.

"That's what I observed, sir," O'Connor replied.

"Who suggested that you say that?"

"No one. That is what I saw."

"Did anyone ever tell you that the Thunderbird probably took off and ran by the Tobin School up through the playground to Tremont Street?" The old man traced that route on the model, using his pointer.

"Yes, sir."

"So when you got on the stand and said that you saw some tracks, were you hoping to help that part of the story?"

"I can only tell what I saw."

"Do you think that would help build up that side of the story?"

"That is what I learned at the scene, yes, sir."

"I see. . . . And you were a friend of Eddie Holland?"

"Yes, sir."

"As you are to this day?"

"Yes, sir."

"When you saw the tracks, did you walk all the way up to Tremont Street and follow them?"

"No, sir."

"You can't even say how long the tracks were, right?"

"No, sir," O'Connor replied sheepishly.

"Keep your voice up." The old man paced from side to side: "So, when you went for this Ernest Winbush . . . at the time you approached his car, you had in mind he tried to kill your friend and fellow officer Edward Holland?"

"That's correct."

"You were very careful to make a search of the Thunderbird?"

"Yes, sir. We looked for a weapon."

"And *you* searched him?"

"I conducted a frisk of his clothing, yes."

"You found no rifle in the car?"

"No, sir."

"You found no gun on him?"

"No, sir."

"*You* were very thorough?"

"Yes, sir."

"And you took him to the station house?"

"Yes, sir."

"He sat where—on that ride?"

"He sat in the back seat with myself."

"Who found the bullets on that man after he rode to the station house handcuffed?"

"Officer Sullivan."

"*Four rounds* of pistol ammunition in his pocket, and *you* didn't find them."

"No, sir."

"Did you get some demerits or lose some brownie points as a result of making a bum search of this fella?"

"No, sir."

"Officer, you're under oath here. Isn't it a fact they were planted on him?"

"No way."

"Is that so?"

"Yeah," O'Connor snapped.

"When *you* searched him, he didn't have any on him!"

"There was no search of his person on the street. He was frisked."

"Oh, patted gently?" The old man patted his own pockets.

"No one entered his clothing."

"I see. You patted him on the derriere?" And the old man patted his own derriere.

There were chuckles in the jury box, and O'Connor's face reddened as he said, "I patted his whole body."

"Well, now," the old man said as he strode to the stand, "how about patting me?" He held his hands over his head. "Just pat these pockets and tell me if you can feel anything."

O'Connor stepped off the stand and patted the old man's coat pockets. When he touched the left one, the old man asked: "Do you feel something in that pocket?"

"Yes."

"Now, by patting me, can you tell me what those are," asked the old man.

With the reluctance of someone who knows he's being played for a fool, O'Connor said, "Three handgun cartridges."

"Three bullets!?" exclaimed the old man in extravagant astonishment.

"Yes, sir."

The old man reached into his pocket and pulled out the bullets. He walked them over to the jury. O'Connor resumed the stand. With the bullets in his upturned palm on the jury rail, the old man said icily, "So, you would feel bullets if you patted someone, right, Officer O'Connor?"

"Possibly, yes, sir."

"It's a practice for all officers to carry extra ammunition, isn't it?"

"Correct."

With a bit more evidence-planting in mind, the old man slipped back to O'Connor's arrival on the scene. "You saw Holland and McKenna moving around Smith Street?"

"I did."

"And you had a conversation with Holland."

"As part of a group, yes, sir."

"You [heard] about the fellow in the Buick trying to shoot him?"

"I heard that, yes, sir."

"You knew a big search was going on?"

"Yes, sir."

The old man snatched the Fabrique Nationale from the defense table, held it up, and said, "Now it's so, isn't it, Officer O'Connor, that you know it was part of the plan to throw a gun under a car?"

"I have no knowledge of any plan or anything else about what you're talking about, counsel."

"They threw it there!"

"Who threw it there?"

"The Tactical Patrol Force planted it there!"

"Not to my knowledge, no, sir."

The old man got away with an explosion of hearsay: "As a matter of fact, you know that it was a sergeant on the Tactical Patrol Force who said to Joseph Fagone, 'Hey, look under there.' And lo and behold. Did Joseph Fagone ever tell you he was furious at being told that? That he figures he was set up?"

Fagone hadn't told the old man that, but you get away with what you can in street fights and in trials.

"No, sir," replied O'Connor unsteadily. "I had no conversation with him."

"Would it surprise you to hear that Sergeant Byrne gave Officer Fagone instructions to go look under that car?" The old man wanted to poison the atmosphere for Harry Byrne, who, he knew, was waiting outside to testify.

"I don't know who gave the order," said O'Connor.

"Incidentally, being with that group, you know, don't you, sir, what a throw-away gun is?"

"I've heard the term, yes."

The jury hadn't, though, so they couldn't have known what to make of O'Connor's acknowledgment of the term.

The old man found his way back to the Winbush story for his last fifteen minutes with O'Connor.

"And you gave him the so-called Miranda warnings: You don't have to talk to us. If you want a lawyer, you can have one. If you can't afford one, we will get one for you. [And] he talked to you?"

"Yes."

"And he was a cooperative guy?"

"He answered what I asked him, yes, sir."

"None of the information that he gave you did you find to be false?"

"I never investigated it."

"You would check out a fella like this. He tried to *kill* a policeman, your pal Eddie Holland. You would check him out, right?"

"Yes, sir."

"He has *no criminal record.*"

"I don't know whether he does or not."

"It would be normal procedure for you . . . to make the determination of whether or not this guy is a hood, a convict; does he have a criminal record? did he kill any other policemen? You would find that out."

"Yes, sir."

"At some time you discovered that this Ernest Winbush was a married man?"

"Yes, sir."

"You discovered he had some children?"

"Yes, sir."

"And you discovered that . . . he had his *kidney* removed around 1972 . . . and that he was on a *dialysis machine* on January 29, 1975, out at the Kidney Center on Commonwealth Avenue?"

"Yes, sir."

"And that is the testimony you heard in Roxbury [Court], right?"

"Yes."

"And having in mind that you talked to Winbush and he was a friendly-type guy, did you ever say to him, 'Hey, Ernie, do you own a rifle?'"

"No, sir. I didn't."

"As a matter of fact, you never said to him, 'Look, Ernie, it's nice of you to talk with me after I give you these Miranda warnings. Did you drop off a man on Smith Street around six-thirty?'"

"I had no knowledge of whether he possessed that at that time," O'Connor replied faintly. The answer made no sense to anyone.

"Try to keep your voice up, Officer O'Connor," said the old man. "You can put it up to the pitch of when you told Winbush to get out of the car that night."

Cohen liked that one.

"Did you ever say to him, 'Hey, Ernie, did you shoot at my buddy Eddie Holland?'"

"No, sir. I didn't."

"That would have helped, if he had told you he did, wouldn't it?" The old man sat down.

"It sure would," replied O'Connor.

Skinner invited redirect, and Keefe declined.

"Next witness," said Skinner.

Keefe turned around and said, "Mr. McKenna."

Mary and Bill collected Eurina and Jamil as Denny came through the bar enclosure, past the defense table to the witness stand. It was twelve-thirty-five. We had only twenty-five minutes left in the trial day, because as Skinner had already announced, the court was committed to an afternoon of hearing arguments on motions in other cases.

Denny's first few minutes of testimony—the autobiography— went smoothly. His voice was as coarse as ever, and his face kept its scowl firmly in place—his facial muscles must be involuntary ones—but he still came across as sort of a regular guy when he was saying: "I went to Saint Anthony's Grammar School. . . . Saint Columbkille's High School . . . I was an Air Force policeman for four years. . . . I have six children. . . . I'm separated. . . . I pay my wife a hundred and fifty-three dollars a week."

After a two-minute review of Denny's thirteen years on the force, Keefe said, "Calling your attention to January 29, 1975, where were you working that day?"

And here the pausing began. It was the first of the strange silences Denny created after almost every question, no matter how simple. Unlike Eddie, Denny never appeared to be searching his memory or even thinking at all. He simply stared close-mouthed at the floor for a long time—five, ten, fifteen seconds—before, and often in the middle of, responding. Because he sat very close to the microphone, when he wasn't talking the loudspeakers carried the sound of his strained breathing. The effect was eerie.

Presently he looked at Keefe and said, "Uh, my mind was, uh, someplace else. I'm sorry. Please repeat that."

Cohen and the foreman exchanged glances. Number six's eyes widened. The old man whispered to Michael. I dropped my pen. And Pat said to me, "I *cannot* believe it."

In the twenty remaining minutes, Keefe dragged Denny up to the point where, as Denny put it, "Officer Holland and I met Molloy and Dwyer. And the photographer and the reporter then got into our motor vehicle. And this was sometime shortly after four o'clock, as I best recall."

"All right," said Skinner. "I think this is a good point to break, so when we get into the critical events we won't be interrupted. . . . We will start at nine o'clock tomorrow."

At lunch, in the middle of all the trial talk, the old man said, "Today's my father's birthday, you know."

We didn't know.

Michael and I spent the afternoon and evening getting ready for Denny and for final argument.

Not long after lunch, the old man disappeared.

CHAPTER 19

Day Six: Thursday, February 23, 1978, began with a bench conference. Keefe had told Skinner's clerk that in order to plan the defense he had to know first thing this morning whether the judge was going to allow Ethel and Desi to testify. Knowing a long discussion was in the offing, Skinner had the marshal keep the jury in its conference room—with a good supply of coffee and donuts.

When Skinner took his seat at the side bar, Keefe handed him what he said was a "memorandum on the admissibility of the Cambridge robbery identification."

"We have a memorandum in opposition," said Michael, handing it over.

"That lends a certain symmetry to the occasion," said Skinner.

Without fear of being overheard by the jury, everyone spoke in his conversational tone. Almost every word was audible to us in the spectators' benches. Eddie and Denny weren't interested enough to listen, though. They were outside with Dwyer, Molloy, Harry Byrne, and newcomers Frank MacDonald and Jim O'Connor. Loman McClinton was conspicuously absent.

Skinner flipped through the memos. Keefe's said that Ethel and Desi's testimony that Bowden was indeed one of the robbers would suggest a motive for his attack on Eddie and Denny: He knew Eddie and Denny were after him for the robbery, and he was of no mind to surrender peacefully. Michael's memo said that whether Bowden was involved in the robbery was irrelevant to the trial issue of what happened on Smith Street, and that Ethel and Desi's IDs of Bowden were suggestive identifications and demonstrably wrong. When Skinner finished reading, Keefe was the first to speak: "Here the question is the motive of Bowden as the police surround his car. . . ."

Skinner's eyes wandered and landed on Michael. He didn't like what he saw. "Finish dressing *before* coming to court," he said.

Michael had not buttoned his vest. "Excuse me, Your Honor."

I could see the back of his neck turn a vivid pink.

"Button your vest and get into uniform."

"Sorry."

A minute later, the bench conference was going better for us. The pressure was on John Keefe and Tom McKenna as Skinner turned to the credibility of Ethel and Desi's IDs.

"The evidence is this man was five feet four inches tall," said Skinner. "Isn't that what the autopsy shows?"

"Yes, Your Honor," said the old man.

"And he's fat," Skinner added.

"Right," said the old man. "A hundred and eighty pounds."

"It strikes me that this identification is inherently suspect," said Skinner.

"The well was poisoned," said the old man. "There wasn't one scintilla of due process used in this situation."

"Your Honor," said Keefe, "as a [former] assistant district attorney, I don't think the quality of identification is very poor."

Tom McKenna responded more forcefully: "Your Honor, you haven't heard the two eyewitnesses. [They] were in the store for ten minutes with these fellows [and] had a clear view of them."

"All right," said Skinner. "Then give me their depositions. I read fast."

He called a recess and took the depositions into his chambers.

Keefe and McKenna stepped outside to explain what was going on to Ethel and Desi, who had just arrived and expected to take the stand later in the morning.

After forty minutes of reading, Skinner returned to the side bar. The old man gave him the mug shots of the three men variously reported by Sergeants Geagan and Petersen to have been identified by Ethel and Desi as the other robber.

"On this matter," said Keefe, "I would like to comment.... From these two parties ... the testimony will be ... they each picked one photo."

"Did they pick that photo?" Skinner asked in amazement, pointing to the picture of the middle-aged white man.

"I don't know which of the three photos they picked," replied Keefe.

"Sergeant Geagan says this is it," said the old man, pointing to the Wardell Washington picture.

"And that is of Washington, who's in the can," said Skinner.

"Obviously," said Keefe, "there were mistakes made by the police in regard to these photos and which ones they picked."

"Well," said Skinner, putting down the pictures, "there are some basic problems with the identification [of Bowden]. The most critical being the height. Mrs. Caragianes says that [he] was about six feet tall."

"She is a very short woman," said McKenna.

"Okay," said Skinner. "Desmond Callahan says he's five ten or thereabouts."

McKenna told Skinner of Pat Bowden's interrogatory answer saying that James was "approximately five feet ten inches."

"Luongo measured him," said the old man.

"You know how tall your husband is," said Keefe.

"Do you know how tall your wife is?" asked Skinner.

"Certainly do," said Keefe. "Five two."

"I don't know," said Skinner. "She's pretty tall—my wife is—but I don't know exactly how tall."

"I know mine," McKenna chimed in.

"I'm sorry," said Skinner, "I will have to take [the autopsy] as an official description of his height. . . . The medical examiner measures and weighs with substantial accuracy."

Keefe and McKenna scrambled to what they thought was firmer ground. Callahan "identified the car," said Keefe.

"He's positive of that, Your Honor," added McKenna.

Desi's deposition in hand, Skinner said, "He says very positively that the car he saw in Cambridge was a Buick Century, and [Bowden's] car has been clearly identified as a Buick Electra. Now a Buick Century—I know because I happened to rent one once upon a time—is the smaller, intermediate Buick. The Electra is a monster Buick."

Keefe switched to Ethel. "The identification with respect to Mrs. Caragianes is strong because of the extent of time she had the opportunity to observe the person."

"When she says the guy was six feet tall," said Skinner agreeably, "I'm inclined to believe her."

"She kicked Bowden," said McKenna.

"Any evidence of a bruise?" asked Skinner. "I read an awful lot of medical examiners' reports in my youth, and they mention every defect that they find on the body. Let me see the medical examiner's report."

"Nobody was looking for a bruise," said McKenna, as Skinner scanned the report.

" 'External genitalia, negative,' " said Skinner, quoting the report. "I wouldn't say that that was critical, but nothing shows up."

Keefe tried to start the argument over again, saying Bowden's participation in an armed robbery shows he had a "tendency" to be violent.

"As a matter of fact," said Skinner, "it has an opposite effect. Here is a guy who gets kicked in the balls and he doesn't respond by any violence."

Skinner continued: "If I'm going to permit to be introduced a collateral matter of this sort, it has to be on a basis of clear and convincing evidence. Otherwise it is extremely prejudicial" to the plaintiff, he explained, because Bowden was not there to defend himself against the robbery charge.

"It is not a collateral matter," said Keefe.

"I think," said Skinner, "this is a conditioned, indeed possibly somewhat hysterical, identification by this woman. I just don't think it has any value."

"This is not a hysterical woman," McKenna protested. "This is a woman who was operating this store for a long time. It was not the first time this store was held up."

"Precisely," said Skinner.

"Mr. O'Donnell has a right to cross-examine her," said Mc-Kenna, "and rip her to shreds if he can."

Skinner explained: "This isn't just the ordinary kind of evidence that can automatically come in and be subject to cross-examination. It's a matter in which I think the court has to exercise some screening as to whether it is relevant and reliable. . . .

"Everything is wrong," Skinner added. "The number is wrong. The car model is wrong. . . ."

"That's the whole point!" said Keefe, becoming more and more animated. "The number is wrong because it was the right car."

Only Tom McKenna appeared to grasp that logic.

"Here's another thing that makes all of this terribly shaky," said Skinner. "The gun that they saw is not the [automatic Fabrique Nationale]. There is no question that it's a revolver in Cambridge."

"We are not attempting to demonstrate that Bowden himself had a gun in that robbery," said McKenna, "but his partner did."

To the old man, Skinner said, "You have [submitted] evidence that he was in the hospital up until something like—"

"Three-seventeen," said the old man.

The discussion continued to bounce from Ethel to Desi to Bowden's height to legal doctrine. Tom McKenna moved out in front for the defense. At some point during McKenna's zealous arguing, the old man and Michael, who were standing aside and watching contentedly, had a moment of revelation. As Michael later put it: "Bowden robbing the store was Eddie and Denny's real defense. That's all there was to it. That's why the City never made us a settlement offer. That's why the City let Keefe try the case. How could they lose? They had positive IDs of Bowden as a robber. Positive IDs! They didn't give a shit about anything else. They figured that as soon as Ethel and Desi tell the jury that our guy robbed them, it's all over for us, we don't have a chance. McKenna never imagined he was gonna have any trouble getting them on the stand. So, he was in there fighting with Skinner for his whole goddamn case."

Skinner: "These identifications are so poor and so unpersuasive and [were made] under such terrible circumstances. . . . There is no way—looking at these pictures [the autopsy photographs]— that that man can be tall and skinny. . . . That man has got to be short and fat."

McKenna: "They think they have the right man. Both of them do. . . . Now, these are two terribly courageous people. One of them kicked the robber. The other one ran after them. Those [robbers] could have turned around and blown him away! But he did it. These are very strong people!"

Skinner: "Strong is not the same as right."

McKenna: "Well, they have an opinion, Your Honor. They were there and we weren't. They think they have the right man! I don't want to get emotional about it, but . . ."

Skinner, looking at the autopsy pictures: "He just looks fat."

McKenna: "The way you appear in terms of your weight is determined very much by what you're wearing. These men were wearing dungaree outfits. When I wear a dungaree outfit, I look a lot thinner than when I wear a suit. . . . If you saw me in civilian clothes or dungarees, you'd think I am ten or fifteen pounds less than I am."

Skinner: "I don't think so."

McKenna: "You can look shorter or taller, depending on the clothes you wear."

Skinner: "You can't gain eight inches."

Musing on the weaknesses of eyewitness identifications, Skinner said, "You know something—there may be forty young lawyers, all of whom affect moustaches and suits with vests. They come in here, and I can't tell one from the other. They all look the same to me."

"They don't hold you up, Your Honor," said Keefe.

"In a way"—Skinner smiled—"they do sometimes."

"Perhaps you would make a bad witness," said McKenna, the only moustache affecter in the room.

"I certainly would," Skinner agreed. "As to the fungibility of some of these people, I certainly would."

In desperation, McKenna returned to the subject of Ethel and revealed something better left unsaid. "What you are seeing there is a deposition of a witness, an *unprepared* witness!"

The old man stiffened at the word *unprepared,* but McKenna plunged on: "My point is that she did not go through the story with a lawyer before she went to this deposition. . . . She has, since that time, spoken to both Mr. Keefe and myself and, in our judgment, is a prepared witness . . . a solid witness."

Many lawyers "prepare" their witnesses, but admitting that to a judge is rather indiscreet. Skinner glanced at the old man, who was happy to let McKenna go on making such reckless statements.

Skinner took a deep breath and said, "If there were some correspondence here. If the guns were the same or the plate numbers or the car models . . ."

"The day after the shooting he identified the Electra," said Keefe. "Two years later he said, 'Century.'"

"There's a big difference," said Skinner. And, "He already talked to the Boston police about this situation."

"I don't believe so," said Keefe.

"He says so in his deposition," said Skinner.

"I see," said Keefe.

"The well was poisoned," said the old man. He added, "The defendants today have demonstrated no foundation or persuasive position in law or in fact for allowing this in."

"I don't like this," said Skinner. "I don't like the circumstances of the identification. . . . I don't think it's clear and convincing by a long shot. . . . I'm very suspicious of identifications that don't have any kind of corroboration. . . . There is no corroboration in terms of size. Nothing like a scar or glasses or anything. The only thing is [he's] black . . . along with eight million other blacks."

"Not according to the interrogatory," said Keefe.

"Let me see it," said Skinner. He read aloud: "'Plaintiff Patricia Bowden's answers to interrogatories . . . Interrogatory Nineteen . . . Q: Please state the height and weight of James

Bowden on January 29th, 1975. A: Approximately five feet ten inches and two hundred pounds.'" Looking up, he said, "She's here. Let's put Mrs. Bowden back on the stand."

Suddenly Pat was on the witness stand again. Having had no time to get worked up about it and no jury to face, she was at ease this time. Skinner asked the questions.

"Mrs. Bowden, can you describe your husband's size and build for us, please?"

"Well, he weighed about one-ninety. About five five in height."

"He was substantially shorter than you?"

"Yes."

"Did you ever discuss his height with him?"

"No."

"Okay. Does either counsel want to interrogate?"

The old man asked, "Do you have any reason as to how you put down five ten [in the interrogatory]?"

"I don't know. At the time I was very upset and everything. I was probably thinking about myself. I'm five ten."

"You're five ten?" Skinner came back, as the old man stepped aside.

"Yes."

"How much shorter was he than you?"

"Not that much shorter. About five inches, maybe."

"All right," said Skinner. "Mr. Keefe, do you want to inquire?"

"I don't think I have any questions," said Keefe.

"Thank you, Mrs. Bowden," said Skinner.

Pat came back to the bench and asked, "How'd I do?" as Skinner was saying: "Well, it's clear to me that Mrs. Bowden is not an expert measurer of people's height and that Doctor Luongo is."

Nodding toward Keefe and McKenna, the old man said, "They didn't challenge Luongo's height."

"I'm going to accept that measurement in the autopsy report—sixty-four and five-tenths inches. And that measurement makes these purported identifications so unreliable [that] I'm going to exclude them."

"Your Honor," cried McKenna, "may we just—"

"Your objections are noted," said Skinner with cold finality. "The circumstances of the identifications, the more or less dramatic facts which were known to Callahan and probably to the lady, their descriptions of the [robbers] and what we know to be Bowden's actual dimensions led me to the conclusion. . . . And under what strikes me as just plain sound sense, I'm going to exclude this evidence."

He told the marshal to bring in the jury.

Walking away from the bench, Keefe looked crushed. McKenna was livid. He went out to tell Ethel and Desi that they were out of the case.

A minute later, the old man got no reactions to his good-morning smile to the jurors because their attention was on Skinner, who was apologizing for having kept them "in limbo for a few hours." He explained: "There was a very perplexing legal question that was presented to me this morning. . . . It had to be resolved before we could go forward.

"Now, we are going to go on from where we left off yesterday—with the direct examination of Mr. McKenna."

Denny resumed the stand. It was 11:20 A.M. In just under an hour of rocking back and forth on the balls of his feet and holding the lectern, Keefe elicited Denny's story.

Denny: "After we picked up Kobre and O'Brian . . . we cruised around . . . the Mission Hill housing project. . . . At some point, . . . we turned into Smith Street. And we proceeded down Smith Street, which was one-way. . . . As we proceeded down Smith Street . . . Officer Holland commented about an automobile. . . . He thought that the car was a car used in the holdup in Cambridge. And as he relayed this information to me, I stopped the unmarked car, . . . turned around, and drove back . . . going the wrong way on Smith Street. As I drove by . . . Officer Holland said, 'That's the car.' . . . I continued down Smith Street . . . crossed Parker Street onto Gurney Street, and turned the car around and parked on the corner of Gurney Street.

"Officer Holland transmitted a radio message on the walkie-talkie, which he had in a paper bag. And he transmitted to the TPF base that we had a car that we were watching and it had a particular license plate on it and would they check that car and see if that car had been involved in a holdup earlier that day in Cambridge.

"Shortly thereafter, a matter of minutes, an answer came from the TPF base—I recognized the voice over the air at the time as Officer Monroe—that the car was in fact the same car that was used in the holdup in Cambridge and it was occupied by two black males and they were armed with a shotgun and a pistol.

"We notified the other TPF units in the area.

"We then again made another call to the TPF base. We asked them if we should stay on the car. Our tour of duty was about to be ended. And at this time we were told to sit on the car. We requested of the TPF base further that they bring a shotgun out to the scene. And we continued our surveillance.

"About six-thirty, about six-thirty a green Thunderbird with a black roof turned from Parker Street . . . turned right onto Smith Street. And it had a Massachusetts number plate on it. And it drove up Smith Street. And it stopped parallel to the blue Buick which we were watching. And it stopped.

"I observed the passenger door of the Thunderbird open up and a man get out of it. I then observed the door of the Buick being opened. And the man got into the Buick.

"It was a black male.

"The Buick backed away from the sidewalk out into the middle of the street and proceeded in reverse.

"Officer Holland stated over the walkie-talkie, 'He's moving. Get the T-Bird.'

"I had placed the car in gear and was crossing Parker Street and entered Smith Street. . . . The Buick was coming down towards me. And the Buick was in the middle of the street. And I was in the middle of the street. And the Buick came to a stop about ten or twelve feet away from the front of my car. At this time, I opened my wallet, which was hanging around my neck, to display my badge. I drew my service revolver and I got out of the car that I was in and approached the Buick from the driver's side. . . . I called on the driver: 'Boston police. Get out of the car.'

"The Buick moved backwards and forwards. As the Buick moved backwards, I jumped away from the Buick. At this time, I had my service revolver in both hands and I was pointing it at the window of the Buick. I then observed the Buick back up. Again. I called on it as he backed up and I jumped back, away from him. Again. I observed the Buick strike Officer Holland. Officer Holland was standing—when I saw him—in the rear. The right side of the Buick. He was in the rear area of the Buick, between the bumper and the fender, and he was spinning. At this time, Officer Holland fell below my vision—below the fender of the Buick. And I called on the driver—the Buick started forward—and I called on the driver of the Buick: 'Police. Get out of the car.' At this time, the driver of the Buick was coming back out in my direction. I began to fire into the Buick. As I was squeezing the pistol which I had—holding it in both of my hands in front of me and pointing it at the driver—I observed from within the Buick a flash and a report, a gunshot. The flash illuminated the driver's arm, which was in this position pointed this way, to the right side of the car. At this time, the action I already initiated with my service revolver. I fired into the closed window of the Buick. The window of the Buick shattered, and the driver of the Buick lunged forward to the right. I fired again. The Buick straightened out and took off up Smith Street. I held my service revolver in my hand and fired at the rear window, aiming at the driver of the Buick. I then turned and ran back to the police car and got into the police car."

Keefe: "After you got back to your vehicle, what next did you hear or observe?"

Denny: "I observed, as I was going up Smith Street, that the Buick had left the roadway. . . . It had apparently struck a light pole . . . and was partially straddling a chain link fence."

Keefe: "What next did you do, Officer?"

Denny: "I got out of the police car. I put my service revolver back in my hands and I approached the Buick from the left side.

The driver's side. Again. As I went up to the window of the Buick, I pointed my service revolver into the Buick and I determined that the operator of the Buick was incapable of attacking myself and Officer Holland.

"I turned and saw Officer Holland on the opposite side of the Buick, and I said, 'Get an ambulance.'

"I then observed Officer Molloy and Dwyer standing at the front of the Buick. At this time, they were asked by Holland or myself—I'm not sure which—'Where is the T-Bird?'

"And they said, 'It never came out the end of the street. What was the number?'

"At this time, I told them the number that was on the T-Bird, which I had observed when the T-Bird had turned in front of me when I was parked on Gurney Street.

"The wagon from District Two . . . pulled up. . . . The other officers got ahold of him and placed him in the stretcher."

Keefe: "What next did you do, Officer, or what next occurred?"

Denny: "Sergeant McHale and Sergeant Byrne, my supervisors, were on the scene, and we had some conversation as to what had occurred."

"I was directed by either Sergeant Byrne or Sergeant McHale to go back to District Two.

"I went to District Two . . . to the second floor. To the Detectives' Room. . . . There were quite a few people coming and going up there. . . . The entire time I was there was perhaps four to five hours. Maybe six hours.

"At some point—perhaps an hour after the incident, I'm not sure of the time—Sergeant Hudson, who was the Homicide investigator, and Sergeant Geagan came into the Detectives' Room. . . . I accompanied them back to Smith Street. Showed them the physical scene from where the car was originally parked, where it backed up to, where the shooting occurred, and where the car finally came to rest. I did this with Sergeant Hudson primarily, and Sergeant Geagan was taking notes."

Keefe: "After you finished at the scene with Sergeants Geagan and Hudson, what did you do?"

Denny: "I returned to District Two.

"I met Captain MacDonald—Captain William MacDonald—who was second in command of the TPF. And he was with Officer O'Connor and Officer Keegan, and Sullivan. . . . And they had a black male who they were having conversation with. And at this time, Captain MacDonald asked me about the shooting from the Thunderbird. And I had no awareness of the shooting from the Thunderbird. And I stated such to him. And I said, 'I think that you want Eddie Holland.' And I went upstairs. And I saw Eddie. And I said, 'Captain MacDonald wants you downstairs.'

"And then I remained in the Detectives' Room . . . preparing the report of the incident.

"At some point, Eddie Holland came back upstairs, and Sergeant Byrne told him that he had better go to the hospital and get his leg looked at because he was limping around.

"A patrolman's [union] representative had come into the Detectives' Room. . . . We had a short conversation with him. . . . And he had a conversation with Frank McGee relative to whatever. I didn't listen to the conversation, much of the conversation. . . . He relayed to us whatever information he determined from McGee. And subsequently I left District Two after completing my report."

Keefe: "Did you have occasion to be involved in court proceedings with respect to the person in the Thunderbird?"

Denny: "Yes. . . . Officer Holland had sought a complaint against James—I'm sorry—Ernest Winbush, who is the owner of the Thunderbird. And I appeared in court, and I testified [that] I had no previous awareness of having seen Mr. Winbush."

Keefe had Denny show the jury how he was wearing his badge on Smith Street. Denny took out his wallet and opened it to reveal a badge pinned inside. A long shoelace was looped through a hole in the edge of the wallet. Denny put the shoelace around his neck, and the wallet hung open on his chest.

Skinner asked, "Were you wearing it in that manner?"

"Yes, sir," Denny replied.

"I have no further questions," said Keefe.

The old man rushed onto the floor. He had fifty minutes left before lunch. From the outset, he appeared to be fighting for control—of himself. He wasn't in his library this time. There could be no lunges at Denny now that Skinner and the jury were watching.

"You said yesterday," the old man began, "you had some military service?"

"Yes, that's right."

"And that was of a noncombatant nature?"

"Yes, that's right."

"But during military service, you did have some firearms experience?"

"Yes, sir. . . . I'm an expert, sir."

"I see. . . . And you do some target practice, do you, on your free time?"

"Yes, sir."

"And you have your own guns besides the department's guns?"

"I own two guns, sir. I own a twenty-two target rifle. . . . The manufacturer is Savage-Anshutz . . . in Germany. It has a wooden stock with a Monte Carlo cheekpiece on it. It has a hooded ramp front sight . . . and I own a twelve-gauge shotgun . . . manufactured in Czechoslovakia. It's a Brno."

"And I would assume that you're licensed for those personal guns?"

"I have a firearms identification card, sir."

That was all Denny needed legally to possess a rifle or a shotgun, but he did not legally possess the firearms identification card. In Massachusetts, local police departments issue the cards, and according to state law, anyone who "has been under treatment for or confinement for drug addiction or habitual drunkenness" is not allowed a gun permit of any sort. We weren't aware of this legal detail at the time, and it is not at all clear that Skinner would have allowed the old man to mention it anyway. Relevance is a tricky concept in a courtroom.

"Did you ever own an automatic?"

"No."

Turning to the defense table, the old man said, "Attorney Mc-Kenna, do you have that Fabrique?"

Tom McKenna had neglected to put it on display that morning. Now he took it out of a briefcase and handed it to the old man.

"Thank you."

He carried it over to the witness stand, dropped it in front of Denny, and said, "Let me ask you this, Mr. McKenna: Did you ever own *that gun*?"

"No, sir."

The old man stayed at Denny's side and slipped into a discussion of the workings of automatics—something already adequately described by Walter Logue. It was one of those moments when the old man has no idea what to do next and stays on something that allows him to think ahead. He asked baby questions—"Is that the barrel?"—and called Denny "Mr. Expert." The jurors couldn't tell he was stalling for a brainstorm. By now, they probably always assumed he was on his way to something worth hearing. And unbeknownst to the old man, he was.

Certainly, we always knew that the old man was the great, shall we say, *peculiarity* of the Bowden case. In Boston, civil rights cases usually feature black plaintiffs represented by black or Jewish lawyers, Irish cop defendants represented by Irish lawyers, and always some Irish jurors. And the defense naturally has a them-versus-us feeling going for it among those jurors who use the word *jew* as a verb and shudder at the sight and sound of black people. Here, however, was a civil rights case with every role typecast except that of plaintiffs' counsel, who was a smiling Irishman—not embarrassed to call his little firm O'Donnell, O'Donnell & O'Donnell—*and* an ex-cop. His Irishness was obvious enough, but his past as a BPD patrolman was not. And that's what we most wanted the jury to know about him. It would let him challenge the cops' credibility with the unique authority of someone who has worn the same badge, made arrests, handled guns, written reports, learned the rules and regulations. But he couldn't just come out on cross or in argument and say something like "I used to be a police officer and I can tell you . . ." The defense would object and ask for, and probably get, a mistrial on the grounds that the comment was unfairly harmful to the defendants. Before the trial we had been counting on the press's help here. We would tell the reporters covering the case that the old man is an ex-cop, they would print it, and the jurors—despite the judge's instructions to ignore newspaper accounts of the trial—would read it. Without the press, we were stuck . . . until the old man asked Denny to explain something about the Fabrique Nationale in terms understandable to "someone inexperienced like me."

In his one quick response on the stand, Denny smirked and said, "I thought you were a policeman, Mr. O'Donnell."

David Cohen grabbed the jury rail. Number six looked at me. I nodded. Pat asked, "What's he talking about?" She didn't know. Skinner's jaw dropped. He knew—it was common knowledge in the business—but he couldn't believe Denny had brought it up.

Even the old man fell back a step. In a fast recovery, he bellowed, "You said to me you thought I was a policeman once?! Of course! You knew I was, didn't you? You knew I was out at Station Fourteen, didn't you?"

Keefe and McKenna had no grounds to object to the colloquy, since their guy had started it.

"I heard about you," said Denny, blithely unaware of the damage he was doing.

Skinner tried to break it up: "We'll get away from that. It's of no particular consequence."

He was asking too much of the old man, who did not acknowledge the interruption. He started toward the jury, then walked back to the stand and picked up Denny's badge, which was still on the counter. "Having in mind this badge, you know I'm familiar with it and lived behind the badge!"

"Yes," said Denny.

Skinner held up both hands to stop the old man and cried, "Excuse me!"

The old man turned to the judge, who told the jury, "Mr. O'Donnell's familiarity with life behind the badge is not [relevant] in this case. You will disregard all of that." To the old man, he added angrily, "And you stay away from it!"

"I will, Your Honor."

The old man is nothing if not a man of his word. With judges anyway. Nearly delirious from this stunning coup only ten minutes into his cross, he sallied forth. The jury sat wide-eyed for the minute or two it took to digest what it had just heard. Even stone-faced number three, an elderly Irish gent, was noticeably surprised. I imagined Cohen telling himself that he should have guessed it. Denny's answers were scarcely going to matter now. The jury would be taking all its information from the questions from here on in. At least, that's how I read the looks the old man was getting.

"When you got down to that Buick at the Tobin School, you searched for any ballistics evidence that would be inside that Buick, didn't you, sir?"

"I looked for a gun."

"And you also looked for a discharged shell from an automatic?"

"I looked to see if it was there."

"And it wasn't."

"I didn't see it."

"It would [be] inside that car," the old man pointed out, if Bowden had fired the Fabrique Nationale.

"I would think that it would discharge into the car," said Denny.

"And [no one] in the entire Boston Police Department . . . ever found one?"

"No."

"About your being on Smith Street jumping out of the police car [the first time]. You left the door open?"

"I don't know."

"You just don't know?"

"I don't know."

"All right. We'll leave it like that."

The old man skipped over to Frank McGee: "He advised you . . . on the very night this happened at Station Two?"

"Yes."

Then to Denny's report: "You didn't approach making out this report in a casual way, did you?"

"I was not casual about it, no."

"You were very serious about it?"

"I was serious about it."

"That night, after consultation with your lawyer down at Station Two, you never said anything about Officer Monroe giving you that information."

"No, I didn't."

"Isn't that a recent contrivance you thought would help you on the stand, help bail you out?"

"No, sir."

With the time remaining before lunch, the Old Man reviewed the shooting. I had left an index card on the lectern which said:

Denny—1st Buick move backward.
Eddie—1st Buick move forward.
Denny—5 Buick moves.
Eddie—3 Buick moves.

The old man read it, winked a "Thanks," then forgot about it and asked his own questions.

"Having in mind your expertise in weapons and handling them, what provisions did you [and Holland] make so you wouldn't end up blowing one another's heads off?"

"That I would go up on the driver's side and he would go up on the passenger's side."

"So you didn't discuss it as a matter of tactics—'You go so far, and I'll go so far.' You never even talked about it. . . . One another's line of fire?"

"No, we didn't."

"You never saw him out in front of the car, did you?"

"I didn't notice him one way or the other."

"And you're taller than the car. You can look over any car. Incidentally, how tall are you?"

"Five nine."

The old man pointed to Eddie. "He's bigger than the car."

"He's taller than the car," Denny agreed.

"So, you were right there at the driver's window."

"Yes."

"And where is Eddie? Is he up there to the right with the headlights shining on him?"

"I don't know."

"What did [Bowden] do? You're out there with a gun in your hand; you yell like that—did he look out at you?"

"I don't recall. I believe he looked. Yes. The first time, he looked at me. Yes. . . . He turned and looked at me."

"I see. . . . And you're saying that after he'd seen you outside with a gun in your hand, he then *took his eyes off you* and backed up and hit Eddie Holland?"

"He backed up the car."

"You were [there] with your gun out, and . . . he then took his eyes away from you?"

"I didn't say he did that. I don't know."

"Well, you said he pointed a gun at Eddie Holland."

"At some later point. Yes."

"Do you think he took his eyes away from you?"

"At some point, yes."

"And so, as you describe it—two police officers, [guns] out like that—this man *stayed there* in that car, and tried hitting both of you?"

Denny didn't answer, and the old man didn't care. He beckoned Denny off the stand for a demonstration. He took Denny's old gun from the clerk and handed it to him. "Take this and show us how you held the gun with both hands."

The old man pulled out his chair again, sat on it, and said, "I'm behind the wheel. I'm on Smith Street."

Denny moved to the old man's left and stood about four feet from him, facing him.

"Now you're going to let go," said the old man. "Squeeze off two rounds on me."

"You want me to point this at you?"

"Sure. You won't hurt me."

"I had the gun in both hands like this," Denny explained. "And I brought the gun and pointed it like that, directly at the driver of the automobile." The gun was not more than two feet from the old man's head. "And I squeezed the trigger."

And, thinking who knows what, Denny did exactly that. The hammer hit the cylinder with a chilling metal-on-metal click. Cohen winced. Denny held his firing position. No one moved.

"Twice," the old man said softly.

"Twice," said Denny. And he did it again.

Skinner recessed for lunch.

At the start of the afternoon session, Skinner called a bench conference. "I'm thinking about my scheduling," he said. "How much longer on cross-examination?"

"I can wind up anytime, Your Honor," said the old man.

Skinner asked Tom McKenna: "What do you have for additional testimony?"

"I haven't discussed it with John at all."

"What I'm getting at," said Skinner, "is are we going to finish testimony today?"

"Would we argue tomorrow?" McKenna asked.

Skinner nodded. "If it was just going to be arguments and charge, I would start at ten o'clock."

"That would be terrific," said McKenna. "Nine o'clock is awful."

"There's nothing like seeing that sunrise." The old man beamed.

"I have a six-month-old that isn't sleeping during the night," Keefe said, without eliciting any sympathy.

"You think there's a reasonable chance you'll be able to finish with the evidence?" asked Skinner.

"We'll try," said McKenna.

"I'll have no rebuttal to speak of," said the old man.

Everyone was already walking away when Tom McKenna said, "When you say nobody to speak of?"

The old man ignored him.

The old man did another ninety minutes of cross with Denny. "You were on Gurney Street for roughly a half hour?"

"Yes."

"And during that half hour . . . maybe twenty-four cars turned from Parker Street into Smith Street?"

"No. . . . My best recollection is a couple of cars turning into Smith Street. . . . Two or three. Four maybe. Not many. Very few."

"All right."

Michael passed the old man Denny's deposition, open to a red-underlined page.

"Now, I show you this deposition . . . Mr. McKenna." After letting Denny read it, the old man read it to the jury: "Question: 'Well, would you estimate how many turned from Parker Street into Smith Street?' Answer: 'If I were to, I would estimate it. I don't think there were more than two dozen cars from the time we began the surveillance.'"

Turning back to Denny, the old man said, "So, you're going to *change* your testimony today and say to the jury: 'Two dozen cars turned from Parker Street into Smith Street.'"

"My best recollection *today* is that it was a few cars."

The old man pointed to the deposition: "That's testimony given under oath!"

"That's correct."

"And then the next question says—see that?—it says: 'Two dozen would be an outside figure?' Answer: 'I think so, yes.'"

The old man gave the deposition back to Michael and took up a leaning position on the jury rail. "Now, when did you last see [the Thunderbird]?"

"The last time that I was aware of it was when the man alighted from it when it stopped alongside the Buick."

"What did you see the Thunderbird do after the man alighted from it?"

"I don't know what the Thunderbird did."

"It's so, isn't it, you were the only person that got the number of the Thunderbird?"

"Yes. That's right."

"And that's something you never wrote down. . . . You had that committed to memory?"

"It was in my memory, yes."

"Because the Thunderbird made a particular impression on you?"

"At some point it did, yes."

"Well, it didn't do anything frisky going around from Parker to Smith, did it?"

"No. [But] it became very important to me when I saw somebody enter the Buick after alighting from the Thunderbird."

"Right. [But] you couldn't make out the [plate number] from that distance, could you?"

"No, I couldn't. . . . I recalled whatever observations I had made prior to it."

"But as it made that turn, it was just another car on the street making a turn?"

"Yes."

"Had all its lights on, drove nicely, obeyed the law?"

"It didn't do anything unusual."

"Now, you have utterly no knowledge of the Thunderbird on Smith Street when you ran up to the Buick and when you were shooting."

"I have no recollection of it at all."

"I now ask you: Did you see a man take a rifle out of the Thunderbird and shoot at Eddie Holland?"

"No, I did not."

"Did you hear the discharge of a shotgun behind you?"

"I did not hear—I was not aware of a—"

"Did Eddie yell at you: 'Denny, watch out! There's a fella with a rifle!'?"

"I didn't hear Eddie say anything at that time."

"Now, it was down at the crash [scene that] you gave Eddie the number of the Thunderbird?"

"Yes."

"Isn't it a fact that it was Molloy and Dwyer that picked up the number of the Thunderbird?"

"Molloy and Dwyer got the information of the number of the Thunderbird from me."

"And you know Mr. Holland . . . got a complaint against Winbush for assault with intent to murder, the next day?"

"I heard that."

"And you knew that day in court—Mr. Holland and you discussed it—you had absolutely no case against Winbush."

"If we didn't have a case against Mr. Winbush, I don't think Edward Holland would have sought the complaint."

"I see. . . . Incidentally, you're a union representative; you're an expert about guns; you know the Boston Police Department rule governing the use of firearms."

"I have a good understanding of it, I think. Yes."

"All right."

The old man got the rule from Michael and read portions of it: "'Deadly force is that degree of force likely to result in death. . . . The law permits police officers to use physical force . . . but only to the degree required to overcome unlawful resistance. . . . The discharge of a firearm under street conditions by a member of the Department is permissible only when there is no less drastic means available to defend himself or another from an unlawful attack which he has reasonable cause to believe could result in death or great bodily injury. . . . Under no circumstances shall members of the Department apply deadly force to effect an arrest on *mere suspicion* that a crime has been committed or that a particular person has committed a crime."

The old man offered the deadly force rule as an exhibit. Keefe objected and asked for a bench conference. At the side bar he said, "Your Honor, the witness hasn't shown any capacity to know what the rules were."

"Didn't he say he was familiar with it?" Skinner asked.

"Yes," said the old man.

"I presume they were sent to him," said Skinner.

"I don't think we can presume that, Your Honor," said Tom McKenna.

Denny could hear all this a few feet away on the stand, so he knew what to say when Skinner asked him: "Were you familiar with this set of rules that has just been read to you, as of January 1975?"

"I don't know that I was familiar with that particular rule, at that time, sir."

"Your Honor," said the old man, "we have a man [under subpoena] from the commissioner's office, who will come right in here and say that that's the rule."

"Then it's excluded for the time being," said Skinner. "I'll find out whether [Officer McKenna] was responsible to know about it."

I told Bill to call George Haskell, a detective assigned to the commissioner's staff, and have him get to the courthouse immediately. Haskell was out in the hall before Denny left the stand.

The old man dropped the rule on the plaintiffs' table and changed the subject.

"During the tour of duty you had various radio communications and you wrote them down."

"I don't recall writing down anything."

"Did you see Eddie Holland ever write anything down?"

"No, I have no recollection of him writing anything down."

Voice rising: "Now, Mr. McKenna, did Edward Holland write down matters concerning the robbery?"

"I don't recall if he did or he didn't."

"Did he have something to write with or some kind of paper?"

"I don't know."

Michael held out the Geagan interview open to the relevant page. At the sight of it, Keefe objected and asked for a bench conference. At the side bar, Tom McKenna insisted that the old man couldn't use the Geagan interview against Denny because "it wasn't done under oath."

Skinner's reply closed the matter even before Michael reached the side bar. He looked at McKenna and said, "Nonsense."

The old man went to Denny's side, held the transcript so they both could read it, and said, "Now, you were asked a question by Sergeant Geagan: Q. 'Do you know if the number was written down at the time it was given out on the radio that afternoon?'

"A. 'We wrote down this number . . . 4-Frank-6838 [Bowden's number].'

"Q. 'Did you personally write it down or did your partner write it down?'

"A. 'Eddie Holland wrote it down and I believe I also wrote it down. . . .'

"Q. 'You don't happen to still have the paper you wrote it down on?'

"A. 'I don't know. I haven't been able to locate it, so I can't honestly say that I have it. I might have it. . . . I know that [Eddie] checked [the Buick's number] with the paper that he had.'"

The old man stopped reading, and Denny said, "That's the statement I made at that time."

The old man started reading again. "Q. 'Why did you remember the number of the T-Bird?'

"A. 'I can't honestly say why I remembered it, but I did remember the number.'"

The old man then asked, "Did Eddie Holland ever tell you, after . . . the car crash, that he was okay?"

"He may have."

Reading again: "A. '. . . I asked Eddie Holland if he was all right, and he responded that he was okay. . . .'"

The old man dropped the interview transcript on the stand, took a deep breath, and said, "Mr. McKenna, insofar as 841A is concerned, it's so, isn't it, that the three cars were—you were 841, Molloy and Dwyer were 842, and over at Station Street was 843?"

"No, sir. That's not true."

"So, who do you say was 841?"

"Molloy and Dwyer."

Taking a piece of paper from the clerk: "And plaintiffs' exhibit

23F shows that 841 called [the turret] about 4F•6368 about six-thirty. . . ."

"The call that was logged by Mullen that you have on that document, yes, I don't quarrel with that," said Denny.

"Can you tell the court and jury where Molloy and Dwyer got [that] number?"

"Where they got the number?"

"Yes."

"I don't know where they got the number."

The old man gave the Mullen report back to the clerk, and, hands in his pockets, he took little steps around the room. "Was it necessary to fire the third shot [after] you got [him] at close range?"

"I fired at him because I wanted to stop him. I regarded him as a threat to the safety of Officers Molloy and Dwyer at the end of the street."

"All right. . . . Now . . . did you see a Spanish man rifle through the glove compartment of the Buick?"

"No."

"Now, you never saw the trunk of the Bowden car opened."

"I don't recall one way or the other."

The old man brought Ken Kobre's pictures to the stand. "I show you the plaintiffs' exhibit number one-nineteen. Does that show the Buick?"

"Yes."

"Is the trunk opened?"

"No."

"Plaintiffs' exhibit one-twenty. Trunk closed?"

"Yes."

"Plaintiffs' exhibit one-twenty-eight. Trunk closed?"

"Yes."

"It's so, isn't it, Mr. McKenna, you *never* saw that trunk open?"

"I don't recall if I did or I didn't."

The old man took the center of the floor for his final series. "Mr. McKenna, you had a David O'Brian in the back seat?"

"Yes."

"You found him a personable man?"

"He was all right."

"And you had a conversation with him after the car crashed at the Tobin School."

"I don't recall."

"Do you recall him asking you: 'Did you get hit?' And you said, 'No. It's his blood. As soon as he turned the wheel, I said, "Fuck him" '?"

Denny locked into a long pause, and the old man yelled, "Do you recall *that* conversation?"

"No, sir."

Still yelling: "So, your testimony is you don't recall it?"

"That's my testimony."

Even louder: "Your testimony is *not*, 'I never said it! It's false!' You say, 'I don't recall it'!"

"Objection," said Keefe.

"Wait a minute!" Skinner shouted into the microphone. Then he said very calmly—no doubt hoping his manner would be contagious—"The objection to that question, in that *form*, is sustained."

The old man kicked the carpet, turned to Denny, and in a low roar said: "That's the way you're gonna leave it with this court and jury! *You just don't recall!*"

"That's right," said Denny.

Keefe had no redirect.

Denny left the stand at 3:25 P.M. and stayed out in the hall for the remaining ninety minutes of the defense case.

Keefe surprised us by calling Henry Smith as his next witness.

"Wasn't this witness here before?" asked Skinner, and the old man said yes.

Keefe asked Smith whether he had any records "concerning the employment of Donald Shaw in January of 1975?"

Smith said yes, and Skinner asked Keefe: "Donald Shaw, did you say?"

"Yes, Your Honor," said Keefe.

"Tell me what this is all about," said Skinner, waving the lawyers into a bench conference.

"What is relevant about this?" he asked at the side bar.

Keefe replied, "Elsie Pina . . . testified that she saw Bowden at two-thirty that afternoon. The reason she recalls it was that afternoon was because James Bowden was taking the place of Donald Shaw. I propose to show Donald Shaw was working that day."

Skinner nodded and returned to the center of the bench.

Through Smith, Keefe introduced the City of Boston's 1975 payroll record for Donald Shaw. It indicated that Shaw was at work on January 29, 1975. The City had no time card to support the summary sheet.

The old man did not cross-examine. Later, when we were going over what we wanted in the final argument, he asked me, "What was that Donald Shaw thing all about?"

"They think it impeached Elsie Pina because she said he was out sick that day. But even if Shaw was at work, James could've still worked for Pina. Donald Webster says he did. It's nothing. Forget it."

Henry Smith left the room, and Keefe and Tom McKenna conferred—apparently on what to do next. Now they had Dwyer, Molloy, Harry Byrne, and a fourth cop we didn't recognize waiting outside. Frank MacDonald had left. Skinner waited impatiently. He was still hoping to finish the testimony today. Soon he said, "Next witness."

Keefe looked up and said, "May we approach the bench?"

"Yes," said Skinner.

Keefe began the bench conference by saying: "Your Honor, the first day of trial . . . the Fabrique gun . . . was offered, and I'd like at this time to offer the gun in evidence."

"I don't think [it is] tied in yet."

"Your Honor," Keefe said, "there is testimony to show: There is a shooting [on] Smith Street; the car goes down the street; the officers don't see the continuity of the car; there is a crash; it's dark out, the police investigate and find a gun there. . . . It certainly is relevant!"

"But," said Skinner, "you don't explain to me how a man who has a gun in his right hand, [and] has been shot three times, manages to get it through the window to the left and all the way across the street."

"How do you explain how he drives up the street?" Keefe countered.

"He falls forward on the accelerator," said Skinner.

"He didn't," said McKenna. "Your foot relaxes when you're dead."

"I've never been dead," Skinner replied, "so I don't know."

Keefe protested. "I don't think it's fair to my clients not to introduce the gun."

"You have to tie it in," said Skinner. "I don't see how you tied it in to that car. It wasn't found until what? An hour later?"

"Eight-fifteen," said the old man. "An hour and forty-five minutes."

"There is no other evidence that we can present to tie the gun in," said McKenna.

Keefe gave up, admitting: "We can't prove how it got there, Your Honor."

Tom McKenna hung on, though. With a nod toward the jury, he said, "They've already seen the gun, Your Honor. They are going to wonder why it isn't in there." (All exhibits go into the jury room during deliberations.)

"I'll tell them," said Skinner. "There's no problem about that. I will instruct them to disregard the gun because it hasn't been tied in to the occupant of this car."

"That's the court's way of telling the jury he didn't have a gun!" said McKenna.

Skinner did not reply.

"What did he shoot with?" McKenna asked contentiously.

"It may well be," said Skinner coolly, "he didn't shoot with anything."

Michael spurred him on, saying softly, "It was not found at the shooting scene."

Skinner nodded and said, "[Officer McKenna] says [Bowden] slumped forward. He already has all these slugs in him." Turning to Tom McKenna, he asked incredulously, "You mean to say that we are to infer that he took the gun that he had in his right hand and managed to fling it across here?" Skinner swung his right arm across his chest.

McKenna replied with a theory that got Michael and the old man chuckling, but did not amuse or impress Skinner: "It just flew out of his hand. Maybe he tried to grab the steering wheel and it flew out the window. Very strange things happen in life, Your Honor."

"Yes, indeed," said Skinner. "But when they are beyond the ordinary, they have to be proven by positive evidence."

"In a situation like this," McKenna averred, "there is no such thing as ordinary."

"I don't think it's a proper inference," said Skinner. "How did [the gun] get from here to there?"

Keefe came back in with a party: "How did the car get from here to there?"

"That's easy enough," said Skinner. "If it were in gear and the guy had his foot on the accelerator or the weight of his leg goes on the accelerator, off it goes. . . . And that seems perfectly logical and clear."

"Aren't these things the jury should sort out?" asked McKenna.

"You just don't shuffle everything over [to the jury]," said Skinner wearily. "That's the purpose of the rules of evidence. . . . I have *some* function."

McKenna had been growing ever more excited. Now he exclaimed, "*Both officers* testified they heard or saw a gun!"

Citing Eddie's and Denny's testimony as a credible link between Bowden and the gun was apparently more than Skinner could bear. "They saw and heard each other's guns," he snapped. "That's what happened."

"I don't think that's the case," said McKenna.

"They managed to incite one another," said Skinner, "perhaps accidentally, perhaps not, but that's what I think happened."

That knocked McKenna into a moment of silence. Then he said, "If the jury wants to find against our clients, fine. But we have to be able to present a case!"

"Nothing matches up in your story," said Skinner. "Nothing that ties this gun to this man."

That sounded like the final word.

McKenna was despondent. "This is very damaging, Your Honor, to our case."

Skinner suddenly softened. "Maybe I'm holding too strict a standard."

That brought the old man to life. He stressed that Eddie and Denny, "two trained men in an excellent position to observe" a gun flying out of the car, saw "nothing coming out of the car."

"Oh, yes," said Skinner.

Both Keefe and McKenna started again. Skinner seemed not to be listening. Eventually he cut them off. "I guess," he said slowly, "here there are really only two possibilities, and . . . by excluding it, I'm in effect assuming one—that it was a plant. . . . I don't think I'm entitled to make that assumption." He paused and said to Keefe, "I guess I will allow your motion."

Keefe thanked him effusively, and he and McKenna walked back to the defense table looking not so much triumphant as relieved.

Skinner told the jury that the Fabrique Nationale was now "admitted as evidence in the case."

The old man smiled at the news as if it didn't matter. But Michael's face belied the old man's calm. Later, Michael said, "That fuckin' gun can kill us."

Keefe called George Hoey. Michael and I remembered the name from Sergeant McHale's list of cops who showed up on Smith Street. He was the police photographer on the scene that night. He had sixteen photographs of the crashed Buick, the spot where the shooting occurred, and the Fabrique Nationale on the pavement. None of them showed any people. Keefe started the routine introductory questions for admitting photographs, and Skinner cut in to ask the old man if he had an objection to the pictures, which added nothing to the Kobre rendition of the scene.

"None whatsoever," he replied.

"All right. They are admitted."

"May I show them to the jury?" Keefe asked.

"They'll be seeing them very shortly, I think," said Skinner, meaning they would be deliberating very shortly.

The old man asked George Hoey only two questions. "What time did you arrive there?"

"Seven-forty-five P.M., sir."

"So, these pictures—like the gun under the car—they were taken *after* seven-forty-five?"

"Yes, sir. They were."

The old man sat down, and Skinner told Hoey, "You are excused."

There was another point worth raising with Sergeant Hoey, but none of us thought of it that day. It was years later, on a sweltering summer afternoon in Hoey's air-conditioned Charlestown dining room, that I asked him who told him what to photograph that night. He said Harry Byrne did. I asked whether he remembered Byrne or anyone else mentioning any tire tracks that he should photograph. "If anyone did," he said, "I would have." He had photographed tire tracks countless times before, he said. When I asked whether Joe Jordan or any of the deputies and captains on the scene mentioned something that should be photographed, he laughed at the thought. "They were just interested bystanders," he said. "When you have a homicide or a shooting like this or whatever you want to call it, nobody wants to get involved. Nobody wants to touch it."

"Do you have another witness?" Skinner asked.

"Yes, Your Honor," Keefe replied. "I have several more."

He had two more: Mark Molloy and Harry Byrne.

At 4:03 P.M., Molloy took the stand wearing dark slacks and a tight brown V-neck sweater—no jacket, no shirt, no tie, and now no beard. He sailed through direct examination in seven minutes.

Molloy: "About six o'clock we received a radio call from the 841A unit informing us they had a motor vehicle under observation that was used earlier in the day in a holdup in Cambridge."

"We told them we'd go to the . . . circular driveway . . . at Seventy-five St. Alphonsus . . . about seventy-five feet [from the end of Smith Street].

"We called back . . . and asked them for the description of the motor vehicle. They gave it to us as a light-blue Buick with a black top—black vinyl, I believe—Mass. registration 4F•6838 [Bowden's number]. With that I went over to Channel One and asked the dispatcher to verify it, which he did.

"A short while later a transmission came over the air. Said a black male was approaching the vehicle. 'Suspect getting into the vehicle.' . . . We went to Smith Street. . . . As we were pulling in, a call came in: 'Stop the T-Bird. Stop the T-Bird.' "

Keefe: "At this time, what did you do?"

Molloy: "I got out of the car. My partner pulled right into Smith Street, put the high beams on, and got out of the car. A short while later, a little transmission came over: 'Get us an ambulance at the Tobin School.' "

"I began jogging down Smith Street towards the school. . . . I was looking in the separate courtyards for the T-Bird. No T-Bird came down to us.

"I went to the Tobin School. And up on the wall, resting on the fence, was the Buick. . . . Officer McKenna was beside the door. Officer Holland asked me if we got the T-Bird. I said no. With that, I walked back down Smith towards St. Alphonsus, looking for it.

"At the end of the Tobin School I observed the driveway leading up into a park. With that, I walked up into it and the tire tracks there and followed it up onto Tremont Street."

"How far up did you go, Officer?"

"All the way out to Tremont Street."

"What did you observe as you were going up?"

"Tire tracks."

"No further questions."

"Now, on May 12, 1977, you were in my office, under oath, and you gave a deposition, right?" There was the usual jarring volume change in the sudden switch from Keefe to the old man.

"Yes, I did." Molloy turned quieter. His neck sank into his shoulders and he leaned his face on his left hand.

The old man put the deposition on the stand. "On page twenty-four, line twenty-two: Q. 'What was the number of your car, incidentally?' A. 'I think 842. I'm not sure of that.' That's what you said?"

"I think."

"Well, you said it *under oath!*"

"I said I think it's the 842. I'm not sure on that. Either 842 or 843."

"Now, when you gave this testimony that you've just given about tire tracks . . . In front of this court and jury you're not suggesting that you looked up there and found some tracks of a car?" The old man was at the model now with his pointer.

"Just that, yes," said Molloy.

"That is what you want them to understand?"

"That is what I want them to understand."

"You're friends with Eddie Holland and Denny McKenna?"

"Yes."

"You feel that will help them?"

"Do I feel that will help them?"

"You want to help them."

"Yes. Of course I want to help them."

"When you wrote to your captain . . . on January 29, 1975, did you tell him about the tracks?"

"I surely did."

The old man took Molloy's report from Michael's hand and put it in front of Molloy, saying, "Is it in there?"

Molloy read his report and softly said, "No, it's not."

"Well, that's *your* report! You told me you surely did! It's not part of your report!"

"No, it's not."

"All right . . . Now . . . you were taking down and writing down numbers [during the stakeout]?"

"Not necessarily, no."

"Well, you had a pencil with you?"

"Yes."

"And you—when you're up at St. Alphonsus Street—never saw the number of the Buick?"

"No, sir."

"Where did you get that?"

"From Holland and McKenna."

"Did you call in and check it?"

"Yes."

This led the old man back to what had become an obsession. "Mr. Molloy, isn't it a fact that the units were 841, 842, and 843?"

"I believe it was 841, 841A, and 842."

"Take your hands away from your mouth," said the old man. "What you heard over the radio was Bowden's number, 4F•6838?"

"Yes, sir."

Skinner cut in. "Well, now, the turret report, Mr. Mullen's report, says it's 4F•6368 that was called in. Does that refresh your recollection with respect to the number that was called in?"

"Your Honor, the only number I know I called in or I recall that I called in is 4F•6838."

"Did you have any notes when you made that report?" Skinner asked.

"No, sir."

"I see," said Skinner. "When you made up the report that you have before you, what did you rely on for the number that you say you called in?"

"Talking to my partner."

"Did you talk to Mr. Holland and Mr. McKenna?"

"No, sir."

Skinner gave Molloy back to the old man. Torn between wanting to please Skinner by finishing quickly and wanting to keep swinging at Molloy, he raced through his remaining questions in a frenzy that disconcerted Molloy.

"You're lying under oath; that's so, isn't it, Mr. Molloy?"

"I doubt that."

"Did you sit down with Dennis McKenna and Edward Holland before you took this witness stand?"

"Did I sit down with them?"

"Did you talk to them?"

"Surely."

"Did you talk about what you were going to tell this jury under oath?"

"No."

"And when you went up to the tracks, you were out looking for the Thunderbird, weren't you?"

"Yes, sir."

"And you had a conversation with Holland?"

"Just briefly."

"Did he say, 'The fella in the Thunderbird shot at me!'?"

"Nope."

"Who came up—and it's just a gimmick, isn't it? This idea of making an 841A. That's designed deliberately—and you're in on it—to deceive anyone that wants to see this report by Mullen showing that 841 called in and asked for 4F•6368?"

"No."

The old man pointed to Eddie and Denny. "And didn't they say something to the effect: 'Mark, we'll beat it. Stick with the number. Otherwise, we're in dead serious trouble!' Didn't they say that to you?"

"Objection, Your Honor!"

"Sustained."

"Mr. Molloy, what I'm asking you: You are under oath. Did you get together and plan to lie about the number in order to help Holland. I'm talking about—Did you—Molloy, Dwyer, Defendant Holland, and Defendant McKenna—get together on the night of January 29, after the killing, and plan to lie about the number that went in to the dispatcher?"

"Objection, Your Honor!"

"Overruled."

"No," said Molloy. "I did not. At no time."

"That's all."

With Molloy headed for the door, John Keefe and Tom McKenna went into another of their whispered strategy sessions.

Skinner gave them a minute, then asked, "Any more witnesses?"
Keefe called Harry Byrne.

His story took five minutes to tell on direct: "At about a little after six P.M., while I was in the TPF office, a call came in
from . . . the 841A unit. That was Officer McKenna and Officer Holland. . . . They had a car that was used in a holdup in
Cambridge . . . and they wanted the number checked.

"It was checked, and it was called back that that was the car
used in the robbery.

"During roll call, a call came in there was a shooting in Roxbury; the unit in Roxbury needed some help. We went from roll
call out to Smith Street.

"When I got to the scene . . . Officer McKenna and Officer
Holland were there with other officers, and they told me the story
of what happened.

"Officer Holland said they had already searched the car, and
there was no weapon in the car. I called for the Emergency Services Unit to come out with some light, so we could make a search
of the area.

"Sometime later, the gun was found."

Keefe: "Did you have a conversation with Officer Molloy?"

Byrne: "Yes, I did."

Keefe: "As a result of that conversation, what did you do?"

Byrne: "I went down Smith Street by the Tobin School and
looked up toward Tremont Street. . . . I saw in the mud, going up
toward Tremont Street, car marks. Tire marks."

Keefe: "Did you have occasion to walk up there at that time?"

"No, sir, I did not. . . . I went back there the next day . . . and
went up that alleyway up to Tremont Street just to see the direction the car was supposed to have gone."

"Thank you," said Keefe.

I put an index card on the lectern. It said:

BYRNE was at Winbush hearing.
Did not testify.
Q—Why didn't he testify re: *tire tracks*?

O'CONNOR & MOLLOY did testify at Rox. Ct.

Both said *nothing* re: *tire tracks*.

Q—Why didn't BYRNE tell SCHROEDER of *tire tracks*? NO
 TIRE TRACKS IN ANY *reports*.

Unfortunately, the old man didn't come near the lectern this time. He stayed between the model and the stand for a seven-minute cross examination.

Tracing a route on the model, he asked, "Sergeant Byrne, did you say you *drove* all the way up there?"

"Yes, sir."

"What did you run into when you got up this way?"

"We didn't run into anything, sir."

"How about steps?" The old man was pointing to the tiny steps on the model.

"No."

"Did you take some pictures [of the tracks]? You had a photographer there that night."

"No."

"Were you in the Roxbury Court when Winbush was being prosecuted?"

"Yes, sir."

"Did you hear Officer Holland in the Roxbury Court say he couldn't identify Winbush?"

"Yes, sir."

"And isn't it so that [when] Winbush was brought into District Two, Holland identified him that night?"

"I don't know, sir."

The old man took two quick steps toward Michael to grab the paper being thrust at him, and came back asking: "Now, in regard to all this, you had an interview with Deputy Francis B. Schroeder on February 26, 1975?"

"Yes, sir."

"And here you are answering Deputy Schroeder: 'He was brought into District Two, and he was identified by Patrolman Holland, to the best of my recollection, as the operator of that car.'

Now, *that's true!* And that's what you said to Deputy Schroeder at that time!"

Byrne paused and said, "Yes."

"That's all."

John Keefe and Tom McKenna huddled as Byrne left the room. In a few seconds, Keefe asked for permission to approach the bench "for a minute."

"All right," said Skinner with an eye on the clock. It was 4:45 P.M. We were probably the only people left in the building.

Tom McKenna excitedly led off the bench conference. "We found that there is a doctor's report, an examination that he took when he went to work for the City."

"Who?" asked Skinner.

"Mr. Bowden," said McKenna. "It's listed in this medical examination. His height was five foot *six* and one half!"

McKenna handed a piece of paper to Skinner, who glanced at it and passed it to the old man. It was a physical examination form filled out in 1967 when Bowden landed his job. We had never seen it. His weight was listed as 190 pounds, and in a markedly different handwriting from the rest of the notations, his height was listed as 5 feet 6½. The old man looked at the physician's signature, recognized it, and said, "That doctor hasn't been sober for the last forty years."

Skinner thought that the two-inch height difference, even if true, couldn't mean that Bowden was anything but short and fat.

McKenna thought the two inches were enough to make Ethel and Desi's ID credible. He had a theory to explain how Bowden could have been fat in 1967 and thin in 1975: People lose weight as they age. "I weigh less than I weighed eight years ago," he claimed.

Keefe—of all people—said to him: "You are unusual."

"I'm not going to change my view," said Skinner. "I've made a ruling on this. Right or wrong, I've made it, and I'll stick with it. I think I'm right."

He called a five-minute recess.

I checked the hall for potential defense witnesses. Only Billy

Dwyer was still there. I reported to Michael and the old man that Keefe had only Dwyer left.

"Are they crazy enough to give me a shot at Dwyer?" the old man asked, hoping we'd say yes. We did.

"Oh, I hope so," he said. "Let me see that picture of him laughing."

The jury started to file in. I hurried back to the spectators' section.

As soon as Skinner was seated, Keefe rose to say, "Your Honor, the defense rests."

Skinner nodded, and to the old man said, "Rebuttal?"

"I have a rebuttal witness, all right." Turning to the jury, he smiled and said, "Ernest Winbush."

Winbush had arrived during the recess. He had spent the afternoon at the office—waiting. He made the walk to the courthouse surrounded by Bill, Kevin, Kim Bonstrom, and an armed private detective. Of course, Winbush didn't need bodyguards—the cops wouldn't have tried anything at this point—but Winbush wasn't so sure of that, and the old man wanted to show him that he was serious about protecting him. At Winbush's pace, walking the three hundred yards to the courthouse took fifteen minutes. It was five o'clock when the marshal swung the door open for him. Everyone studied him on his way to the stand. Even the stenographer turned to get a good look at him. He wore a light-blue suit without a tie. He was a thin, stooped man who seemed slowed by age.

"Kindly state your name," the old man began.

"Ernest Winbush." He spoke softly but stayed close to the microphone, so his voice carried well in the hushed room.

"Are you married or single?"

"Married."

"How old are you?"

"Thirty-four."

"At some time, Mr. Winbush, did you have a medical procedure involving your kidney?"

"Yes. Around 1972. . . . I went to the hospital, and they discovered I had a kidney ailment. . . . I had a transplant, but it didn't work."

"And on January 29, 1975 . . . did you receive some treatment?"

"Yes. . . . dialysis treatment."

"And that's where—do they inject something into you?"

"They inject two needles into you, and your blood goes out through the tubes and into the machine. The machine is like a washing machine and purifies your blood and brings it back to your body."

Skinner interjected: "That's what your kidney would otherwise do for you."

"Right," said Winbush.

"How long were you on the machine that day?" asked the old man.

"Well, that day I went for five hours. They've cut it down to four hours now."

"Did you have occasion to meet James Bowden [that day]?"

"Yes."

"Around what time?"

"Around six, six-thirty. I was on my way to a school meeting in Brighton. The Edison Middle School. My wife was going to go with me, but she decided to stay home that particular night. She wasn't feeling very well."

"Did you give Bowden a ride in your car that night?"

"Yes."

In his haste, the old man forgot to ask Winbush how and where he happened to meet Bowden that night.

"Did you drive into Smith Street?"

"Yes."

"Did you drop him off in front of his own car?"

"Yes, I did."

"After you dropped him off, where did you go?"

"I went up Smith Street to St. Alphonsus, from St. Alphonsus to Tremont Street . . . to a gas station there. It was called Fill Up Fast. . . . And from there to the PTA meeting."

"While you were on Smith Street, right after you dropped off James Bowden, did you take a rifle and shoot at a man in the vicinity of the Buick?"

"No."

The old man sat down.

When Tom McKenna finished whispering to him, Keefe went to the lectern and began cross-examination with a trick.

"Mr. Winbush, didn't you tell the police officers you didn't know James Bowden?"

"I didn't know James Bowden," Winbush replied. "I only knew him by seeing him in the project. . . . His mother lived in the same building where my wife's aunt lived. And I knew his mother, but I didn't actually *know* him."

"Didn't you tell the police officers you didn't give him a ride that night?"

"No, I didn't," said Winbush after a pause. He appeared uncertain now of what he did tell the police.

I realized that at the recess I should have reminded him of O'Connor's version of their conversation, which he had heard once at the Roxbury Court three years ago. We had spent the recess getting ready for Dwyer, and none of us—not the old man nor Michael nor I—had spoken to Winbush. The old man's report on Winbush was that he was going to be a solid witness. But now we knew that the one thing we should have reviewed with him was his conversation with O'Connor.

Keefe stayed with it, and in a minute his trick worked.

"Didn't you tell them that you didn't let anyone use your car that night?"

"No one was using my car. I had the car myself."

"Were you trying to make them think that you weren't with Bowden that night?"

"Well, I was so mixed up when they arrested me—and I knew I hadn't done anything wrong—that I probably told them that."

Skinner interrupted. "When were you asked about whether Mr. Bowden was in your car?"

"When I was arrested. I wasn't told anything except—they

started questioning me: Where was I during the night? Did I go up Smith Street? I went up Smith Street, but I didn't know what I was being held for or questioned for."

"All right," said Skinner—sympathetically, I thought.

"Where did you get Bowden?" asked Keefe.

Winbush pointed to the model. "Outside the store there on Parker Street."

"What's the name of that store?"

"Paul's Market."

"Would you tell us about the bullets in your pocket?"

"I don't know anything about the bullets."

"Did you have them when you were driving your car?"

"No."

"How did the bullets get in your pocket?"

"Well, I don't know," said Winbush facetiously. "I didn't have any."

Keefe checked his notes, looked at Winbush, checked his notes again, went to the defense table, talked to Tom McKenna, and sat down.

Skinner asked, "Do you own a gun, Mr. Winbush?"

"No, I don't."

And Winbush was finished. He carefully stepped off the stand and shuffled to the door, looking not a bit like the assault-with-intent-to-murder type. The old man stood and watched him go, adding to the import of the moment. The marshal held the door for him, and Winbush disappeared into the hall.

It was 5:15 P.M.

"Anything further?" Skinner asked the old man.

"Yes. George Haskell. This is on Rule 303, the deadly force rule."

"All right."

Haskell was a three-minute witness.

Name.

Address.

Occupation.

"In response to a subpoena from me, did you bring in the rule governing the use of deadly force in the Boston Police Department?"

"Yes, sir."

"And the one you've got there—was it in effect on January 29, 1975?"

"Yes, sir."

"I'm going to offer it, Your Honor."

"No objections, Your Honor," said Keefe.

"Plaintiffs' exhibit one-fifty-seven is in evidence," said Skinner.

"That's all," said the old man.

"Tell me, Mr. Haskell," said Skinner, "what is the method for distributing these rules to the men on patrol?"

"This is distributed through general orders, sir. It's distributed throughout the Department."

"Does everybody get a copy of it?"

"Everybody has a copy."

"Is it the duty of each police officer to be familiar with the rules and regulations, Mr. Haskell?"

"Yes, Your Honor."

Haskell left, and the old man offered as an exhibit "a certified copy of the U.S. Weather Service report for January 29, 1975." It was corroboration of Jessina's testimony that it was warm enough for her to be at her window that night. Keefe didn't object. Skinner admitted it. Then the old man said, "And the plaintiffs rest their rebuttal case."

"Any surrebuttal, Mr. Keefe?" asked Skinner.

"May we approach the bench, Your Honor?" asked Keefe.

Skinner said nothing and moved to the side bar. McKenna started the bench conference by saying, "We had not anticipated this witness—Winbush."

Skinner smiled. "I was wondering where Winbush was all the time."

Keefe said, "I would like to have the opportunity tomorrow morning, Your Honor, to put on a rebuttal witness to Winbush."

"Like whom?"

"I have, Your Honor, the officers that were with Winbush in the car. With respect to his conversation with them."

"You already had that guy on."

"There were two other people in the car," said McKenna.

"You tell me what they're going to add," said Skinner.

"I really don't know," said Keefe.

"Could we check their depositions?" McKenna begged.

"Check them right now," said Skinner. "Hurry up."

McKenna ran to the defense table, pulled out the Sullivan, Keegan, and Foley depositions, flipped through them for two minutes, and returned to the bench empty-handed.

"You put O'Connor on," Skinner told him. "Now they've rebutted that, and all you want is to repeat what was said before."

"We'll withdraw the request," said McKenna.

The bench conference broke up, and Skinner turned to the jury to announce: "The evidence is completed. Closed. And what is left in the case is the arguments of counsel and the court's instructions.

"I hope we can start the arguments at ten-fifteen." With a glance to Keefe and the old man, he said, "You can have forty minutes apiece." Turning back to the jury: "I expect you will get the case for deliberation some time late tomorrow morning.

"Until that time, the court is in adjournment."

I told Pat not to bring Eurina and Jamil to court the next day.

CHAPTER 20

I spent the night at the old man's house. The plan was for me to pump him up with information for the argument. But he fell asleep on the couch at eight-thirty—about ten minutes after we walked in the door. I spread my notes out on the living room floor, and while he snored I wrote one-liners on index cards.

It must have been well after midnight when I fell asleep. My mother found me sprawled on the floor at seven.

"Where's the old man?" I asked.

"He's in the shower. He's been awake since three."

My notes and cards were exactly where I had left them.

Soon the old man came bouncing down the stairs—tie tied, vest buttoned, hair combed—carrying a couple of old sport coats.

"Hey, I found these in the attic," he said. "What do you think? Will they fit you? Try them on. They've gotta be twenty-five years old, the both of them."

One was a blue-gray cashmere. It fit. I took it. The other was a Harris tweed. It was too big, but I took it. It seemed that nothing could have made him happier.

He pulled a handful of cards out of his pocket, gave them to me, and said, "Tell me which ones I should use." There were eighteen cards. On each, in his surprisingly careful handwriting, was a line by Shakespeare, Abraham Lincoln, Plato, William Butler Yeats, or another of a flock of sages.

"You don't need these guys," I said. "You need evidence." And I handed him my cards.

"No, come on now. I wanna use some of them. I know I can't use them all."

I gave him the Byron and one of the Daniel Websters. He wanted more, but I was adamant.

He studied all the cards as we crawled along the Southeast Expressway and, at some point, said, "How the hell did I ever try cases alone?"

On the elevator in the parking garage, he started doing that little dance that boxers do before coming out of their corners. It suddenly occurred to me that the one athletic thing he ever tried to teach me was how to hit a punching bag—the speed bag. He could make it go like a propeller. Still can. I never caught on.

"It's the case of a lifetime," he said. "I mean it's the case of *my* lifetime. . . . I mean I've lived my whole goddamn life for this case. . . . I mean . . . You know what I mean?"

Kevin showed up for the arguments, as did my mother, who hadn't been in a courtroom since the Brink's case.

On Eddie and Denny's bench were two reporters assigned to the Federal Court—one from the *Globe* and one from the *Herald*. Word had spread through the building that the O'Donnells—of all people—were putting on a pretty good civil rights case against a couple of cops and actually had a chance of winning.

Eddie and Denny were inexplicably absent—not out in the hall either—when Skinner entered at 10:10 A.M. And they didn't arrive during the ensuing half-hour bench conference that Skinner convened to discuss points of law he wanted to mention in his charge to the jury.

At 10:40 A.M. Skinner had the marshal bring in the jurors.

The old man did not look at them.

Skinner apologized for the delay and for the temperature of the courtroom. "We're back in our freeze-and-fry sequence of heating in this room," he said, "and it got pretty hot." I hadn't noticed. "I've opened this window, here. . . . If that's uncomfortable or drafty for anyone, let me know." No one complained.

"Now," he said, "we're at the point where the lawyers have a right to argue as to the version of the facts that you should accept, the testimony that you should believe or reject, and the conclusions which you should draw from the evidence. And to the extent it differs from your recollection of the evidence, you should disregard it, because it is your memory of the evidence that governs. . . . And that is true with respect to the remarks that I may make later on, if I talk about the evidence. . . .

"Pay attention to the lawyers. They have studied the case. They've lived with it and will undoubtedly be helpful to you in reviewing the evidence. . . . So, I urge you to pay careful attention to what they say. . . .

"The defendants go first. . . . Mr. Keefe, are you ready?"

"Yes, Your Honor."

Forcing the defense to argue first is a procedure that courts instituted long ago as an advantage to prosecutors. Every other time I had seen the old man argue, he had gone first. I always thought it unfair. But now, as Keefe stepped up to the lectern, well . . .

He carried only a single legal pad with him. He moved the lectern to a spot between the counsel tables and turned it around to face the jury. The old man's back was about six feet to Keefe's right and the jury rail was about eight feet in front of him. The old man leaned back to listen. Michael hunched over to take notes. Tom McKenna gave Keefe rapt attention. Eddie and Denny were still absent.

Keefe coughed and, in his most hard-to-hear tone, said, "Madam Forelady and gentlemen of the jury, I would like to thank you for listening over this long period of time. . . . I would like to review with you some of the issues in the case [and] to summarize the evidence . . . in order to help you in your determinations. . . .

"Here we have many many witnesses trying to determine whether a certain few things happened on Gurney Street and on Smith Street."

Judges are extremely reluctant to interrupt final arguments, but Skinner had to respond to the pained expressions in the jury box. "Mr. Keefe," he said gently, "I think if you expect all of the jurors to hear you, you have to speak more loudly. Possibly you may want to get closer to them because they are not hearing you very well."

Keefe smiled, nudged the lectern forward a few inches, and continued. Skinner leaned forward and cupped his ear. Keefe turned out to be more a suggester than an arguer. He sometimes spoke with feeling but stopped far short of passion. And he used the Socratic method lawyers often use when they have weak cases: give the jury questions instead of answers. He didn't cover all the evidence, but lawyers seldom do in summations. The idea is to drill the jury on your strong points and glance over, and sometimes ignore, your weak points.

Most of the first half of his argument—twenty minutes—was devoted to the plate number controversy. He launched into it right after the Skinner interruption, saying, "You have to consider whether the police officers on Gurney Street had a reasonable suspicion [that] the person getting into the Buick might be involved in the Cambridge robbery or in illegal activity. And you have to consider to what extent a mistake might have been made, who it was made by, and what the effect of the mistake might have been. Was it proven to have been made by these officers? If it was, was the mistake so significant in light of all the circumstances? . . . [Would] a reasonable man . . . have considered it reasonable to approach the vehicle to ask the person in the vehicle questions concerning the Cambridge robbery?"

Skinner was going to answer that one in his charge to the jury.

Keefe went on: "You have to consider the good faith of the police officers. Is there anything that has been demonstrated to you that they were not acting in *good faith?* . . .

"Before I start to summarize the evidence, I would like you to consider [that] the plaintiffs are seeking damages. We had an economist in here who testified. When you are to consider damages, if you so find, you should consider, as the economist did testify, that personal consumption is a factor, taxes are a factor . . . and you have to consider [at] what interest rate the money could be invested. . . .

"Now, we're going to start to discuss the circumstances . . . starting from the Cambridge robbery, the communications that were made, and the knowledge of the officers in their patrol car going down Smith Street. . . . You should consider, in this regard, the different lines of communication. Here you have a report coming in from victims in the Cambridge robbery. . . . It's possible that a number can be made a mistake on in that time. You then have the first person who receives it at the police station reporting it to the next person—the person who perhaps receives the telephone call reports it to the radio operator. You have another juncture at which a number can be made a mistake about. Each time you have a juncture, you have two possibilities for a mistake—the sending and the receiving.

"With respect to Officer Mullen receiving a call . . . you should consider whether Officer Mullen wrote down what he heard. You should consider whether Officer Molloy reported the number correctly. . . .

"Officers McKenna and Holland . . . called the TPF base. They called in the description as best they knew it. They called in the plate as best they knew it. And there has been no evidence to show that *they* called in the wrong plate. . . . You, once again, have to consider the junctures. Officer Monroe took the call. Did he take the call correctly? He called the Cambridge Police. Did they even listen to the whole plate? Did they hear blue Buick Electra with the plate Four-F, and say 'That is the one'?" There is *no evidence* to show the mistake in the plate was made by *these officers!*"

Keefe turned to point to Eddie and Denny, only to find them still missing.

"I submit to you there is no evidence that the defendant officers, McKenna and Holland, made that mistake."

With half of his time gone, Keefe moved into the action.

"The officers are entitled to rely on the information they receive. . . . I ask you: Are they entitled to suspect the person who comes to the car if he matches the categorical description that they have? The man . . . was a black man, and this categorical description . . . matched the categorical description they had received over the radio. . . . It is their duty to follow up and to pursue this dangerous situation. . . .

"They approached the Buick. . . . Both of the officers have testified that they each announced their office. . . . You will recall the diagram with the little cars on the witness stand that showed that Officer Holland had taken a position in front of the car. You recall his testimony that the car came at him, the car struck him . . . came back at him, struck him, hit him in the knee, struck him hard. . . . It brought tears to his eyes. . . . He was down. . . . He grabbed the handle of the car when he came up.

"It's interesting to consider that the little girls, or the schoolgirls, that were in the project testified that they had seen something, that they looked away, and they had looked back, and then saw some shooting. . . . One thing that the little girl did testify to was that she noticed the hand of a person on the car door. . . . That does, in fact, substantiate Holland's testimony with respect to that aspect.

"You should also, with respect to the schoolgirls, consider that . . . they were unable to recall any details as to color, or any details as to what they saw. And when you think of that, you should consider the distance . . . they are looking from [and] that it is dark and it is at night and Smith Street is not that well lit. . . .

"You should consider the danger to undercover plainclothes police officers, in that they are not able to let people know as well as uniformed officers that they are police. . . . The announcing of the office by plain-clothesmen is something they do for their own protection. . . .

"You heard testimony from the reporters, O'Brian and Kobre, [that] they didn't hear any noises except the shooting. I submit to you [that] with them scrunched down in the back seat . . . they were unable . . . to hear anything on the street except for the very loud noise of the shots. . . .

"Try to place yourself in that scene, trying to carry out your duties, the duties of a police officer. . . .

"You should consider the treatment by Doctor Creeden of Mr. Holland. When Doctor Creeden first saw Holland, [he] was still able to observe objective signs of the injury that Officer Holland received on Smith Street when the car struck him."

Now Keefe had one minute left, and Skinner broke in to warn him: "Your time is about up, Mr. Keefe. Do you want to wind up?"

"Yes, Your Honor."

At that moment, Denny entered and slid into the front bench.

"With respect to Mr. Winbush," Keefe continued hurriedly, "you should consider that there is testimony from the police officers that there were tracks. . . . And you should consider that Mr. Winbush acknowledged to you that he had *lied* to the police officers! And I ask you to consider why he would want to do that. . . .

"You should consider the testimony of the girl that works at the hospital with respect to having James Bowden under her supervision on the twenty-ninth. She said that the reason she remembers that James Bowden was working for her that day was because James Bowden took the place of Donald Shaw. You should consider the testimony of Mr. Smith, the administrator . . . that Donald Shaw was working on the twenty-ninth. . . .

"Lastly, you should consider the gun that was found on the street. . . . You should consider whether this is the weapon that was observed by Officer Holland just prior to the window going out. . . . With respect to the ejection [of a shell], there was a possibility there was not a thorough search inside of the vehicle, or it's possible it went out the window when the window blew out. . . .

"You should also consider that the vehicle's motions are independent acts from the firing of a weapon. . . .

"Finally, you should consider the time references that were made with respect to what happened on Smith Street. You have the report of O'Brian. . . . I ask you to consider the accuracy as to the time he would estimate with respect to how long it took for the shots to start. He said three to five seconds. I submit to you, if you consider what actually happened out there, it *would* happen very fast! Perhaps it would take *twelve* seconds. And I ask you to consider Mr. O'Brian is *wrong* when he says three to five seconds! . . .

"Finally, I ask you to consider all the testimony of all the officers that you have heard. Consider their demeanor. Consider their jobs. And ask yourselves how did they impress you when you saw them talking on the stand. And I ask you to consider the *reasonableness* of the conduct of Officers McKenna and Holland! To consider the *danger* that's involved in their duties as police officers in the city of Boston! And to make your deliberations carefully.

"Thank you very much."

Keefe strode back to the defense table and took his seat just as Eddie came through the door and skulked over to Denny, as if hoping no one would notice his tardiness.

Conventional wisdom has it that defendants should always try to convey to juries an abiding interest in their trials. Steady attendance is one very good signal of that. Eddie and Denny had been irregular attendees since Day Two, but at least they had been in their seats at the beginning of each day. There was no point in speculating about why they were late this morning. (They were excused from work during the trial.) I was just glad they arrived in time for the main event. The old man needed them more than he needed my cards.

The old man dumped a pile of legal pads, cards, and exhibits on the lectern. He tried to organize the material neatly but gave up in a few seconds. He stepped back, looked at the clock on the back wall—11:22—and checked his silver pocket watch. He spoke slowly. "Your Honor, Madame Forelady, members of the jury, on behalf of the plaintiffs, thank you for your attention throughout this long, difficult trial. We also [thank] the United States marshal. And the court reporter. And the clerk." He bowed to each person he mentioned.

Pause. "I look to the rear of the room, and there is a portrait of a judge on the left. . . . That is the Honorable George C. Sweeney, who served this court between 1935 and 1966. . . . He was appointed by Franklin Delano Roosevelt. . . . I want you to notice the frame that the portrait artist used. Beautiful gold leaf. Hand carved."

Turning back to the jury, he drew a deep breath and whispered, "In this case you're getting a *perjury frame!*" Louder: "And the perjury frame is around James Bowden and disabled Ernie Winbush!" Louder: "That's a perjury frame! It's a nefarious frame! It's made of fraud, deceit, and perjury!"

The old man had thirty-nine minutes left in a three-year job. Michael slouched and just listened. The entire argument went on behind his back. No matter. His work was done. Mine was too. I put down my pen and held on to the bench. Pat was expressionless.

"But preliminarily, I say this is not the usual civil case. . . . The plaintiffs take the position that there was willful, wanton, reckless conduct here. . . . We have a wrongful death statute in Massachusetts. Chapter Two-twenty-nine. And in that statute there is a provision [for cases of] 'willful, wanton, reckless conduct,' [which allows] you to give punitive damages. . . . Now insofar as that is concerned, we have to tell the world, we have to tell the Commonwealth, we have to tell the City of Boston: 'Don't kill people just because'—the only characteristic Holland and McKenna ever knew was he was black. They never once stated here that he conformed to the description given out by Cambridge. They never said that. . . . He got killed because he was black! . . . Willful, wanton, reckless conduct will be found here. It reeks of it! It's in this very courtroom." He glared at Eddie and Denny.

Back to the jury again: "And we come to you under the federal law, which His Honor will discuss with you, Section 1983. . . . Now, that civil rights statute was passed in 1871 [and] it gives *you* the power . . . to police those who are charged with policing us all. . . .

"There isn't a sane, fair-minded person who doesn't support policemen. There isn't. It is a sensible, civilized thing to do. And it's the same way we support our armies. With our armies, we decorate. . . . We reward. We give Congressional Medals of Honor.

We give Silver Stars. . . . Nevertheless, that same army that gives those rewards holds courtmartials, and they punish wrongdoers within their ranks. . . .

"Can anyone go into the jury room and say, 'I'm voting for Mr. McKenna and Mr. Holland because James Bowden robbed the store in Cambridge'? He never did anything in his life! . . .

"Cambridge teletype. One black male, six feet, thin build, wearing a dark-blue denim jacket, white *sneakers*. Sneakers give you a lot of height? And the other: five-ten, thin build, wearing a hat, white sneakers.

"So what does the one man they can't fix [do]? He measures James Bowden. . . . Sixty-four point five inches . . . That is a careful measurement. That is the measurement of a pathologist. . . . I admire Doctor Luongo . . . a public officer who will tell the truth. . . .

"There was not one piece of evidence brought in by this big police force that showed James Bowden wasn't in the City Hospital [at 2:30 P.M.]. . . . No one ever got on that stand and said James Bowden robbed them in Cambridge! Nobody ever got on that stand and said James Bowden robbed them! . . .

"The pieces in this case can't fit together. . . . The very first witness, Walter Logue . . . Does something go wrong there? He testifies, 'At seven o'clock I found the Fabrique Nationale.' And then I said, 'Look, do you know Fagone?' He jumps up to eight-fifteen! . . .

"What possible reason could an honorable, decent man like James Bowden have to do anything on Smith Street? They have him in a Buick automobile doing things that a prima ballerina couldn't do. With that big car? Back up, go forward, make it go sideways, do this, do that? . . . This ballet around the car, it's just ludicrous. . . . See, the defense case is: The cow jumped over the moon." And the old man jumped.

"They thought they would come in here and impress you with their superior police work. . . . Let me give you an example of police work. . . . We had the biggest robbery known to mankind on

January 17, 1950. The Brink's robbery at One-ninety-one Prince Street."

Skinner leaned forward with a knowing gleam in his eye. There was no great revelation coming. The few members of the Brink's gang still living had recently admitted guilt—in exchange for book and movie money.

"It happened in 1950. There were no arrests until 1956. Eleven perpetrators of that crime were arrested by the FBI and not a shot was fired. Now . . . these men had been suspects all the time. Two of them were fugitives, [and when they] were caught, they had guns. Not a shot was fired. It's been done. . . .

"There is not a shooting and killing in every arrest. . . . That's only on TV. That distorts police work. . . . Men serve thirty years and never pull out their guns. It's a rare, unusual thing. . . .

"I'll tell you what we've got here. We've got people who killed and went for the cover-up—don't recall; don't remember; have no records; we don't know how to write. Couldn't give you a piece of paper. Wrote on a newspaper. A multimillion-dollar turret system? . . . You didn't hear a whisper from it! . . .

"There's nothing important on those tapes. Just a black guy got killed. (They're still calling him colored—a colored male.) So what? We'll beat the rap. We'll cover it up. Who the hell can penetrate the Boston Police Department? We've got the patrolmen's union. Let them try to press this case. Let them try to get any of these records.

"It wasn't easy. . . .

"When they were down on Smith Street, they said, He's black; he'll be a drug pusher; he'll have a record a mile long; he'll live in a housing project; he'll be on welfare. The vicious stereotype! Class libel! Vicious!"

Then, in a low voice: "What did they get? A twenty-five-year-old man . . . Worked continuously for seven years . . . Married . . . Paying rent in a three-family house." Long pause. "Son, six months." Voice cracking: "A daughter, three years . . . Sure, it moves me! I tell you what I want to do! I want those kids to be able to grow up and say, 'My father wasn't a *robber*. He's not here, but he left us his name, and we . . . want to go along and not have that on us. We loved our father.'

"Jamil, the boy. Six months. You saw them in here. They're plaintiffs. Eurina, the daughter. What do you think? Do you think she felt her father's arms around her? Do you think at three years old there was something there she wanted? Do you think she misses it?

"The poor widow sitting there . . . Who does she turn to now? . . . Nobody."

The old man's eyes leaped from Pat to Eddie and Denny. "They were just two orphans in the storm, two little orphans in the storm. They found themselves out on Smith Street. It was *so* awful. . . . Terrified poor little Eddie Holland had tears in his eyes. Oh, God, it was awful." The old man ran to the clerk's desk, grabbed the TPF guns, and came whirling back with one in each hand. "But let me tell you they were out there with *these things*! Two orphans in the storm. Two killers! They put it right into him! Bang!" He pulled the triggers. "Poor man was shot and killed. They didn't give him a chance! They blew him to kingdom come! . . . Miserable, mean, cruel killers . . ."

He dropped the guns on the defense table and raced to the model. Pointing to Dwyer and Molloy's stakeout position: "They had an armament up there." Pointing to MacDonald and McClinton's stakeout position: "They had armament down there. . . . What the *hell* have they got a team for if they don't act like a team? One little suspect on Smith Street. . . . To pick him up, why, it would've been nothing. Absolutely nothing. What the hell did he have in the car? Nothing. Nothing! . . . Firing those bullets there that night was crazy! Jessina Stokes could have been killed. . . . Crazy. Not justified. . . .

"Poor little Mark Molloy. Undernourished little fella with the red hair, sitting on the stand. Eight-forty-one. What a bold way to come into a federal court. . . . You get the conspiracy? . . . All those reports are alike because they all consulted, obviously. . . .

They knew there was a bad number that very night. . . . They just figured they were close enough.

"Go down to the sweepstakes if your number is close [to the million-dollar winning number]. Try to get them to give you five hundred thousand because you're only a couple of numbers off. . . .

"What about Ernie Winbush? . . . Four of them nailed him— no criminal record, no wrongdoing—and they lugged him into the station house. What did Eddie do? (Tears in his eyes. So sensitive . . .) He only charged him with assault with intent to murder.

"It's surprising that Winbush didn't die. That was a tough spot for him to be in [that night]. That man in that physical condition. . . .

"Sergeant Byrne, in talking to Deputy Schroeder . . . said Holland identified him in the station that night. And he quit in court because he couldn't bag the case. . . . They had an able judge over there by the name of Philip Tracy, a Harvard Law grad. He wouldn't buy it. He threw it out. . . .

"Expert in weapons. That was a death trap! They set up a death trap. . . . Why, he didn't have a chance. . . . That foot went on the accelerator as he was going down to his death. . . . They absolutely willfully killed . . . and they've been running the cover-up ever since. . . . They were squirming on that stand with their perjury frame."

He wandered around, head down. "Byron once said: 'Guilt, Oh that pang, where more than madness lies, the worm that will never sleep and never dies.'" Pointing to Eddie and Denny: "It will be with them forever. Forever! . . . They are men of depraved hearts and diseased minds from this. And it showed on the witness stand. . . . When they were on that stand, they twisted, they squirmed, they were perjuring themselves. They were trying to put something over. They were liars! They were perjurers! Did you get a feeling of confidence as they spoke to you? Did you feel they gave you everything they could to help you? Did you feel that they wanted to be forthright? . . . Guilt. Guilt is in them. . . .

"And then we get the contrivance that a Spanish man was down at the car, putting his hands in there."

He looked at Eddie. "You never said *that* before, Eddie! Who told you to say that?"

He waited as if expecting an answer, then looked at John Keefe and Tom McKenna, and then turned back to the jury. "Can you think of a more Humpty Dumpty—they can't put the pieces together. All the City's horses, all the City's talent, all the Boston Police Department can't put Humpty Dumpty together. Because the facts are against them!"

Eventually the old man mentioned money, but only briefly. "What is Jim Bowden worth?" he asked, unable to answer. The rules wouldn't allow him to suggest a figure to the jury. All he could do was refer to the actuarial testimony. "Mr. Marshall gave an estimation of a million dollars plus. He gave lesser figures for present value . . . a significant and substantial amount of money. . . . But there is no money that can bring back James Bowden."

He took the autopsy photographs from the lectern and held up one in each hand. "And there he is. You meet him in death." Nodding to Pat: "That lady knew him in life."

He put down the pictures. "His kids are entitled to him. . . . You can't take a man away from children . . . and think you can get away with it. They're entitled to have those killers of their father punished. . . . And, as Daniel Webster said in this Commonwealth, 'Every unpunished killing takes away something from the security of every man's life.'"

Skinner looked at the clock. Two minutes left. The old man hadn't been keeping track of the time. I was ready to signal him, but he was facing the jury.

"That was willful, wanton slaying! . . . Stupid! Stupid and willful and wanton! . . .

"They thought: He's black; he'll never be able to fight this case; he'll never get it to a court of law. We'll trip him and put up every obstacle—which they didn't hesitate to do. . . .

"When you're in that jury room, say to yourselves: 'Show me

one, show me *one honest man* who took that witness stand and condemned James Bowden! . . .

"What I want to do—*most important*—I want to vindicate the name of James Bowden. It should be cleared. . . . James Bowden was an honest man. And he went too soon. . . .

"Men can be evil and men can kill, but they can't and shouldn't . . . get away with it."

Suddenly he spun away from the jury, charged toward Eddie and Denny—five or six steps—and shouted, "You're not gonna beat the rap!"

Back to the jury, with his voice steadily falling from a shout to a whisper: "Teach what has to be taught: Man values life, and . . . kids like to have a father, and wives like to have their husbands.

"They took him away; let them pay."

The old man held an accusing finger on Eddie and Denny for a long, silent moment, then slowly walked back to his chair, sat down, and turned away from the jury.

Cohen rubbed his eyes.

Skinner said softly, "We will take a brief recess."

Michael and the old man stayed in their seats during the nine-minute recess. Pat and I did too. We said nothing. Kevin and my mother went back to the office.

At 12:13 P.M., Skinner began his charge to the jury. After an introductory explanation of Title 42, Section 1983, he gave the standard lecture on evidence: There are two kinds: direct and circumstantial. "Direct evidence consists of testimony [which] describes what [the witness] perceived. Direct evidence may also [be] physical exhibits or documents. . . . Circumstantial evidence establishes facts from which . . . an ultimate fact in issue may reasonably be inferred. The law [gives] circumstantial evidence and direct evidence . . . equal weight. . . . Now, I'm [going] to give you an example of the two kinds of evidence.

"The defendants here seek to establish that James Bowden had a gun."

I perked up.

"Now they offer direct evidence through Officer Holland. . . . He saw a gun pointed at him. . . . And Mr. McKenna . . . saw a flash of the gun in the car. . . . That is direct evidence. . . . They ask you to draw the inference that [that] was the gun found on the street. . . .

"Now, you can consider what the [circumstantial] evidence was: . . . that it wasn't found for some considerable time . . . that no discharged shell was found inside the car . . . what James Bowden's physical condition was [when he would have had to] fling it out the window . . .

"The plaintiffs suggested . . . that this was a throw-away gun that the police planted. . . . It's for you to decide which inference you think is more likely."

Skinner turned to the problem of deciding who told the truth. "That is your most serious task. That is why you're here. . . . How do you do it? . . . You listen to the story. Does it hang together? Is it consistent? Is it in accordance with the laws of physics and the laws of nature? You listen for tone of voice. Is the tone of voice forthright? Does it suggest hesitation or attempt to fabricate? You look at the expression of the face. You look at the body English. . . . You do this all the time. You listen to salesmen. You listen to political campaigns. You listen to squabbling neighbors. You listen to your children or in-laws who may be at one another over something. And you try to find out who is telling the truth. . . .

"With respect to all of the witnesses—the newspapermen, the policemen, the little girls, Mr. Winbush, everybody else—you can consider whether they . . . have any motive for telling you something other than the truth. . . .

"You can reject part of a witness's statement and accept part. Or you can consider that if a witness is not telling the truth in one respect, he may not be telling the truth in another."

Skinner defined the trial issue clearly. "What we're dealing with is what the officers did when they got out [of their car] on the street. . . . There was justification, in my view—and I so instruct you—for the officers to at least make an inquiry of the occupant of the [Buick] at that point. . . .

"Now, what constitutes justification [for the officers' shooting]?

If the police officers were being fired upon or were being attacked with an automobile or both, *or* had reasonable belief that they were being fired upon or being attacked—a *reasonable* belief— then they would be justified in defending themselves by the use of deadly force."

Thirty minutes into the charge, Skinner took up the matter of damages. "I wish to make it clear that you don't get to the issue of damages until you determine liability. . . . One measure of [compensatory] damages is loss of earnings." He adopted the figures Keefe elicited—between "$183,000 [and] $164,000"—"as being the present value of the lost earnings." He added, "You are entitled further to assess a dollar value for the loss of the care and love and affection and companionship. . . . How you put a dollar value on these things is something of a mystery. . . .

"Punitive damages have nothing to do with the plaintiffs' loss. The purpose is to punish and *deter.* Deter not only these defendants but others similarly situated from unjustified acts, willful assaults . . . There is a minimum amount. If you find a willful killing which is not justified . . . then you must find *at least* five thousand dollars of punitive damages."

I didn't like the way Skinner said that. It sounded as if $10,000 would be a lot of punitive.

"If you make a finding for the plaintiffs," he continued, "damages—compensatory and punitive—are to be *reasonable.* I'm not going to try to tell you what reasonable is. . . . That is for you to decide."

Skinner glanced at his notes, then raised his final point. "You may find that only one defendant should be liable. There is not much in the evidence that would warrant that result, but I can't say that it's impossible."

He looked at his notes again and said, "Your verdict must be unanimous."

He explained that the marshal would soon deliver lunch to the jury room and then said solemnly, "All right, jurors, you are excused to commence your deliberations."

It was 1:06 P.M. on Friday, February 24, 1978.

We went back to the office. No one wanted to have lunch. Michael tended to some long-delayed paperwork. The old man returned month-old phone calls. Pat and Bill and Mary and Kim Bonstrom and I sat in the library and talked—about anything but the case. The weather was a recurring topic. I'd been marveling at the blinding sunshine since we left the courthouse. I felt as if I'd been in a movie theater for a week.

At two-forty-five, the clerk called. The jury had a question.

We were all in the elevator in a minute. Only Pat and Mary had grabbed their coats. The old man, Michael, and I ran down Devonshire Street and over the melting snowbank in front of the courthouse.

I waited with them at the plaintiffs' table.

"It's got to be a damages question," said the old man.

I agreed. Michael said nothing.

"It's got to be something like 'Can we give more punitive than compensatory?'" said the old man. "Something like that."

Michael still said nothing.

"Michael, listen to me. I'm tellin' ya it's a fuckin' damages question."

We waited forty minutes for the defense to arrive. The clerk tried unsuccessfully to reach Keefe and left word for him at City Hall.

Skinner decided not to wait any longer and had the jury brought in at three-thirty. Their question had come to him as a handwritten note from the foreman. With everyone seated, and the defense still missing, he began.

"Madam Foreman and gentlemen, I'm sorry to keep you waiting so long for a question, but there are certain procedural formalities that have to be attended to before I can address you. And that's what we were doing.

"Your questions are as follows: 'Was a McKenna report entered as evidence like Holland's report, plaintiffs' exhibit seven-B?'

"The answer is no. There was no such report introduced.

"The second question: 'If there is a McKenna report, may we have it?'

"And the answer to that question is, I have no idea whether there is a McKenna report, and in any case, you can't have it because it hasn't been introduced into evidence. You can only deal with those matters that have been offered by the parties.

"The third part: 'If no report, may we have a copy of his testimony?'

"At present, the only copy of his testimony is a strip of paper that comes off that [stenotype] machine, which you would not be able to read. . . . There is no copy of his testimony that you can have. . . . You will have to simply rely on your recollection of his testimony. . . .

"I'm sorry not to be able to give you more satisfaction in response to your questions."

"I excuse you once again to continue your deliberations."

"Thank you very much," said the foreman, and the jury left.

Cohen had been expressionless for the four minutes that he was in the courtroom.

John Keefe, Tom McKenna, Eddie, and Denny arrived as Skinner was leaving. He waved the lawyers into a bench conference and told Keefe and McKenna about the questions. They turned away jubilant, of course.

No one left the courthouse. In the men's room, I tried the it's-not-your-fault line, but I didn't mean it, and Michael wasn't listening anyway. He kept repeating, "I can't believe I left that fuckin' thing out."

The old man stayed in the courtroom. A wise choice. He probably would have gotten into trouble in the hall. The defense was out there, leaning against the wall and doing a lot of laughing. Eddie and Denny were taking big drags on cigarettes. The old man hates cigarette smoke.

When Michael and I returned, the three of us gathered at the table.

"Well," said the old man wearily, "maybe they're gonna let Mc-Kenna off. He wasn't in so deep on the Winbush thing, so they figure he deserves a break. And they probably think Holland fired first, so . . ."

"No," said Michael. "Skinner charged them on that. He said there was no difference between them."

"Cohen will at least give us a hung jury," I said with feigned confidence.

"Hey," said Michael, "we got by a directed verdict, for chrissake. That's more than most people do in these goddamn things."

A long silence followed. Then Michael muttered, "Nobody's ever won one."

I started thinking about cold-looking number three and the foreman and our hippie mechanic and number five and number four. We never had any indication that they were on our side. Oh, they were always riveted to the old man, but who else was there to watch?

How were we supposed to keep racism out of the jury box? A Boston jury box. How was Cohen supposed to stand up to it? Boston racism.

The day after Martin Luther King, Jr., was assassinated, there was a march of mourning and protest in Boston. Marchers wore black armbands. Kevin was in the Suffolk University contingent. A television camera randomly picked him out of the crowd on Tremont Street and zoomed in on his face and armband. The next day, down the corner, I had this conversation with a high school friend who had just picked up his senior prom tuxedo:

"I saw your brother Kevin last night on the news!"

"Yeah. I heard they had a shot of him."

"Uh, what's the story?"

"What d'ya mean?"

"You know—doesn't he hate niggers?"

"Uh, well, uh, I guess not."

"What the fuck's the matter with him?"

No reply.

"Do you?"

"Do I what?"

"Hate niggers."

"No."

"Jesus! You fuckin' guys. Me and my old man fuckin' cheered when we heard they shot that fuckin' nigger."

I bumped into that friend some years later in a courthouse. "Drunk driving?" I guessed.

"Nah, I got jury duty."

Fifty minutes after the jury had resumed deliberation, the clerk came in and said, "They're ready."

"Well, I guess that's it," said the old man, forcing a smile. "If they were still on evidence an hour ago, they couldn't have figured out damages by now."

"Ask for a Judgment Notwithstanding the Verdict," said Michael.

In civil cases, judges have a limited and rarely used power to overturn jury verdicts on the spot.

"I gotta talk to Patricia," said the old man.

She smiled nervously as he approached.

"Patricia, uh, it doesn't look good. But there are still things we can do. Appeals, uh . . ."

The jury started to file in. The old man quickly walked away.

I took Pat's hand and spoke to her. Neither of us remembers what I said.

The defense scrambled into place. Eddie and Denny were on the edge of their bench.

The jurors—including Cohen—looked at the floor.

We stood for Skinner's entrance. He asked the foreman whether the jury had reached a verdict. She nodded and handed a folded piece of paper to the clerk. He passed it to Skinner, who read it in a second and returned it. The clerk looked at it, cleared his throat, and read it aloud: "We find the defendants, Edward Holland and Dennis McKenna, liable to the plaintiffs in the amount of two hundred and forty thousand dollars in compensatory damages and ten thousand dollars in punitive damages." And the clerk smiled.

As I remember it, the jurors filed out rather abruptly. The old man stood and bowed and thanked each of them as they walked by him. I don't know when I let go of Pat's hand. I don't think we said anything. I know I shook the old man's hand. And Michael's. I may have said, "Congratulations." The old man hugged Pat and spoke to her. Mary ran up and hugged him. I shook hands with Bill. With Kim. I patted someone on the back. Over someone's shoulder, in the distance, I saw Judge Skinner smiling. We were out of there in a minute or two, and I'm almost sure that Keefe and McKenna and Eddie and Denny hadn't moved.

There was no celebration in the offing. The old man has never celebrated the outcome of a trial.

Back at the office, Pat used Michael's phone to call her mother. "We won," she said softly. Her lips trembled. "We won," she said again. Then she put down the telephone and cried.

Epilogue

The next day, the Bowden case was in the newspapers again. Weeks later, seemingly embarrassed not to have covered the trial, the *Sunday Globe* ran a long report on it.

David Cohen told the *Globe* that the jury had immediately agreed: "They had no reason to shoot him, no reason at all." Chester Cederholm, the alternate juror who was not in on the deliberations, told the *Globe*, "The policemen were a bunch of damn liars."

Joe Jordan told the *Globe* he was "the most probing" investigator of the Bowden case and stood by his conclusion that Eddie and Denny were right to shoot. He scoffed at the verdict: "I don't think the jury in this case got all the facts. They didn't get the information that Bowden was identified as one of the robbers."

John Keefe took the case to the United States Court of Appeals for the First Circuit and pleaded for a new trial, claiming that Ethel and Desi should have been allowed to testify and that it was unfair of the old man to have capitalized on their exclusion by saying to the jury: "Nobody ever got on that stand and said James Bowden robbed them." Keefe submitted a typed fifty-page brief, which was perfectly professional in every respect except that it actually referred to Ethel and Desi as "Ethel" and "Desi." (When lawyers are on a first-name basis with their supposedly impartial witnesses, they usually don't let judges in on their intimacy.) The brief said, "Without the eyewitness testimony, a central pillar was torn from the structure of the defendants' case."

Michael responded with a forty-one-page printed and bound brief which supported Judge Skinner's every ruling and maintained that if the old man had left the controversial comment out of his argument, the verdict would have been the same. "If certain comments by plaintiffs' counsel constituted error," wrote Michael, "they were no more than harmless error."

The appeal was decided by a three-judge panel that included Bailey Aldrich, an old bow-tie Yankee Republican who had been appointed to the federal bench by President Eisenhower in 1954. The old man had been anti-Aldrich ever since he had tangled with him in the Lester case, which was the case a friend had mentioned to Pat Bowden when suggesting she approach the old man.

In a 1957 federal court trial, the old man had defended Donald Lester, a twenty-five-year-old black man charged with the armed robbery of a suburban bank. Two other black men, represented by separate counsel, stood trial with Lester. All three were convicted on the strength of an eyewitness's testimony. During the trial, the old man had made an unprecedented motion: He wanted to see the FBI's report of what the eyewitness had said the day after the robbery. The trial judge treated this as the most impudent request ever to come his way—which, in 1957, it certainly must have been. With Lester starting his twenty-five-year sentence in a federal penitentiary, the old man appealed, saying he should have been allowed to see the FBI report. The United States Court of Appeals for the First Circuit disagreed and affirmed the conviction. So the old man petitioned the United States Supreme Court, and to the legal community's astonishment, it agreed to hear the case in 1960. The old man's written brief and oral argument persuaded the Supreme Court to order the trial judge to reconsider the motion and, if necessary, hold a new trial. The judge reconsidered the motion and again denied it. The old man appealed again. The Court of Appeals this time stepped aside and referred the case to a judge who eventually ruled in the old man's favor.

Then the Court of Appeals—and this is what really infuriated the old man—took the case away from that judge and, in an opinion written by Bailey Aldrich, rejected his ruling and again affirmed the conviction. Again the old man petitioned the Supreme Court. Again the Supreme Court agreed to hear the case. This time—1962—the Justice Department, shuddering at the thought of having to open FBI files to outsiders, sent its big gun, Solicitor General Archibald Cox, to put a stop to the old man's mischief. The two went head to head in oral argument. Michael and I went down to Washington for the show. Being ten years old at the time, I was more concerned with taking in the majesty of the room than in listening to Cox pontificate on the sanctity of government documents or the old man going on and on about "fundamental fairness." Michael, then eighteen, seemed to get every word, though, and was even able to discuss it with the old man on the way home.

Months later, the Supreme Court vacated all three convictions and ordered the FBI report turned over to the old man in the event of a retrial. There was a retrial in 1963. The old man introduced the FBI report. It quoted the eyewitness as having said, the day after the robbery, that he saw only two robbers and that he did not get a good look at either of them. Donald Lester was acquitted. The other two defendants were again convicted. Released from prison after serving six years, Lester told reporters that he owed his freedom to "the perseverance of Attorney O'Donnell." The old man, in turn, said Lester owed his incarceration to the intransigence of Bailey Aldrich and his Court of Appeals.

The other judges on the Bowden Court of Appeals were also Harvard Yankee republicans—one appointed by Eisenhower, the other by Richard Nixon.

The day the Bowden opinion came down—May 9, 1979—Michael sent me to the courthouse to pick it up. "Just look at the last sentence," he said anxiously.

A clerk handed it to me. It was an eight-page printed pamphlet written by Senior Circuit Judge Aldrich. The last sentence said: "There must be a new trial."

The old man profaned Bailey Aldrich every day for over a year after that.

Michael went to work on a petition to the Supreme Court. I talked a friend of mine, Sanford Frank, then a student at Harvard

Law School, into volunteering to help with the research. Michael put in 305 hours on the petition, had it printed and bound, and personally carried the 44-page booklet to Washington on August 7, 1979.

The linchpin of Bailey Aldrich's opinion was that there was no precedent for excluding suggestive identifications in *civil* trials. To the Supreme Court, Michael wrote: "Surely, in a [Section] 1983 suit, an action created by Congress to deter police from engaging in certain types of unwanted behavior, those same police should not be allowed to establish a defense by engaging in other forms of unwanted behavior. Suggestive identifications are undesirable when used as a basis for prosecution; certainly they are no less undesirable when used as a basis for a cover-up of a police shooting."

On October 9, 1979, we received a one-sentence letter from the Supreme Court. It said: "The petition for a [hearing] is denied."

The Bowden case went back on the trial waiting list. This time, by lottery again, it was assigned to Judge W. Arthur Garrity, Jr., who five years earlier had become the most famous, and infamous, judge in local history by bringing court-ordered school busing to Boston.

The prospect of a new trial that would include Ethel's and Desi's IDs of Bowden did not fill the City's Law Department with confidence. On January 11, 1980, a Law Department attorney not previously involved in the case called the old man and offered a settlement of $150,000. The old man, with Pat Bowden's after-the-fact approval, said he would settle for no less than the $250,000 the jury had awarded. No deal resulted.

The case came to trial again in October of 1980. John Keefe had resigned from the Law Department by then and had entered private practice. The City hired outside counsel for Eddie and Denny from the prestigious firm of Parker, Coulter, Daley & White. Senior partner James Meehan, who has been on one side or the other of more million-dollar lawsuits than anyone can remember, led the defense. At his side was James Polianites, a young lawyer who had just joined the firm after a year as Judge Garrity's law clerk. We got along well with Meehan and Polianites. The old man and Meehan liked, respected, and, I think, feared each other.

We impaneled another all-white jury of five men and one woman.

We presented essentially the same case-in-chief. The old man ran into trouble on the first day, though. Meehan was using well-placed objections to break his momentum. As a result, the old man often lost his train of thought and ended up on tangents that led nowhere. By late afternoon, Meehan's favorite objection became: "Unintelligible question, Your Honor." Garrity sustained it every time.

Late that night at the office, I had a screaming run-in with the old man. He started it by yelling at me for something, and I, for the first time in my life, unloaded on him. I outyelled him in the first few seconds—his being in a brief state of shock helped—and kept going for most of a minute or so. He sat looking at me with that evil eye he gives people on cross. Michael jumped in and said something reasonable, to the effect that we were both right . . . or maybe it was both wrong. When I got home, I couldn't remember what the fight had been about, but I knew that what was bothering me was the awful realization of how good Jim Meehan was.

The next day the old man took off like a rocket and stayed on target the rest of the way. Meehan still objected whenever he could, but he was overruled as often as he was sustained. And he never altered the old man's course.

As usual, the old man fought with all the grace of a gladiator. Meehan, a handsome, elegant, compact man, stood his ground with the dignity of a warrior prince, but he had no more luck cross-examining our witnesses than Keefe had had, even though his resonant voice was heard by all.

Meehan streamlined the defense case to five witnesses: Eddie, Denny, Molloy, Ethel, and Desi. He conceded the obvious: Eddie may have made a mistake calling in the Buick's plate number; and James Bowden was five feet four and a half inches tall. He dressed his clients in plain dark suits and had Denny get his hair cut. But Eddie, Denny, and Molloy fared no better on the stand this second time around. And Ethel and Desi turned out not to be the strong "central pillar" of the defense that Keefe had convinced Bailey Aldrich they would be.

In a bench conference, Judge Garrity, a thin, bald man ever careful in his choice of words, said he was "tending toward Judge Skinner's appraisal" of Ethel's and Desi's testimony. "A sideshow," he called it contemptuously, "a trial within a trial." He said Meehan was prosecuting Bowden for armed robbery, but "you can't prosecute a dead man because he can't defend himself." Nevertheless, Garrity was bound by the Aldrich opinion to allow Ethel and Desi to take the stand.

On cross, Desi did what I had always expected him to do: In effect, he retracted his positive identification of Bowden. The way the old man set him up made it inevitable. He asked Desi how he had estimated the robbers' heights. Desi said that they were both taller than he was.

"How tall are you?" asked the old man.

"Five nine," said Desi.

The old man put the autopsy report in front of him and asked whether he knew that Bowden was five feet four and a half. Desi's eyes widened as he looked at Doctor Luongo's measurement. He said he did not know it and volunteered, "If someone brought it to my attention, it would have been different." He said that someone four and a half inches shorter than he could not have been one of the robbers.

For her part, Ethel stubbornly insisted that Bowden was one of the robbers—the one without a gun, the one she kicked. On cross, she said Bowden was "not much taller" than she. (Ethel is five feet two and a half inches.) When shown her deposition statement that Bowden was six feet tall, she said, "I never meant to say six feet." When shown the mug shots that Geagan and Petersen had said she chose for the other robber, she said she couldn't remember which pictures she had selected. When shown her statement to the Cambridge Police saying she was "positive that the pictures I identified are those of the second robber," she said that she had meant to say "*not* positive." When shown the Cambridge Police description of the robbers as being five ten and six feet, she said she never gave the police a description of the robbers. She said that the officer on the scene took the descriptions only from Desi.

In our rebuttal case, the old man called Nicholas Arancio, the Cambridge patrolman who was the first cop in the store after the robbery. Arancio, a middle-aged man with an earnest manner, took the stand in his patrolman's uniform and brought with him the notes he had taken that afternoon. They had been kept in Cambridge's file on robbery. Arancio's easily legible description was: "2 B/Ms . . . #① 6', THIN BUILD . . . #② 5'10". . . THIN BUILD. . . ." Arancio, who had then known Ethel and Desi for years, testified that Desi gave him the description and "Ethel backed up what he said."

For more rebuttal, we brought on the City Hospital people. When Meehan got Elsie Pina on cross, he tried to use Donald Shaw's attendance record against her, but she pooh-poohed it, saying there was always confusion about Shaw's attendance in 1975. He was a very sick man, she said—he died later in 1975— and he would frequently report to work, be marked present, but spend most or all of the day in his doctor's office in another wing of the hospital. The old man called Adolph Grant this time. Grant was his imperturbable self in the face of Meehan's close cross-examination and piercing glare. He was unshakable on his claim of "duckin' work" with Bowden from two-thirty until punch-out time.

Meehan's final argument was only twenty minutes long. There was a sensible ring to it—as far as it went. He kept it simple: Bowden, for whatever reason, tried to kill Eddie and Denny by shooting and running them down. In closing, he warned that the old man would get "emotional" in his argument and asked the jury not to be swayed by that. A master of subtle inflection, Meehan made the word *emotional* sound like the name of a disease.

Garrity let the old man argue for an hour. He actually used my cards this time. They paved his way through a twenty-five-minute coherent review of the evidence, then left him on his own. Nicholas Arancio became "the policeman of the year, the policeman I salute, the policeman who is a credit to the Cambridge Police De-partment." He contrasted Arancio's "conscientious note-taking" with Eddie's and Denny's "sloppy, stupid policework." Toward the end, when his voice cracked, he said proudly, "Sure there's emo-tion in me. I don't apologize for it." After a flurry of bombast, he finished in a whisper: "If James Bowden, rather than being a humble hospital worker, had been a high public official, what happened to him would have been called an *assassination*! And I assure you it was an assassination in the eyes of his family. His mother. His wife. His daughter. And the son who never got to know him."

In his charge, Garrity raised a point that we were embarrassed to have overlooked. He asked the jury to consider how Bowden could have had a gun in his right hand if he was using that hand repeatedly to shift gears and using his left hand to steer, as Eddie's and Denny's testimony indicated.

The jury got the case on the afternoon of Friday, October 31, 1980—Halloween. The jury was out longer this time. No one left the courthouse. The old man and Meehan, both pretending to be relaxed, filled the passing hours by exchanging war stories. The old man's were mostly boastful, Meehan's mostly self-effacing.

As the wait dragged into the evening and it became clear that Pat would not get home in time to take Eurina and Jamil trick-or-treating, Bill drove out to the house, where Pat's mother had them waiting in costume. He took them by the hand and led them door to door.

Pat and I fell into a discussion of this book. How long would it take me to write it? Would I find a publisher? Things like that. When we exhausted the subject and silence seemed about to set in, she said, "Well, he was in a book before."

"My father." I nodded, thinking she was referring to one of the many Brink's books.

"No, I meant James."

"What?"

"James was in a book when he was a teenager. Before I met him. They didn't give him a copy, so I don't have it, but it was some kind of photography book. He and Walter Lee took pictures for it."

Houghton Mifflin Company had published *The Image Is You* in 1969. It is a collection of photographs of Roxbury with an accompanying text by Harvard Professor Robert Coles. The photographs were taken by Roxbury boys and girls, who were supplied with cameras and film by Polaroid Corporation and left to their artistic instincts. The editor's preface says they "uncovered the moods of the neighborhood and its black community with disarming simplicity and frightening accuracy." The list of ten photographers includes the names Walter Bowden and James Bowden. They were selected for the task by someone at the Cooper Community Center. No one now working at Houghton Mifflin remembers the book, much less Walter Lee or James Bowden. And those two names apparently mean nothing to Robert Coles, who has never answered my letter of inquiry nor returned my many telephone calls. Actually, the book bears no indication that Coles ever met his photographers. At least Polaroid let the kids keep the cameras. Walter Lee used his to take James and Pat's wedding pictures.

Bill made it back to the courtroom just as the jury was filing in. The foreman handed the folded piece of paper to the clerk, who passed it to Garrity, who read it and handed it back to the clerk, who read it to us: "We find the defendants, Edward Holland and Dennis McKenna, liable to the plaintiffs in the amount of two hundred fifty thousand dollars in compensatory damages."

The jury did not return punitive damages this time.

Two of the deciding jurors and one of the alternates granted me interviews a few weeks after the trial. Number four, Richard Beal, a production supervisor in a computer manufacturing company, said, "There was no disagreement as we went through the whole thing. We just wanted to make sure to be completely fair. That's what took the time. There was no disagreement. We all said, 'Yes, they're guilty.'" Beal admitted that the jury was initially prejudiced in Eddie and Denny's favor. "We all know police officers have a tough job," he said, "and we went into the trial with the attitude that we were not about to find these guys guilty unless they *really* were."

The jury found all our witnesses credible. Dave O'Brian was the key man for us. "I believed O'Brian right in the beginning," said alternate juror Norman Wordell, an engineer with Raytheon Company. "I was impressed with him. He told the truth, and I took his elapsed-time estimate as factual."

But Eddie and Denny had no credibility with the jury. Wordell told me: "If it was up to me, Holland and McKenna would be in jail."

The jury liked Meehan and the old man. "I'm for less emotional type people," said Wordell. "Meehan came across well. I felt sorry for him after a while." The foreman, William Edgerly, Jr., an executive of New England Telephone Company, told me: "After the first day, we all thought Meehan was great and your father was, well, pretty confused. But by the end of the trial, we all agreed that if we were ever in trouble, we'd want your father."

Interestingly, the jurors—some very much to their surprise—came out of the trial with strong admiration for Judge Garrity, a man who is one of the leading recipients of public hatred in the history of the American judiciary. He has been burned in effigy at many anti-busing demonstrations. Beal and Edgerly said Garrity was "completely fair." Wordell was effusive: "I was very impressed with him. He seemed to be fair and smart—everything you'd picture a judge to be."

Of Bowden's involvement in the robbery, Beal said, "We actually didn't feel that whether he held up the store had much to do with the case at all. That was incidental because it didn't matter whether he was a crook or not. But we were convinced that he did *not* participate in the holdup."

Alternate Wordell was gravely disappointed by the verdict. He said that if he had a voice in the deliberation, he would have argued for at least an additional $250,000 in punitive damages.

Beal explained why the jury did not award punitive damages. "We all felt that the whole Police Department was to blame. The Police Department surely should've found something wrong here.

There was too much covering up. So we felt that a lot of people knew something wasn't right here, but they simply overlooked it. And if we came back with punitive damages, it would really look like it was only Holland and McKenna we were blaming and not the whole department. If we could've made a statement and said that the punitive damages were against the Police Department, we would've done it."

There was no appeal of the second verdict.

When, in another case, Jim Meehan next appeared in the Court of Appeals, Bailey Aldrich looked down at him and (surely knowing the answer) asked, "Are you *the* James Meehan?"

"My name *is* James Meehan," came the modest reply.

"Are you the same James Meehan who tried the second Bowden trial?"

"I am."

"Well," said Aldrich, "it looks like we wasted our time with that one."

Meehan agreed.

The day after the trial, Garrity's clerk added to the jury's $250,000 a mandatory 8 percent noncompounded annual interest calculated from the day the complaint was filed. The five and a half years of interest came to $115,231.62. That brought the total judgment against Eddie and Denny to $365,231.62.

It was hypothetical money, of course. Collecting it from Eddie and Denny was impossible. So, the City naturally expected the old man to be receptive when, six weeks after the trial, it volunteered, through Meehan, to step in and settle the matter for $250,000. Expecting the City to make such an offer on Eddie and Denny's behalf, the old man had conferred with Pat and found, to his delight, that she was adamant about holding out for every penny of the judgment. "Too late," he told Meehan. "My client won't take anything less than what the court says she has coming to her." A week later, the judgment increased again.

It happened in Judge Garrity's motions session on Decem-

ber 22, 1980. The courtroom was packed that day with prominent criminal lawyers waiting to argue pre-trial motions in a huge
marijuana smuggling case, but the Bowden business came first.
Garrity was going to add to the judgment an amount that would
cover O'Donnell, O'Donnell & O'Donnell's fee and expenses. He
was empowered to do this by a new law designed by Congress to
reward a plaintiff's lawyer who wins a civil rights case (because in
doing so the lawyer acts "as a 'private attorney general' vindicating
[rights] that Congress considers of the highest priority"). Garrity
had scheduled the hearing to determine what the fee should be.

The old man gave him a list of expenses and a log of the hours
he and Michael had spent on the case. The $13,221.55 in expenses
was a modest sum. It did not include the cost of having me on the
team, for example, though it would have been perfectly proper to
add that amount.

One of the factors Garrity was required to consider in setting
the fee was the "undesirability" of the case from the standpoint of
a lawyer being approached by Pat in 1975. In his opening comments he said, "I can't imagine a more undesirable case than this
one. . . . This case was both novel and difficult. . . . Three quarters
of the lawyers in Boston wouldn't touch this case with a ten-foot
pole."

The old man pulled the rug out from under himself on that
point. He was supposed to say, "That's right, Your Honor. It
seemed like an impossible case, but my conscience overcame my
reluctance to take it." Instead he stood and said, "I'm not insensible to the remarks made by His Honor, [but] when Mrs. Bowden
walked into my office, I was going to take the case. . . . It was my
lot. I'm happy I took it . . . and I say to the court"—he looked
down at Michael, who was shaking his head in a signal of disapproval that the old man missed—"we would do it again."

Meehan had nothing to say. He left the talking to his assistant.
Jim Polianites's job was to keep the fee low. He said that his research of attorneys' fees awarded by courts in civil rights cases
revealed that the hourly rates judges had used to calculate them
did not "even approach one hundred dollars."

The old man glowed when Garrity replied: "I'm less interested in what other [judges] have awarded than in what your top criminal trial lawyers and plaintiff tort lawyers get on an hourly basis because this was a case that demanded tops in the way of representation."

Garrity, a former prosecutor and private practitioner, added with apparent disdain: "Some of your big law firms today charge two hundred dollars an hour for office work . . . shuffling correspondence from some corporate headquarters."

Polianites went on to persuade his former boss that, since fees can be awarded only for winning efforts, the 305 hours Michael had worked on the petition to the Supreme Court were "noncompensable" because the plaintiffs lost that round.

Garrity recessed to confer with his law clerk. When he returned to the bench, he spoke without interruption for thirty minutes. In that time, Wendell Arthur Garrity, Jr., a jurist well respected by the bar if not the public, provided the old man, in front of an audience of his peers, with the most delightful experience of his career.

"Well," Garrity began, slowly and deliberately, "I will state the court's findings on the fee. The total is two hundred thousand dollars. . . . Mr. Michael O'Donnell's portion . . . I have computed at seventy-five dollars an hour [and] Lawrence O'Donnell's portion [at] two hundred dollars per hour."

A buzz went through the spectators' section.

Two hundred an hour—the highest hourly ever awarded by a federal judge—had to be justified on the record. Garrity did so with pleasure. First, he said, "I think the verdict was a fair one. The amount awarded was not inflated unreasonably. It was within the range of figures testified to by the actuarial expert. . . .

"I turn now to the various factors which underlie the court's decision. . . . I start off with the proposition that the two-hundred-dollar and seventy-five-dollar hourly rates are reasonable and by no means excessive [for] Lawrence and Michael O'Donnell, considering their experience and reputations and abilities. . . . Here you needed the trial capability of an unusually skillful and committed nature to present this case. . . . I think that Mr. O'Donnell's experience and standing at the bar and his ability to project the feelings and the justness of his clients' position are very high . . . and a two-hundred-dollar hourly rate of compensation is not at all out of line. [But] I don't know of any lawyer who would not require assistance in attacking a case of this complexity. . . . If ever there was a trial where trial counsel needed someone at his elbow, it was this case. . . . You might say trying to maintain the emotional high . . . to communicate righteous indignation . . . is where Lawrence was trying to focus. And Michael was feeding him the page numbers of depositions, the next exhibit, et cetera. He was the detail man. Lawrence was the overall advocate. . . .

"I am not suggesting that Michael O'Donnell's services could not be worth one hundred or one hundred and twenty-five or perhaps one hundred and fifty dollars per hour. . . . For example, his work on the Court of Appeals brief obviously should be compensated at the rate of one hundred dollars, one hundred and twenty-five dollars, or more. But . . . I am setting what seems to be a reasonable [average] fee for the mix of [his] services in this particular case. . . .

"Very few lawyers possess the skill requisite to try this case properly, in my opinion. It required knowledge of a practical sort that was acquired over years. . . . All the books written on the law would not confer on an advocate the skill he needed to try this particular case. . . . There are very few who could have conducted the case with the same vigor and dedication that the O'Donnells brought to this one. . . .

"This is a unique case. I don't think there is another similar case. . . . It involved a frontal assault on the integrity of *portions* of the Boston Police Department [and] persons in it who would trample the rights of inconsequential citizens. . . . [It] involves an alleged cover-up implicating not only the officers who were on that street on the evening in question but their superiors and colleagues, who, according to the plaintiff, deliberately sought to protect the defendants in this case from the lawful claims of the widow and the children. . . . There was no disposition on the part of the Boston Police Department to take any action against the individuals who were involved in this shooting or this cover-up. [The O'Donnells] did it alone. . . .

"Even today, the police [are not] interested in using their resources to uncover the truth. . . . There is no attitude within the department that Mr. O'Donnell and his son have by this case helped the Police Department by uncovering a violation of someone's civil rights. Not at all . . . Is there any doubt that the majority of the police and the majority of the superiors in the Police Department still support the action of the defendants in this case? . . . In my opinion, many persons—members, or sympathetic to the membership, of the Boston Patrolman's Association and the Boston Police Department—will blame Mr. O'Donnell for bringing the Association and some of its members into disrepute. It will be a long time before some persons in the Boston Police Department, in my opinion, forgive Mr. O'Donnell for the obloquy that he brought upon the police in this case. [But] I don't know how he could have tried it without doing so. . . .

"The consequences were costly to Mr. O'Donnell and may trail him for years." We took this as a reference to my arrest and the attempted A and B prosecution of the old man. In an affidavit submitted a week earlier in anticipation of this hearing, Michael had mentioned these things as elements of the "undesirability" factor. Garrity added, "I think there was a cost to Mr. O'Donnell . . . in this case that goes far beyond the cost that a lawyer pays when he undertakes the average civil rights case . . . a special cost to Mr. O'Donnell and his family. . . .

"Mr. O'Donnell undertook this representation at considerable risk—the risk of getting nothing. . . . Counsel risked untold numbers of hours and effort—with the full awareness that he might, at the end of the road, have been out roughly thirteen thousand dollars of expenses—all undertaken in the hope that he would obtain justice for a lonely widow.

"I don't know how to characterize Mrs. Bowden but as a woman who had no place to turn except to counsel who might undertake this type of case. . . . Counsel who in the old tradition of the bar are willing to lend their dedication and energy to the representation of poor people [are] to be encouraged. . . .

"Therefore, the fee is two hundred thousand dollars plus expenses of thirteen thousand, two hundred and twenty-one dollars and thirty-five cents. . . . The clerk is ordered to prepare an amended judgment. . . .

"Now, I have kept these lawyers in the criminal case waiting an additional half hour, so that concludes this matter today."

"Thank you, Your Honor," the old man said faintly.

Garrity's ode had a strange effect on him. As his pals, including Meehan and Polianites, were shaking his hand, he managed only a smile. This great braggart was, by this great praise, reduced to speechlessness.

Of course, the amended judgment of $578,452.97 was still all theoretical money.

Two weeks after the fee hearing, on January 8, 1981, Eddie and Denny signed identical letters to the police commissioner. Composed by Jim Polianites, they said: "I hereby request that I be fully and completely indemnified by the City of Boston . . . for civil money damages incurred by me for actions which I performed in the course of my duties as a Boston Police Officer. . . . I believe that full and complete indemnification is appropriate in my case." Being at least as hopeful of indemnification as Eddie and Denny were, we patiently waited for Joe Jordan's reply.

Six months passed. In the meantime, the commissioner's lawyer, Nicholas Foundas, tried to settle the matter for $350,000. I was with the old man when he said to Foundas, "Nick, tell Joe that we've got a judgment. I know he's never seen one before, but try to make him understand what it means. He has to pay full price. My client thinks he owes her that."

With the City's offer on the rise, the old man grew confident that full payment was on the way. Pat did too. But a week later, Foundas retracted the offer and put nothing in its place. Then, on July 30, 1981, in letters to Eddie and Denny, Joe Jordan wrote: "I regret to inform you that your request for indemnification must be denied. The reason for this denial is based upon financial circumstances."

Had Jordan chosen to indemnify them, the money would have come from the police budget. The judgment, which would continue to have interest added to it while it remained unpaid, was then approaching $600,000 but was still less than 1 percent of the annual Boston Police Department budget.

The old man sent an angry letter to Mayor White, asking him to intervene and expedite "the ethically inevitable full payment of the judgment."

The mayor did not reply.

A few months later, in October of 1981, O'Donnell, O'Donnell & O'Donnell's second civil rights lawsuit came to trial. In 1978, using the Bowden complaint as a model, I had written the complaint for this one, only a few days before the three-year statute of limitations would have made it impossible. After languishing on the federal court docket for three years, *Lawrence Francis O'Donnell, Jr.* v. *Mark Molloy, William Dwyer and Frank Kelly* was called for trial on three weeks notice by a judge named Herbert Maletz, whom we had never heard of. He had been sent from New York City's Federal Court to lend a hand in Boston for a month or two.

Other than a couple of rounds of interrogatories, neither side had conducted any discovery.

Appearing for the defendants were Jim Meehan and Jim Polianites.

In a pre-trial conference, Judge Maletz explored the chance of a settlement. Concerned only with the principle of the thing, we would have accepted anything. One thousand dollars? One hundred? One dollar? Assault and battery and false arrest aren't worth much. Meehan had no offer to make.

The trial ran three and a half days. We called one witness in our case-in-chief—me—and one witness in our rebuttal case— me again. Meehan did a fine job of intimidating me on cross, but I'm told that I never conveyed that impression to the jury.

The defense put on four witnesses: Molloy, Dwyer, Frank Kelly, who was in their team that night, and John Ricci, the patrolman who booked me. Cross-examination was rather turbulent for all of them.

When Dwyer, red-faced with humiliation and anger, returned from the stand to his seat beside Molloy, I, from just across the aisle, heard him excitedly say to Mark in a voice enough above a whisper that it seemed intended for my ear: "Why the fuck did ya just hit him? Ya shoulda killed him!"

I assumed that Billy was speaking figuratively. Molloy chuckled. I caught Dwyer's eye and smiled. He didn't.

The jury stayed out a day and a half before coming back with $7,500 in compensatory and punitive damages for me. The verdict was against Molloy only. The foreman told Judge Maletz that the jury was hopelessly deadlocked on Dwyer and Kelly. Maletz accepted the partial verdict, such as it was, and said there would have to be a new trial for Dwyer and Kelly.

The following month, Maletz tacked a $5,000 attorneys' fee onto the judgment, based on $150 an hour for the old man and $75 for Michael.

Since the judgment against Molloy was small enough to be squeezed out of him, we didn't wait to see whether Joe Jordan would indemnify him. Michael went after Molloy's house immediately, and the City swiftly—in four months—stepped in to pay the debt. With interest, it amounted to $13,069.15.

Ignored by City Hall and Police Headquarters, the Bowden judgment remains unpaid as of this writing. With interest still accruing at $190.18 per day, the judgment has now—June 1983—risen to just over $730,000.

The old man has tried approaching collection from the political angle. Once. In the summer of 1982, when the NAACP was weeks away from holding its national convention in Boston, he wrote to its outspoken executive director, Benjamin Hooks, asking him to raise the issue with Mayor White. In an encouraging letter of reply, Hooks thanked him for "bringing to [his] attention the tragic story of the murder of James Bowden" and promised a meeting when he came to town. The old man tried to arrange such a meeting during the week-long convention, but was rebuffed by Hooks's assistants, who explained that their boss had no appointment time available. The old man persisted, but the closest he came to a meeting was the night he and Pat prowled the convention hall and got within a bodyguard or two of Hooks for about a minute.

On another night, Kevin White addressed the convention from center stage after being introduced by Benjamin Hooks. The mayor's speech was warmly received.

Since Kevin White has decided not to seek reelection, Boston will have a new mayor in 1984. Pat hopes for "one with a conscience."

The old man and Michael have been chasing the judgment's rainbow from the only legal angle: collecting from Eddie and Denny.

In the fall of 1982, when Eddie and Denny were first summoned into Federal Court for an evaluation of their assets by Magistrate Cohen, neither of them showed up. Jim Polianites explained that Eddie had been off duty for weeks with another on-the-job injury and so was unfit to travel to the courthouse. (Purely by coincidence, my mother and I had spotted Eddie a couple of nights earlier driving through Dorchester in an aging Chevrolet with the license plate SHOGUN. The car belongs to a woman friend of his.) Denny, Polianites went on to explain, had for the past two weeks been confined to an alcoholism treatment center.

Magistrate Cohen rescheduled the hearing for the following month. Eddie appeared and testified about his assets—essentially none. Denny was absent again. This time Frank McGee came to explain. He said that Denny had returned to duty for a few weeks but became troublesome at a recent union meeting and was packed off to an alcoholics' ward in a suburban hospital. McGee said that a patrolman at the meeting took Denny's gun from him.

Cohen scheduled another hearing for Denny and threatened to send U.S. marshals out to arrest him if he failed to appear. Denny showed up and testified that he was "broke." He said that personal expenses and child support payments deplete his $25,000 annual income. When the old man asked Denny whether he has cash income that he does not mention on his tax returns, Denny cited the Fifth Amendment and declined to answer.

Michael is now moving in on Denny's largest asset: the small house his wife and children occupy. It is worth perhaps forty to fifty thousand. Frank McGee is opposing Michael on the house.

With Bowden expenses still piling up as the collection attempts proceed, O'Donnell, O'Donnell & O'Donnell's foray into civil rights litigation has been a costly one. Not long ago I asked Michael whether, considering he might never be paid for it, he had any regrets about working on the Bowden case. "Course not," he said. "I learned a lot." As I left his office, he added, "It was a terrific fight. I don't think I'll ever be involved in anything that'll be as much fun."

"Would you take a case like that again?"

Michael makes most of the decisions now on what civil cases the firm will handle. "I don't know," he said. He turned to the window. "They'd have to have a Dave O'Brian in the car again."

I walked around the corner to the old man's office, knocked, and swung the door open as he was hanging up the phone. I said, "Okay, Bowden is the oldest open case you've got. And you've spent about fifteen thousand on it. You don't have a penny to show for it. Don't you wish Pat never found you?"

He looked at me as if I were crazy.

In the eight years since her husband's death, Pat Bowden has taken business courses at Roxbury Community College, found work as a bookkeeper, and been laid off when business slumped. She is now a computer operator.

Eurina is a pretty, bright-eyed twelve-year-old. She is a fine student, and Pat has high hopes for her.

Jamil, now eight, is also doing well in school. He's a lively little fellow who captures people's affection immediately. Pat says he asks about his father a lot.

I talked to Bob di Grazia for four hours one autumn afternoon in 1980. He had, by then, lost his police chief job in Maryland after becoming too irritatingly controversial for the Fraternal Order of Police, which lobbied successfully for his firing. The Fraternal Order was outraged by such impolitic public comments by Di Grazia as: "Most cops view the community as the enemy. It's a simple them-us thing for cops." And: At least a third of all police officers "are psychologically unsuited for police work." When he was fired, he told the *Phoenix:* "I think a change agent, particularly in an archaic, conservative type of business like the police business, is always gonna be in trouble." Di Grazia was out of trouble and self-employed when I spent the afternoon in his Washington, D.C., office. I had found him through his advertisement in the *American Bar Association Journal,* in which he was offering himself as an expert witness for hire, ready to "testify for defense and plaintiff attorneys in police malpractice, brutality, firearm abuse, etc. matters." Di Grazia's new business hadn't gotten off the ground yet in 1981, but it has now. He gets $120 an hour plus expenses as an expert witness, and his testimony is much in demand.

I had all the police reports with me that day and, as it turned out, just enough tape to record all of our conversation. At the outset, Di Grazia was buoyant. An hour later, he was sad-eyed. His baritone had softened considerably. He said that he now regretted accepting the conclusion of the department's investigation.

We went over the reports, all of which—except Joe Jordan's—he claimed he had never seen. Di Grazia said, in essence, that he had approved of the Bowden killing because Joe Jordan did. "I relied on him to a great degree. . . . Unfortunately, you have to delegate. And you place good faith in someone that it'll be done right. . . . I had reasonable faith in Joe Jordan. He was a good foot soldier. . . . His ties with the department were strong. Thirty-two years. He had all of that weighing down on him, I guess. . . .

"What happened in the department for years was they just didn't want anything bad ever said about it, so they allowed bad things to happen. . . . They could almost write it off as a poor investigation here. Except that they're so poor at the cover-up."

When I asked Di Grazia whether he was in on the cover-up, his denial was vehement, and he added angrily: "I really felt that if the goddamn city had to blow up, it blew up! But a goddamn cop did not get away with that sort of stuff!"

After stressing that he always considered Jordan "a nice guy," Di Grazia said, "He was probably misled too. He was pretty busy on other things and probably took recommendations as they were without checking them out."

Joe Jordan is now in his seventh year as Boston police commissioner. Though he has often been criticized for being shamelessly servile to Mayor White, Jordan's fundamental integrity has never been publicly doubted.

Joe Jordan refused to be interviewed for this book.

"I always laugh at tough Internal Affairs investigations on TV cop shows," Di Grazia told me. "I was never happy with [Boston's] Internal Affairs. . . . They would whitewash whatever they could. Internal Affairs was called 'whitewash alley.' . . . Even with a known bum in the department, they'd defend him. . . . When they go into this kind of investigation, it's to find someone innocent instead of guilty. It's the complete opposite of what they do on a criminal case. . . .

"The situation of Geagan helping with some questions that really elicited answers in a certain way—that's all part of the game that's played. They want to get these things over with. . . . Geagan was providing them with outs. . . . Geagan, I guess, just felt it was necessary to play the game. What was necessary to get ahead, he would do."

John Geagan now has two of Joe Jordan's old titles. He is the superintendent of the Bureau of Field Services. He is also the chairman of the Firearms Discharge Review Board. No one in the Department will be surprised if Geagan becomes the next Boston police commissioner.

John Geagan refused to be interviewed for this book.

Di Grazia told me Bob Hudson is "the best homicide detective in Boston." But, he added, "With the past record of the Boston Police Department, I had great doubts about all of them—the ones who'd been around for a while."

Bob Hudson is no longer with the Homicide Unit. He is the chief of detectives assigned to the Suffolk County District Attorney.

In 1981, Joe Jordan gave Hudson a general commendation "in special recognition of exemplary performance while providing police services to the City of Boston."

"I just call things as I see them," Hudson told me. "And I felt at no time that this was a criminal homicide case. If I found something criminal, I would've gone for a complaint."

Michael says Hudson could have found a manslaughter or second degree murder if he had looked hard enough.

Hudson said he spent little time on Bowden because he (Hudson) "was tied up on other matters. When you have two or three years behind you on Homicide, your cases back up on you and you're in court almost every day. And you have other investigations going on all the time."

Hudson has logged more time in court than any other cop in this story. He knows what it takes to get a unanimous verdict out of a jury, and he accepts the Bowden verdicts: "The federal juries heard all the evidence and saw the demeanor of the witnesses. They were in the best position to judge what happened."

The TPF is gone now. Eleven months after the first Bowden trial, on January 18, 1979, Joe Jordan disbanded it. The commissioner denied that his move was related to a fresh stack of brutality complaints lodged against the TPF for its crowd control maneuvers during the preceding New Year's Eve.

The Bowden case was on appeal then and had drifted so far from public consciousness—as it has once again—that the *Globe*'s farewell salute to the Tactical Patrol Force said admiringly: "No member of the TPF has fired his weapon outside the target range."

Former TPF patrol supervisor Sergeant Harry Bryne is now assigned to a district. He refused to be interviewed for this book.

Sergeant Ed McHale retired shortly after the TPF broke up. Before I could locate him, he suffered heart failure and died in 1981.

Jim O'Connor is the only one of the four Winbush arresting officers who has spoken to me about the case. Daniel Sullivan angrily turned me away from his door, and James Keegan (who has some scary-sounding brutality complaints in his file at Headquarters) chased me away from his. Thomas Foley has resigned from the force and, so one rumor goes, moved to Arizona. O'Connor has resigned, too, but I found him in Colorado, where he joined a small-town police force in 1979. When I interviewed him in 1981, he had left the police job and was prospering in the lumber business. Apparently very happy to be out of police work after fourteen years of it, O'Connor told me: "I'm a white man again."

When I turned to the night of January 29, 1975, O'Connor said, "I can't think of what the hell went on. . . . I really don't have anything to add to what you probably already know because I don't know anything more than what I put down on paper and what I testified to."

I asked him why he didn't ask Winbush better questions, like: Do you know James Bowden? Did you fire a shot on Smith Street? How did you get away?

As if he had been puzzled by that, too, O'Connor replied, "Beats the shit out of me."

He was just as unenlightened about why, if Harry Byrne actually thought Winbush had fired at Eddie, he didn't send half a dozen unmarked cars with twenty or so ACU men to close in on him. People who try to kill cops usually get that kind of attention.

O'Connor did have some Colorado experience to bring to one point. It enabled him easily to envision Bowden dumping the Fabrique Nationale after the shooting. He told me: "You oughta see what an elk does after it gets shot dead."

O'Connor, who comes from a police family—his father and

brother—is the staunchest defender of Eddie and Denny I encountered. "I'm pissed that they lost the case," he said. "What were they guilty of? Guilty of being policemen! . . . Losing the case shows why so many people are leaving police service. You can't do the job anymore. Frustrating . . . I don't think that anyone but God should sit on a jury as far as policemen go myself, because the policeman is the guy that's facing all the problems; not Joe Shit, the ragman! . . . That doesn't sound very good, I guess—calling jurors Joe Shit. But if they haven't lived it, they don't know it. . . . How dare they say those police officers were wrong? . . . They don't have much faith in their appointed authority, do they? . . . I don't believe anyone has the right to second-guess the police officer on the street. . . . How can anyone second-guess the policeman who's there trying to make a decision in a second?"

"But, Jim," I asked, "can't a cop ever be wrong?"

"Never."

"Never?"

"Never!"

Frank MacDonald, still a patrolman, refused to be interviewed for this book. But his former TPF partner, Loman McClinton, did talk to me. He's now assigned to the Mounted Unit and patrols downtown Boston atop a handsome light-brown horse.

The summer afternoon when I interviewed McClinton on his front porch in Roxbury, he said he had recently, by coincidence, met Ernest Winbush through mutual friends. He was sure Winbush—who has now moved thirty miles from Boston and lives with the hope of having a successful kidney transplant—"is not the type to be involved in robberies and shootings."

He told me nothing more than his report said about what happened on January 29, 1975. But he did say that the Fabrique Nationale now "looks like a throw-away" and that he felt he was "being kept in the dark" that night.

Through Jim Meehan and Jim Polianites, their clients Eddie Holland, Denny McKenna, Billy Dwyer, and Mark Molloy refused to be interviewed for this book.

Eddie and Denny are still patrolmen. Eddie is assigned to District 14 but has been on the injured list since the summer of 1982. When, in October of 1982, we saw him in Magistrate Cohen's courtroom, he showed no apparent sign of being incapacitated.

Denny is assigned to District 2. Pat Bowden occasionally used to see him patrolling the streets of Roxbury when he was first transferred there. But for over a year now, Denny has been kept inside at the booking desk.

He did make at least one arrest in 1982, though. Everyone agrees on this much: While on duty on December 20, Denny left the booking desk and, with another uniformed patrolman, climbed into an available police wagon. Their mission: pick up Denny's black leather jacket at Fred's Tailor Shop, just outside the district. Fred was to have done some minor repair work on the jacket, but as he found himself apologetically explaining to Denny, it had somehow fallen into the dry-cleaning pile without a tag and was now lost. Fred offered to buy Denny a new one. Denny was prepared to settle for nothing but his old jacket. A sentimental attachment, perhaps.

The disagreement comes with the question of who punched whom. The cop with Denny reported that he didn't see how the scuffle started. Fred, a short round man, says that Denny attacked and beat him and that he, Fred, never raised a finger in provocation or defense. Denny arrested the tailor for Assault and Battery on a Police Officer.

Denny was the first witness called to testify in the West Roxbury District Court on January 20, 1983, in Commonwealth versus Fred. Denny was much steadier on the stand in that drab little courthouse, where the police almost always have their way, than he had been when I last saw him in Garrity's courtroom. But his credibility had not improved. The judge didn't have to hear the defense. Ten minutes into Denny's testimony, he dismissed the case.

If Fred's turn on the witness stand had come, his lawyer told me, I would have heard him quoting Denny as having told him: "Next time, I'll use a gun."

During my trial—*O'Donnell* v. *Molloy et al.*—my brother Bill often chatted with Billy Dwyer. I kept my distance. But in the excitement after final arguments, when the jury had just left to deliberate, Michael and I sidled up to Bill and Billy. The old man was with Meehan and Polianites. Nothing could make him talk to the old TPF gang. Dwyer was denouncing the claim we had put to the jury that my beating and arrest were a TPF conspiracy aimed at the old man for his handling of the Bowden case. Of course, Dwyer was the key man in the conspiracy theory because he was the only one who knew who I was at the time. The four of us were smiling.

"You fuckin' guys know that conspiracy line is bullshit."

"Makes sense to us, Billy."

Dwyer tried his best to make it sound nonsensical by stressing how little he ever cared about the Bowden case. "Mark and I weren't really involved," he said. "Why were we supposed to care that your father was suing Holland and McKenna?"

We were unmoved. He glanced over both shoulders. No one else was close enough to hear. We tightened the circle. Still wearing that disarming you-gotta-believe-me smile, Billy Dwyer said, "Okay. It never should've happened. Everybody knew that. There was no way for the Buick to get away. We would've blocked the street. We were all set to go in; then we got a call for an ambulance. They never should've approached the car that way. They didn't need to."

He shook his head. "It never should've happened. But what the fuck should me and Mark care? It was no skin off our nose. We didn't give a shit."

Afterword to the Paperback Edition

When this book arrived in Boston bookstores in the late summer of 1983, most of the news media learned about the Bowden case for the first time, and they learned much more than the trials could reveal—things like Joe Fagone's admission to me that he thought the gun he found at the scene was probably planted by police, Commissioner Jordan's hands-on involvement in the investigation, and former Commissioner Di Grazia calling the investigation a "cover-up" after I presented the evidence to him. With the media suddenly taking a new look at the Bowden case, the Boston Police Department went strangely silent. No one could reach Commissioner Jordan for a comment. For days I did Boston newspaper, TV, and radio interviews with no response from the commissioner who I insisted was implicated in the cover-up. Joe Jordan was always available to the media and now in the middle of the biggest crisis of his career—the first time his integrity was being challenged—he disappeared. Then I got a call from a friend who was visiting a relative at an alcoholism rehabilitation center in Rhode Island. He told me he saw Joe Jordan at the rehab center. Jordan wasn't a visitor. He was a patient.

I immediately called the *Boston Globe* and told them where they could find Joe Jordan. The *Globe* wasn't interested. They said if the police commissioner was being treated for alcoholism, that was a private matter. I was stunned. I didn't think I was going to have to explain to a newspaper that it was newsworthy that the police commissioner checked into rehab in reaction to a book implicating him in a scandal. It seemed the *Globe* was stunned too—stunned by the novelty of what I was telling them. A public official going to rehab was unthinkable then. The *Globe* didn't have a rule for this. My next call was to the *Boston Herald* and as soon as I said the name of the rehab center, they had a reporter and photographer on the way to Rhode Island. I called back the *Globe* to give them another chance. I told them the *Herald* was already on the way to Rhode Island. The *Globe* apparently did have a rule about not getting beaten by the *Herald*. So thanks to good old-fashioned newspaper competitiveness, rehab was suddenly not a private matter at the *Globe* and they rushed a reporter and photographer to Rhode Island. The next day, a picture of Joe Jordan, as we had never seen him, was on the front page of the *Globe* under the headline: "Jordan in R.I. hospital." He was sitting in a lawn chair in the summer sun in casual clothes. The *Globe*'s photographer got the shot with a telephoto lens through a fence outside the rehab center. The *Herald*'s front-page headline was more specific: "Hub's Top Cop In Drink Clinic."

The Commissioner was appointed to a fixed term of five years. Removing him from office would be legally complicated but a determined mayor could do it. Mayor Kevin White made the choice most Boston politicians of that era would make—protect his friend. With the unprecedented double scandal of a police cover-up and checking into rehab, Joe Jordan was still not in trouble with the mayor. A month later, when the commissioner returned to headquarters, the *Globe* greeted him with a sympathetic front-page story headlined: "Comr. Jordan back on job, 'in charge' and 'on the wagon.'" The *Globe* story had only one short paragraph about this book, just enough for Jordan to insist the book was "definitely not" a factor in his decision to check in to rehab for twenty-eight days out of state. He also denied he was an alcoholic. He told the *Herald*, "I haven't read the book but I intend to. If he has lied and libeled me, I expect to take whatever action I consider to be just." I repeatedly challenged Jordan to dispute anything in the book, even a single sentence. He never did.

My objective in dealing with the news media then was to illuminate the problem of police use of deadly force for the first time, both locally and nationally, and to force the city to pay the judgment that the jury awarded the Bowden family. The Bowden judgment seems small now—less than a million dollars—when cases like this are sometimes settled for millions of dollars today without even going to trial. New York City paid $5.9 million to the family of Eric Garner who was choked to death by an NYPD officer in 2014. As soon as that wrongful death case was filed, the city started settlement talks with the Garner family lawyers. Cleveland settled with Tamir Rice's family for $6 million. Chicago settled with Laquan McDonald's family for $5 million. As with everything, there has to be a first. And the Bowden family was first, long before anyone thought juries would second-guess police officers in shootings, long before most cities thought they would ever have to pay anything for lives taken by police.

Getting the judgment paid was a political objective, the first one of my career, a career that I did not then know would turn entirely political at times. Leaders of the black community reached out to me and offered their help, especially religious leaders. I was invited to "preach" in black churches about what happened to James Bowden. I got a lot of Amens from those congregations, but I didn't get much surprise. They had heard stories like this before. They knew what bad police officers could do and they knew that the police always served and protected themselves much better than they served and protected the black community.

Ray Flynn became the front-runner to succeed Mayor White who was not running for reelection that fall. Flynn was a member of the City Council from South Boston who knew he needed to make an extra effort to reach out to black voters who saw Southie as the city's most racist neighborhood, the place where black children's school buses were viciously attacked when Southie High was integrated. During the campaign Dave O'Brian asked Ray Flynn whether he would pay the Bowden judgment if he became the next mayor. Flynn said he would. No other reporters covering the campaign ever asked any candidates about the Bowden case. When Ray Flynn won, I tried to turn that one sentence to Dave O'Brian into an unbreakable campaign promise.

The ministers told me they were going to demand a meeting with Ray Flynn as soon as he was sworn in and they had some surprising news: Don X wanted to join them in that meeting. Minister Don Muhammad, then known as Don X, is the long-time Boston leader of the Nation of Islam, a position once held by Malcolm X. The ministers were surprised Don X wanted to join them because the Nation of Islam then shunned politics—many members refused to even vote—because they thought American government was a hopeless route to social justice. The ministers asked me to join them in the meeting with the mayor. When we gathered at City Hall, Don X was clearly the man in charge, not by choice, simply by the deference others offered him. Don X was a man of few words. The classic quiet man except when something had to be said. As we were being guided to the mayor's office, Don asked me what I wanted to say to the mayor. I said I was hoping to say nothing unless some detail of the case had to be clarified. I told Don I thought he didn't have to request or demand that the mayor pay the judgment. Instead he could just assume the mayor was going to pay it because he promised he would during the campaign. Don could thank him for paying it instead of asking him to pay. That would force the mayor to raise doubt about his own promise if there was any doubt. Don liked that, not just as a strategic device, but because, like Malcolm X before him, he didn't want to ask a politician for anything.

Ray Flynn knew this was his most important meeting of the day for two reasons: It was Don X's first time in City Hall and right outside the mayor's office door was as big a collection of reporters and cameras as City Hall had ever seen, including Fox Butterfield, Boston bureau chief of the *New York Times*, Ray Flynn's ticket to national press attention.

The mayor began the meeting by saying he wasn't going to say anything to the press afterward. I thought that was a very bad sign. That meant the mayor knew he would have nothing to announce after the meeting because he already decided he wasn't going to agree to anything in the meeting. He then said he knew the city's lawyers had made an offer to pay the judgment. I said,

"The city has never offered to pay Mrs. Bowden the full amount she won in court from two all-white Boston juries." In a room full of black men, I wanted the mayor to feel the injustice of what we all took for granted in Boston courtrooms then—all-white juries. And I wanted him to see that no one in this room was willing to compromise on payment in full.

Don's big voice filled the room when he spoke. He told the mayor the Bowden family had suffered too long and that he was glad the mayor was finally going to bring the case to a close by paying the judgment. There were no question marks at the end of any of Don's sentences, just the assumption that the mayor was going to deliver on his campaign promise. Don cornered the mayor perfectly. If the mayor was not going to deliver on that promise in full, now was the time for the mayor to say something. The mayor said nothing. The other ministers echoed Don and told the mayor that his campaign promise to pay the Bowden judgment was an important issue for their congregations. The ministers then changed the subject to the firing of Joe Jordan and now the mayor had something to say. Flynn had already publicly asked for Jordan's resignation but Jordan refused to resign. Flynn said he was still quietly trying to get Jordan to resign because firing him for cause would be a long and untested legal process that could get tied up in court for years. Ray Flynn's quiet, behind-the-scenes approach eventually paid off a year later when Joe Jordan finally resigned.

During the meeting I was impressed at the mayor's ability to speak without saying anything. He filled what could have been awkward silences with words, sometimes lots of words, but he mostly said nothing. He didn't say he would pay the judgment or not pay the judgment or make another settlement offer. Nothing. No hint of what he would do. It turned out to be a preview of meetings in my then unforeseen future working in the United States Senate where the decider—a committee chairman, the Majority Leader, the President—would say the fewest words of anyone else in the room and usually not even hint at what he was going to do. The first time I saw Bill Clinton do that in the Oval

Office in 1993, I flashed back nine years to watching Ray Flynn do it. I didn't realize that day in the mayor's office how important that skill is for a political decider. I've been in the room with the best of them, and I've seen no one do it better than Ray Flynn. And so we got up to leave with nothing—no renewed promise by the mayor.

We had seconds to decide what to say to the press waiting just outside the door. Don was going to speak for the group. He leaned toward me, "What do you think?" I was about to advise a deeply religious man, who I had just met, not to tell the truth, the whole truth and nothing but the truth. I had to rush my whispered advice: "The mayor said he's not gonna speak to the press, so what happened in there is what you say happened in there. You can just say what you said in there, 'I'm very happy the mayor promised to pay the judgment in full.' The press will assume the mayor said that today. And what's the mayor gonna do? He's not gonna come running out here after you and say 'Oh, no, I didn't promise to do what I promised I would do during the campaign.'" For the first time, Don smiled.

Don stepped up to the microphones and said it was a very good meeting and he was very glad the mayor promised to pay the full judgment "in compliance with the court's decision." And so the lead story on local TV news that night was that the mayor promised to pay the judgment in full and the next day's newspapers said the same thing with the *New York Times* headline saying "Boston Mayor Is Said to Agree to Pay Widow of Man Shot by Police." The bad news for the mayor was that Don had boxed him in with the press. The mayor had no choice now. The good news for the mayor was it looked like the *New York Times* was ready to make him a national hero in the final chapter of this story. And so it did.

A few weeks later, the mayor, with an army of news media in tow, knocked on Pat Bowden's front door. Michael opened the door for the mayor and the image of the two of them at the Bowden front door was captured by all the cameras. I had arranged for two reporters to be in the house waiting for the mayor:

Dave O'Brian and Fox Butterfield of the *Times* whose front page headline the next day was "Boston Mayor Takes Action To Promote Racial Harmony." Standing at Pat Bowden's kitchen table, Ray Flynn handed her a check for $843,498.00. He said, "As mayor, I want to say we're very very sorry for what's happened."

Pat said, "God bless you."

Eurina Bowden, who had just turned fourteen years old, looked outside at the horde of reporters and cameras and TV trucks, then sat down, put a piece of paper in her typewriter, and typed a note. She showed it to Michael and said she wanted to go out and tape the note to the front door. He read it, smiled, hugged her, and said, "Let's just stay in here." Eurina's note said, "Please go away. Don't bother us. Where were you nine years ago?"

The old man wasn't there that day. He told me he wanted Michael to have the limelight on the biggest day of media coverage of the Bowden case. It worked. It was Michael's face that Boston saw on TV news that night and in the papers the next day. I suspected there was another reason why the old man decided to stay out of the final moment of the case. He knew he would cry. And he didn't want the mayor to see him cry. He stayed at the office with my mother and busied himself by pretending to care about what bills they could pay now that some money was coming in—a subject that never interested him before that day and never interested him again. That's how he chose to deal with the emotion of the final day of the most important case of his life.

I guess I'm a little like the old man that way and maybe cry more easily than I should. I cried when I was writing certain passages of this book. I've cried while writing certain fictional scenes in TV dramas. I've come close to tears on TV when discussing mass shootings and other tragedies, but we always cut to a commercial just in time for me to hide most of that emotion from the audience. So I was afraid I was going to cry when I had to deliver the eulogy at my father's funeral in 2009. I wanted to fondly recall the best things about his eighty-seven years of life while following the Irish eulogy tradition of winking at his weaknesses and conveniently overlooking his worst moments. And, through it all, I wanted to smile. Crying would make the moment about my emotions instead of his life, just like a TV anchorman crying would make the story about him instead of the tragedy he is reporting.

I began writing the eulogy the same way I begin writing everything—thinking it's impossible, thinking I don't know what to say, and hating that I got stuck with this assignment. The first day, nothing came to me. Not a single sentence. Hoping I would find something to borrow, I read the brilliant, multi-layered eulogy my cousin Kirk O'Donnell had delivered for my father's identical twin brother a few years earlier. I then realized that "identical" was not the right word for these twins. They were each unique bundles of human complexity. Kirk had beautifully written his father's story and now I had to write mine. I thought about what my father would say if he could write his own eulogy. Then I realized it had already been written—by Judge Garrity at the end of the second Bowden trial. And so I finally had it. I knew what to say. All I had to do was tell the story of a little boy who lost his father in tragedy, wasn't a good student but had the audacity to push himself through college and law school, the audacity to try what everyone thought was impossible. Then I could let a judge tell the story of who my father turned out to be in the courtroom, who he turned out to be on his life's stage, the place where he was most alive:

". . . All the books written on the law would not confer on an advocate the skill he needed to try this particular case . . . Mr. O'Donnell undertook this representation at considerable risk . . . all undertaken in the hope that he would obtain justice for a lonely widow . . ."

I knew, and every O'Donnell in the church knew, beyond a shadow of a doubt, as I was saying those words at his funeral, that if he could have heard me, the old man would have loved it.

Acknowledgments

My first gratitude is to the Sisters of Saint Joseph for teaching me how to read and write. My last gratitude is to my editor, Bruce Lee, for teaching me how to write this book. Between the first and the last are many gratitudes to many faithful friends. To each, I am in perpetual debt.

Index